T0247881

BRUNO SCHULZ

Bruno Schulz on the steps of his home, Drohobycz, Poland, 1933
(Bertold Schenkelbach)

BRUNO SCHULZ

AN ARTIST, A MURDER, AND THE HIJACKING OF HISTORY

BENJAMIN BALINT

W. W. NORTON & COMPANY
Celebrating a Century of Independent Publishing

For information about permission to reproduce selections from this book,
write to Permissions, W. W. Norton & Company, Inc.,
500 Fifth Avenue, New York, NY 10110

For information about special discounts for bulk purchases, please contact
W. W. Norton Special Sales at specialsales@wwnorton.com or 800-233-4830

Manufacturing by Lake Book Manufacturing
Book design by Patrice Sheridan
Production manager: Julia Druskin

ISBN 978-0-393-86657-5

W. W. Norton & Company, Inc., 500 Fifth Avenue, New York, N.Y. 10110
www.wwnorton.com

W. W. Norton & Company Ltd., 15 Carlisle Street, London W1D 3BS

1 2 3 4 5 6 7 8 9 0

For Ida

CONTENTS

BRUNO SCHULZ

PROLOGUE

The fragmented murals I saw that morning at Yad Vashem, Israel's Holocaust museum in Jerusalem, seemed both perishable and permanent. Formally untutored in painting, the artist had used a *fresco secco* ("dry fresco") technique, applying paint directly to dry plaster to create fanciful figures held in lucid stillness. The technique allows for an immediacy of gesture. Though the gaily colored fairy-tale scenes painted in 1942 had been muted by time, even today, eight decades later, and even to my untrained eye, something alive inhabited the brushstrokes, traces of a past espousal of passion that had not quite disappeared. In their dissolving contours, the murals support contemplation and require our complicity; they invite us to speculate, to fill in what's missing. They merge in the mind more than in the eye.

One rough-hewn fragment depicts a seductively dressed, resplendent Snow White surrounded by red-hatted gnomes. One gnome seems to bear the time-ridden face of the painter's father, Jakub. Another tableau features a colorful carriage drawn forward on clattering wheels into an uncertain distance by two splendid horses ready to canter away, their progress brought to a halt, their forelegs suspended in midair. The vigilant, proud, blue-helmeted driver holding the reins like a charioteer is the painter himself. It is the doomed artist's last self-portrait, and maybe, too, a last act of resistance against the effacement of his individuality.

Throughout his life, this artist had drawn horse-drawn carriages sweeping through the dark. He once wrote to a friend of his earliest scribbles:

> Before I could even talk, I was already covering every scrap of paper and the margins of newspapers with scribbles that attracted those around me. At first, they were all horses and wagons. The action of riding in a carriage seemed to me full

Bruno Schulz, "Bianca and Her Father in a Coach" (c. 1936), an illustration for his book *Sanatorium Under the Sign of the Hourglass* (CREDIT: Yad Vashem)

of weight and arcane symbolism. From age six or seven there appeared and reappeared in my drawings the image of a cab, with a hood on top and lanterns blazing, emerging from a nocturnal forest. That image belongs to the basic material of my imagination and to this day I haven't exhausted its metaphysical content.[1]

During the Holocaust, the Polish Jewish artist and writer Bruno Schulz was coerced by a Nazi to paint these murals on the walls of a children's room in an SS villa in the then-Polish, now-Ukrainian city of Drohobych. (References in this book to the city at a time when it belonged to Poland will use the Polish spelling, Drohobycz.) Long before the war, Schulz had created unnerving masochistic scenes, depictions of men groveling at women's feet. These caught the eye of the sadistic SS officer with a Jewish stepfather who would serve as Schulz's "guardian devil" and would determine Schulz's fate. In this uneasy alliance, Schulz's art became the currency with which he bought life.

When I stood before those murals at Yad Vashem, I couldn't help but imagine the artist sapped of his vitality, compelled to flatter the fancies of his master, forced to flounder somewhere between *Lebensraum* and *Todesraum* (living space and death space), hourly reminded of his status as a disconsolate prisoner of an enemy who wished to dehumanize him. I wondered whether he painted his desire to seize the reins of his own narrative, to reclaim dignity. (One of the verbs in the Nazi vocabulary of Jew hatred, itself an outrage against dignity, was *entwürdigen*, to deprive of dignity.) "By my very nature," Schulz remarked, "I am not made to offer resistance, to stand up for myself, to defy the will of another person. I don't possess the necessary strength of conviction, the narrow faith in the rightness of my cause, for that."[2] Yet if the art he had earlier created with the free play of his imagination is servility made visible, the art he created under the most coercive conditions depicts unflinching freedom. Did he manage to control his brushstrokes without letting the fear slip out through his fingers? Could he summon dignity, even defiance?

Schulz's story did not end with the bullet that took his life in November 1942. Nearly sixty years after Schulz was murdered, his murals—witnesses to human cruelty—were miraculously rediscovered. Several months later, three Israeli agents—aided by bribery, spycraft, and diplomatic immunity—chiseled them from the villa's walls and secretly spirited the fragments to Yad Vashem, perhaps the only museum in the world guided by the injunction to remember as both a national and a religious imperative. The ensuing international furor, and its excursions into competitive martyrology, revived questions about Schulz's life and went to the very heart of Jewish and European memory (or how Holocaust memory becomes an object of realpolitik) and of the political implications of who controls cultural heritage.

Drawing on extensive new reporting, archival research, interviews (in Poland, Ukraine, and Israel), and scattered letters and memoirs, *Bruno Schulz* chases these inventive murals—the last traces of his vanished world—into multiple dimensions of Schulz's life and afterlife.

———

SCHULZ WAS BORN AN AUSTRIAN, LIVED AS A POLE, AND DIED A JEW. His life began under the banner of the Austro-Hungarian double-headed eagle and ended in the genocidal dehumanizations of Nazi occupation. Born a citizen of the Habsburg monarchy, Schulz would—without moving—become a subject of the West Ukrainian People's Republic (November 1918 to July 1919), the Second Polish Republic (1919 to 1939), the USSR (September 1939 to July 1940), and, finally, the Third Reich. Yet to use his own metaphor, Schulz remained throughout a citizen of the Republic of Dreams.

The cartographer of that republic was both a graphic artist and a master of twentieth-century imaginative fiction, a powerful writer who mapped the anxious perplexities of his time, who used the Polish language as dexterously as if he had made it—or even as if the language had been invented for his sake. His polysensual prose, to use his phrase, was "touched by the divine finger of poetry." It may very well be the most beautiful ever written in Polish. Modernist classics—Joyce's *Ulysses*, Proust's *In Search of Lost Time*, Musil's *The Man Without Qualities*—tend to be sprawling. Schulz's literary reputation rests on two slender volumes (some thirty short stories): *Cinnamon Shops* (1934, published in the United States. as *The Street of Crocodiles*) and *Sanatorium Under the Sign of the Hourglass* (1937). Yet his elegant verbal art, with its inexhaustible inventiveness, transcends the confines of its chronology. Alternately claustrophobic and boundless, his fables are peopled with an uncanny congress of characters who dream febrile dreams, with streets that turn into labyrinths, with time that circles and eddies. To borrow his own phrase again, Schulz's work represented an "enormous, magnificent, colorful blasphemy." That blasphemy made Schulz a venerated and tutelary spirit for a procession of better-known writers—including Philip Roth, Cynthia Ozick, Nicole Krauss, Jonathan Safran Foer, David Grossman, and Polish Nobel laureates Czesław Miłosz and Olga Tokarczuk. Each felt profound affinities with his many-sided fiction, and with the motifs that course through it. Along with filmmakers and actors, they wove stories out of Schulz's private mythology.[3] Schulz's fiction has been translated into forty-five languages. Yet Schulz, today lionized, would never know his own international success, his afterlife in the brushes and pens of other artists, or the ways posterity would consecrate him into myth. He was killed before he finished saying what he had to say. "If Schulz had been allowed to live out his life," said the Polish-born Yiddish writer Isaac Bashevis Singer, "he might have given us untold treasures, but what he did in his short life was enough to make him one of the most remarkable writers who ever lived."

This book conjures a portal into the haunted life of this virtuoso of language and image. By summoning the artist's milieu at a crossroads not just of Jewish and Polish culture but of art, sex, and violence, and by recovering his utterly individual idioms and imagery, it stands as an act of belated restitution, an attempt to decipher the scattered signs he has left us without projecting our own notions onto the past. Between Bruno Schulz and us, a history of organized forgetting has intervened to, in the words of the French poet René Char, rob the deceased of his death. This has made both the man and his message a telling example of the Shoah as seen through the self-aggrandizing ideological prisms of "official" memory. Can this breach of memory be remedied?

"Unlike a biography," Schulz wrote, "which presents its subject in a process of sequential dynamic development, the portrait has the contours of its physiognomy fixed from the start."[4] *Bruno Schulz* recounts a life, with all its paradoxes and curtailed possibilities. But I invite you to read it not so much as a biography as an attempt to restore the obliterated lines of continuity between him and us, as a portrait of a man who in his own distinctive way seized the reins, like a charioteer, and rallied under impossible circumstances for his freedom. Or maybe in the triumph of his imagination over brutality he was free all along.

CHAPTER 1
MUROMANCY

February 2001

In some sense we derive a profound satisfaction from the loosening of the web of reality; we feel an interest in witnessing the bankruptcy of reality.[1]

—BRUNO SCHULZ

Searching for Schulz

VILLA LANDAU, DROHOBYCH, UKRAINE, FEBRUARY 9, 2001

A pair of documentary filmmakers from Hamburg—Benjamin Geissler, thirty-seven, and his stepfather, Christian Geissler, seventy-three—stood in the cheerless stairwell and knocked on the door of apartment 3. They had come in search of Bruno Schulz's last known artworks, lost for decades behind the Iron Curtain in a three-story building in Drohobych, a town near the Poland-Ukraine border. Built for the Jochman family, the villa had served as a police headquarters before World War II, and as home during the war to Felix Landau. (Before the war the address was 12 Jana Street, afterward 14 Tarnowski Street.) When the area was absorbed into Soviet Ukraine, Villa Landau, as the building has been known ever since, had been divided into five apartments. Its stern gray walls and steeply gabled roof, unchanged since the war, suggested a fairy-tale castle.

The Geisslers had been brought here not by curiosity but by penance. Christian Geissler was the son of a "convinced Nazi" (in Benjamin Geissler's description) who died in battle on the eastern front near Poznań in World War II. This heritage weighed on him. Christian titled his first novel *The Sins of the Fathers*.[2] A committed left-wing Catholic social critic in his youth, he became a Communist in late 1960s, and an anti-imperialist radical leftist who sympathized with the Red Army Faction (RAF), a left-wing terrorist organization, through the 1970s and 1980s. He began making documentary films in 1969. Benjamin Geissler, born in Ohrbeck in 1964, belonged to a younger generation, the members of which, in the words of Chancellor Helmut Kohl, had "the blessing of late birth." (Ohrbeck, a town in the German region of Lower Saxony, was the site of a Gestapo-run forced labor camp from January 1944 to April 1945.)

Christian had harbored a fascination with Bruno Schulz since the autumn of 1961, when he read a German edition of *Cinnamon Shops*. In the spring of 1992, he went to an exhibition of Schulz's drawings in Munich and learned from the show's catalog about Bruno Schulz's lost murals, his last known artworks. In May 1999, he suggested to his stepson that they make a documentary about the murals. "The old man goes from door to door," he told Benjamin, "and the boy makes a film." Benjamin Geissler and his wife would later name their son Bruno.

The Geisslers made their first trip to Drohobycz in December 2000. After two years of sleuthing, they concluded that the kitchen pantry in a second-floor apartment in Villa Landau had once served as the playroom of Felix Landau's two children. They approached Schulz's former student Alfred Schreyer, then seventy-eight, a survivor of the Płaszów and Buchenwald concentration camps. He said that together with his musical talents, the craft skills he'd learned in Schulz's classes had more than once saved his life in the camps. Schreyer was the last

Jew living in Drohobych born before World War II. "I was born in Drohobycz," he told an interviewer, "which was a Polish city at the time. I went to a Polish school. Polish was the only language spoken at home. I was brought up in the spirit of Polish patriotism. I always felt, I feel, and I assure you that until the last day of my life, I will feel attached to Polishness."[3]

Schreyer led the Geisslers to Apolonia Klügler, a former postal worker whose husband, Artek, had studied with Schulz; she, in turn, located Vladimir Protasov, the son of a high-ranking military official, who'd lived in Villa Landau immediately after the war. Protasov disclosed that he had seen Schulz's murals with his own eyes in the room he had once used as a photographic darkroom. Protasov pointed out the room on a diagram of the apartment.

Two months later, on February 3, 2001, the Geisslers drove their Volkswagen van from Hamburg via Lviv to Drohobych. Christian deliberately took a route past the sites of former concentration camps: Neuengamme, Oranienburg, Gross Rosen, Sosnowiec, Płaszów, and Józefów. On arriving in Drohobych, the Geisslers met up with their Polish sound operator, Marek Śląski, and Jurko Prochaśko, their translator and "fixer." For Prochaśko, a highly educated native of western Ukraine and a practicing psychoanalyst, this was a dream assignment. At age twelve, he had been enraptured by a Polish edition of Schulz's work on his parents' bookshelf and taught himself Polish by reading it. During his university studies, Prochaśko had come across a Ukrainian translation of some of Schulz's stories in a literary magazine and found in it a "revelation."

Nadezhda Kaluzhni, a short, solid woman wearing an apron over a loose house robe with fraying hems, answered the door. Alfred Schreyer introduced himself and Geissler. She peered at the unexpected visitors through thick-lensed glasses and reluctantly admitted them. Her mind was elsewhere: on grieving for her son, who had died a short time earlier, just short of his fiftieth birthday, from a blocked coronary artery, and on caring for her cancer-ridden husband, Nikolai, seventy-nine, confined to his bed. The elderly couple had lived in the drab apartment for forty-four years. Nikolai was a World War II veteran; he had been conscripted to fight against the Germans near Stalingrad. Originally from Soviet Ukraine, the Kaluzhnis had been resettled here as part of postwar Sovietization. Other than their two daughters, Larissa and Nadia, they were unaccustomed to visitors. Nadezhda became suddenly ashamed of the squalor. "We live like beggars," she said.

At the mention of Schulz, Nadezhda clasped her knobby fingers tightly over her chest. She told the Geisslers that decades earlier, Polish researchers had searched for Schulz's murals in vain. "They asked questions, scraped paint off walls, but found nothing." (In 1965, Poland's leading Schulz expert, Jerzy Ficowski, had come to this very apartment in search of the murals.) "Nothing," she said. "They can't be here. How can they be in this closet?"

Nonetheless, the Geisslers and Schreyer crowded into her narrow pantry (240 centimeters long by 180 centimeters wide, or just under eight feet long by six feet wide), which had a single small window at the far end. In the catacomb-like dimness, their eyes scouted faint but discernible shadows of figures behind shelves swelling with tarnished pots and half-forgotten pickling jars, behind creviced bunches of garlic, beneath smudges of mildew and several layers of pale pink paint. It was as though father and son were practicing muromancy, the obscure art of reading the spots on walls. For a moment, as the past reasserted itself and in its unrushed way let itself be seen again, they were struck mute.

"I can't see a thing," Kaluzhni said, wiping her thick glasses. "I can hardly see." And then, looking again: "Thank God you found it. May God help you."

"It's a miracle," Alfred Schreyer said, his voice trembling with emotion.

Christian Geissler recalled how staggered he was to find Schulz's images "in the shadows of degradation" (*"in den Schatten einer Erniedrigung"*). Invoking a line from the poet Paul Celan, "death is a

master from Germany," Christian said he felt as though they were witnessing at that moment an encounter between Schulz and "the master
from Germany."

This wasn't the first time Schulz's art had unexpectedly resurfaced.
In June 1957, a hitherto unknown drawing of three figures Schulz had
made in 1935 was donated to a small private museum in Israel. Nothing was known about the drawing's provenance except a name and
profession stamped on the reverse: Dr. Michał Chajes, Adwokat.[4] It's
not clear when or how Chajes acquired the Schulz drawing, nor why
the Drohobycz-born lawyer sent it to Israel, a country he'd never visited.

A parcel containing more than seventy of Schulz's drawings (and
a notebook of sketches Schulz had done at age fifteen, peopled with
clowns, imps in top hats, and circus strongmen) resurfaced in 1986.
During the war Schulz had entrusted it to Zbigniew Moroń, a math
teacher at the Drohobycz high school where Schulz taught. Moroń
claimed to have believed that it had been destroyed when Nazis looted
his home in 1945. His heirs found it in a timeworn suitcase in Gdańsk,
Poland, and arranged for the works to be sold to the Adam Mickiewicz
Museum of Literature in Warsaw.[5]

Finally, Schulz's only surviving painting, *Encounter* (1920), had
mysteriously appeared at an auction in Łódź, Poland, in March 1992.
It, too, was purchased by the Adam Mickiewicz Museum of Literature.[6]

But of all these discoveries, the reanimation of Schulz's fairy-tale
murals—like Snow White opening her eyes again—would prove by far
the most sensational.

"As a German"
DROHOBYCH LIBRARY, TARAS SHEVCHENKO STREET,
FEBRUARY 16, 2001

Immediately after discovering the murals, Benjamin Geissler alerted
Drohobych mayor Oleksy Radziyevsky; Ukraine's minister of culture,

Bohdan Stupka; Poland's undersecretary of state in the Ministry of Culture and National Heritage, Stanisław Żurowski; German secretary of culture Michael Naumann; Schulz expert Jerzy Ficowski; Michael Krüger of Hanser Verlag, publisher of Schulz's work in Germany; and representatives of Yad Vashem in Jerusalem. The immediate response from the latter, according to Geissler: "Listen, who visits Drohobych? But two million people visit Yad Vashem annually."

A week after the discovery, on the evening of February 16, Benjamin Geissler convened a confidential meeting at the Drohobycz library—in the very room where Schulz had been obliged to sort books for the Nazi occupiers. On the agenda: how to restore the murals, secure them against theft, compensate the Kaluzhnis, and offer them alternative accommodations. In attendance: Schulz's former student Alfred Schreyer; three art experts (Agnieszka Kijowska and Wojciech Chmurzyński from Poland, and Boris Voznytsky from Ukraine); the Drohobycz official in charge of cultural affairs, Mikhail Michatz; the Geisslers' assistant Jurko Prochaśko; their translator Roman Dubassevych; and the Polish consul in Lviv, Krzysztof Sawicki. Two decades earlier, Sawicki had written his master's thesis on Schulz at the Catholic University of Lublin. Now he took a hectoring tone toward Geissler: "As a German," the consul said, "you have the least rights to this heritage." An audio recording of the meeting would later be handed over to Ukrainian prosecutors.

Pentimento

VILLA LANDAU, DROHOBYCH, FEBRUARY 17, 2001

The next day, February 17, the team of Polish and Ukrainian art experts crammed into the pantry and began the unhurried work of removing layers of paint to reveal Schulz's brushstrokes beneath. The team included Wojciech Chmurzyński, an expert in Schulz's art and a former head of the art department at the Adam Mickiewicz Museum of Literature (where he had curated a major Schulz exhibition in 1992); Boris Voznytsky, a Ukrainian art historian and the director since 1962 of the Lviv Art Gallery; and Agnieszka Kijowska, an art conservator at the National Museum in Warsaw and a specialist in wall paintings.[7] Kijowska had been part of a team that used advanced techniques (X-ray fluorescence spectrometry and laser ablation) to recover decorations painted between the seventh and fourteenth centuries in churches in Nubia (today's southern Egypt and northern Sudan). Weeks before coming to Drohobych, she had restored murals in a pharaoh's crypt in Egypt.

Kijowska lifted her eyes and caught a first glimpse of Schulz's murals. Dim presences seemed to gather palpability. She beheld a miraculous case of pentimento (the word is derived from the Italian *pentirsi*, "to repent"), a reappearance in a painting of an original that had been painted over, in this case not by the artist but by other hands.

After a tremulous silence, Kijowska said: Mr. Wojciech . . . here's a little face.

Wojciech: Wonderful! Oh my God! It's typical. Oh my God! Isn't it? It's reminiscent of his self-portraits. Oh my God!

[Kijowska laughed in delight.]

Wojciech: This is it!

"There is no dead matter," a character says in one of Schulz's stories; "lifelessness is only an external appearance behind which unknown forms of life are hiding."[8]

That same day, news of the rediscovered murals, leaked by Sawicki, appeared on the front page of the Polish right-wing daily *Life* (*Życie*). According to Jurko, Nadezhda Kaluzhni had said, "I'm at the end of my days. Just promise me this will remain quiet." Benjamin Geissler had given his assurances. Betraying Geissler's trust, Sawicki had taken the liberty of informing the press, and journalists were soon swarming outside the Kaluzhnis' door.

"This flat was privatized, it's our property, we can do what we want," Nadezhda Kaluzhni told the *Guardian*. "No one told us these paintings were valuable. They're not even paintings, just smears on the wall. It would be different if they were frescoes, Italian, Michelangelo or something."

"We knew about this house's past," Nadezhda told another reporter, "about that Gestapo monster [Felix Landau] shooting people from the balcony, but who could have imagined we'd never get any peace thanks to some old smears on the wall?"[9] Her husband, Nikolai, threatened to "take an ax" to the remaining murals in his apartment, if he and his wife were not given "inviolable" peace from reporters.

A Museum in the Executioner's House?
DROHOBYCH TOWN HALL, FEBRUARY 19, 2001

Benjamin Geissler sensed that some were prepared to go to great lengths to get those "old smears." He wrote a letter to the mayor, Oleksy Radziyevsky, to assert copyright over images of the murals and to implore the mayor to prevent anyone not authorized by the expert team, especially television crews, from entering the Kaluzhnis' apartment.

On February 19, Geissler met the mayor at the town hall to deliver the letter in person. He was joined by Christian Geissler, Alfred Schreyer, Mikhail Michatz, and deputy mayor Taras Metyk. The mayor told the Geisslers:

> The Drohobych city council welcomes the filming of your documentary "Finding Pictures." We are particularly happy about

the first results: the discovery of the murals of the world-famous writer and painter Bruno Schulz from our city. Since the end of the war, many experts have searched for this unique work of art. We hope to have a good cooperation with you. We are thinking on the one hand of the successful progress of your shooting, but on the other hand also of building a memorial for Bruno Schulz in the former Villa Landau. Since there are no funds for such a measure in the city budget, we ask you to work internationally to raise such funds.

Finally, the mayor gave assurances that Schulz's murals would be protected in situ and suggested having the room containing the murals sealed for reasons of security. Benjamin Geissler replied that since the Kaluzhni family still used the room as a pantry, sealing it wouldn't be right.

The next day, the Geisslers returned to Hamburg via Kraków (where they reported their discovery to leading Schulz scholar Jerzy Jarzębski). On returning home, Benjamin Geissler began to look for funding to relocate the inhabitants of Villa Landau and to repurpose the building as the Reunion and Reconciliation Center and Bruno Schulz Memorial Museum. "Not just a museum," Geissler said, "but also a place of encounter. For contemplating, talking, and being silent."

To inquire about funding, he called Matthias Buth, a senior official at the Federal Commissioner for Culture and Media Affairs (Beauftragte der Bundesregierung für Kultur und Medien) in Bonn. Buth replied that while the German government recognized a moral obligation to help, it could act only if it received official requests from Ukraine and Poland, preferably at the ministerial level. Geissler next approached Joseph H. Domberger, a real estate entrepreneur in Munich and honorary president of B'nai B'rith Europe, who offered to help underwrite the proposed Schulz museum. Domberger was born in Drohobycz in 1926 and lived there until age thirteen. Geissler asked Boris Voznytsky to meet the prospective donor in Drohobych in early June.

On February 23, Geissler contacted the German industrialist Berthold Beitz, then eighty-seven, a former adviser to Konrad Adenauer and then head of the Krupp Foundation, a major German philanthropy based at Villa Hügel in Essen. "Beitz was initially very interested," Geissler told me. Geissler knew of Beitz's personal interest in the matter. During the German occupation, he had been assigned to supervise the Carpathian Oil Company in Borysław, the town adjacent to Drohobycz. In August 1942, Beitz had saved 250 Jewish men and women from a transport train to the Belzec extermination camp by declaring them essential "petroleum technicians." He also gave local Jews advance warnings of Nazi roundups, issued and signed fake work permits, and, together with his wife, Else, hid Jews in his home.[10]

Władysław Panas, a prominent Schulzologist from Lublin, objected that establishing a Schulz museum in "the executioner's house" would be in bad taste. But according to Anne Webber, a representative of the European Council of Jewish Communities and the Commission for Looted Art in Europe, "the planned museum would have provided an ideal opportunity to strengthen awareness in the Ukraine and beyond of what befell the Jewish people and would have helped build relations between Jews and the local communities."[11] "Schulz is for us an iconic cult figure," said Andriy Pavlyshyn, a Ukrainian translator of Schulz and the editor of a cultural journal in Lviv:

That is why everything that is happening in Drohobych is very important for us emotionally. . . . From the first step Benjamin Geissler took here, his position was: to act legally, in coordination with all stakeholders, and in such a way as to bring

the greatest benefit to the Ukrainian people and our international image. . . . The plan was that after the restoration of the
murals, they would create a museum in Drohobych, the birthplace of Schulz . . . the homeland of the great Mitteleuropa culture, to which we, Ukrainians, belong as an essential element!
But this museum should be not a dead collection of images or
artifacts but a place of living communication, a center of unity,
where the people of Drohobych could learn more about the
wider world, and people from abroad could learn more about
Drohobych.

Several months before the discovery, Jerzy Jarzębski, the author
of the introduction to the standard Polish National Library edition
of Schulz's works and the co-editor of the four-hundred page Schulz
dictionary, had lectured at the Hebrew University on Polish literature
(including Schulz).[12] He told me how the museum was envisioned:

Maybe it was naïve, but our intentions were the best. The
paintings were to play a very important role in this, as the
only works by Schulz whose fate was not thrown beyond
Drohobych. As our Ukrainian hosts made me the chairman
of the Scientific Council of the Schulz Museum, I initially
designed this museum not so much as a repository of the writer's memorabilia but, rather, as a study center for which the
area of activity would be the entire Drohobych, its "Schulz
sites," and in the very core of it the paintings. . . . All this on
condition that the fairy tales would not be torn off the wall
and taken to another country.

Which is precisely what was about to happen.
Bruno Schulz once wrote: "The knot the soul got itself tied up in

is not a false one that comes undone when you pull the ends. On the contrary, it draws tighter. We handle it, trace the path of the separate threads, look for the end of the string, and out of these manipulations comes art."[13] The competing claims that arose so long after Schulz's death are like the ends of separate strings that trace their origins back into Schulz's life.

CHAPTER 2

THE REPUBLIC OF DREAMS

1892–1919

The books we read in childhood don't exist anymore; they sailed off with the wind, leaving bare skeletons behind. Whoever still has in him the memory and marrow of childhood should rewrite these books as he experienced them.[1]

—BRUNO SCHULZ

Maturing into Childhood

DROHOBYCZ, POLAND, 1892–1902

The cityscape of his childhood exerted a lifelong hold on Schulz's phantasmagoric imagination. Both the cityscape and the childhood, with its flood of impressions, continually replenished the adult artist's wide-eyed wonder.

Bruno was the youngest child of Henrietta and Jakub Schulz.[2] The family started off well with two children, Hania (b. 1873) and Izydor (b. 1881), but the next two children died while they were toddlers (Isaac at the age of three years and four months and Hinda before she was three). On July 12, 1892, Henrietta, forty-one, gave birth to

Bruno. She may have named him after her father, Berl, a man of meticulous piety who had died in Drohobycz nine years earlier.

Bruno grew up in a world dominated by women. He was raised by his doting mother and his sister, Hania, nearly twenty years older than Bruno. Henrietta Schulz (née Hendel Kuhmerker) came from an educated family that traded in timber and owned a steam sawmill. She read Goethe's ballads to her youngest son in German. When he was eight years old, she read to him "Elf-King" ("Erlkönig"), Goethe's poem about a fearful boy carried through the night by his father on horseback. Bruno, "idolatrously loved by his mother," remembered that the story left him in tears, "shaken to the bottom of my soul."[3]

The Schulzes lived above their ground-floor textile shop on a corner of the town's market square (10 Rynek), next to Café Boulevard, run by Ida Schechter, with its blue awnings. Behind the shop was a courtyard crisscrossed with clotheslines. An 1896 advertisement taken out by Schulz's mother promised "linen and woolen goods in a great selection in the latest designs." The shop overflowed with rolls of wool serge and embroidered brocade, with bolts of felt and velvet, with shelves of fringed scarves, starched ribbons, tulle veils, and haberdashery. Scraps and trimmings carpeted the floor. Mute unjointed mannequins looked out through the uncurtained windows onto the square, their reflections disappearing into the panes.

As a child, Schulz would stand in the shade of the square's acacia trees and watch merchants hawking an array of goods, itinerant organ grinders cranking out their songs, shop assistants leaning on balustrades, lawyers' apprentices in bowler hats gliding by, beggars pressing into the shadows, and horses hauling carts of firewood. (The first cars arrived in Drohobycz only in 1904.)

In one of his stories, Schulz describes the enchantments of that square in the luster of an August afternoon:

Etching by E. M. Lilien, "Market Trading in Drohobycz," ca. 1892. The building at the right housed the Schulz family shop and home. (CREDIT: Israel Museum, Jerusalem)

The market square was empty and yellow from the heat, swept clean of dust by hot winds, like a biblical desert. . . . The old houses, polished by the winds of many days, took on the reflected colors of the great atmosphere, the echoes and memories of hues diffused in the depths of the colorful weather. . . . Now the windows, blinded by the radiance of the empty square, were sleeping; the balconies confessed their emptiness to the sky; the open vestibules smelled of coolness and wine. . . . So, Mother and I strolled down the two sunny sides of the market square, leading our broken shadows across all the houses as if across piano keys.[4]

Schulz imparted special meaning to childhood—"the genial epoch," as he called it. "The most beautiful and most intimate thing in a man," he told a student, "are his memories from youth, from childhood."

Were it possible to turn back development, achieve by some circuitous path a repeated childhood, one more time have its fullness and limitlessness—that would be the realization of an "age of genius," of "messianic times" which through all mythologies are promised and pledged to us. My ideal is to mature into childhood.[5]

If, as Baudelaire said, genius consists in the ability to recapture childhood at will, then Schulz was irrefutably a genius. This incomparably gifted explorer of his own inner life succeeded by the cultivation of profound powers of imagination to evoke childhood and its protean possibilities. Many of us mythologize childhood, sometimes in the service of a merciful forgetting of our origins. Schulz did something else: he tried to "catch up" with his childhood and translate its perceptions, unsupervised and unsanctioned, into images. His art aimed not to reproduce or ratify reality but to evoke childlike (not childish) longing; his creative work is the satisfaction of that longing. Schulz would remark that everything artists have is given to them in childhood in the form of images,

> like filaments in a solution around which the sense of the world crystalizes for us. . . . They do not discover anything new after that, they only learn how to understand better and better the secret entrusted to them at the outset; their creative effort is an unending exegesis, a commentary on that one verse assigned to them.[6]

The decisive verse of Schulz's childhood took the form of a dream he had at age seven:

> In my dream I am in a forest at night, in the dark; I cut off my penis with a knife, scoop out a little cavity in the earth, and

bury it there. . . . I come to my senses, bring my conscious mind to bear on the atrocity, on the horror of dream sin I have committed. I refuse to believe that I really committed it and keep finding to my despair that it is so, that what I have perpetrated is irrevocable. I seem already to be beyond time, sub specie aeternitatis, an eternity that cannot be anything else for me now but a dreadful consciousness of guilt. . . . I am condemned forever. . . . How is one to explain, at such an age, the symbolic charge, the semantic potential of this dream, which I have been unable to exhaust to this day?[7]

Half-Banished Land: Galicia

Two centuries before Bruno Schulz's birth, Drohobycz had been associated with a martyr: the exceptionally beautiful daughter of a merchant named Moses Kikinesh. On the first night of Passover 1718, the family's Catholic maid accused Adela Kikinesh of murdering the maid's child to use Christian blood for matzoth. Arrested, imprisoned, and pressured to name accomplices, Adela refused to cooperate. Adela (a name we'll encounter again) was sentenced to a cruel death: her tresses would be tied to the tail of a wild stallion, which would be whipped along the unpaved streets until she died. Horrified by the pronouncement of this sentence, the maid recanted and confessed to perjury. The judges refused to overturn their verdict. As a last-ditch effort, Adela was told that her sentence would be suspended if she would convert. Again, she steadfastly refused.

Brought from Drohobycz to Lwów, Adela was executed with much pageantry before tens of thousands of spectators on a Friday evening, September 2, 1718. (I use "Lviv" and "Lwów" in accordance with whether the city was part of Poland or Ukraine at the time of the events described.) The archbishop asked whether she had a last wish. She requested that the guards untie her hands and give her some pins. She pinned the hem of her dress into the flesh of her calves to ensure that when the horse dragged her through the streets her nakedness would not be exposed.[8]

The city of Schulz's birth in 1892 belonged to Galicia—originally a Polish territory annexed to Austria in 1772 (after the First Partition of Poland)—the largest and most densely populated province of the Austrian Empire. It was also commonly considered by those in the capital, Vienna, to have been that empire's most peculiar and poverty-stricken province. The Viennese called this borderland at the far eastern edge of the empire *halb-Asien* (half-Asian), as though it were halfway between Occident and Orient. They took the very name Galicia as shorthand for squalor, as in the common phrase "Galician misery."[9] To call someone "a typical Galicianer" was to lob an insult. When Emperor Joseph II set out for Galicia in 1773, Empress Maria Theresa asked her son to reconsider "this terrible voyage" so distant from the precincts of power and to stay in Vienna: "Here is your place, and not in those Carpathian hills."

Fourteen years later, a Habsburg officer, Alphons Heinrich Traunpaur, who had lived in Galicia for eight years, imagined a meeting between an officer, "a second Robinson [Crusoe]," and a Galician rabbi.

"How were the Jews treated before the partition of Poland?" asks the officer.

"We always suffered blows," the rabbi replies, and recites a litany of brutal beatings and persecutions.

"These atrocities have vanished," the officer declares.

"Our posterity will bless those who have made them vanish," says the rabbi.[10]

A century later, that posterity, the last generation of Galician Jews, would include a trio of first-rate writers: Bruno Schulz in Polish, Joseph Roth in German, and S. Y. Agnon in Hebrew. Roth observed that

Galicia, that "half-banished land," had "the sad allure of the place scorned."[11]

A Land Flowing with Salt and Oil

Drohobycz drew its nourishment from the land, first in the form of salt, and then of crude oil. In or about 1869, the sleepy semi-industrialized area pivoted from salt production to oil production and reinvented itself as the Klondike of Galicia (or as Joseph Roth called it, "the Polish California").[12] Drohobycz became important enough for Emperor Franz Joseph to visit during his tour of Galicia in 1880. He was welcomed with a cantata that included the line "Welcome to the land where salt and oil flow." The Canadian oil-rigging entrepreneur William Henry McGarvey came to Galicia in 1883 and would make his fortune there. Two decades of oil boom followed, attracting the notice even of John D. Rockefeller's Standard Oil Company. By the eve of World War I, Galicia's refineries, centered around Drohobycz and the Borysław basin, would supply 60 percent of the Central Powers' petroleum. Schönholz's café served Drohobycz as a kind of stock market where traders and brokers met each morning to buy and sell shares in oil wells and to read German and Polish petroleum industry newspapers over their cups of tea or coffee with *Schlag.*

Schulz's childhood coincided with the industrialization of Galicia. As capital flowed in and derricks began to dot the bucolic landscape, and as modernization swept over the traditional merchant ethos, elegant mansions for the nouveau riche and theaters replaced the city's tawdry brothels. Schulz avoided the streets where the oil barons built their art nouveau villas, recalled a friend of Schulz's, the Polish translator Izabela Czermakowa: "He disliked their pseudo-elegance even more than he disliked their legendary owners, who mostly lived abroad." In his short story "The Street of Crocodiles," Schulz would write, "The spirit of the time, the mechanism of economics, had not spared our city, either, and it had put down greedy roots on the patch that was its periphery, where it developed into a parasitic quarter."[13]

Although the name Drohobycz nowhere appears in his prose, as both microcosm and metaphor Schulz's native city's "rich but empty and colorless vegetation of vulgarity," as he called it, was his *locus inspirationis*, toward which all the tendrils of his imagination reached. Like James Joyce's Dublin, Thomas Hardy's Wessex, William Faulkner's apocryphal Yoknapatawpha County in Mississippi (that "postage stamp of native soil"), and Isaac Bashevis Singer's Krochmalna Street in Warsaw, Schulz's Drohobycz was a universe in itself.[14] As a boy, Schulz imagined that beyond its borders lay only terra incognita. "The garden plots at the outskirts of town are planted as if at the world's edge and look across their fences into the infinity of the anonymous plain," Schulz wrote. "Just beyond the tollgates the map of the region turns nameless and cosmic like Canaan."[15]

To call Galicia a "borderland" is to adopt a gaze from the center. For Schulz, the borderland *was* the center. In the opening of his story "The Republic of Dreams," Schulz calls his home "this chosen region, this singular province, this city unique in all the world. . . . This city and this region locked themselves into a self-sufficient microcosm, installed themselves at their own risk on the very brink of eternity." Schulz saw in his native town a coalescence of life, with himself as the chronicler of its manners and modes. "How to express it?" he asks. "Here, nothing happens in vain, nothing occurs without profound meaning and without premeditation."[16]

To describe how Schulz's fascination tapered toward his native town, Izabela Czermakowa recalled his description of Drohobycz as "a marvel and mystery of anachronism, a reserve of Time." She added:

At times it felt as if he was separated from the rest of the world by some invisible, impenetrable wall which he himself tried in vain to pierce. . . . Schulz was lonely in Drohobycz. And yet despite the prospects then opening up to him in Warsaw or Lwów, Bruno did not want to leave his town. I myself once persuaded him to quit his hermitage. But I understood the artist's unshakable decision only when he showed us around the crooked dust-encrusted streets. With a sparkle in his eyes, he showed us orgies of weeds behind houses made of clay and fantasy. He initiated us into dead-end alleys that rocked his imagination and cultivated his reverie. We walked as though captivated. Bruno was pulling us into the world of his poetic vision. . . . His painterly eye perceived the play of colors and light, discovered beauty in ugliness. He showed us specimens of medieval Talmudic mystics hermetically sealed within the ghetto's non-existent walls. . . . Once we climbed a hill which offered views of the entire oil basin; the countless lights of drilling towers flickered in the early autumn twilight. "I can't live anywhere else," Bruno said then. "And here I will die."[17]

"One and a Half Cities": Jewish Drohobycz

When Bruno Schulz was fourteen, his brother handed him a copy of a book illustrated by the Zionist painter and art nouveau illustrator artist E. M. Lilien, *Songs of the Ghetto* (*Lieder des Ghetto*, 1902). "I borrowed it for you," said Izydor (Bruno called him Lulu), "but I have to return it tonight." "Unable to tear myself away," Schulz remembered thirty years later, he fell into a "solemn silence." Lilien, born on Żupna Street in Drohobycz eighteen years before Schulz, would later help found the Bezalel Academy of Arts and Design in Jerusalem. Schulz reported that he "powerfully fertilized my inner world, which manifested itself in early, failed youth. Lilien was the first spring of my sensitivity, my mystical marriage to art."

The encounter also initiated Schulz into the ways the Jewish messianic impulse had been "pressed deep into the soul of the people, where it smolders with a faint flame." For Schulz, Lilien's style illuminated "the transition from religious, mythical, messianic Jewish nationalism to modern and realistic nationalism." It imparted in images how "Zionism, born among Europeanized intellectuals . . . longed to take root in mythical ground." Hence it is a "creation born of the longing of *golus* [exile]." Lilien's Zionism, as Schulz pictured it, "was not only an attempt to solve the economic and political problem of Jewry, not only a question of making mystical and religious Jewish nationalism real, but also, at least in its intentions, an idealistic movement like any deep movement aimed at life, based on the principles of good, truth, and beauty."[18]

The Jews of Galicia inhabited the same region they had for centuries; the borders, not the Jews, shifted. "I am a public employee," Schulz would remark, "an Austrian, a Jew, a Pole—all in the space of an afternoon."[19] Schulz also believed that "there are no dead, solid or bounded objects. Everything diffuses beyond its borders, lasting only for a moment in a certain form, only to abandon it at the first opportunity."[20] Just as his home province of Galicia was a place of fluctuation, at the heart of Schulz's art is a blurring of borders between animal and human, animate and inanimate, instinct and intellect, high and low, and (to use his phrase) "between the darkness of myth and the sharp contour of actual history."[21] He transgressed the boundaries between pallid reality and blinding dream, receding lucidity and rampant madness, domination and submission—the very borders that would be so violently and irrevocably thrust upon him.

Toward the close of the nineteenth century, just around the time of Schulz's birth, Galicia's Jews—until then allied with the Poles against the Ukrainians—developed their own national movements.

Zionist groups of many varieties proliferated in Drohobycz: radical, socialist, right-wing Revisionist, and religious Zionist. Turning their faces toward Jerusalem, all of them dreamed in one way or another of a Palestine they had never seen, and all of them scorned those undignified or self-deceiving enough to wish to shed their Jewishness and disappear into Polish society.

In 1883, Aron Hirsh Żupnik, a devoted Zionist and a relative of Schulz's mother, began publishing the biweekly *Drohobyczer Zeitung* (in German using Hebrew letters). In 1893, the Zionist Union of Palestine Settlement Societies was founded here with seventy-one members, soon to be joined by an organization simply called Zion, a society for settlement of the Land of Israel (then under Ottoman rule).[22] Children in colored scarves came together in Zionist youth groups like Einigkeit (Unity), Ha'ivri, and Hashomer Hatzair youth scouts; the Bundist Zukunft youth club; and the Beitar Jewish sports and gymnastics association.

At the same time, the town teemed with a motley assortment of *maskilim* (adherents of the Jewish Enlightenment, or Haskalah),[23] Hasidic dynasties,[24] ultra-Orthodox defenders of the faith, assimilationists and diasporists (believers in a Jewish future in Poland),[25] and socialists steeped in a Marxist faith in progress. Charity associations supported the needy. A Jewish cultural council (*Kulturrat*) elected members for six-year terms. The Jewish community established schools (including the Tarbut Hebrew school on Bednarska Street), kindergartens, libraries, an old-age home (Mickewicz Street), a hospital (founded by the Drohobycz Jewish oil industrialist Moses Gartenberg, today a kindergarten), and an orphanage (Izydor Schulz, Bruno's brother, was one of the engineers who oversaw its construction).

In a world of rising nationalisms, Drohobycz, a satellite of the regional capital, Lwów, was described as "one and a half cities": half Polish (the gentry), half Jewish (the merchants), and half Ukrainian (the peasantry). Its streets resounded with a mixture of Polish (the language of prestige), Ukrainian, German, and Yiddish. During Schulz's childhood, more than 40 percent of the town's inhabitants were Jews, some 30 percent Catholic Poles, and 30 percent Ukrainians. By decades-long tradition, Drohobycz was administered by a Catholic Polish mayor and a Jewish vice mayor. Some 80 percent of the employees and managers in the city's oil refineries were Jews. It was rumored of one of the wealthiest of the Drohobycz "oil kings," Moses Gartenberg, that wherever he threw his yarmulke he would find a deposit of black gold. In 1914, a popular travel guide referred to the town's population of thirty-eight thousand as "primarily Jews."[26] Most shops were closed on Shabbat.

On a visit to Drohobycz in 1924, the German Jewish writer Alfred Döblin found himself jostled by a rowdy rabble in the market square.

> Male and female vendors, Jews, only Jews, with German names, chat and shout. Groups of peddlers in soft caps, dirty clothes, talk in the square, outside the one-story houses. Stooped old men, greasy, in dreadfully tattered caftans, raggedy trousers, burst boots, poke sticks in the garbage on the ground. One old-ster has a long yellowish-white beard, a stiff hat full of holes, its brim half torn off; he keeps murmuring, playing with his thick fingers, begging. . . . They all murmur in Yiddish: "Give me something."[27]

In one story, Schulz portrays those Yiddish murmurers with a more muted palette:

> Groups of Jews in colorful gabardines and fur kolpiks stood in front of high waterfalls of bright materials. They were the men of the Great Assembly, distinguished gentlemen full of solemnity, stroking their long, well-cared-for beards and conducting restrained, diplomatic conversations. But even in this ceremonial conversation, in the glances they exchanged, there was a twinkle of smiling irony. . . . The city fathers, the men of the

Great Sanhedrin, promenaded in grave and dignified groups, engaging in quiet, profound debates.[28]

By the 1930s, some twenty synagogues stood in Drohobycz.[29] The Choral Synagogue, the grandest in Galicia, took twenty-three years to build. It rose above Lan, a neighborhood of working-class Jews, in 1865.[30] Each May 3, a Polish national holiday called Constitution Day, the town's chief rabbi, Yaakov Avigdor, would deliver a lecture in Polish there in honor of the occasion.[31]

"A Need to Order the world"
DROHOBYCZ AND LWÓW, POLAND, 1902–14

In 1902, Bruno Schulz enrolled in the Drohobycz junior high school, where he took classes in gymnastics (the bane of his days), Polish language, Latin, mathematics, natural history, drawing, and "Mosaic religion" (taught by Baruch Margulies). He shared a bench with Stanisław Maczek, the son of a local lawyer and a future highly decorated Polish tank commander of World War II.

For his Polish language class, Schulz concocted a fairy tale about a horse. Struck by its inventiveness, his teacher brought it to the principal, Józef Staromiejski, who publicly praised it. Even then, Schulz's classmates noticed his drawings, including one depicting "a woman-tigress, its tail triumphantly raised, joyfully clawing apart her male victims." One classmate remembered Schulz's elegant fingers, "bony yet strangely soft, as if caressing and guiding a pen or a brush. These fingers moved with so much charm, so much beauty, and at the same time so much energy, that the most casual observer was provoked to wonder about the mystery they concealed."[32]

For his final exams (the so-called *matura*), Schulz was given three hours (and a dictionary) to translate passages of Virgil's *Aeneid* from the Latin and sections of Demosthenes's oration "On the Crown" from the Greek. He graduated high school with honors in June 1910.

Later that year, Schulz's brother-in-law, the oil industrialist Moses Hoffman, slit his throat with a razor. He left his widow, Bruno's sister, Hania, in deplorable financial condition. Hania, a calm woman who had always shown great tenderness for Bruno, fell ill with "a nervous disorder." She began to suffer seizures and convulsions and major depressive episodes. The burden of her care fell on Schulz's nearly sixty-year-old mother. Thereafter, Bruno shared a gloomy house with his father, who was in declining health; his mother; his sickly widowed sister, Hania; an elderly female cousin; and several cats. One visitor remembers creaky carpet-lined floors, plush ottomans, faded pillows, and "paintings so wrapped in cobwebs that it was hard to tell what they were actually representing."[33] Another visitor observed that Schulz lived "in a fairly closed circle, as if in constant mourning or exile. . . . He was afraid of the brutality of the outside world; he hated the clamor and noise."[34]

Schulz dreamed of studying the fine arts; he wished with all his heart to be a painter. Instead, in October 1910, at the urging of his pragmatic-minded brother, Izydor, Schulz enrolled without much enthusiasm in the Lwów Polytechnic to study architecture. Izydor, himself a graduate of the engineering program there, had by then married Regina Liebesmann and spread his wings in the oil business (elected a member of the National Council of Oil Exporters). Izydor was a man of action and tact, an entrepreneur who threw himself into a whirlwind of profitable businesses in Warsaw, Lwów, and Vienna. A cinephile, he established movie theaters in Drohobycz (the Urania cinema on Ślusarska Street), Kraków (also called the Urania, on Długa Street), and Warsaw (the Corso on Wierzbowa Street and the Nirvana on Three Crosses Square). He was also an active member of the Polish branch of B'nai B'rith, the Jewish humanitarian organization.[35] Izydor and Regina's son Jakub Schulz would say of those years (using the family nickname for Bruno): "We knew Brunio well, because he often came to visit us in Lwów. . . . Because Brunio liked to fantasize, he enjoyed our company (the company of children) more than talking to adults. His main topic was life on an uninhabited island—without women."[36]

After his first year of studies, Schulz returned from Lwów to Drohobycz for the summer. On the unseasonably rainy afternoon of June 19, 1911, he happened to witness an election-day massacre, sparked by accusations of electoral fraud. More than two dozen unarmed citizens were shot or bayoneted to death on the streets by panicked troops from two infantry regiments, and scores of others were wounded. The massacre made international news: in London, the *Times* ran an article headlined "The Austrian General Election: Fatal Riot in Galicia." "Believe me," an independent socialist lawmaker, Ernst Breiter, said in Parliament,

> the innocent blood spilled in the streets of Drohobycz did not fall on fruitless ground. On June 19, for the first time, a real equality came about. Jewish blood for the first time mixed with Polish and Ukrainian blood. The unworthy system treated Poles, Ukrainian, and Jews completely equally, when it came to the elections, pushing through a candidate acceptable to the executioners of Galicia! And believe me the memory of that murder in Drohobycz will not disappear without allowing this teaching back into the human heart: only the combined strength of the Polish, Ukrainian, and Jewish peoples can push aside the ruling system![37]

As he watched the violence from the windows of his home on the market square, Schulz was amazed at "the ease of unleashing misery and

Bruno Schulz as a student (CREDIT: PAP)

hyena in man." According to Schulz's student (later a poet and novelist) Andrzej Chciuk, Schulz remarked that the shock of that bloody
day made him want to become a writer. "Writing? It is a need to order
the world."[38]

Among the Refugees: The First World War
VIENNA, 1914–18

After several terms, Schulz's studies in Lwów were interrupted by a
bout of pneumonia, by his father's illness, and by the outbreak of
war. He later said of himself that he had "never studied anything
thoroughly."[39]

　　At the outset of World War I, Russian troops of the Third and
Eighth Armies, led respectively by Nikolai Ruzsky (nicknamed the
"Conqueror of Galicia") and Alexei Brusilov, swept across Galicia.
Residents of Drohobycz first heard the cannons on September 11,

1914. Fearing the Russian offensive, Schulz (accompanied by his sister, Hania, and his twelve-year-old nephew, Ludwik) fled Drohobycz by train several days later. It was the last time he saw his father. A month later, the Schulz shop and home—together with many other buildings on the market square—was burned down by rampaging Russian soldiers, a conflagration witnessed and later evoked by the Drohobycz painter Felix Lachowicz.[40]

Schulz made his way haltingly via Prešov (then in Hungary) to Vienna, where he found an apartment in a large tenement on Seegasse 3 (in the ninth district), a couple doors down from the Jewish-run Rothschild Hospital. After the defeats of the Austro-Hungarian Empire in the Lwów region, some three thousand refugees like Schulz were arriving daily to seek shelter in the capital, part of a massive migration from the east. (Figures of Jewish war refugees in Vienna vary between 75,000 and 120,000. They helped make Vienna the second-largest Jewish community in Europe, after Warsaw.) Joseph Roth said at the time that there was "no harder lot than that of the Eastern Jew newly arrived in Vienna." The Viennese press, especially the Christian Social newspaper *Reichspost*, portrayed Galician Jews as parasites, as collaborators with the Bolsheviks, and as shirkers of military service.[41] (To escape from Austrian military conscription, the failed painter Adolf Hitler had left Vienna a year before Schulz's arrival.) Most able-bodied men were at the front, including Izydor Schulz, who oversaw fortification construction projects for the Austrian army. Those who remained felt the sting of rampant inflation.

In March 1915, Schulz moved to a ground floor apartment nearby, overlooking the Danube canal (Elisabethpromenade 29, today Rossauer Lände). In June, after fierce fighting, the Austrians drove back the Russians from Galicia and reconquered Drohobycz. Bruno's father died that month, at the age of sixty-nine. Bruno, still in Vienna, would have the narrator of a short story say:

I bore a hidden grudge against Mother for the ease with which she moved on past the loss of Father to daily routine. She never loved him, I thought, and because Father was not rooted in the heart of any woman, he also could not grow into any reality and floated eternally on the periphery of life, in half-real regions, on the edges of actuality.[42]

Hit hard by his father's death, Schulz spent nearly two months that summer recuperating and taking the waters in Marienbad, a Czech spa town. Only in mid-December, after more than a year away, did Schulz return to Drohobycz to console his mother.

An attempt to resume his studies in Vienna in 1917–18 proved abortive. Schulz preferred to spend mornings at the Kunsthistorisches Museum and other galleries, acquainting himself with the paintings of Gustav Klimt, Egon Schiele, and Oskar Kokoschka—and with the decadent finale of the empire.

By the time Schulz returned again to Drohobycz in August 1918, the imperial order had unraveled and Austrian Galicia had disappeared. The dreams of a multinational Habsburg K. & K. (*kaiserlich und königlich*, or imperial and royal) were giving way to nationalist nightmares. Suddenly, Joseph Roth said in *The Wandering Jews*, former subjects of Emperor Franz Joseph, the longest-reigning monarch in Europe, became "constrained by the nationalism of others to become a nation." But the decay of the monarchy's patchwork of small homelands also proved fruitful. In various shades of nostalgia, many Habsburg authors—including Joseph Roth, Robert Musil, and Gustav Meyrink (the author of *The Golem*)—mythologized their decomposing world.

The bloodshed did not cease with the war's end in November 1918. Drohobycz briefly came under the rule of the Western Ukrainian Republic. A shortage of coal reached almost catastrophic proportions. Oil factories were paralyzed. Though they declared their neutrality, Jews found themselves caught in the middle of widening Polish-Ukrainian antagonisms. On November 22, a three-day carnivalesque pogrom raged in nearby Lwów (Lemberg, in German) after Polish soldiers had secured the city. At least seventy-three Jews, accused of siding with the Ukrainians, were slaughtered by Polish soldiers, militia volunteers, and ordinary civilians. Dozens of others were robbed and raped. Three synagogues in the Galician capital were desecrated. "Never was Lemberg so far from us as it is today," Vienna's leading paper announced.[43] When word of the harrowing brutality reached Drohobycz, thousands of Jews filled the Choral Synagogue and the courtyard for a memorial service, then formed a spontaneous, black-bannered procession through the streets. When the procession stopped in front of the Jewish council building, a communal leader, Dr. Josef Friedman, expressed "the hope that the victims' spilled blood and their new graves would hasten the arrival of a better, happier future for the Jews."[44] Over the next three years, at least one hundred thousand Jews (according to some estimates up to two hundred thousand) would be murdered in similar ethnic riots in Ukraine and Poland, rehearsals for the mass murder to come.[45]

The Ukrainians were, in turn, ousted by the Poles in June 1919, and Drohobycz became once more a Polish city. In welcoming Polish independence, a new generation of writers would loosen the reins of nationalism and liberate literature from patriotism. "And in the spring," the poet Jan Lechoń wrote in 1920, "let me see spring, not Poland."[46]

CHAPTER 3

THE SENSUOUS SAINT

1919–1930

The role of art is to be a probe sunk into the nameless.[1]

—BRUNO SCHULZ

On All Fours

BAD KUDOWA, GERMANY, AUGUST 1922

After World War I, Schulz joined the Kalleia club (from the Greek Καλη, or beauty), a salon of impassioned Jewish artists and writers who met in Drohobycz for heady discussions of contemporary art.[2] In the summer of 1919, one of the founding members, Maria Budratzka, happened to be sitting on a stool eating freshly fried potato pancakes in the kitchen when Schulz walked in. Schulz asked to draw her, "just as you're sitting."

> He especially liked my clothes, my slippers—black lacquer edged with green fabric—and black silk stockings, then seldom worn by girls in bourgeois circles. My dress was black velvet with black and green crêpe georgette. Bruno Schulz depicted it in his fantasy as somewhat transparent. Soon he returned, had a little drink of wine from my slipper, and after two or three hours the figure and face were already completely drawn.[3]

For the 1920–21 academic year, Bruno Schulz, twenty-eight, enrolled in the School of Fine Arts in Warsaw and rented an apartment on Grzybowski Square. (Twenty years later, the square would be enveloped into the Warsaw ghetto.) The more exhibitions he saw, the greater he doubted his own artistic ambitions. "Due to the many new things I've seen," he wrote to the vice president of the Polish Writers' Union, "I'm under the depressing impression of my own shortcomings and backwardness."[4]

In August 1922, in the spa town of Bad Kudowa, Cecylia Kejlin and her twelve-year-old daughter, Irena, were sitting on a park bench flipping through the pages of Irena's sketchbook. They weren't far from the Basilica of Wambierzyce, a popular pilgrimage site nicknamed "Silesian Jerusalem." According to legend, a blind man had regained his eyesight after praying to a wooden statue of the Virgin Mary there. Irena, a tiny girl with wire-rimmed glasses, looked up and noticed a strange figure on the bench opposite, a man huddled into himself, legs and feet together, palms flat on his knees, dark head tucked between his shoulders. Schulz noticed her curiosity and approached. "If you please—I'm from Poland and I'm also an artist . . . actually, I also draw." He sat down on the edge of the bench, looked over Irena's drawings, and praised them.[5]

For the next three weeks, Schulz would be waiting every morning on that bench in the garden of their guesthouse. He and Irena began to draw together. "Bruno taught me to look and to simplify. . . . The best teacher I ever had." Once she made an ink sketch of Bruno on the bench, his hands between the knees. "He said it was the first time someone had drawn him—which I didn't believe—and kept telling me that it was thanks to me he draws here at all, because he didn't intend to and didn't take any drawing materials with him—which I believed." One morning, he wasn't on the bench. He had disappeared. When the family returned home to Warsaw, several letters from Schulz were waiting for Cecylia, and a lively correspondence began.

A year or two later, when Schulz visited Warsaw, Irena's parents commissioned him to paint portraits of them (Irena said Schulz's portrait of Cecylia reminded her of the style of the French artist Pierre Bonnard) and then of the daughter as she held a red rose. Schulz gave her a lilac instead. "Mum went out somewhere for a meeting," Irena recalled.

> Suddenly Bruno puts down the palette, kneels before me, leans over, and kisses my legs somewhere near the ankle. He is motionless; only the hands move, as though they had independent life, and glide higher and higher over the calves, reaching the knees. From the first moment I froze; I didn't let go of that lilac. . . . But when I felt his hands under my dress, I jumped to my feet. A terrible thought pierced me—not fear (I wasn't afraid of Bruno), but the thought that Bruno would discover that I wear warm woolen panties in spring. . . . Bruno stayed on the carpet on all fours.[6]

After a brief visit to Berlin, where he stayed in the Charlottenburg district with his mother's relatives, the Kuhmerker family, Schulz returned to Vienna for six months in 1923 to prepare for entrance exams at the Vienna Academy of Fine Arts. Denied admission, he returned home, his studies once more left incomplete, and looked for a job.

Clamor and Creation: The Artist as Teacher
DROHOBYCZ, POLAND, SEPTEMBER 1924

Despite his lack of formal training, in September 1924 Schulz began to teach arts and crafts, draftsmanship, and woodworking for thirty hours a week at the high school he himself had attended from 1902 to 1910.[7] About half of his students were Polish Jews.

In November 1924, at the standard request of the Lwów school

Bruno Schulz, "Self-portrait," 1921 (CREDIT: Tomasz
Prażmowski/PAP)

district, Schulz received a signed police approval: "Bruno Schulz, resid-
ing at Floriańska St. 10 in Drohobycz, behaves in a politically and
morally flawless way and enjoys a good reputation among local high-
school professors."

Schulz experienced teaching as a torment; almost from the first he
chafed at the stultifications of his tasks. "I submitted to the demands
of a school routine alien to my temper," he complained, "and how
much I suffered under this yoke."[8] To get through the school day, he
sometimes took drops of valerian root extract (often referred to as

"nature's Valium"). "Boys, a little quieter please," Schulz would say in the carpentry workshop, above the din. "My head is going to explode." Students noticed him pensively chewing roasted coffee beans, which he seemed to keep somewhere in reserve. "When I have to prepare a lesson for the next day, buy materials at the lumberyard," he said, "the entire afternoon and evening are ruined for me already."

Schulz felt a deep need for what he called "my own musical quiet, a stilled pendulum, subject to its own gravitation, along a clear line of track, undistracted by foreign influence. This substantial quiet, positive—full—is already itself almost creativity."[9] Sometimes he fantasized about withdrawing into hermetic seclusion, "like Proust, finally to formulate my world."[10] "Loneliness is the catalyst that makes reality ferment," he said.[11] Schulz could suddenly become witty and chatty, then just as suddenly absent himself and lapse again into pensive silence, into what he called "a state of spellbound suspension within a personal solitude."[12] He made of his solitude a way of seeing.

Throughout his seventeen-year teaching career, he struggled with bouts of debilitating depression, with pains caused by wasted powers, and with the need, as he put it, to "fence off one's inner life, not to permit the vermin of ordinary cares to infest it."[13] Most days, he felt that need unfulfilled.

> I don't know if I can stand this drudgery much longer. School today is not the school of an earlier day, that veritable idyll among professions—almost a sideline, maintaining a modest position on the backdrop of life. . . . It lost long ago that beautiful modesty which predestined it to be the income-yielding profession of people possessed of some mission, some lofty but unprofitable task. . . . Every day I leave that scene brutalized and soiled inside, filled with distaste for myself and so violently drained of energy that several hours are not enough to restore it.[14]

In a letter to the Polish writer Tadeusz Breza, Schulz groused:

> My nerves have been stretched thin like a net over the entire
> handicraft center, have crept along the floor, smothered the
> walls like tapestry and covered the shops and the smithy with a
> dense web. This phenomenon is known to science as telekinesis,
> which makes everything that happens in the shops, the planing
> shed, and so on seem to happen on my skin as well. . . . I can't
> stand people laying claim to my time. They make the scrap they
> touched nauseating to me.[15]

Painting with Words: The Teacher as Storyteller

His students remembered the unobtrusive manner of their timorous
teacher and came to love this shy, half-hidden man, so rich in abili-
ties, who bore not a trace of haughtiness. According to Schulz's
student Leopold Lustig, whose parents owned a market stall where
they sold flour, grains, sugar, and coffee, "he walked sloping towards
the walls, obliquely, almost sidelong, with his head lowered, making way for everybody."[16] Another student compared his frail form
to "a kite oscillating in the wind, held only by precarious ties."[17]
"He deeply understood the process of spiritual growth in children,"
a fellow teacher recalled, "and treated them all with seriousness
and respect."[18]

Students nicknamed him Storyteller (*Bajcarz*). As though to allay
his dread of teaching, Schulz would sit on his chair backward, as if riding a horse, or perch sideways on a carpentry table, looking toward the
wall, and embellish unscripted fairy tales. "We listened spellbound,"
Lustig said. "We'd put a kopeck under a fuse so that the light would
go out. 'Tell us a story, Professor, tell us a story.' He was never angry,
never raised his voice. A silken man, too silken."[19]

Alfred Schreyer, the son of a chief chemist at an oil refinery, began studying with Schulz in 1932, when he was ten years old. Schreyer said his teacher was "modest to the point of exaggeration," but also that improvised storytelling came to Schulz as naturally as leaves to a tree:

> "Professor, maybe you can tell us a fairy tale?"
> "Very well, clear away the shavings," said the teacher.
> Then he sat in profile, not looking at us but at the wall, and started to talk. Nobody moved until Schulz had finished. Unfortunately, all those fairy tales have been lost. If they could be collected, they would constitute a beautiful part of his literary legacy.[20]

Andrzej Chciuk remembered that "Schulz recounted these extraordinarily beautiful and unique stories in an exquisite Polish with a fluency that no one would have suspected of this melancholiac. We all loved these tales and didn't even realize how time flew during them."[21] "We all sat so fascinated," said Emil Górski, "that the school bell signaling the lesson's end would wake us as if from a beautiful dream."[22]

Ze'ev Fleischer, who studied with Schulz for two years, elaborated on the enthrallment:

> In general, he was one of those people who kind of apologize for their very existence, so you can only imagine what went on during his lessons. . . . I think he realized very fast that he could save himself only if he did something different. So he had this brilliant idea—he would tell us stories. Extemporaneous stories, on the spot, and that's what he did, and it was like he was painting with words. He told stories, and we listened—even the wildest animals listened. He did nearly nothing else. I don't think he drew one line on the blackboard the whole year. . . . But he told stories. . . . The wildest kids sat there enchanted. . . . We could smell the things he described. I remember how, for

example, he described the smell of cinnamon, which was dominant in the commercial area of Drohobycz, and I, all my life,
never could stand the smell of cinnamon, but only when he
described it, I loved it.[23]

The teacher often bought sweets for his "little devils" from Mrs.
Liberova, the school watchman's wife, who kept a tiny shop downstairs by the door leading to the schoolyard. He also helped students
who were less well off. According to one student: "Among the students
was a ward of the Jewish orphanage. . . . Schulz would bring the boy
a sandwich every day, and often gave him something to wear. He did
so discreetly."[24]

Ma-zo-chist

Less discreetly, Schulz drew portraits of his students. A student named
Joanna Nestel took private lessons at his home. "Once, when I was
sitting there [in Schulz's house], I noticed that he was drawing my legs,
which was not what I expected. I think it was something he always
liked. He liked women's legs."[25]

His student Harry Zeimer recalled a visit to Schulz's home on
Floriańska Street (named after one of Poland's most venerated saints,
Saint Florian).

> "Please sit down." . . . And there hangs a large picture painted
> by Schulz and there is a naked woman with French black fish-
> net stockings. This is intended sexually. Of course the breast,
> the breast outside, without anything. And with a whip. And
> on her feet, so crouched, is Schulz. . . . Somehow, he looks like
> some kind of animal, but still like Schulz. . . . I never dealt with
> a woman. I was fifteen years old. . . . I was innocent. And seeing
> something like this was uncomfortable for me.[26]

Another student who visited Schulz's home remembered his half-sad, half-playful smile "as he looked at us standing in front of one of his paintings. Its contours break through the fog of memory: a woman with a whip in her hand and a man perversely pleased with the blows given to him. We seventeen-year-old brats goggled our eyes at it." One of the students told Schulz that it was "against nature." Schulz looked at him, and without a word retreated into his room. "We were left alone in the dark, slightly eerie corridor."[27]

Regina Silberner, another Schulz student, remembered that in the 1920s and 1930s Schulz visited his friend Mundek Pilpel nearly every day; his house (Taras Shevchenko Street 8) was next door to the Silberners.[28] The walls featured portraits Schulz had painted of Mundek and his redheaded sister, Trudzia, and several of his drawings. "One stuck in my memory," Regina Silberner recalled. "It depicted a nude woman stepping into a bath into which a black man was pouring blood from a headless body. At her feet were the heads of Mundek, Staszek Weingarten, and other men I knew, and, naturally, Bruno Schulz's head."[29] (All of these works are now lost.)

Schulz's student Andrzej Chciuk remembered the gossip:

"Do you know? He's a masochist."
"What do you say, madam? Ma-zo-chi-what?" . . .
Then, with blushed cheeks, a flipping through the encyclopedia.
Ma-zo-chist.

On a December evening, a group of students returning from a hockey game in Borysław happened to see their teacher in front of the Hotel Europejski, near the Drohobycz bus station. According to one student (with what veracity it is hard to say), Schulz raised his hand in greeting, accidentally revealing a whip hidden under his coat.[30]

Schulz's friend Izydor Friedman spoke of his *vita sexualis*: "His fetishism was in the adoration of beautiful long legs that were necessarily sheathed in black silk stockings. Kissing such legs was—as he told me more than once—the greatest delight. He spoke contemptuously about the sex act itself, though he hardly shied away from it."[31]

The narrator of the title story of Schulz's collection *Sanatorium Under the Sign of the Hourglass* admires young ladies who walk "full of focus and dignity," their "feet in immaculate footwear." He notes, "And then it becomes clear that what they carry above themselves with such care and excitement is but a certain *idée fixe* of their own perfection, which through the power of their conviction almost becomes reality."[32]

Graven Images: *The Booke of Idolatry*
DROHOBYCZ, 1924

> Oh, those luminous drawings, springing up as if under a stranger's hand.[33]

—BRUNO SCHULZ

In one of Schulz's stories, the narrator, Joseph, says of his own bewitching drawings, "From the start I was assailed by doubt as to whether I am in fact their author. At times they seem to me to be involuntary plagiarism, something that was hinted to me, handed to me."[34] The same might be said of Schulz's artworks, rendered in a style of grotesque realism in a line reaching back through Max Klinger and Francisco Goya all the way to the German Renaissance painters Albrecht Dürer and Lucas Cranach the Elder. (According to one friend, Schulz "spoke in superlatives of Goya as his own unsurpassed prototype and ideal.")[35]

Some of Schulz's visual art appeared innocent enough: a series of drawings on Jewish themes featured Jews gathered around festive tables or around a well, with titles like "Hasidim at the Passover

Table," "Hasidim at the Well," and "Two Boys in Yarmulkes and a Naked Woman in a Town Street." And Schulz excelled at portraits and self-portraits.[36] ("I have long had the idea," Schulz said, "that you could distill an entire story or novel from the face of a person you meet.")[37]

"I believe that Schulz was first and foremost a great artist," Drohobycz native Henryk Grynberg told me, "who tried to translate his visual art into words to the point of impossibility." As in his writing, in his graphic art Schulz equates femaleness with fecundity and maleness with inadequacy. The drawings and etchings feature imperious and unattainable long-legged women, as though etched out of darkness. Sometimes they stand, their heads held high, with ermine fur stoles across their shoulders. Sometimes they recline in sumptuous serenity on an altar-like divan (often with a partial view of Drohobycz visible in the background, as though in a symbiosis of the real and the imagined). In his titles, Schulz gives these statuesque women mythic names: Undula, Susannah, Circe, Infanta. Others carry titles like "Girl with a Briefcase Stepping on a Prostrate Man" and "Maid Flogging a Naked Man with a Birch Whip." Mannequins have a prominent place in Schulz's fiction. Like them, the women of his etchings are speechless idols—aloof, unpropitiated, and sufficient in themselves. They scorn their worshipful male idolaters, who in sublime surrender both await pleasure and expect pain. The coquettish women, luxuriating in their own beauty, give the men no more than a passing glance. They are insensitive to male obeisances and prostrations. In their demonic dominion they remain arrogantly heedless of the abject, self-abasing men—sometimes rendered with more than a touch of self-portrayal, just as medieval artists lent their own features to faces of saints—supplicating and entreating at their coveted feet.

Sometimes Schulz's emasculated men—stylized representations of self-denigrated and self-marginalized masculinity—kiss or wash the women's feet in erotic exhilaration. More often, unable to worship the idealized goddesses directly, they genuflect with exaggerated gestures and surreptitious or beseeching glances before a ritual substitute: a beribboned shoe, a fetishized foot, or a slender ankle in stockings. These stunted figures want chastisement. They assume postures of unfulfilled yearning.[38]

Schulz reverses Nietzsche's oft-quoted line from *Thus Spoke Zarathustra*: "You are going to women? Do not forget the whip!" In one etching, a young woman wields a whip to tame male circus performers. In another, "On Cythera," Schulz depicts a whip-wielding woman riding a carriage drawn by three naked cowering men.

Still others feature hybrid man-beast creatures, sometimes leashed, like a crawling man with a leopard's hind legs. (Schulz's story "The Sanatorium Under the Hourglass" features a dog-man: "a dog, certainly, but a dog in human shape.") The same obsessive eroticism suffuses ex libris bookplates Schulz designed for Stanislaw (Staszek) Weingarten and Maximilian Goldstein.[39]

Many of Schulz's startling works were born in vitro, etched onto glass plates, as though scratched out of darkness. As Schulz described it:

> It isn't aquafortis etching but the so-called *cliché-verre* technique, using a glass plate. You draw with a stylus on a black gelatin layer covering the glass, and the translucent negative drawing obtained in this way is treated like a photographic negative, i.e., it is printed in a photographic copying frame onto light-sensitive paper, developed, fixed, and rinsed.[40]

Schulz bought the plates from his friend Bertold Schenkelbach, a Drohobycz photographer whose studio at 3 Mickiewicz (now

Bruno Schulz,
"Ex Libris Eroticis,"
1920 (CREDIT: Yad
Vashem Art Museum)

Shevchenko) Street became a hub of the city's artistic life. Bertold's
son Erwin, born in 1929, told me that he remembers Schulz's frequent
visits and his "slantwise vaulted face that looks like a bird gearing
up for take-off." Erwin credits his father with giving Schulz the idea
for this technique, which Schulz was the only graphic artist in Poland
to use.[41]

In 1924, Schulz attached twenty-six of these prints to white card-
board folios and bound them in canvas under the title *The Booke of
Idolatry*. (Schulz used the archaic Polish word *xiega* ["booke"], which
suggests a sacred text.) Each copy featured different prints and different hand-illustrated covers. Of the several dozen copies, he gave a

few to friends and tried to sell the rest. The first print in *The Booke of Idolatry* is a self-portrait of the artist, hunched over in deference, carrying a tray on which lies a golden crown. The last print portrays Schulz holding an open book while abjectly approaching a half-naked woman who carries a whip in her right hand. In staging these surrender scenes—images of his private phantasms—Schulz is both director and actor.

Schulz's artworks can be seen as comments on what previously had been hidden (sexual and social female power). In Schulz's art—an autodidact's visual vocabulary of degradation that unmistakably pulls toward the masochistic—pain becomes pleasure when it involves submission to an idealized figure. It reflects his obsession with what he called a "world

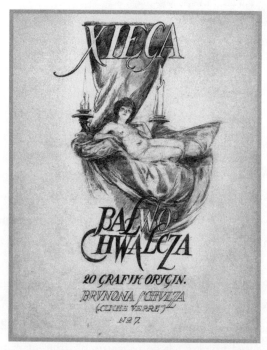

Bruno Schulz, frontispiece of *The Booke of Idolatry*, 1920s (CREDIT: Biblioteka Jagiellońska, public domain)

Bruno Schulz, "Procession," from *The Booke of Idolatry*, 1920s (CREDIT: Biblioteka Jagiellońska, public domain)

of sewers and gutters . . . a compost." It is in such marginal and undignified places, he added, that life teems and tumbles most abundantly.

> While under the shield of adult and official forms we pay homage
> to more elevated and refined values, our actual life runs secretly
> and without more elevated sanctions in this dirty indigenous
> region. . . . It is better to develop under the hundredfold pres-
> sure of disgrace and shame than on the plateau of sublimation.[42]

Schulz's friend Maria Chazen remembered her surprise at his depictions of a figure who had been run over in the street by a horse-drawn carriage or a car. She asked Schulz who this man was. "This man is me!" he said, without a hint of sublimation.[43]

A Slave to Art

TRUSKAWIEC, POLAND, SUMMER 1928

Afflicted with an inferiority complex, agoraphobia, and hypersensitivity to sounds, Bruno Schulz was as anxious in life as undaunted in art. "He suffered from all the inhibitions that a writer can suffer," said Isaac Bashevis Singer. "When you look at his picture you see the face of a man who never made peace with life."[44]

Schulz sought in his art a confirmation of his existence; art for him was something sacerdotal. Schulz considered art—and its magical relation to reality—from the point of view of its creator. In time he became inextricably bound up with his art and its disinhibiting effect. He saw that art as his true element, as an expression of his inmost self. One of the foremost figures of twentieth-century Polish literature, Witold Gombrowicz, appraised Schulz as "a false ascetic, a sensuous saint . . . a monk without God." Gombrowicz said that Schulz was consumed by art "with a zeal and concentration I had never seen in anyone else— he, a fanatic of art, its slave. . . . He preferred to lose himself in it, to vanish altogether."[45]

At first, Schulz gave his art a pretext: he told friends and colleagues that his outré drawings were illustrations for Sacher-Masoch's novella *Venus in Furs* (1870), which had appeared in Polish in 1913. In the novella, the urtext of masochism, the protagonist, Severin, finds the highest form of delight in being dominated by beautiful women.[46] When Schulz began to exhibit his artworks under his own name, he preferred to do so outside Drohobycz, in galleries in Warsaw (1922), Lwów (1922, 1930, 1935, and 1940), Vilna (1923), and Kraków (1930 and 1931), often in group shows alongside other Jewish artists.[47] The National Art Gallery in Lwów bought two of his works. An acquaintance, Juliusz Flaszen, said Schulz had little penchant for publicity and often sold his works "at wretched prices. His self-esteem was so low that he always feared to overcharge and felt sufficiently rewarded by people's buying his work at all."[48]

If some were baffled by Schulz's graphic art and its tawdry preoccupation with servility and subservience, others were scandalized. In the summer of 1928, Schulz exhibited fifty or sixty works in the banquet hall in a resort in Truskawiec, the spa town just south of Drohobycz. Schulz spent summers here to "take the waters," listen to the murmur of the forest streams, and stroll along streets lined by white-blossomed cherry trees. "It's my favorite place," he wrote. "One day I'm going to write a novel about it."[49] Maksymilian Thullie, seventy-five, a mustached Christian Democratic senator and a former rector of the Lwów Polytechnic, where Schulz had studied, happened to stop by. He was stunned by the indecency of Schulz's works. Schulz was enraged. "Can you imagine?" he said to a friend at the resort. "I was called in to the spa administration and told that some senator who is taking a cure has categorically demanded that my exhibition should be closed since in his view it's abominable pornography!" "If the senator succeeds in closing the exhibition," the friend replied, "the resulting scandal would make your name famous overnight."[50] Another visitor to the gallery was outraged to recognize his wife depicted among the seductresses in one of Schulz's more lascivious drawings. As a result, Schulz was suspended from teaching for two months.

A critic who reviewed that exhibition for a Polish-language Zionist daily described Schulz as "one of the most talented and subtle artists in contemporary Poland . . . a visionary of feverish dreams, a painfully high-strung man vibrating with the sound of deeply hidden feelings."[51]

An exhibition in Lwów in the spring of 1930 drew mixed reviews. One critic lauded Schulz's prints for their "marvelous talent for combining fantastic elements surrounded by a mysterious charm of vision and dream phantoms with the most real shapes and forms." Another, referring to Belgian artist Félicien Rops, pronounced Schulz's style as

"marked by Rops-like satanism."[52] "As a draftsman and graphic artist," S. I. Witkiewicz said, "he belongs to the realm of the demonic," to
those who paint "with the delight of debauchery scenes that are more
hellish than heavenly. . . . His graphics are poems of pedal atrocity. . . .
In Schulz's case we find ourselves if not in the realm of genius . . .
then certainly at its border."[53] Kazimierz Majewski, writing in *Gazeta
Lwowska*, predicted that Schulz's work would no doubt prove as valuable to a psychoanalyst as to an art historian.

Those who wished to overcome male vulnerability were offended
by an artist who embraced it. What was it that struck viewers of
Schulz's art as "indecent": its sexual explicitness or its honesty?

CHAPTER 4
THE WRITER DISCOVERED

1930–1939

This is the best kind of reading, when between the lines you read yourself, your own book.[1]

—BRUNO SCHULZ

Minds Meet: Bruno and Debora
ZAKOPANE, POLAND, SUMMER 1930

One morning in the summer of 1930, in Zakopane, a resort town known as the winter capital of Poland, two modernists met—one writing in Yiddish, the other in Polish.[2]

Bruno Schulz, thirty-eight, the self-effacing high school teacher from Drohobycz, had come to get away from his native city's "rich but empty and colorless vegetation of vulgarity," as he called it. While in Zakopane, Schulz saw the versatile poet and painter S. I. Witkie-wicz (known as Witkacy), a brilliant figure of the Polish avant-garde. Witkacy and Schulz had met in Drohobycz five years earlier through Emmanuel Pilpel. "My inventiveness," Schulz confided to him, "leans, just like yours, towards aberration, persiflage, buffoonery, and self-irony."[3] Witkacy had drawn a portrait of Schulz in charcoal and pastels, his head grafted onto a fish tail.

Heedless of Schulz's wish to be free of distraction, Witkacy invited his fellow artist to his atelier, where he was painting a portrait of the avant-garde poet Debora Vogel (nicknamed Dosia), thirty, the "wandering star" of Yiddish literature. Born in a Galician town called Burshtyn, Vogel was educated in Vienna and Kraków, where she earned a doctorate in philosophy with a dissertation on Hegel's aesthetics. "The more conservative poets mocked and mimicked her obscure style," Isaac Bashevis Singer said. "A woman with a Ph.D. in philosophy was highly suspect in this circle." Her father, Anshel, was a Hebraist; her mother, Lea, a teacher. Her uncle Marcus Ehrenpreis, the chief rabbi of Stockholm, had worked closely with Theodor Herzl at the First Zionist Congress.[4]

Vogel had published her first story, "Messiah," at age nineteen. The year she met Schulz, she had published her first collection of free-verse poems in Yiddish, *Day Figures* (1930), and had started her second, *Mannequins* (1934).[5] Her condensed painterly poems aimed, she said, at "a lyric of cool stasis and geometrical ornamentality with its monotony and rhythm of return." Her Yiddish poems were preoccupied with *shund*; this Yiddish term encompasses "lowbrow" literature, tacky mass culture, and kitschy commodities. One cycle of poems, called "Shoddy Ballads," features streetwalkers, Parisian vagabonds, and trashy novels. She wrote essays—many with polemical bite—on photomontage and literary montage; on abstract art; on the painter Marc Chagall (whom she knew personally); on racism and anti-Semitism ("Exoticized People"); and on the history of secular Yiddish writing in Galicia—a relatively young tradition "initiated," Vogel noted, "and for a long time cultivated by, women poets who as a rule did not have access to the Hebrew language and the philosophy of the Talmud."

Vogel's style reflected her vast erudition in Yiddish, Polish, German, and Hebrew. "Every word Debora writes," said the Yiddish poet Melekh Ravitch, "is lined with at least three books she has read. She knew several languages, all as fluently as a native tongue. Only when it came to *mame-loshn* did she understand every nuance and speak it in a way that showed she was prepared to learn more and more, with great devotion and love."[6] "These are no artworks," Vogel said to Ravitch of her poems, "no surface 'experiments,' but extracts from life and experiences for which I paid a high price." Those extracts, with their austere and dispassionate coolness, offered no solace to conventional taste. "I am used to being disregarded by poetic ignoramuses," Vogel confessed to Schulz.

Moving between gravity and levity, Vogel experimented with what she called "the method of simultaneity" (*simultanishkeyt*), in which "cast-off, 'small' events receive the same importance as 'great' heroic life events." Vogel called her final book, the prose collection *Acacias Bloom* (Yiddish 1935, Polish 1936), a "montage novel." In his review of it, Schulz admired the way Vogel allows human fates to be expressed only "once they pass through thousands of hearts, when they become colorless, impersonal, and representative—coins for exchange, anonymous, worn-out, and banal formulae." In this blooming of forms, Schulz adds, Vogel captures "the sound and sweetness of banality."

The two writers understood each other by mere glances. An easy eloquence developed between them over long Sunday strolls, a form of intimacy that catalyzed an incipient literary creativity. "Our conversations and our interactions then," Vogel said, "were one of the rare wonderful things that happen only once in a lifetime, perhaps only once in several hopeless, colorless lives."[7] Schulz described her as "a dear, noble, wise person."[8] Schulz's mother had earlier tried to match Bruno and his cousin Ernestina (Tinka) Kupferberg. Tinka, seven years younger than Schulz, did not take a liking to him.[9]

In 1931, about a year after they met, Schulz proposed to Vogel. His mother, Henrietta, had died that April, and could not object. Vogel's mother, Leonia, fearing a mésalliance, opposed the match for her only daughter. According to Vogel's friend Rachel Auerbach, "depressive, hypochondriac Schulz of course agreed with [Leonia's] opinion that he was not a suitable candidate for a husband and father."[10]

Vogel married another man in October 1931, and her relationship with Schulz took an epistolary turn. Schulz's letters, sent from Drohobycz to Lwów, at once seduced Vogel and kept her at a distance. ("There was a time when I put everything I had into letter writing," Schulz confessed to a friend, "then my only creative outlet.")[11] The postscripts of Schulz's letters to Vogel—descriptions of Drohobycz through the eyes of a child—grew more fantastical and unmoored from the contents of the letters, like boats pushed away from the shore of reality.

The literary critic Walter Benjamin, Schulz's exact contemporary, once remarked that in the Jewish concept of time, "every second was the narrow gate through which the Messiah could enter."[12] Vogel found in the slant of Schulz's syntax—faultlessly tuned to his secularized messianic hungers, to his way of transmuting the mundane into the transcendent—an unerring example of this understanding of time. She heard in the postscripts the reverberations of a new if still muffled melody, undulating motifs that meandered through different keys. She became entranced by how those postscripts dissolved the familiar into the unfamiliar. ("Some event," Schulz wrote, "perhaps minor and modest with regard to its provenance and its own means, may, when brought close to the eye, reveal in its interior an infinite, radiant perspective.")[13] Vogel showed them to her friend Rachel Auerbach, who agreed that they should be published to the widest audience.[14]

Emmanuel (Mundek) Pilpel—a portly, balding, nearsighted friend of Schulz's—had in parallel reached the same conviction. In his free time, Schulz used to burrow into the bookshop run by Jacob Pilpel, Mundek's father, and bury his head in the pages of Marcel Proust, Rilke, and Thomas Mann. (Schulz read *Buddenbrooks* and the four-part novel *Joseph and His Brothers* in the original German, and later corresponded with Mann).[15] Long before Schulz's literary debut, Mundek recognized the sumptuousness of Schulz's letters to him. "Delighted, Mundek would read these letters to me," Regina Silberner recalled, "lifting his majestic index finger and saying: remember what I tell you. Bruno will become a famous writer."[16]

Amid the ferment of interwar Poland, two opposite motions guided Jewish writers who followed the torches that lit the way toward modern culture. The first impulse, Schulz's, surged outward toward a sublime mastery of Polish, sometimes with self-assertion and sometimes with worshipful self-abasement vis-à-vis an idealized majority culture. The second, Vogel's, traveled inward to find ways of importing the innovations of European modernism into a newly unfettered Yiddish. Each would be tragically truncated.

"An Encounter Between a Comet and the Sun"
WARSAW, POLAND, APRIL 16, 1933

With a sureness of touch that surprised him, Schulz transformed the postscripts into a collection of voluptuous short stories called *Cinnamon Shops*, a singular book addressed in intimacy to a single reader. He called the book

> an autobiography, or rather a spiritual genealogy, a genealogy par excellence in that it follows the spiritual family tree down to those depths where it merges into mythology. . . . In a way these "stories" are real, they represent my way of living, my personal fate. The overriding motif of this fate is a profound loneliness, isolation from the stuff of daily life.[17]

Moved by an autobiographical impulse, Schulz put pen to paper to overcome that loneliness, "to feel that my world borders on other worlds, that at those borders these worlds cross and interpenetrate."[18]

Schulz had long concealed his literary ambitions; beset by insecurities, he had written in isolation (as the Poles say, *do szuflady*, "for the desk drawer"). He neither dared think of himself as destined for acclaim nor expected to be read by generations yet unborn. But on Easter Sunday 1933, on leave from teaching, Schulz traveled to Warsaw in the hopes of showing his short stories to the urbane grande dame of Polish letters, Zofia Nałkowska.[19] Nałkowska—a feminist, an accomplished novelist, the vice president of the Polish PEN Club, a member of the Polish Academy of Literature, and an editor with the prestigious Rój publishing house (named after the Polish for "beehive")—had long experience in turning away provincial scribblers and literary malingerers. But she also had a reputation for sniffing out new talent, for being one of those publishers who seek out the books that they themselves would have wanted to write. Schulz coveted her approval.

Taut with anticipation, Schulz approached the sculptor Magdalena Gross, a friend of both Debora Vogel and Zofia Nałkowska's sister, Hanna Nałkowska-Bick. They met in a guesthouse on Nowy Świat Street run by Magdalena's mother. Having arrived the previous day, Schulz intended to catch the evening train back to Drohobycz. "The fate of my book depends on you," he said to Magdalena. "I know that you are a friend of Zofia Nałkowska and that if you phoned her and asked her to meet with me, she would not refuse you. Please do it; I have only this afternoon—the return train leaves tonight and I've no time to lose."

With some reluctance, Magdalena agreed; she left the room to call Nałkowska and returned a few minutes later in triumph. "Grab a taxi right away and go to this address." She handed Schulz Nałkowska's address on Marszałkowska Street. Schulz, his hands trembling, rushed out of the guesthouse only to realize he'd forgotten his manuscript. "My briefcase!" He retrieved it, ran downstairs, and hailed a taxi.

He returned to the guesthouse an hour later. "Nałkowska asked me to read a few of the first pages, then she interrupted and sent me out, asking me to leave the manuscript with her. She wanted to read it through herself. It was an encounter between a comet and the sun. The comet burned up."

That evening, Nałkowska telephoned Magdalena. "This is the most sensational discovery in our literature! I'll run tomorrow to Rój so that this book can be published as quickly as possible!" Magdalena relayed Nałkowska's verdict to Schulz. He stood stupefied, momentarily robbed of his voice.[20]

In June and August of that year, Schulz, forty-one, returned to Warsaw to spend time with Nałkowska, forty-eight. The woman-about-town found his Drohobycz diffidence refreshing. Soon enough she nonchalantly dropped her affair with a married Croatian writer and became Schulz's protectress and lover.[21] *Au fait* with literary circles in the capital, she used her clout to grant Schulz entrée to a world of avant-gardists, authors of Futurist manifestos, and proletarian poets who inhabited Warsaw's interwar bohemia.

The Father, the Son, and the Alluring Adela: *Cinnamon Shops*
DECEMBER 1933

Cinnamon Shops appeared in December 1933. Its publisher, Rój, was infamous for offering low advances and unfavorable contractual terms to debut writers like Schulz.[22] Izydor, who supported his younger brother's writerly ambitions, helped defray the costs of publication.

Asked about the book, Schulz resorted to the third person and preferred to say what his aims were not:

> It is the author's conviction that there is no way to plumb the deepest level of biography or make out the true shape of personal destiny either by describing the external curriculum vitae or by psychological analysis, however deeply the latter might probe. The ultimate given data of human life, he submits, lie in a spiritual dimension, not in the category of facts but in their transcendent meaning.[23]

The book's voluptuous verbal architecture takes its torque from Schulz's steady and seamless sentences, a mellifluous flow of metaphors—metaphors not as literary decorations but as a way of thinking. Schulz draws from within himself strange sentences that snake back to the origins of things. Realistic descriptions accumulate to fantastic effect and feverish ferment. Images cascade as though searching for concordances and discordances. Time itself, undisciplined, forks into detours, plays practical jokes, and keeps "getting lost amid a thousand subterfuges."[24] It's an idiom easy to praise and impossible to imitate.

The book's thirteen interlaced stories constellate around three protagonists. The sensitive boy Joseph (named after Jacob's son in the book of Genesis) narrates the stories—in effect narrating his own birth as an artist. Seeking escape from the tedium of daily life, freeing himself from causality, Joseph plunges into a world of picturesque plasticity. He yields to the joy of finding the hidden life in inanimate things—like tailors' dummies—and endows them with an opulent mythology.

In one of the stories, Joseph (the artist as a child) watches a magician pull endless streams of ribbons from his top hat. It was clear, Joseph says, "that he was drawing this abundance not from his own resources, that celestial sources not in accordance with human measures and accounts had simply opened up for him."[25] An apt description, perhaps, of Schulz's own creativity.

The second protagonist, the father, is an eccentric cloth merchant who wavers between mercantilism and mysticism. (Schulz's working title for what became *Cinnamon Shops* had been *Reminiscences of Father*.) Schulz describes him as a "heresiarch" possessed of heretical doctrines, "a voluntary outcast" who, in failing health, "floated eternally on the periphery of life."[26]

> At that time, my father's health began to fail. Already in the
> first weeks of that early winter there were periods when he spent

entire days in bed surrounded by bottles, pills, and the account books that were brought to him from the office. A bitter odor of illness settled on the bottom of the room.[27]

Father "waged war on the boundless element of boredom stupefying our city"[28] by breeding birds—an extravagant collection of peacocks, pheasants, and pelicans—in the attic aviary and by experimenting with electricity and mesmerism (like a tailor animating his dummies) before an audience of "elegant female disciples and male followers with waxed mustaches." Schulz would call him "a quintessential victim."[29]

Father also flirts with ideas as though they were alluring women. He delivers his metaphysical monologues in his shop to giggling seamstresses (the undifferentiated duo Pauline and Poldine), their hips framed by garter belts, as the sewing machine purrs in background. He lectures them, for instance, on the properties of matter: "lasciviously submissive, malleable like a woman, compliant in response to every impulse. . . . Matter is the most passive, defenseless being in the cosmos. Anyone can knead it, shape it; it obeys everyone. . . . Herein is the starting point for a new apologia for sadism."[30]

Father reserves his main attentions for the third main character, his arch-adversary: the sassy, seductive, slender-limbed housemaid, Adela, who appears in nineteen of Schulz's thirty-two stories. (Her figure is likely based on a real-life maid in the Schulz household named Rachela, or Ruchla, who prepared dinners, scrubbed the tin pots, swept the parquet floors, pulled open the heavy curtains in the morning, did much of the household shopping, and often punished Bruno.)[31] In her prosaic and down-to-earth way, this unmeek maiden also delights in her mysterious dominance over Father as she interrupts his disquisitions and ridicules his flights of fancy.

Sometimes the flow of ideas allows Father to forget about Adela, and sometimes not. Her cleaning of his room, for instance, was a great and important ceremony for him that he never neglected to witness, following all Adela's manipulations with a mixture of terror and delight. He ascribed deeper, symbolic meaning to all her activities. When the girl, with youthful and bold movements, pushed a brush on a long pole over the floor, that was almost beyond his strength. Tears would flow from his eyes, his face would be overwhelmed with quiet laughter, and a delightful orgasmic spasm would shake his body. . . . Thanks to this, Adela had almost unlimited power over Father.[32]

In another scene, Adela lifts her dress to reveal a foot covered in black silk. "Adela's outstretched slipper trembled slightly and glistened like a serpent's tongue."[33] Confronted with this titillation, Father falls helplessly to his knees.

"Like Meteors"
1934

The appearance of *Cinnamon Shops* vaulted Schulz to the summits of Polish prose. The novelist and essayist Tadeusz Breza (a longtime member of Zofia Nałkowska's salon) called *Cinnamon Shops* "an incredibly beautiful book . . . embodied poetry."[34] The "ravishing" book, said S. I. Witkiewicz (Witkacy), "left me thunderstruck." He hailed the author's "facility born of real inspiration and the simplicity and earnestness of a child." He announced that Schulz's sentences, "like meteors, illuminate unknown landscapes, which we, usually sunk in the sea of daily trivialities, are unable to see. . . . Schulz shows the unfathomable strangeness of everyday life." In a letter to his wife, Witkacy wrote, "If Szulz [*sic*] described the whole world in this way, and not just one corner of it, he would be the most brilliant writer in the world."[35]

Avant-garde Polish poets—including Julian Tuwim, Aleksander

Wat, Antoni Slonimski, and Józef Wittlin—immediately sighted the
blaze of Schulz's genius. "In the circles of young Polish poets to which
I belonged in the late 1930s," Czesław Miłosz said, "Schulz's name
was surrounded by a special, magical aura."[36] Those circles regarded
Schulz, Witold Gombrowicz, and Witkacy—close friends and peers—
as the three musketeers of the Polish avant-garde; their names were
so inseparably linked, one critic remarked, as to make them Poland's
"literary Marx Brothers."[37] Yet Schulz's writing, which oscillates out
of sync with any canon, is perhaps better described as a modernist
movement of one.

Rokhl Korn, a leading Yiddish poet from Galicia and a friend of
Debora Vogel's, reviewed *Cinnamon Shops* for a Yiddish-language
weekly:

> While reading this short novella, in which the imaginary takes
> on the fixed forms of reality, one has the impression that Schulz
> wants to lead the enslaved word out of its ages-long *golus*. Schulz
> breaks down the hardened shell that had, over the course of
> years, formed layers around the kernel of the word, and restores
> to it its own meaning, its form, sound and aroma. Entering
> between the covers of the Book of Genesis, Schulz has found a
> way, through the spirit of words, to the essence of things. . . .
> This is not a grotesque stage play of Andersen's fairy tales for
> children. It is a revelation.[38]

Alongside such hymns of praise, *Cinnamon Shops* also attracted slings
and hatchets. Under the headline "One Strange Book," a reviewer in
Chwila (Moment) remarked on the exaggerated "morbidity" that put
the book "beyond evaluation."[39] A Polish Marxist critic caustically classified Schulz's prose as a "literature of sick maniacs . . . exhibitionists
and psychopaths, degenerates . . . hypochondriacs, misanthropes."[40]

In January 1934, just after his literary debut, Schulz met Zofia

Nałkowska in Zakopane. She took "personal pride" in Schulz's new-found success and lavished on him a maternal protection. When he returned to Drohobycz, Nałkowska said that "he left behind him a huge empty space, even though he is so small. I correspond to his great-est need, which would seem to be for adoration [for adoring others]— I am charming and kind, and I allow him to idolize me. . . . Even if the erotic confessions have not all been made, our mental bonds are very taut."[41]

They next saw each other in Warsaw in April, when he stayed with her for a week at her apartment on Marszałkowska Street. They listened to Stravinsky and Mahler on her record player and attended theater performances, including an adaptation of Dostoyevsky's *Crime and Punishment* and *Krasin*, an experimental Yiddish play by Michał Brandt. Schulz sent a bouquet of roses for her name day (May 15).

By May, however, Nałkowska's feelings had shifted.

Certainly I am not the essence of his existence as it might seem from his letters, from his pretty words. It was not even called love. Rather it was worship, giving praise to me. And it origi-nated not in my quality (not only in it) but in his nature, in the craving to be humbled and lost in adoration.[42]

Mismeasure of a Man
DROHOBYCZ, 1934

The flattering reviews of *Cinnamon Shops* did not fundamentally alter Schulz's frame of mind. "You ask, 'What the hell is depressing you?' I don't know how to answer that," he wrote to a friend in the spring of 1934. "The sadness of life, fear of the future, some dark conviction that everything is headed for a tragic end. . . . I don't write anything. I even feel deep revulsion towards copying something already written. And such an improbable spring has just come to the world, with all its breezes, lights, presentiments—only to make me realize that I am already on the other side of all springs."[43] Half a year later, he wrote to the same friend: "For a month I've written nothing, painted nothing, and sometimes I have the feeling that I'll never again write anything good. I really feel sorry about wasting such success that I achieved with *The Shops*, and I will waste it if I don't publish something at least at the same level this year."[44]

Even now, Schulz's hometown treated him deafly at best.[45] "He was very shy and bottled up," his student Ze'ev Fleischer said. "His stock was very low in the eyes of others, of strangers. . . . And someone like Schulz, who wrote 'nonsense,' counted for nothing. At most they regarded him as human sawdust."[46] Emmanuel Weintraub, who lived in Drohobycz then, remembered a similar indifference: "In Drohobycz itself one did not know very much about him, and one was not interested either, because these were oil people. Imagine this was a little Texas."[47]

Just after his literary debut, Schulz, suffering from what he called "hypochondriacal musings," wrote to the Ministry of Religion and Public Education in Warsaw to request paid leave for the 1934–35 school year. He had no high expectations of the pen pushers there.

> The undersigned art teacher at Drohobycz Public Secondary School is the author of the recently published book *Cinnamon Shops*. According to the enclosed press reviews, unanimous critical opinion has acclaimed that book as an achievement in the area of Polish prose, which obliges the author to further pursue his literary endeavors. Recently, I have undertaken certain steps and made plans for a larger work, which cannot be accomplished during random hours on the margins of my duties at school. Trapped between the difficult tasks of the teaching profession and a responsible artistic career—far from any artistic aids and stimuli provided by large cultural centers—I notice

with despair that my energy has dissipated fruitlessly, and the
realization of my goal recedes into an unattainable future. . . .
I must focus my energy on a total artistic deed, of which I am
fully capable. The pressure of unrealized goals encourages me
to request the following: Could the Ministry possibly grant me
a paid leave of absence for one year?

Schulz's request was denied without explanation in May 1934.

The next year, he again attempted to reason with the board of
education, and again expressed a vacillation between duty and dream:

I am a painter by education and professional calling, but as sometimes happens during an artist's evolution, an inner impulse and
expressive need prompted me toward literary experiments. . . .
Haphazard, intermittent efforts undertaken on the margins of
my teaching responsibilities have resulted in the dispersal and
loss of the artistic impulse which should be channeled entirely
in one direction. On the other hand, the tasks and duties of an
art teacher require that I concentrate fully on the subject. They
dictate an inner attitude which is incompatible with the artist's
work, full of inner tension.

Later, Schulz appealed not for a leave but for a transfer:

The countryside where I live would be perhaps beneficial for
the artist already mature in his development, the artist who
only weaves his thread out of the material collected over years
of studies and experiences. There is no such sense of completion, readiness, and maturity in my case. On the contrary, I am
haunted by a scorching sense of the inadequacy of my knowledge. . . . My present situation does not solve the problem of
spiritual nourishment, of inner regeneration, without which a

developing artist must wither and perish without succor. . . . This concern for contact with intellectual life, and a sense of responsibility toward my work, incline me to extend the following request: Could the Board of Education kindly consider the possibility of transferring me to an equivalent job, i.e. as a teacher in a secondary, vocational, or even elementary school in Lvov?[48]

His entreaties again fell on deaf ears.

"She Enslaves Me": Józefina
DROHOBYCZ, 1933–36

> This beauty regenerates rapidly through the medium of distance and becomes painful, unbearable, and beyond all measure.[49]

—BRUNO SCHULZ

In the spring of 1933, Schulz came to idolize Józefina Szelińska, twenty-eight, a teacher in Drohobycz's Teachers' Seminary. Schulz wanted Józefina—Juna, as he called her, after the Roman goddess of marriage and fertility—to pose for a portrait, the first of many he would make of her. Too shy to ask her in person, he sent his colleague Aleksy Kuszczak, a math and physics teacher, to arrange a meeting. "He put away his pastels and we talked," Józefina recalled. "These meetings at my house and then our walks through the meadows behind the house, in the birch forest, gave me a foretaste of something miraculous, inimitable experiences which so rarely occur in life. It was the sheer essence of poetry."

Schulz told Józefina that he saw in every person some kind of animal resemblance.

"Which animal do I resemble?" she asked.

"An antelope," Schulz said.

"And you?"

"A dog," he answered.[50]

As she discerned the apparent contradictions of his personality, Józefina came to see Schulz not as a dog but as a kobold—a mythological sprite neither boy nor man, alternately virtuous and mischievous. She remarked on Schulz's "extraordinary kindness, modesty, and apparent humility, and at the same time high sense of his own artistry. . . . The artist absorbed the human being in him. The term *kobold* was thus no mere metaphor."[51]

Thirteen years younger than Schulz, Józefina had grown up in Janów, a town near Lwów. Her parents, Zygmunt and Helena Schrenzel, had converted from Judaism to Catholicism. In 1919, she formally "Polonized" her last name to Szelińska. (Her biographer Agata Tuszyńska told me that during a visit to Janów, almost seventy years after the war, she asked a passerby if he knew where the Szelińska family had lived. "Oh, those Jews?" came the reply. "Sure, they lived right over there.") She had earned a master's degree in Polish Romantic poetry and a doctorate in philology and art history. She read fluently in German and French.

After returning to Drohobycz from her summer 1933 holidays on the Baltic coast, she was visited by Schulz nearly every evening. They discovered a shared love of Rilke ("godlike Rilke," as Schulz called him), Franz Kafka, and Thomas Mann. He read to her from unpublished drafts of his stories. She visited his home on Floriańska Street only twice. "In both cases," she said, "I was impressed by the silent morbid atmosphere that pervaded the whole house, as if on the margins of life."[52]

In 1934, Józefina Szelińska lost her teaching job in Drohobycz and moved to Janów and then to Warsaw. From then on, she saw Schulz only intermittently on holidays (winter holidays in Warsaw, summers in Zakopane), and they communicated through what she called "passionate letters that saved Bruno from his depressions, full of mothering protection and care for this man, helpless in the sphere of life."[53]

On one summer holiday, Bruno and Józefina visited Maria Kasprowiczowa, the daughter of a tsarist general and the widow of the poet Jan Kasprowicz, at her villa outside Zakopane. In a letter to Maria, Schulz made clear why something more profound than shyness kept him apart from others:

The word "human being" in itself is a brilliant fiction, concealing with a beautiful and reassuring lie those abysses and worlds, those undischarged universes, that individuals are. There is no human being—there are only sovereign ways of being, infinitely distant from each other, that don't fit into any uniform formula, that cannot be reduced to a common denominator. From one human being to another is a leap greater than from a worm to the highest vertebrate. Moving from one face to another we must rethink and rebuild entirely, we must change all dimensions and postulates. None of the categories that applied when we were talking about one person remain when we stand before another. . . . When I meet a new person, all of my previous experiences, anticipations, and tactics prepared in advance become useless. Between me and each new person the world begins anew.[54]

In January 1935, Schulz's brother Izydor died of a heart attack, at the peak of his career, at age fifty-three. "My brother supported my home," Schulz wrote, "that is, my sister and my nephew; he was the breadwinner for a number of families that are now left with nothing to live on. It will be hard now; I don't know what I'll do."[55]

Bruno and Józefina announced their engagement several months later. One of Schulz's students remembered that "students and professors collected for wedding gifts, gave them to Schulz, and he thanked them."[56] Józefina "enslaves me and obligates me," Schulz noted.[57] "My fiancée represents my participation in life; only by her mediation am I a human being and not just a lemur or a gnome. . . . With her love, she has redeemed me, already nearly lost and marooned in a remote no-man's-land, a barren underworld of fantasy."[58] He added, "Is it not a great thing to mean everything for someone?"[59]

In January 1936, Schulz was at last granted a six-month paid leave. He spent it mainly in Warsaw with his fiancée. To enter into a civil marriage with a Catholic woman, Schulz placed an announcement in the local papers in February, announcing with clipped formality his withdrawal from the Jewish community. Overcoming any lingering loyalties, he registered himself "without denomination."

Józefina Szelińska, photograph by Bruno Schulz (CREDIT: Central State Historical Archives of Ukraine in Lviv)

Even before taking this step, his friend Izydor Friedman said, Schulz "had nothing to do with Judaism, apart from some *sui generis* mysticism. . . . He had no idea about the Jewish religion. . . . Though not a believer, he was more of a deist than an atheist."[60] Still, a couple of years previous, Schulz had consulted a wonder-working rabbi, Aharon Rokeach from Bełz, who'd visited Drohobycz in 1934. Schulz asked the sage to foretell the family's fortunes. He did not record the reply.

Metamorphosis: Kafka and Schulz
THREE CROSSES SQUARE, WARSAW, JANUARY 1936

One evening in January 1936, Bruno Schulz—then in Warsaw on paid leave—attended a book party hosted by the writer Maria Kuncewicz. She was celebrating her new novel, *The Stranger*, which Schulz had warmly reviewed. He filled his plate with neatly arranged asparagus stalks garlanded with capers and red Cumberland sauce. As the party wound down, Schulz took a stroll in the company of two promising young writers, Hanna Mortkowicz-Olczakowa and Jerzy Andrzejewski. The conversation turned to Franz Kafka. Schulz spoke of having read the Prague author's "great writing" as early as 1927, three years after Kafka's untimely death, and remarked that for Kafka women are "intermediaries between the human and the divine."

Absorbed in conversation, the three strollers found themselves ensnared in a dark, narrow alley leading to an unused side entrance to the monastery of St. Kazimierz Church. "Schulz stopped and screamed," Hanna recalled. "We were standing in a place that seemed to have no exit, in front of a high wall that blocked the entire width of the street and a closed gate. . . . It was not easy to reassure Schulz that no, it was not a trap. . . . He took note of our explanations, but for a moment he stood frightened, his hand touching a wall as gray and mute as a prison wall."[61]

As the acclaimed author of *Cinnamon Shops*, Schulz lent his name
to his fiancée's Polish translation of Kafka's *The Trial*. The first Polish edition of the novel appeared in the spring of 1936 as a translation
"by Bruno Schulz." "We received 1,000 złotys," Józefina Szelińska
said, "600 for me and 400 for Bruno—a fair division, since without his inspiration there would be no translation, and Bruno needed
the money."[62]

In his afterword, Schulz offers an overture to *The Trial*:

> Kafka is able to render the atmosphere—the climate and
> aura—of a human life coming into contact with the superhu-
> man, with the highest truth. . . . The perceptions and insights
> Kafka means to give expression to here are not his exclusive
> property. They are the common heritage of the mysticism of
> all times and nations. . . . Kafka sees the realistic surface of
> existence with unusual precision . . . but these to him are but a
> loose epidermis without roots, which he lifts off like a delicate
> membrane and fits onto his transcendental world, grafts onto
> his reality. His attitude to reality is radically ironic, treacher-
> ous, profoundly ill-intentioned—the relationship of a presti-
> digitator to his raw material.[63]

Schulz and Kafka, born nine years apart, are often compared.
Both were Jewish citizens of the Austro-Hungarian Empire. Both
feared conventional matrimony and suffered broken engagements.
Both were driven by an unswerving and self-sacrificial devotion to
literature. Both writers had father fixations, and both gave their alter
egos the name Joseph (Kafka's Joseph K., protagonist of *The Trial*
and the short story "A Dream," and Schulz's child narrator Joseph).
Both were sons of self-made fathers who went into the textile business
and moved as young men from the countryside to the city (Hermann
Kafka from Osek to Prague, Jakub Schulz from Sądowa Wisznia to

Drohobycz). In the eyes of his tubercular son, Hermann Kafka, a vig-
orous, dominant, larger-than-life figure, symbolized authority. In the
Schulz family, the bed-ridden, tuberculosis-stricken father, his authority deflated by the maid Adela, demanded his son's care. His decline
and decrepitude stand in for an Austro-Hungarian world in decay.
(Czesław Miłosz observed that Schulz's exuberance "differentiates him
from the ascetic Kafka . . . [but] his feeling of decay is no less strong
than Kafka's.") If for Schulz the paternal figure (alternately inspired
and weak-willed) collapses, in Kafka the filial bond dissolves.

And both writers, with uncanny alchemy, descended into what
Schulz called "the lairs of language" to conduct a dialogue with metamorphosis.[64] Like the biblical Joseph, the interpreter of dreams, Schulz
makes clear he is no believer in material permanence. He describes
reality as a masquerade:

> Reality takes on certain shapes merely for the sake of appear-
> ance, as a joke or form of play. One person is a human, another
> is a cockroach, but shape does not penetrate essence, is only a
> role adopted for the moment, an outer skin soon to be shed. . . .
> This migration of forms is the essence of life.[65]

In his semi-autobiographical book *The One Inside* (2017), the
American actor and playwright Sam Shepard has the protagonist, a
laconic actor, delve into a rare edition of Schulz's *Sanatorium Under
the Sign of the Hourglass* over breakfast at a diner. The character relates
how he "turned to the chapter called 'Father's Last Escape,' where Bruno
describes his dead dad as having metamorphosed into a scorpion." In
Schulz's imagination, masochism becomes metamorphosis—not of the
son (Gregor Samsa, in Kafka's "The Metamorphosis," who wakes up
one morning to discover that he has been transformed into a monstrous
bug) but of the father, who departs and returns in new forms. In one
of Schulz's stories, Father turns into a helpless cockroach. "Perhaps he

was among those dead insects that Adela found every morning lying belly up, bristly with legs, that she collected with loathing on her dustpan and discarded."[66] In others, Father turns into a watchful condor ("Visitation" and "Birds"), a huge fly ("Dead Season"), a scorpion, or a (non-kosher) crab, which the mother serves to the family for dinner, as though he were a patriarch eaten by the tribe, which wishes to incorporate his qualities ("Father's Last Escape").

In Kafka's world, metamorphosis is sudden and irreversible. In Schulz's imagination, it is gradual and fluid: Father, who exists in a twilight of time, might be a fly in the morning and, having reverted back to himself, be bent over the shop's accounting ledgers in the afternoon, "seated once again in the shop's back office, in a small room with a vaulted ceiling, a room divided, like a hive, into squares, into the many-celled boxes of file cabinets, perpetually shedding layers of paper, letters, and invoices."[67]

"From This Flour No Bread Would Rise"
WARSAW, JANUARY 1936

In the winter of 1936, Regina Silberner was invited to dinner at the Warsaw home of her cousin Herman Horowitz. Bruno Schulz and his fiancée were the only other guests. Józefina spoke with excitement about her dream of living in Paris after the wedding. Bruno kept his eyes fixed on his plate.

"And you, Bruno," Regina said, "where would you like to live?"

"Me?" Schulz mumbled, as though startled from a reverie. "In Drohobycz."

Józefina fell silent.

"I realized then," Regina said, "that as the farmers say, from this flour no bread would rise."[68]

Józefina pleaded with Schulz to live with her in Warsaw, where she had taken a monotonous office job at the Central Statistical Office in order to save for their life there. She wanted nothing more than to bring balm into his life. Schulz—who, in any case, never felt fully in his element in Warsaw—was reluctant to abandon his ailing sister. "The feeling for fatherhood was alien to him and his needs," his fiancée said. "The need for his own home, his own family, was alien to him." He also dreaded lapsing into inaction and destitution. Józefina remembers him "repeatedly returning to the same image: [he imagined himself] as a beggar wandering the city, reaching out his hands, and I would turn away from him contemptuously."[69]

By January 1937, his indecision had led her to despair. "I became perfectly aware," Józefina later confided, "that contrary to appearances, of the two of us I was the weaker party. He had his creative world, his high regions. I had nothing." On January 5, Józefina turned thirty-two. A few days later, she swallowed handfuls of sleeping pills. Just before losing consciousness, she called for help and was rescued. Schulz rushed to Warsaw to be with her in the hospital. While there, still reeling from shock, he fell ill with the flu and was bedridden for ten days. When Józefina recovered, she returned to her parents' home. In February, Schulz showed up there, bearing figs and dates. "He showed me great care and devotion," Szelińska recalled years later. "He felt guilt—completely unfounded, for he was nothing but goodness."[70]

Realizing that she could not count on his constancy, Józefina Szelińska ended the engagement in the spring of 1937 and stopped answering Schulz's letters. "I'm sorry to have to sadden you with the news that my relationship with Józefina has completely broken down," Schulz wrote to friends. "She finally grew tired of my hopeless situation, the difficulties in the way of a move to Warsaw, which she attributed—rightly, I admit—to my lack of practical sense. I don't even know where she is now, since she's broken off even written communication with me."[71] His vexed relationship with Józefina—his "excursion into matrimony," as he called it—had curdled.[72] Like Kafka, Schulz was an *homme à femmes* who ultimately could not trade in his solitude for a life *en deux*. Despite his susceptibility to feminine charms, Schulz never married. Nor did Józefina, though she would outlive him by nearly forty-nine years. "She never became emotionally involved with another man, never had a family," notes Józefina's biographer. "She decided to stay with him, for better and for worse, forever."[73]

"Barometer of Happiness": Romana
1936–37

Though expressing outward "relief that she finally broke up with me," Schulz was stalked by depression. "Even though I should be pleased with this break-up," he confessed, "I now feel a terrible emptiness, the nothingness of life. I can't do anything. I can't pick up a book; it makes me nauseous."[74]

Schulz admitted to another friend that he often asked himself,

> Do I have the right to be satisfied, is the undertaking "Schulz" worth carrying on, does it justify further investment? And from the answer to this happiness questionnaire, I deduce a defeatist or optimistic attitude—mostly a defeatist one. . . . To build a life on work, on activity, declaring independence from the barometer of happiness—this is the right way to organize a life.[75]

To mitigate the misery to which he'd consigned himself, Schulz turned his attentions to Romana Halpern, a beautiful divorcée in her thirties whom he met through Witkacy in 1936. The daughter of a well-known Warsaw journalist, Aleksander Kenig, Halpern would become the addressee of the largest surviving collection of Schulz's letters. Many of Schulz's startlingly unguarded letters to her churn with self-chiding—even self-flagellation. "My attempts to write are really agonizing," he admitted in his first letter to her. "A writer (my type of writer, anyway) is the most wretched creature on earth. He has to lie

incessantly, has to represent as valid and real what is actually in a mis-
erable state of disintegration and chaos within him."[76]

In April 1936, the Arab Revolt broke out in Palestine. A youth
committee in Drohobycz called Bitzaron u'Bitakhon collected dona-
tions for the Jewish victims of the riots. Schulz was too preoccupied
to make mention of such events. In September, he wrote to Romana
Halpern:

> My great enemy is lack of self-confidence, of *amour propre*.
> Long months pass when nothing that I do wins my approval, no
> idea that comes up satisfies me, nothing pleases me. This state
> of discontent with myself condemns me to inactivity. But some-
> times I think that this severity is justified and that I'm right to
> consign immature and imperfect things to perdition.[77]

In another letter to Halpern, Schulz ascribed his depression to "inactivity, unproductiveness. And the cause of my inactivity, in turn, is the
mistaken idea that I am able to work only when everything is in good
shape and I am content and have some peace of mind."[78]

Mostly Schulz pondered whether marriage would disturb that
peace of mind, enfeeble his artistic potency, and, as he wrote to
Halpern, "throw me out of the right climate for my creativity." He
wondered whether it would impede "the solitary life [that] may have
been the source of my inspiration."[79] In the spring and summer of
1937, soon after his engagement was broken, he shared with Halpern
his fear of loneliness: "I'll never find someone else like her." He also
confesses, "I search for a medicine against my incapacity for love
rather than for love itself. I envy people who know how to love."[80]
Later that summer, Schulz wrote to Halpern: "Like an insect released
from its cocoon, exposed to the tempest of an alien light and the
winds of heaven, I commit myself to the elements, in a way for the
first time."[81]

Sanatorium Under the Sign of the Hourglass
1937

In January 1937, Schulz signed a contract for his second collection of
stories with Rój. The advance payment of 1,500 złotys did not allow
him luxuries like a typewriter (then about 1,200 złotys).[82] Submit-
ting the manuscript brought him little reprieve. "I want those periods
of depression which paralyze me to stop coming back," he wrote to
Romana Halpern that August. "Maybe I should seek treatment by a
psychiatrist. These depressions disorganize me, making continuous
work impossible. Out of seven days a week they may poison six."[83]

Sanatorium Under the Sign of the Hourglass (the Polish word
klepsydra of the title can denote both an hourglass and a black-framed
obituary notice) went to press in November 1937, accompanied by
thirty-three of Schulz's illustrations. The dust-jacket copy, likely composed by Schulz, reads:

> The keynote of this new prose fiction of Schulz's is the dream of
> a renewal of life through the power of delight, the unleashing
> of inspiration, the primeval human belief that the dammed-up
> loveliness of things, hampered and hidden though it is, only
> awaits an inspired being to break its bonds and release a flood
> of happiness over all the world. This ancient myth of the mys-
> tics becomes flesh in this work, takes the shape of a peculiar
> eschatology, a wreath of legends plaited from strands from all
> cultures and mythologies and transformed into a fascinating
> tangle of fabulation. It is worth emphasizing that this fabula-
> tion, for all the wealth of its cultural elements, is strictly pri-
> vate and *sui generis*, that a wholly novel terminology is used,
> that a new organ, as it were, has been created for age-old
> human dreams.[84]

Schulz harbored ambivalence about his second book, dedicated to Józefina. He described it as "an attempt at eliciting the history of a certain family, a certain house in a provincial city—not from documents, events, a study of character, or of people's destinies—but by a search for the mythical sense, the essential core of that history. . . . These mythical elements are inherent in the region of early childish fantasies, intuitions, fears, and anticipations characteristic of the dawn of life."[85]

Schulz's search for mythical origins rattled some readers. One reviewer harangued Schulz for writing as "impure at the source . . . blooming at the edges with bizarre delusions and phantoms."[86] The eminent literary critics Kazimierz Wyka and Stefan Napierski published vicious attacks on Schulz—and on *Sanatorium* as the fruit of Galician decadence—in the monthly magazine *Ateneum*. Expressing surprise at the "warm reception of this book by various representatives of the so-called intelligentsia," Wyka concluded that the burning of Schulz's volume would cause little loss to literature.[87]

At the time, Schulz's student Andrzej Chciuk wrote a satire for the high school paper *Tramp*, on the lack of recognition accorded to Schulz by those who were bewildered by his books. He imagined a conversation with Schulz, who complained about the permanent puzzlement that greeted his writing in his hometown. The fictional Schulz promises to write some new, more accessible collections entitled *Cinnamon in an Hourglass, Cinnamon Sanatorium,* and *Hourglass with Cinnamon.* The real Schulz was amused.

"Sweet Slavery" and Sublime Surrender
DROHOBYCZ, 1937

Bruno Schulz believed that human weaknesses—carnal and otherwise—allow human beings to find companionship. "Without flaws they would stay locked inside themselves, not needing anything. It takes their vices to give them flavor and attraction."[88]

Soon after *Sanatorium* came out, Witkacy took Alicja Mondschein to meet Schulz—and his vice. Alicja, a young woman from Warsaw, had found work as a dancer in a Zakopane. Witkacy hired her as a hostess. "She had only two tasks," a friend of hers recalled. "Keeping the glasses neither full nor empty, and second, every five minutes she would burst into sparkling laughter regardless of the topic of the conversation."[89] On the train from Zakopane to Drohobycz, Witkacy said, "When we reach Schulz's house, I will knock and step back. As soon as he opens the door and sees you," he instructed, deadpan, "you will slap him as a greeting." Witkacy rapped on the door, took two steps back, and pushed Alicja forward. Schulz opened the door, peering out from under his eyebrows. Before Schulz could utter a word, Alicja slapped him, almost robotically. He fell at her feet, flustered with a pleasure he'd had no chance to anticipate.

Through the ensuing friendship, Bruno and Alicja would stroll in Zakopane, at the time a fashionable hub of Polish culture. Deliberately courting attention, they would hopscotch down the sidewalk or caper in zigzags and syncopated steps. He was then a slight man in his forties, wearing a jacket, his head half-hidden in a beret; she, a tall woman in her twenties in a short orange skirt, showing off an exposed midriff and "my tanned, long legs." Passersby would stare and mutter about "those two weirdos."

Once, as they were lying in the sun in Zakopane, Schulz asked, "Do you think that one day I will be famous and rich and happy?"

"Yes, of course, but after death."

At that Schulz turned pale, curled up in a fetal position like a sick animal, and for a long time covered his head with his hands.[90]

That phrase, "after death," must have aroused Schulz's delight in prolonged disappointment and deferral, the pleasure in something that is bound to be late (à la messianic anticipation, in which misery climaxes in redemption). In one of Schulz's stories, the narrator names "the exquisite terror of consummation."[91]

Many friends remarked on Schulz's "vice." Witold Gombrowicz called him "a relentless, untempered masochist."[92] Even children could sense something. Ola Watowa, the wife of the futurist poet and Marxist intellectual Aleksander Wat, recalled that during Schulz's visit to their home, their small son, Andrzej, looked with curiosity at the guest and suddenly left for the bathroom. He returned holding a piece of wood and said, "Mommy, beat me!" "Telepathy?" the mother wondered. "Or perhaps simply the whimsical act of a child?"[93]

Schulz himself took pains to deflect perceptions that he suffered from a common perversion:

> My creativeness differs in this respect from the stereotyped creativeness of perverts like Sacher Masoch or [the Marquis] de Sade. . . . It doesn't represent direct imaginative satisfaction of a perverse drive but reflects rather my entire inner life, the focal center of which is formed about a certain perversion. Creatively, I express this perversion in its loftiest, philosophically interpreted form as a foundation determining the total *Weltanschauung* of an individual in all its ramifications.[94]

That inner life comes through openly enough in his writing.[95] In the first story in *Sanatorium*, young Joseph notices an advertisement on the last page of the Book: a certain Miss Magda Wang declares "from the heights of her tight décolleté that she laughs at masculine resoluteness and principles, and that her specialty is breaking the strongest character. . . .That was the final word of the Book, which left a taste of strange stupefaction, a mixture of hunger and arousal in the soul." The next section begins with these words: "Bent over the Book, my face aflame like a rainbow, I burned in silence from ecstasy to ecstasy."[96] The sacred and the masochistic have become one.

"Before the Gate Closes"
DROHOBYCZ, MARCH 1938

> Something wants to ferment out of the concentrated noise
> of these darkening days—something immense beyond mea-
> sure. I test and I calculate what kind of event might...
> equal this catastrophic barometric drop.[97]

—BRUNO SCHULZ

Despite the occasional rumbles of anti-Semitism, Polish Jews in the
interwar years had enjoyed a cultural renaissance. Many of the country's 2.1 million Jews, the second-largest minority after the Ukrainians, had welcomed the revival of Polish independence after 123 years
of partitions, the 1921 constitution, which declared "all citizens equal
before the law," and the tolerant regime led by Józef Piłsudski from
1926 to 1935.

In 1932, Ozjasz Thon, a leading rabbi in Kraków, gave voice to
this optimism:

> There were moments when the genius of the Jewish people
> reached its full flowering in Poland. I am convinced that the
> events are again creating a situation in which in Poland there
> will emerge one of the great centers of the Jewish spirit.[98]

In the early 1930s, Schulz painted a colorful portrait of Piłsudski, a
brilliant military leader and first chief of state of the newly independent
Poland, to be displayed for state ceremonies. Though he kept his political proclivities to himself, Schulz wrote an encomium after Piłsudski's
burial alongside Polish kings in May 1935, comparing him favorably
to Napoleon.[99] One historian goes so far as to call Schulz "an exegete
of Piłsudski's greatness."[100]

Yet Schulz, by nature full of foreboding, could not share Thon's optimism; nor, in the months after Piłsudski's death, could he ignore recurrent strains of Polish anti-Semitic pathologies, of bigotry disguised as patriotism and violence masked as self-defense. A wave of anti-Jewish violence swept through Poland between 1935 and 1937, including a notorious pogrom in Przytyk, a small town near Radom, in March 1936.[101] In January 1937, students at the University of Warsaw organized and enforced "A Day Without Jews." The poet Czesław Miłosz remembered that time as one in which "gangs of students would attack their Jewish colleagues" and anti-Semitic nationalists "seemed to encounter no open resistance."[102] Poland's parliament, the Sejm, began restricting Jews' practice of medicine, law, and engineering. Polish professional guilds, which begrudged Polish Jews their share of desirable jobs, adopted "Aryan clauses." The National Democratic movement (Endecja) led a boycott of Jewish shops and stalls. Under the slogan "Poland for the Poles," members of the Camp of National Unity (OZN) and the National Radical Camp (ONR) portrayed Jews— perceived as economically powerful but politically powerless—as alien to Polish soil; they clamored for the Jews to leave Poland. In 1936, one of Poland's leading writers, Zofia Kossak-Szczucka, declared:

> Jews are so terribly alien to us, alien and unpleasant, that they are a race apart. They irritate us and all their traits grate against our sensibilities. Their oriental impetuosity, argumentativeness, specific mode of thought, the set of their eyes, the shape of their ears, the winking of their eyelids, the line of their lips, everything.[103]

A year later, the Supreme Council of the ruling party, the OZN, declared, "The Communist party of Jewry is the open enemy of our Nation and State. . . . It is a foreign body, dispersed in our organism so that it produces a pathological deformation."[104] Jews who vocally protested such libels were criminally charged with "insulting the Polish nation."

As the Nazi frenzy gripped Germany, Schulz remarked that "some fever and restlessness has taken hold of me, and panic 'before the gate closes.' "[105] These words, addressed to Romana Halpern, were put to paper in March 1938, a week before Nazi Germany annexed Austria. Schulz called the *Anschluss* a "shattering historical event." On March 15, Hitler delivered his triumphal speech at Vienna's Heldenplatz (Heroes' Square). "The oldest eastern province of the German people," he announced, "shall be, from this point on, the newest bastion of the German Reich." Five days later, Schulz again wrote to Halpern: "The spring was so beautiful; one should live and swallow the world. And I spend days and nights without a woman and without the Muse and I waste away fruitlessly."[106] A month later, Schulz linked political calamity with his own. "Can the demon of creativity," he wondered, "be fed with one's own defeat?"[107]

In an essay published that year, Schulz pondered the links between the political and the creative:

> Political programs are only the rationalized surface, an internal index of the deep transformations taking place in the depths of collective consciousness. These transformations do not take place in the categories of political thought alone, but they ferment in the mythical depths where the longings, raptures, ideals, and forms of the collective imagination are born. Art operates in the same depths; hence its tremendous role.[108]

And hence, too, Schulz's tremendous sensitivity to the political climate. Schulz's student Alfred Schreyer said that Schulz occasionally came to paint the poor Jews who lived near the Choral Synagogue. "Professor," a student asked, "why are you painting those horrible old houses and those old Jews with their big beards?"

"Children, I have to record it. Soon there will come a terrible storm, and all this will disappear."[109]

"A Debauched Babylon": We'll Never Have Paris
PARIS, AUGUST 1938

In January 1938, Schulz had made a five-day visit to Poznań, where he'd stayed with Egga van Haardt, an artist, and discussed her illustrations to his stories "Comet" and "The Homecoming," and to his novel in progress, *Messiah*.[110] On returning to Drohobycz, feeling stalled in his writing and increasingly irritated with living with his family, Schulz wanted to move out into a "bachelor pad" of his own. Renting an apartment, however, proved beyond his means. Finally, in the spring of 1938, Schulz rearranged the house on Floriańska Street so that he could have a separate room. He arranged his room neatly, as though it were himself that he was putting into a certain order.[111]

Now he faced a dilemma: to use the advance for his second book to buy a couch or "to see French art once and breathe the air of pure artistry."[112] In the summer of 1938, on the advice of a painter named Natan Spigel, Schulz drew on his modest book royalties to make his first and last trip to Paris. His plans to travel in the spring were delayed by bureaucracy: obtaining a passport (40 złotys), a certificate of residence signed by Drohobycz mayor Michał Piechowicz, a transit pass through Nazi Germany, and a letter of credit from the foreign currency exchange office (with Romana Halpern's help). Another reason for hesitation, as he confided to Halpern, was his fear of interrupting his work on the manuscript of *Messiah*. "If I had four months off," he wrote, "I would finish the book." Schulz's friend Artur Sandauer, a young literary critic, advised him to go to Paris only if the trip wouldn't blunt *Messiah*'s momentum or put it into permanent suspension.

Schulz had read André Gide and reviewed books by French writers (François Mauriac, George Bernanos, and Louis Aragon), but he didn't speak much French, and he feared being mocked for his French malapropisms. The pianist Maria Chazen wrote to him before he left: "I can give you only one piece of advice: get rid of your stage fright and let Paris rejuvenate your self-confidence. You mustn't be too modest and insecure there."[113] The actress Kazimiera Rychterówna supplied Schulz with the names of some Paris contacts and likewise urged him to overcome his "lack of courage" and to summon "the talent for entrepreneurship and assertive pluck that people need to make real achievements."[114]

After a two-day journey by train from Warsaw, Schulz arrived in Paris on July 31, 1938. He took a room at Hotel d'Orient on Rue de l'Abbé-Grégoire, near the Luxembourg Gardens, then stayed with the Polish surrealist artist Ludwik Lille on boulevard Saint-Jacques.[115] (The two had met in the 1920s when Lille organized an exhibition of Schulz's artworks in Lwów.) Four days after his arrival, the front page of *Paris-soir* (a paper with a circulation of more than two million) featured a map of the Dachau concentration camp near Munich under the headline "Dachau: Danger de Mort!"[116]

The forty-six-year-old artist had brought with him a hundred drawings tucked into a large portfolio in the hopes of arranging an exhibition of his artworks in Paris. The Polish-Jewish artist Menasze Seidenbeutel had assured Schulz that such an exhibition would be a commercial success. Schulz met with Maria Chazen's brother Georges Rosenberg, a Polish Jewish émigré from Łódź. They spent an evening at the famous cabaret Casanova, in Montmartre. "Schulz was overwhelmed with the women's beauty, elegance, and costumes," Rosenberg reported, "and with their dizzying décolletés. . . . I understood that he was a slave to his fantasies."[117] Schulz also arranged meetings with the poet Jan Brzękowski, then press attaché at the Polish embassy; the cubist painter Louis Marcoussis (originally Markus); and the sculptor Naoum Aronson at his studio on rue de Vaugirard. On a late Saturday afternoon, Schulz met the exiled cultural critic Siegfried Kracauer at the Café de Versailles, opposite the Gare Montparnasse ("I'll be carrying a green briefcase," Krakauer had written to Schulz). In the end, the art dealer André J. Rotgé offered Schulz an exhibition that November in his gallery in rue Faubourg Saint-Honoré; Schulz could not afford the 1,600-franc registration fee. "It was naive of me to rush out the way I did with the intent of conquering Paris," he wrote to Romana Halpern, "the most exclusive, self-sufficient, standoffish city in the world." Still, "the lovely women of Paris impressed me greatly, both ladies of society and of the night."[118]

Schulz left Paris—a "debauched Babylon," as he called it[119]—on August 26, empty-handed except for the gift towels from Galeries Lafayette for his sister in Drohobycz. His return trip took him through Nazi Germany. On arrival, he wrote to his host Lille to apologize for not having said good-bye: "For a long time I've had a phobia of farewell scenes and avoid them whenever I can."[120]

Schulz had hoped to receive *Wiadomości Literackie*'s fiction award for 1938. "I'd very much like to get this prize," he had told Romana Halpern, "mainly because it's a bridge to going beyond the borders of the Polish language."[121] The award, however, went to a novel about the Polish astronomer Copernicus. A month or so after his return from Paris, Schulz instead got news that the Polish Academy of Literature had awarded him a Golden Laurel. No money accompanied the prize; in fact, the cost of the gold and red-enamel decoration (30 złotys) was borne by the winners themselves.

Schulz's depressions—and his correspondence with Romana Halpern—meanwhile intensified. "In the past I was defended by a certain kind of blindness," he wrote to her in October 1938. "I had blinkers on my eyes, like a horse in harness. Now reality has defeated me and barged into my inwardness."[122] In his last letter to her, from June 1939, Schulz describes being beset by "the onset of melancholy, despondency, sadness, a sense of inevitable disaster, irreparable loss."[123]

CHAPTER 5

THE ARTIST ENSLAVED

September 1939–November 1942

Loneliness is the catalyst that makes reality ferment.[1]

—BRUNO SCHULZ

The Artist as Propagandist: Russian Occupation

DROHOBYCZ, SEPTEMBER 1939

On September 1, 1939, Wehrmacht troops invaded Poland from the west and Luftwaffe bombers made their first raids from the air. After just twenty years of independence, Poland had ceased to exist.

An intrepid twenty-six-year-old literary critic, Artur Sandauer, was then visiting Drohobycz. That day, he listened to the radio with Bruno Schulz. "Did you know," Schulz said with a twinkle in his eye, "their planes are said to be flown by young women." "To die at the hands of a female bombardier," Sandauer later remarked, "this was apparently the height of his fantasies."

The first German soldiers, arriving on motorcycles on the road from nearby Sambor, reached Drohobycz on September 11. Outside the town hall, locals greeted them with bread and salt.[2]

On September 17—the day Schulz had planned to give a talk on the Drohobycz artists E. M. Lilien and Leopold Gottlieb at the Ossolineum library in Wrocław—Polish radio announced what Sandauer called "joyful news": the Red Army had invaded Poland from the east. "Joyful, because Schulz and I—like the majority of Polish intelligentsia of Jewish origin—believed that after the Germans any change was a change for the better."[3]

In accordance with the Molotov-Ribbentrop non-aggression pact (an agreement that "brought all of Europe's poisons to the surface," Czesław Miłosz wrote), the Germans withdrew from the town after a week-long occupation and handed it over to the Red Army (the Twelfth Army, under the command of Ivan Tyulenev). The last service held in the Choral Synagogue in Drohobycz would be on Yom Kippur 1939. On September 24, the day after Yom Kippur, Soviet armored troop carriers rumbled into Drohobycz.

Later that week, Schulz met a former student on the market square. He looked up at the town hall, festooned with red flags fluttering in the bursts of breeze. "It has all happened so fast," Schulz remarked cryptically to his young companion, "as though history has passed through us at a horrible gallop." He seemed to apprehend that Drohobycz, however provincial, would not escape the great gusts of history—gusts that an artist, however sovereign his imaginative world, would not evade.

As elsewhere in Eastern Europe, many Drohobycz Jews were lured by the Communist promise that differences between nationalities, religions, and classes would dissolve. "The Jews were very happy that the Germans didn't take our town, and they welcomed the rag-tag army with real joy," recalled Leopold Lustig, a student of Schulz's. Lustig remembered that the Soviets used to say, "With us, Jew or not a Jew, *odin hui*, same fuck."[4]

The Soviets nationalized the local petroleum firms and renamed Floriańska Street, where Schulz lived, Sedova Street (in honor of the Russian Arctic explorer Georgy Sedov). In accordance with the freedom of worship enshrined in Stalin's 1936 Constitution (copies of which were freely distributed in the town), synagogue doors were not

Bruno Schulz (standing, center) with his mother, Henrietta (seated next to Schulz), and other family members in the garden of their home, Drohobycz, 1930s (CREDIT: Adam Mickiewicz Museum of Literature, Warsaw)

shut, though the Soviets regarded Zionism as a reactionary ideology and henceforth banned the use of Hebrew in schools and in print.

As the only breadwinner of the house—he supported his ailing older sister, Hania, and her adult son—Schulz could not flee. He was compelled instead to pay lip service to the ludicrous Communist Party pablum to keep his job as a high school teacher. "In Soviet times," Andrzej Chciuk remembered, "Schulz had to endure many humiliations: he was called a typical representative of the rotten bourgeoisie and capitalist decadence." In his application to join the West Ukrainian Trade Unions, Schulz wrote:

> I wish to explore theoretically the teachings of Communism, as I see in it the intellectual system most profoundly expressing

and embracing the entirety of life, and above all a magnificent
programme based on the principles of humanity and ensuring
the liberation of maximal creative forces in the masses and a
magnificent blooming of human creative work.[5]

Schulz continued to teach at the gymnasium (now renamed School
Number 12); on Tuesday and Thursday afternoons he also taught at
the former Sternbach Jewish junior high school (now School Number 3).

In March 1940, a Polish monthly called *New Horizons* (*Novim
vidokruzima*), edited by an ardent Communist named Wanda
Wasilewska, invited Schulz to contribute. "But what can I possibly
write for them?" he asked a friend. "I'm more and more persuaded of
how far I am from actually existing life and how little I'm oriented in
the spirit of the times. Somehow everyone has found a place for themselves,
but I've remained stranded. It comes from a lack of flexibility,
from a certain uncompromising attitude, which I do not laud."[6] Despite
these hesitations, he submitted a short story, the last one he would
write. The editors' reply arrived from Lwów in May: "We don't need
any more Prousts."[7]

In the spring of 1940, Schulz showed six of his works in a group
exhibition in Lwów sponsored by the Office for Art at the Council of
People's Commissars of the Ukrainian Soviet Socialist Republic. The
introduction to the exhibition catalog concludes on a note of exhortation:
"The artists of the western territories of Soviet Ukraine must
become active participants in building a new socialist culture in the
land liberated from the oppression of the Polish nobility and create
works worthy of our great Stalinist era."

During the twenty-one months of Soviet occupation, Schulz proved
more elastic an artist than a writer. On the orders of the Soviet authorities,
he was obliged to work as the sole illustrator for the Ukrainian-language
Soviet newspaper *Bolshevik Truth* (*Bilshovitska Pravda*),

mimicking a prefabricated socialist realist style to glorify parades of Soviet soldiers and cavalry, as well as peasants welcoming the Soviets (these illustrations were rediscovered only in 2016). Schulz's friend Bertold Schenkelbach served as the paper's photojournalist. Fully aware that ideological dictates are anathema to art, Schulz painted portraits of Ivan Franko and a series of off-the-cuff propaganda posters that decorated a voting hall—typical expressions of the slogan-saturated times.

Schulz never got caught up in his own impersonation; he never overdid the part he was forced to play. Trapped in a totalitarian vise, he played his role with a tedium seasoned with terror, with the knowledge that his forays into contrived and banal hackwork were nothing more than exercises in conformity, acts of calculated accommodation to party-sanctioned art. "Do you see any other way out?" he said to Sandauer.[8]

In a letter to a friend from that time, Schulz expressed the numbing pain of feeling his talents depleted and wasted: "A person of my type cannot bear it even for a month; he turns into a soulless machine. Can you save me from physical and spiritual destruction?" In desperation, he implored friends living in Lwów to find him a job there.

In September 1940, Schulz was instructed to create a large oil painting on the theme "Liberation of the Western Ukraine." Because he painted it in the Ukrainian national colors, blue and yellow, the painting earned him an interrogation by the NKVD (the Soviet secret police, forerunner of the KGB) on charges of "Ukrainian bourgeois nationalism." The same month, working on the bare floor of the high school auditorium, Schulz painted a fifty-foot-tall portrait of Stalin to be draped on the Drohobycz town hall. Within the month, by the October 25 anniversary of the Russian Revolution, that portrait had been soiled by jackdaws, and its colors had been streaked by rain. "For once in my life," Schulz said, "the destruction of one of my own works has brought me real satisfaction."[9]

That month, Schulz confided to a friend the toll the first year of the war had taken on him. "I have become anonymous, a stranger to myself, so when someone from the past comes to look for me, it seems to me that he has made a mistake, that he's become lost in time, that I'm long gone."[10]

Greeting the Germans

DROHOBYCZ, JUNE 30, 1941

The Germans had never entirely put Galicia and its resources out of mind. In December 1939, Hermann Göring, Hitler's deputy and commander in chief of the Luftwaffe, had demanded that exploitation of Galician oil be pursued by any and all means.

On June 22, 1941, the Germans broke their non-aggression pact. Thirsty for "living space" in the east, Hitler attacked the Soviet Union in a massive offensive that would become known as Operation Barbarossa. In desperation, some young Jews in Drohobycz joined the retreating Red Army (the Eighth Mechanized Corps), which sabotaged oil wells and pipelines on its eastward withdrawal toward Brody.

Eight days later, at five p.m. on June 30, Drohobycz residents heard the droning roar of the first Luftwaffe Stuka gull-winged dive-bombers above the stippled clouds. At eight or nine p.m., troops from the German Seventeenth Army unceremoniously entered the undefended city. A moment long foreseen and imagined—yet still somehow unfathomable, as if beyond comprehension—had arrived.

What was terrifying for some proved exhilarating for others. That same day, with the arrival of goose-stepping Nazi troops in Ukraine, supporters of Stepan Bandera, head of the proto-fascist Organization of Ukrainian Nationalists (OUN), declared an independent Ukrainian state. Article 3 of the Proclamation of Ukrainian Independence read: "The newly formed Ukrainian state will work closely with the National-Socialist Greater Germany, under the leadership of its leader

Adolf Hitler which is forming a new order in Europe and the world and is helping the Ukrainian People to free itself from Moscovite occupation." The town's Ukrainian nationalists greeted the Germans as liberators from the Soviet yoke. They hung banners bearing the slogan "Glory to Hitler! Glory to Bandera!"

Before beating a hasty retreat from Drohobycz, the Soviet secret police (NKVD) had executed Ukrainian political prisoners—some shot in the back of the head, others bayoneted—and left their corpses in the prisons. On July 1, local Ukrainians, many of whom had accused the Jews of "collaborating with the Bolsheviks," took out their vengeful fury on their Jewish neighbors.[11] Amalia Buchman watched the pogrom reach its crescendo:

> Like unleashed beasts of prey, the Ukrainians, a number of them intoxicated, attacked the homes of the Jews with crowbars, axes, iron bars, knives and every type of weapon that they could lay their hands on. . . . The hoodlums murdered with no distinction between children, women and old people, barbarically and callously abusing their dead bodies. They dragged the wounded victims towards the district courthouse in Drohobycz and there abused them again and again until their souls returned to their Creator. The torture was in revenge for the killing of Ukrainian nationalists by the Soviet regime which had fled the city. The rioting mob of Ukrainian rabble, which was mainly made up of farmers from the region, among them many youths, dragged additional victims from all corners of the Jewish neighborhood, beating and brutalizing them in an inhuman manner, and brought them to the fresh mass grave of the Ukrainians who had been killed by the Russians.[12]

Some fifteen years earlier, the Galicia-born rabbi Simon Bernfeld had published *The Book of Tears* (*Sefer Ha'Demaot*, in Hebrew), an anthology of historical sources on the persecution of Jews since antiquity. The third volume recounts the Ukrainian pogroms led by Bogdan Chmielnitsky the 1640s and 1650s, during which tens of thousands of Jews were massacred. Chmielnitsky had told Ukrainian peasants that the Poles had sold them as slaves "into the hands of the accursed Jews. . . . You know the wrongs done us by the Poles and Yids. . . . You know and you remember." Bernfeld's book ends with the Ukrainian pogroms of 1768, led by Maxim Zheleznyak. The coming calamities were as yet unimaginable.

Draconian Decrees
DROHOBYCZ, SUMMER 1941

Beginning on July 15, two weeks after the pogrom, Drohobycz Jews were obliged to wear on their left arms a white armband with the blue Star of David. With the new lords came new laws. Every day brought an additional draconian decree, a new—and often arbitrarily enforced—edict of discrimination. Jews were soon forbidden to ride in trains, cars, and horse-drawn carriages; then banned from public buildings, theaters and cinemas, and "Aryan" hospitals. They could no longer traverse public parks, use sidewalks, or leave town without obtaining a special permit (*Passierschein*). The Germans restricted Jews' food rations: 70 grams of bread per day (two and a half ounces), 1 kilogram of sour cabbage per month (2.2 pounds), 50 grams of sugar per month (twelve teaspoons). They confiscated Jewish properties, plundered their shops, appropriated their radios and telephones, and suspended their legal rights.[13]

The German occupiers established special branches for the employment of Jews (*Judeneinsatz*) and decreed humiliating forced labor for Jewish men ages sixteen to sixty and Jewish women sixteen to fifty. Forced laborers had to wear a four-inch-wide armband bearing the letter A (for *Arbeitsjude*, "Jewish worker"). The security police in charge of the persecution of the political and racial enemies of the state (the *Sicherheitspolizei* and *Sicherheitsdienst*) issued each Jewish laborer in Drohobycz an identification card (*Ausweis für Arbeitsjuden*).

The SS assigned the management of Jews' internal administration to a Jewish council (*Judenrat*), led by Isaac Rosenblatt and Maurice Ruhrberg, to which the Germans gave an imposture of "Jewish autonomy."[14] Headquartered at 7 Taras Shevchenko Street, the council was forced to provide the Germans with a certain number of Jewish laborers each day (and on occasion to supply alcohol and pornographic materials).

On August 1, 1941, Galicia was incorporated, on Hitler's orders, into a larger administrative unit called the General Government (GG), nicknamed "Gangster Ground." It was led by Hans Frank, the brutal gauleiter who six years earlier had helped draft the anti-Semitic Nuremberg Race Laws. In parallel, the SS and the Gestapo in occupied Poland were commanded by SS-Obergruppenführer (equivalent to lieutenant general) Friedrich-Wilhelm Krüger and his deputy SS-Gruppenführer (major general) Fritz Katzmann.

The first civil governor of the Galicia district and its more than one million inhabitants was Karl Lasch, a ruthless anti-Semite and a close friend of Hans Frank's (and briefly the lover of Frank's wife). In January 1942, after Lasch was charged with corruption, Hitler personally chose Vienna-born SS-Gruppenführer Otto Wächter to succeed him. SS-Sturmbannführer (major) Eduard Jedamzik, who commanded the Drohobycz district, answered to Wächter, who answered to Hans Frank, who answered to Hitler.[15]

According to Amalia Buchman, on August 1, 1941, "Seventeen Jews who worked in Gestapo headquarters broke a mirror and from fear of the punishment awaiting them, abandoned their workplace and ran away. Retribution was swift and cruel. On the afternoon of that same day the Gestapo came to Reich and Brudna Streets and seized people indiscriminately. After they had taken seventeen persons, they lined them up against the wall and shot them." (German soldiers held weekly firing squads on a wall facing Kowalska Street.)

As a boy, Schulz had often played with a deck of cards. One night, the defenselessness of the card figures dawned on him. He drew sabers onto the figures so that they could protect themselves.[16] As an adult, Schulz tended to avoid conflict. According to one friend, "there was lavender water in him where there should have been bile."[17] "There was nothing rough about him," Alfred Schreyer said.

And yet one morning Schulz refused to be cowed. He saw a group of Jews who had been rounded up. His eyes darted toward one of the detainees, his friend Samuel Bergman, a violinist. Schulz steadied himself and took an uncalculated risk. He shouldered past the onlookers and begged a Gestapo guard to spare Bergman's life, to pardon a condemned man. Bergman, startled to be granted reprieve, stumbled away in disbelief, and never forgot this "wonderful proof of true friendship . . . an act which at the time required incredible courage."[18]

The worse the external circumstances, the more Schulz sought comfort from his correspondents. Amid the horrors, Schulz again found solace in the company of a woman: Anna Płockier, a young Jewish painter, a graduate of the Kraków Academy of Fine Arts then living in nearby Borysław. "I am continually under the spell of your charming metamorphoses": this was the opening line of a letter Schulz sent to Płockier in June 1941, at the same time warning her of his misanthropic moods.[19] She read and commented on his unpublished story "The Homecoming"; he read fragments of her literary texts. "You are the partner of my interior dialogues about things that matter to me," he wrote in September.[20]

In his last letter to her, on November 19, 1941, Schulz refers to "the inexhaustible supply" of their shared concerns. "My hunch tells me that we'll meet again soon, and that the history of our friendship is not over." A decree issued on November 20 forbade Drohobycz Jews from leaving their place of residence on penalty of death. A week later, on November 27, Anna Płockier was murdered during a mass shooting in a forest near Schulz's beloved Truskawiec. She was twenty-six.

Messiah in the Ghetto

DROHOBYCZ, NOVEMBER 1941

Mass shootings of the area's Jews began in November 1941. One day the Gestapo (Geheime Staatspolizei, German for "secret state police") asked all Jewish war invalids who had served with the Austrian army in World War I to report to the Jewish orphanage in Drohobycz so that they could receive exemptions from hard labor. Instead, they were brought to Bronica Forest and shot. On November 22, some 250 Jews were instructed to assemble for medical examination at the Labor Bureau at 44 Mickiewicz Street. Instead, they were loaded onto trucks and taken to Bronica Forest, where they were made to strip and stand on the lip of a pit to await a bullet to the head.[21] Six days later, on November 28, a thousand more were transported from Drohobycz to the forest outside a nearby village, Tustanowice, where they were shot.

At the end of the month, Schulz and his family (his semi-invalided sister, depressive nephew, and cousin) were dispossessed of their home on Floriańska Street, where they had lived since 1910, and forced to move to a single-story shanty in the Jewish ghetto (Stolyarska 18). The ghetto had been created in a working-class Jewish neighborhood called Lan (nothing of which remains today), marked off by large notices forbidding Jews from crossing to Aryan neighborhoods and Aryans from entering the ghetto.[22]

"When the Jews were forced to move to the ghetto," Leon Thorne recalls, "they were unable to take their books, and so the volumes were left behind and collected by poor folk who sold them for packing paper."[23] The price of packing paper plummeted dizzyingly.

By that winter, more than twelve thousand Jews lived in the Drohobycz ghetto, stalked by hunger, cold, typhus, and deprivation.

"It was terrible to see hitherto well-off people now swollen with hunger," a survivor recounted, "rummaging like dogs for a piece of discarded bread in garbage dumps."[24]

Destitute and dependent on meager rations, Schulz had to pay for medical treatments with his drawings. He parceled out his manuscripts and remaining drawings in six or seven packages to acquaintances so that, as Horace put it, "non omnis moriar" ("not all of me will die"). One parcel held Schulz's unfinished masterpiece, a novel called *Messiah*. He had been intermittently laboring on it since 1934, blocked from finishing it by the weight of unfulfillable expectations.[25] In the meantime he let a messianic thread unspool through his art. Debora Vogel said that Schulz had shown her a series of drawings entitled *Times of the Messiah*, also now lost. She remembered depictions of "winged, fantastical women, who ride naked through the streets of the city in deep carriages." Schulz's niece, Ella Schulz-Podstolska, said that a large oil painting by Schulz in her family's apartment in Lwów was called *Awaiting the Messiah*.[26]

In 1936, Schulz had read fragments of *Messiah* to the literary critic Artur Sandauer. Sandauer remembered the novel's opening sentences, and their incursion of the miraculous into the mundane: " 'You know,' my mother told me in the morning. 'The Messiah has come. He is already in Sambor [a town twenty miles west of Drohobycz].' " Sandauer did not remember by what signs we would recognize the messiah's arrival, or even whether anything would change by his coming. Some scholars accused Sandauer, himself from Sambor, of fabricating the quote. In a 1938 interview for a newspaper in Poznań, Schulz said that his "eschatological novel" was nearing completion.[27]

Schulz now deposited the manuscript with someone he described to Izydor Friedman only as "a Catholic outside the ghetto." "Unfortunately, he did not give me the person's name," Friedman reported, "or possibly I forgot it." The manuscript has to this day yet to be found; if anywhere, it might be buried in the depths of one of two Moscow archives that served as repositories for material carted away by the Red Army at the end of the war.[28] (My own inquiries with the Russian state archivist, Larisa Rogovaya, were unsuccessful.) It exists only as a metaphor of loss, as proof of the absence of redemption, of the fragility of those things we call culture, and as a reminder that Schulz's lifework has come to be defined more by absence than by presence.

On December 23, 1941, the Gestapo decreed that every Jew in Drohobycz had to give up any fur items, ostensibly for German soldiers fighting on the Russian front. "After some days," Amalia Buchman recalled, "the wives of the Gestapo soldiers were seen in the fox-fur scarves and fur coats which just a few days ago had belonged to Jewish women."[29] And not only women. Schulz, too, was forced to render to the occupiers the fur collar from his threadbare coat.[30]

Sorting Books

JEWISH NURSING HOME, 27 TARAS SHEVCHENKA STREET, DROHOBYCZ, 1942

On the orders of a Gestapo official named Benno Pauliszkis, Schulz, his cheeks gaunt and shadowed with stubble, was put to work cataloging and appraising looted books and art collections at the Jewish nursing home (today the Drohobycz library). He worked alongside several of his former students and his close friend Izydor Friedman. "This assignment lasted several months," Friedman said, "was congenial and full of interest to us, and was paradise by comparison with the assignments drawn by other Jews."[31] They had to sort through about a hundred thousand volumes, including the library of the Jesuits of Chyrów (today Khyriv, Ukraine), and decide which should be rescued and which pulped. Schulz, who cherished books so highly, who wished they could all be left in peace, was forced to make heartrending choices.

By that time, Friedman said, "when his life was constantly in danger, he completely broke down and changed beyond recognition. He ceased to be an artist and thinker. He thought only about food. He was greedy for sweets like a child."[32] Emaciated and weakened from hunger, he could talk for hours, in a barely audible voice, about food.[33]

Schulz had the narrator of one of his short stories voice what he might have been feeling:

> Like a mouse, I thought, "What can hunger do to me? As a last resort I can even gnaw on the wood or shred paper into tiny pieces with my tiny snout. The poorest animal, a gray church mouse—at the tail end of the Book of Creation—I will manage to live on nothing."[34]

Schulz picked up the confiscated books, five or six at a time, and gingerly fingered their frayed spines. Sometimes he recognized a book—something by Goethe or Rilke, by Hölderlin or Horace—that stirred childhood memories and released glimmers of joy. He shut his eyes tightly and allowed himself to riffle through the pages.

The Dramaturgy of Destruction
DROHOBYCZ, SPRING 1942

As the Nazi vise tightened, Schulz happened to meet a former colleague, a high school teacher named Aleksy Kuszczak. They hadn't seen one another in many months. Kuszczak later recalled the encounter.

> In a normal voice but with great sadness he suddenly said: "They will liquidate us by next November."
> I didn't understand, but the tone of his words disquieted me. I looked surprised and asked a bit sharply: "Who?"
> "Us. Jews."
> "What does it mean to liquidate?"

"Liquidate," he repeated.

I understood. . . . But I did not or could not believe that it could actually be true . . . and I said this [to Schulz]. He looked at me as if I were completely alien to him. . . . He nodded his head, once more confirming his message . . . as if he felt sorry for me that I was so blind.[35]

In March 1942, as part of Operation Reinhard (the German code name for the systematic murder of some 1.3 million Jews in the General Government–administered areas of German-occupied Poland), the Nazis began deporting Jews from Drohobycz to the newly completed Belzec death camp, which pioneered the use of gas as a means of mass extermination and which served as the prototype for Sobibor and Treblinka. The deportations were overseen by SS-Sturmbannführer Eduard Jedamzik, who commanded the Drohobycz district until July 1942.

Grotesque rumors of deportations to death factories, often received with irritated incredulity, had reached Drohobycz from Lublin, Warsaw, and Kraków. "At first no one wanted to believe this," Amalia Buchman wrote, "or even to recognize that the catastrophe could reach us too. . . . The optimists among us said, and probably also believed, that these roundups related only to certain areas in Poland and not to Galicia."[36]

On March 25, some fifteen hundred Jews from Drohobycz, most of them elderly, were assembled and told they would be "resettled" in Pinsk. They were shipped instead to the Belzec extermination camp, where they were met by Commandant Christian Wirth and his SS colleagues, assisted by about ninety Ukrainian guards.[37] Like other victims, on arriving at Belzec's gates, the Drohobycz Jews were told that they had arrived in a transit camp and would be disinfected and showered. Men and women were separated, forced to strip off their clothing and to hand over their valuables, and were chased down a path called the "tube" (*Schlauch*, in German), which ended at the gas chambers.

In mid-June 1942, the Nazis halted transports to Belzec for a month in order to enlarge the gas chambers. Some twenty-four hundred Drohobycz Jews were rounded up and deported on August 18 and 19, and a further fifty-eight hundred in October and November. None survived.

The Sokal gymnasium in Drohobycz, 70 meters long by 20 meters wide (230 feet by 65), served as a *Sammelstelle* (assembly place). One survivor described the acrid odors that accosted the nostrils there on October 19, 1942:

> It was forbidden to move; whoever tried to change their position or to get up was beaten on the head with a club by the Ukrainian police guarding the place. A blow like this usually caused unconsciousness, brain damage, or even death. Bodily functions were made where they sat, and people were forced to sit in them. The smell and the stench were unbearable.[38]

With unsparing clarity, Schulz took some hundred pages of notes on the scenes of cruelty in Drohobycz for what he described to his friend Michał Mirski as "a work about the most awful martyrdom in history." Those dense, disjointed jottings have never been discovered.

Sometime that spring, assailed by a sense of the approaching abyss, Schulz handed a folder with 117 of his drawings and etchings to his devoted former student Samuel Bergman (after the war he took the name Emil Górski), who dreamed of becoming a musician. "I am giving these drawings to you. Perhaps you will manage to safeguard them. If you survive, do sell them, please, in case they are of any value. Then buy yourself a decent violin."[39]

Long before the war, Schulz had found in imagination a defense against coerced conformity. In Schulz's story "The Republic of Dreams," the narrator retreats into a bastioned territory:

In those far-off days our gang of boys first hit on the . . . notion of straying even farther . . . into no-man's- or God's-land, of patrolling borders both neutral and disputed, where boundary lines petered out. . . . There we meant to dig in, raise ramparts around us, make ourselves independent of the grown-ups, pass completely out of the realm of their authority, proclaim the Republic of the Young. Here we would form a new and autonomous legislature, erect a new hierarchy of standards and values. It was to be a life under the aegis of poetry and adventure, never-ending signs and portents.[40]

Bergman called this kind of escape from reality "a distinctive personality trait of Bruno Schulz."

I discovered this during the years of Nazi occupation, when nightmarish reality crossed all the limits of human fantasy, when the "surrealism" of those days reached such an intensity that we ceased to believe that what was happening around us was really real, and not some ghastly dream. . . . Even then Schulz was able to tear himself away from reality and create such an asylum that would afford refuge. This was the Citadel, mighty and safe, unconquerable to the enemy. The Citadel—a fantastic product of his imagination. . . . We all were to shelter ourselves there: Schulz and his friends; he described it meticulously, designed a defense system, discussed the organizational aspects of communal living, he even delineated a daily schedule, as well as times of activities and entertainment; he overlooked nothing, not even the kinds of victuals to be stocked in the storerooms and pantries. . . . While telling us of his dreamed-up Citadel, he forgot about reality, ablaze and enlivened, and his eyes—dimmed by hunger and torment—regained their old sparkle. Descriptions of the Citadel were so expressive and art-fully convincing that listening to them, with time we almost began to believe this beautiful fiction.[41]

How else to cope with the coming cataclysm that would soon extinguish the Republic of Dreams?

"Necessary Jew"
DROHOBYCZ, 1942

Bruno Schulz's favorite poet, Rainer Maria Rilke, once wrote to his wife, Clara: "Works of art are always the product of a risk one has run, of an experience taken to its extreme limit, to the point where man can no longer go on."

The masochistic, female-worshipping aesthetics of Schulz's artworks caught the eye of Felix Landau, a sadist beyond Schulz's imaginings who feared becoming engulfed by his own stifled sexual proclivities. Schulz's images did more than attract—his drawings and etchings prompted in Landau something like a rapturous return of the repressed. Perhaps Landau sensed in Schulz that which he wished to overcome in himself. Here the *imagination* of masochism—the fantasies of expiating some indefinite guilt by means of unconditional obedience—met the *actuality* of sadism. The need to provoke punishment met the uninhibited powerful punisher. For many Nazis, exertion of power was the highest art. Nazi propagandist and failed novelist Joseph Goebbels famously said that Nazi politics consisted in "the art of making possible what seems impossible" ("*Politik ist die Kunst, das unmöglich Scheinende möglich zu machen*"). With Landau, the Nazi art of power met Schulz's power of art.

The two men made a contract—not one between equals, but one that established a relationship of protection and predation. In return for Schulz's services, for the abdication of his artistic self, Landau granted Schulz status as a "necessary Jew," the "underman" to his "overman." Landau, the self-designated delegate of death, would henceforth keep Schulz as his lackey, his "personal Jew" (*Leibjude*). This entitled Schulz to extra rations. Landau trained his horses by feeding them a lump of sugar when they obeyed his commands. He now boasted that he kept his "house Jew" alive with a daily slice of bread and bowl of soup. (By this time, twenty to thirty Jews were starving to death in Drohobycz daily.) Landau also allowed Schulz to wear a coveted "safe conduct" armband, though even it gave no guarantee of survival. Zbigniew Moroń recalled: "I remember once, during the absence of his protector, he was hiding in the basement of our villa [on St. Bartłomiej Street]. . . . We had spare keys, and Schulz hid there for four days with his sister and eleven other Jews."[42]

Landau became Schulz's protector, so much so that some superiors suspected the Austrian officer of "favoring Jews" (engaging in *Judenbegünstigung*, or "Jew favoritism") for personal gain. The sadist transformed Schulz into a passive artist-slave; he derived profound pleasure from subjecting "his Jew" to cruelty and from forcing him to participate in his own humiliation. Landau tried to subjugate the "female" element within himself and reinstate male superiority even as he sensed a secret attraction to the truth revealed in Schulz's masochistic subjects.

"Among the Germans," a survivor from Drohobycz said, "Schulz was a painter and a slave."[43] Landau ordered Schulz to paint his portrait, portraits of Gestapo officers' girlfriends, and, beginning in the spring of 1942, to create murals in several buildings in Drohobycz: the SS casino (in Villa Jarosz); on the curved ceiling of the former Jewish orphanage on Sobieski Street; and in the riding hall, or Reithalle. ("It was Landau who made Jews build the Reithalle, which he himself had designed. Who drafted the plans? Most likely Schulz.")[44] Schulz's casino painting, which extended over several walls, depicted banquet guests at a long, richly laid table, as in a medieval pub. In the lower right corner, a servant pours beer from a barrel into mugs. He has the face of Bruno Schulz. None of these portraits or paintings survived the war.

In *One Thousand and One Nights*, Scheherazade, in the royal bedchamber, had to tell her tyrant beguiling stories to delay her execution. However beaten down, however coiled in misery, however scoured was his mind of any thoughts beyond those of survival, Schulz hoped that as long as he continued painting for Landau, he would be spared. At the same time, he questioned whether slavery was not a greater menace than death, whether it might be as dangerous to earn Landau's favor as to incur his disfavor. He had little inclination to cling to life, by any means possible, merely for the sake of life. For now, he had no choice but to acquiesce, to cede his time to Landau in order to buy more time for himself.

The master and slave conversed in German. Landau's tongue never tired of talking with Schulz about art.[45] "Jews trembled at the sight of Landau," Schulz's former student Leopold Lustig said, "but he was kindly disposed toward Schulz, toward his talent. He had him make his portraits and talked to him during the sessions."[46] Sometimes they spoke about Vienna, Landau's hometown, where Schulz had studied art and architecture.

What was the nature of the psychological circuit between these two men, the intimate connection between master and slave, punisher and punished? Could they share a common idiom? How to explain Landau's attraction to Schulz's art?

Landau seems to have believed that he could see through Schulz but Schulz could not see through him. He wished to exalt himself by abasing Schulz. We might be tempted at first glance to see Landau as a man of good taste who is at the same time a wretched criminal. (Clive James, for instance, writes: "A Gestapo officer with good taste, one Felix Landau, had made a pet of him so that he could paint murals.")[47] On closer look, however, Landau appears as a philistine of boorish bad taste whose greatest wish was to be a man of good taste, capable of taking a disinterested pleasure in beauty. So disinterested, in fact, that he might have overlooked the Nazi doctrine that regarded any contact with the condemned and contaminated race as defilement. He might have seen Schulz's artistic talent as disconnected from Schulz as a member of the subhuman Jewish race that in Nazi theory was incapable of anything but derivative creativity. (In his 1850 anti-Semitic tract *Jewishness in Music*, the German composer Richard Wagner claimed that Jews, an essentially uncreative people, could only "imitate art.") For Landau, "commissioning" Schulz's art was an occasion to demonstrate his own good taste, enhance his own prestige, and regard himself as a patron of sorts. Landau's treatment of Schulz sometimes resembled beneficence and sometimes dilated into malice. Did he envy the ability to create, an ability to the brute denied? Did he sense the abyss between taste and genius? Did he wish that he had been the creator of Schulz's art? Perhaps Landau looked upon Schulz as a reproach to his own unlived life.

The SS Officer with a Jewish Name: Felix Landau

Bruno Schulz's "guardian devil" was born in Vienna in 1910, the illegitimate child of Paul Stipkowitz and Maria Maier. A year later, his mother married a Galician-born Jew named Jakob Landau, who gave his surname to his stepson. Felix Landau bore a revulsion for his Jewish surname all his life.

When Felix was eight or nine, after Jakob Landau died, the boy was sent off to study at a Catholic boarding school. At age fourteen, he apprenticed as a carpenter and cabinet maker at the Riesner & Hölzel company, located on Vienna's Schottenfeldgasse. (As of this writing the building houses a restaurant designed by the celebrated Israeli chef Eyal Shani). Like Schulz, Landau learned the disciplines and demands of the craft.

On his fifteenth birthday, in May 1925, Landau joined the National Socialist Worker Youth. He enlisted in the Austrian army (*Bundesheer*) in 1929; his main job was to break in young horses. In March 1931, he joined the Nazi Party (membership number 442571). In June 1933, he joined the SA (Sturmabteilung, Hitler's brown-shirted storm troopers), and in April 1934 he joined the elite SS (Schutzstaffel).

Three months later, Landau was arrested for participating in a coup attempt—the so-called July Putsch—during which the Austrian chancellor, Engelbert Dollfuss, was fatally wounded. Together with a group of Nazi loyalists led by Otto Wächter, Landau stormed the Federal Chancellery and held up the chancellor's staff with a submachine gun. He was imprisoned in the Wöllersdorf detention center (*Anhalte-lager*) until he was amnestied in February 1937. He fled to Germany, trained in an SS-run military fitness camp (*Wehrertüchtigungslager*) in Ranis (a town in Thuringia), and found work as a junior police official (*Kriminalassistent*) in Berlin. After the *Anschluss* of March 1938, Landau returned to Vienna and married Marianne Grzonka. Armed with a Gestapo commission to "secure" Jewish property, he became one of the pioneers of persecuting Vienna's Jews in the name of what the Nazis called "de-Jewification" and "Aryanization" (*Ent-judung und Arisierung*).

In April 1938, the Nazis enacted the Decree on the Registration of the Property of Jews, which legalized confiscation of Jewish property. As head of Vienna's Procurement Office, Landau took to plundering with great rapacity. He seized several homes belonging to the Altmann family—including the exquisite apartment of Fritz and Maria Altmann (née Bloch-Bauer), ten days after their wedding,[48] as well as Bernhard Altmann's villa (1 Kopfgasse). Landau confiscated Maria Altmann's diamond necklace, a wedding gift from her uncle, Ferdinand Bloch-Bauer. (The necklace reportedly found its way to Hitler's deputy Hermann Göring, who presented it to his wife, Emmy, "First Lady of the Third Reich.") Landau personally "Aryanized" more than a hundred artworks from their collection, including paint-ings by Edgar Degas and Gustav Klimt (among them Klimt's mas-terpiece *Lady in Gold*, a portrait of the fashionable Viennese Jewish *salonnière* Adele Bloch-Bauer). "Now he ruled the fates of the people into whose parlors he once would have entered only as a workman," writes Anne-Marie O'Connor in her book on the "Lady in Gold." In June and July 1938, Landau himself orchestrated the public auction of the Altmann's art collection (nearly fourteen hundred lots) at the Dorotheum in Vienna.[49]

In April 1940, Landau was transferred nearly four hundred miles east, to Radom, Poland. In August, he was awarded the Nazi Blood Order (*Blutorden*). It was in Radom that the stout, bull-necked officer met a twenty-year-old shorthand typist and payroll clerk, a brunette named Gertrude (Trude) Segel. The daughter of an SS second lieu-tenant, Trude had joined the Gestapo in Vienna in August 1938 and had been transferred to Radom in February 1941, where she would work until September 1941. "I was asked at the employment office if I wanted to work at the Gestapo," she later testified, "and I agreed since the pay was 175 Reichsmark. I want it to be noted that even after starting work at the Gestapo, I never joined the NSDAP [Nazi Party]."

After the German invasion of the Soviet Union in June 1941, Landau abandoned all other attachments and volunteered for the SS *Einsatzkommandos*, the mobile killing-squad units, part of the *Ein-satzgruppen*. Based first in Lemberg (Lwów), and later in Drohobycz, he took part in *Einsatzgruppen* murders throughout Eastern Galicia, a region that played a pioneering role in the genocide of the Jews, even before the so-called Final Solution, to use the Nazi euphemism, was officially implemented.[50] Given the rank SS-Hauptscharführer (a non-commissioned officer equivalent to master sergeant), Landau partici-pated in mass executions in the Lemberg district. He complained of "Too little combat." (Though resentful that he had been passed over for further promotion, he would keep this rank through the end of the war.)

Felix Landau,
undated
(CREDIT: Yad
Vashem)

Like many Nazis, Landau felt the impulse to record. His journal
from this time is the reverberating record of a mass murderer who represented not so much a triumph of the will as a triumph of brutality.

"General of the Jews"

DROHOBYCZ, JULY 1941–NOVEMBER 1942

Felix Landau's career culminated in Drohobycz, where he arrived at
four p.m. on July 7, 1941, along with about twenty SS men commanded
by SS-Obersturmführer (first lieutenant) Nikolaus Tolle.[51] "We've
occupied a Jewish hotel for a few days," Landau said.

> On our way two Jews were stopped. They said that they had fled
> from the Russian army. Their story was fairly unbelievable. Six
> of our men got out, loaded up and the next minute both were

Felix Landau
on horseback,
Drohobycz,
early 1940s
(CREDIT: Yad
Vashem)

dead. When the order to take aim was given, one of the Jews, an engineer, was still shouting, "Long live Germany." Strange, I thought. What on earth had this Jew been hoping for?[52]

Once settled in Drohobycz, an emboldened Landau took to calling himself the "General of the Jews" (*Der Judengeneral*). Acting the part of a *Herrenmensch*, a man of the nature-ordained master race, he savored his power over the life and death of his subjects.

Years later, a German prosecutor would describe Landau as "a very primitive person, a person who certainly also had feelings of inferiority." He elaborated on this:

He was not born in wedlock, which was a serious social blemish in those days, in the first half of the last century, unlike today. He had a poor education; the death of his stepfather led him to financial difficulties; he was socially outclassed in Austria at the time. . . . He didn't have any friends among his colleagues; they didn't really like him. Even though he was a *Blutordenträger* [bearer of the Nazi Blood Order medal], they held back a bit from him. He was quite isolated. . . . And this man suddenly got a job in Drohobycz—as the *Judengeneral*, as he called himself—where he suddenly got power over other people. . . . A completely insignificant person suddenly got power over other people—but over defenseless people.[53]

Several Nazi traits found their confluence in Landau's inborn instincts. Comrades observed that the *Wille zur Macht* (the will to power) seemed to course through his veins. A stocky man with a curt, clipped manner of speaking and a love of riding (a love, more precisely, of feeling himself benevolent master to an obedient horse), Landau was fanatic in his belief that the flourishing of one group depends on the effacement of another (in this case, Jews). He would strut the streets of Drohobycz in his uniform (as if his clothing partook of his grim purpose), tar-black boots on his feet, a brass ring with a black stone on his little finger, and an impassive expression on his jowly face. His posture was that of a man convinced of his own superior rectitude. "*Du, komm her!*" he would shout—You, come here!—his voice barbed with hauteur and hatred.

Five days after his arrival, Landau shot two dozen Jewish men and women in the nearby woods. He described the incident in his diary:

> Drohobycz—July 12, 1941: At six o'clock in the morning I was suddenly awoken from a deep sleep. Report for an execution. Fine, so I'll just play executioner and then gravedigger, why not? Isn't it strange: you love battle and then have to shoot defenseless people. Twenty-three had to be shot, amongst them . . . two women. . . . I was detailed as marksman and had to shoot

any runaways. . . . We had to find a suitable spot to shoot and bury them. After a few minutes we found a place. The death candidates assembled with shovels to dig their own graves. Two of them were weeping. The others certainly have incredible courage. . . . Strange, *I am completely unmoved. No pity, nothing.* That's the way it is and then it's all over. . . . Slowly the hole gets bigger and bigger; two of them are crying continuously. I keep them digging longer and longer; they don't think so much when they're digging. . . . Valuables, watches and money are put into a pile. . . . The two women are lined up at one end of the grave ready to be shot first. . . . As the women walked to the grave they were completely composed. They turned around. Six of us had to shoot them. The job was assigned thus: three at the heart, three at the head. I took the heart. The shots were fired and the brains whizzed through the air. Two in the head is too much. They almost tear it off. Almost all of them fell to the ground without a sound. Only with two of them it didn't work. They screamed and whimpered for a long time. . . .

Then a few bodies were rearranged with a pickaxe and after that then we began the gravedigging work. I came back dog tired but the work went on. Everything in the building had to be straightened up. And so it went on without respite. . . . So I worked until 11 o'clock and had to make myself a plan like a proper little architect. Everyone admired my work.[54]

A witness named Wajsbord later testified that when Landau returned from such "*Aktions*," he would hand over his blood-flecked boots to be wiped clean.

Landau would ride through Drohobycz in a horse-drawn carriage (called a *biadka*), the horse blinkered, with a horsewhip in one hand and a pistol in the other. Some spoke of him as "the murderer on a white horse." "One day a group of Jews, including me, were gathered

together in the central courtyard of the Gestapo," recalled Wilhelm
Krell, "where, among others, Landau stood in SS uniform and cursed
the Jews and whipped them with a riding whip, including me." Albert
Kolpenicki also witnessed Landau whipping Jews who were forced
to work for him. Savage by training and sadistic by instinct, Landau
referred to his whip as "the interpreter" (*der Dolmetscher*). Increasingly instigated to cruelty, as though he were a law unto himself, at
least once he bridled Jews and harnessed them to horse carts.

Naftali (Tulek) Backenroth, a Paris-educated agronomist and a
leading member of the Drohobycz *Judenrat*, the Jewish council tasked
with liaising with the town's Nazi occupiers, was desperate to "deflect
Landau's brutal energy."[55] To do so, he submitted to Landau the idea
of building an indoor riding arena. Jewish laborers completed it in the
spring of 1942. It had ten stalls, two of which housed Landau's beloved
well-groomed horses: a mare named Erika and a stallion, Caesar. Once
Landau noticed that Erika had a scratch and decided to shoot the Jew
who had taken the horse to pasture. The Jew, forewarned by Backenroth, fled and survived.[56]

Another time, Landau focused his savagery on a servant, Eliasz
Sobel, who had not arranged Landau's saddle to his satisfaction; Landau unleashed his dogs, Asta and Rolf, and incited them to maul the
helpless Jew. (The title story of *Sanatorium Under the Sign of the
Hourglass* features "an enormous German shepherd on a chain, a
terrifying beast, a veritable werewolf of simply demonic ferocity . . .
the machinery of his powerful jaws filled with fangs.")[57] "I saw how
Landau incited a dog to attack children," said Anna Lustman, then
a twenty-nine-year-old woman living in Drohobycz, "and how the
dog had bitten the children and torn bits of flesh from their bodies."[58]
Marela Schwarz was eleven years old the day Landau and a Gestapo
officer named Hübner brought the two dogs to her house to hunt for
Jews suspected to be hiding in the basement. She knew the dogs well;
Landau had forced her father, Marian Schwarz, to take care of them.

"I know you're hiding Jews here," Landau said to Marela's father. "I suggest you take them out. Otherwise, we'll kill them and your entire family as you watch, and then we'll shoot you too."

Schwarz, an oil man, kept his composure. "Officer, sir," he said. "What do you suppose would happen if you and I both say together: 'Asta, sic 'em!' Would the dog attack you or me?"

"You," Landau said.

"Let's try it," Schwarz said.

Asta, momentarily confused on hearing the command issued simultaneously from two masters, bit Hübner instead. "Landau and Hübner rushed out to take care of his wounds," Marela said. "The Jews who hid with us downstairs survived—for the time being."[59]

On other occasions, Landau battered a Jewish glazier because he hadn't finished a task on schedule, and with his bare knuckles bludgeoned a Jewish farmer who had not stepped off the sidewalk in time for Landau's approach. Landau left his insufficiently swift-footed victim bruised and broken in the gutter.

Put in charge of organizing Jewish forced labor, Landau supervised workshops where Jewish carpenters, tailors, shoemakers, and furriers were forced to work without compensation. Others assembled outside the ghetto every morning at six a.m. and labored until four p.m.—digging ditches, carrying heavy railroad ties, or exhausting themselves in sawmills, refineries, ceramics factories, and the Dachów-czarnia brick factory. Landau forced Dr. Liberman and Zecharia Herzig of the *Judenrat*'s labor department (*Arbeitsamt*) to supply laborers, whom Landau treated as dispensable slaves.

July 22, 1941: One of my colleagues from the council came and asked me for my support as the Jews were refusing to work here. I went over. When those assholes saw me, they ran in all directions. Pity I did not have a pistol on me or else I would have shot some of them down. I then went to the *Judenrat* and informed them that if a hundred Jews did not report for work within an hour, I would select a hundred of them *not for work but for the firing squad*. Barely half an hour later a hundred Jews arrived together with a further seventeen for those who had run away. I reported the incident and at the same time gave orders for the fugitives to be shot for refusing to work, which happened precisely twelve hours later. *Twenty Jews were finished off.* . . . Tomorrow I am going to make a concerted effort to ask about my Trudchen coming here. . . . Good night, my dear little rascal; please still love me, think of me, and stay true to me.[60]

Landau arbitrarily selected the twenty Jews himself with his finger: *"Du, du, und du!'"* He boasted to Backenroth that he had shot them himself. "At twelve o'clock," Landau wrote in his diary entry of August 2, "the [Jewish] Council of Elders reported to me that all the uniforms were ready. Since I had twenty of its men shot for refusing to work, everything's been running smoothly."[61]

"My Bunny": Trude Segel
DROHOBYCZ, 1942

Landau's diary from this time intersperses fanaticism with bureaucratic tedium, and matter-of-fact reports of atrocities with cloying longing for his mistress Gertrude (Trude) Segel, whom he calls "my lovely little Trudchen" and "my dear bunny [*Hasi*]." He closes one entry with "Good night Trudchen. Think a little of your Lexi." He writes of Trude, "I could kill her with kisses."[62] The shifts between these two registers, sinister and saccharine, point toward Landau's twin sources of libidinous excitation: eros and death.

On July 3, 1941, for instance, Landau recorded his participation in the methodical murder of five hundred Jews:

While listening to madly sensual music, I wrote my first letter to my Trude. While I was writing the letter, we were ordered to get ready. Einsatzkommando with steel helmets, carbines, thirty rounds of ammunition. We have just come back. Five hundred Jews were lined up ready to be shot. . . . I have little inclination to shoot defenseless people—even if they are only Jews. I would far rather good honest open combat. Now good night, my dear bunny."[63]

Six days later, Landau relapses into soppy pathos: "If only I had post from my Trude. During the day when I am buried in work it is all right, but during the night the loneliness and inactivity simply make me despair."[64] His very faith in humanity depended on her. "If she, who has come to mean so much to me, disappointed me I would be completely devastated. I think that I would lose my belief in humanity right up to the day I died."[65]

The United States entered the war in December 1941, following the Japanese attack on Pearl Harbor. Four days after that surprise strike, Hitler declared war on America. Nazi propaganda chief Joseph Goebbels was overjoyed. "The World War is here," he announced. "The extermination of the Jews must be the necessary consequence."[66]

The next month, Felix Landau, one of the willing exterminators, persuaded Trude Segel to move to Drohobycz, where she served as the only woman typist in the Gestapo office.[67] The lovers installed themselves in a villa, together with Landau's children from his first marriage, to Marianne Grzonka, whom he would divorce in June 1942. Together with the two children, Wolf-Dieter and Helga, ages two and four, they lived in conspicuous luxury amid paintings, furs, jewelry, and porcelain confiscated from Jews. "I'm fine," Landau said with characteristic flippancy. "The Jews take care of me, that's why I send them to heaven."[68]

Felix and Trude regularly brought great gaiety to parties at the indoor riding hall. Jews were made to serve beer and schnapps to the Nazi officers and to clean up afterward. At one of these celebrations, Trude, wearing a gold necklace, danced drunkenly on a table, surrounded by a whirl of upturned faces. Giggling broke out among the Germans. (Bernhard Fischer, a neighbor of Schulz's, said, "From my personal dealings with her I knew that Segel accepted pieces of jewelry from Jews in order to intervene on their behalf for better treatment from her lover.") After Trude's preening performance, several Gestapo men groped her as they helped her down. One of them slipped the necklace into his pocket.

When the revelries ended, Landau accused Jacob Goldsztein, one of the Jews forced to clean up after the party, of the theft. During an interrogation of the accused the next day, Trude lay on a sofa in the office, looking on in inarticulate rage. Suddenly she shouted at Goldsztein: "Don't play stupid, you *Saujud* [Jew-swine]! You took the necklace." Landau, perhaps sensing that Trude wished him to prove his own mettle, pummeled Goldsztein to the ground. Trude egged him on. Landau ordered the panic-stricken man to get up. "He preferred to beat him standing, which he explained was more convenient than bending down to the floor."[69] Goldsztein, who would be forced to serve Landau for more than two years, called him "an unparalleled sadist."

Trude's cruelty rivaled Landau's, though hers took a primmer form, better concealed beneath a demure and maidenly surface. Salo Weiss, a Jewish tailor in Drohobycz, recalled that Trude brought a silver-fox fur stole to him for repair. "If you do it wrongly," she said as she turned her back to him, "you will be shot."[70]

On another occasion, Trude, who prided herself on her cleanliness and good grooming and associated Jews with slovenliness, and who felt sullied by her surroundings in Drohobycz, ordered the deaths of three Jewish maids who worked in the villa. Two other maids survived: Maryla Birman and Stella Backenroth. Leon Wieseltier told me that after Trude had trampled a Jewish child to death, his mother, Stella Backenroth, was ordered to "clean up the mess." "She saw unspeakable things," Wieseltier said of his mother, "and about most of them she has not spoken."

Forty years later, Stella Backenroth allowed herself to speak with Yaffa Eliach (one of the first historians to collect oral testimonies of Holocaust survivors) about an encounter with Felix Landau. Stella had been pulled down from one of the trucks headed to Bronica Forest by a member of the *Judenrat*.

> As she stood there in a daze, a Gestapo man by the name of Landau was practicing target shooting. Instinctively, she bent down. But Stella was not his target that day. He had a pocket full of lollipops. A group of children who were dragged out of hiding were standing around him. He asked them, one by one, if they would like lollipops, and if they wanted one, they should open their mouths. They did. One by one he shot them in their open mouths. Stella fainted.

"Until today," Eliach reports, "she feels faint when she sees dolls. To her, they represent the little, lifeless bodies of the innocent children on that Drohobycz street."[71]

Shooting from the Balcony
VILLA LANDAU, DROHOBYCZ, JUNE 14, 1942

Landau sometimes killed in the course of his official duties, and sometimes on his own initiative. Two balconies jutted from his villa: one gave onto the street and the second overlooked the manicured garden and its gravel path. June 14, 1942, was a pleasantly warm Sunday afternoon. After lunch, Felix Landau and Trude Segel were sunbathing and playing cards on upholstered Kanadier lounge chairs on the balcony overlooking the garden, where a dozen Jews were forced to work. Landau had on white pants and a white shirt. Trude was wearing a yellow swimsuit and had left her hair loose. To amuse himself, Landau grabbed a small-caliber Flobert rifle, one he usually used for vermin control and shooting pigeons. He loaded and cocked the rifle. Several shots rang out.

A Jew named Fliegner, forty-five or fifty years old, had been leaning on his spade in the garden beside a spray of flowers when he was struck. "I called his name," his friend Osias Weidmann said, "but he could no longer answer me. His arms and legs twitched, and he expired in front of my eyes. He was bleeding from a small wound on the left side of his chest and must have died from a direct shot to the heart."

Landau and Segel went inside, turned on the radio, and listened to classical music at high volume. The melodies could be heard in the garden below as members of the *Judenrat* (Jewish council) carted Fliegner's corpse away.

Trude Segel would twice testify about the shooting. (She refers to Landau as her husband, although at the time they were not yet married.) In her first testimony, she said:

> Landau got up and fetched a Flobert rifle that he kept in a chest in the hallway. Back on the balcony he aimed and shot at a pigeon which was sitting on the roof of the house opposite ours; immediately after, he fired two shots in the direction of the garden in which a group of men were working (they must have been Jews because Jews were always brought to work in our garden). After the second shot, a man from the group collapsed. Before my husband fired at that group, I wanted to stop him. I said to him, "You are not allowed to shoot at human beings" or something similar. The accused laughed and explained that it was just a Flobert rifle and that nothing could happen.

In her second testimony, Trude said:

> One Sunday in the summer of 1942, my husband and I were
> playing cards on the balcony of our house. I can no longer pre-
> cisely recall whether Landau or I fetched a Flobert rifle with
> which to amuse ourselves by shooting pigeons. I want you to
> note that it was not I, but Landau, who shot at the pigeons. A
> group of Jews were working about forty meters across the road
> from our house. . . . I witnessed how Landau aimed his rifle at
> the group and shot at them. I saw how one, a man supported
> by his shovel, must have been hit, since he fell forward to the
> ground. . . . If anyone accuses me of shooting into the group of
> Jews out of pure exuberance, I deny it most strenuously. . . . In
> response to repeated allegations, I report that not I, but Landau
> shot the Jew Fliegner with the Flobert rifle.

The following day, Felix Landau boasted of having killed "that
old *Scheissjuden*" ("Jewish shit"). Hans Joachim Badian, a Jew forced
to work for the Germans, asked him why he had shot Fliegner. "It
doesn't matter whether it is a week sooner or later," came the reply,
"you will all be liquidated."[72] According to Leon Thorne, the next
day the head of the *Judenrat*, Maurice (Maciek) Ruhrberg, also asked
Landau why he had murdered the blameless gardener. "Why not?"
Landau answered. "Others are killing thousands of Jews. Can't I shoot
at least one?"[73]

Fairy Tales: Art Under Coercion
VILLA LANDAU, DROHOBYCZ, JUNE 1942

Under certain conditions of artistic partnership, Schulz once remarked,
"the wall admits us to dimensions formerly denied us; the frescoes
painted on the vault of heaven come to life as in a pantomime."[74] In

June 1942, not long after Fliegner's murder, Landau took advantage of the suppleness and the compliance of Schulz's hands and commanded him to paint murals for the children's room in the villa Landau had confiscated.

For the last time, Schulz obeyed Landau's instructions "under the pressure of losing his life," though not without a measure of soft subversion.[75] Did Schulz find any peace in surrendering to subservience and self-annulment before his tormentor, or only great anguish? Did he dream of deferred justice, of delayed rewards, for this patiently endured suffering? Maybe beneath his apparent acquiescence the creation of the murals was an act of resistance. A former student of Schulz's recalled:

> Schulz remained somehow faithful to his creative principle: in the paintings on the wall of the child's room, in the fantastic fairy-tale scenery, the characters of kings, knights, squires had the completely "un-Aryan" features of the faces of people among whom Schulz lived at the time. Their similarity to the emaciated and tortured faces that Schulz had captured in memory was extraordinary. Here these tormented people— transported through Schulz's imagination from the world of tragic reality—found for themselves in paintings brilliant richness and pride; as kings on thrones in sable furs, with golden crowns on their heads; on beautiful white horses as knights in armor, with swords in their hands and surrounded by knights; seated like powerful lords in golden carriages.[76]

Authoritarians either repress artists into stunned silence or co-opt them. Schulz, who painted his murals under duress, embodied the artist under coercion. The murals, and the circumstances of their creation, compel a question: Should they be granted a place in Schulz's artistic output alongside his other works or be treated as evidence of oppression? Are they the transient products of trauma or enduring works that transcend it?

Though some works of art are commissioned, many more emerge unbidden not from external commands but from internal demands, as products of inventive play. Though many artists feel the push and pull of authority and autonomy, true instances of "art under coercion" are few and far between. We know that some artists, including Leo Haas, were forced to illustrate propaganda material for the Germans in Theresienstadt. We know that Ester Lurie was ordered by her captors to paint landscapes and portraits in the Kovno ghetto even as she secretly drew and documented ghetto scenes.[77] We know that a contemporary of Schulz's, the Italian artist Aldo Carpi, survived Gusen, a subcamp of the Mauthausen concentration camp in Austria, by painting more than seventy portraits of SS officers' wives and mistresses (some in the style of Venetian nudes). In return, Carpi was permitted to work indoors and to earn supplementary rations, which he often distributed to fellow inmates.[78] We know, finally, that a year or so after Schulz's death, a twenty-year-old prisoner named Dina Babbitt painted meadows, flowers, and Snow White and the Seven Dwarfs on the walls of the children's barracks in Block 31 of the so-called *Familienlager* ("family camp") at Auschwitz. Those barracks were under the direct supervision of Josef Mengele, the infamous Nazi physician known as the Angel of Death, who ordered Babbitt to make watercolor portraits of Roma (Gypsy) prisoners. (Mengele took an interest in their skin tones and physiognomies.) Babbitt bartered the portraits for her life and the life of her mother.[79]

Five years before he painted the murals for Landau's children, Schulz had watched a screening of *Snow White and the Seven Dwarfs*, Disney's first animated feature film. It is no coincidence that in his last artworks Schulz elaborated on fairy-tale imagery. Fairy tales, when they're not prettified by fairy godmothers and chivalrous rescuers, often feature monstrous scenes of wickedness, cruel separation or imprisonment or rejection, devouring wolves, sadistic stepmothers, terrifying witches, impostors, poisoned apples, ugliness and deformity, and death. By allowing for the obliteration of fear by fancy, the tales let children set their anxieties at a safe distance.

The narrow children's room in Villa Landau became for Schulz a sanctuary of sorrow. The warm colors he used to depict his characters contrasted with the dread-induced foreboding he must have felt at the time. In Schulz's murals we can catch a banishment of his fears.

Escape Date
DROHOBYCZ, NOVEMBER 19, 1942

"Ordinary facts are lined up in time," Schulz writes in one of his stories, "strung onto its course as if on a thread. . . . But what can be done with events that do not have their own place in time, with events that arrived too late?"[80]

On August 6, 1942, Fritz Katzmann, SS commander of the Galicia district, convened a meeting in Lemberg on "the solution to the Jewish question in Galicia." On October 23 and 24, a further twenty-three hundred Jews, including members of the *Judenrat*, were herded like cattle onto trains from Drohobycz to the Belzec extermination camp. At the same time, all three hundred patients of the Jewish hospital were shot.[81] Beginning on November 7, the Gestapo demanded the delivery of a hundred Drohobycz Jews a day to the Komarner synagogue on Gabarska Street to be deported or killed. By the end of 1942, no more than three thousand Jews would remain in the Drohobycz ghetto.

In one of his stories, Schulz remarks, "Fate does not bypass our consciousness and will but incorporates them into its own mechanism so that we permit and accept, as in a lethargic dream, things before which under normal conditions we recoil."[82] Though aware of his own unworldliness and ineffectualness in practical affairs, Schulz refused to reconcile himself to the cruel abnormality of his fate. Marooned in his memories, Schulz was plagued by thoughts of escape. According to Jerzy Ficowski, "He confided to friends that he visualized himself riding on a train with windows darkened with blue paint. At some small station the train halts, there is the sound of the hobnailed boots of military policemen, the beam of a flashlight falls on his face, and the words are heard: *Komm du Jude, komm!* [Come, you Jew, come!]"[83]

According to Schulz's friend Izydor Friedman, friends had sent him a forged identity card (what the Germans called a *Kennkarte*) from Warsaw: "I provided him with currency and dollars, but he kept putting off the departure day. He could not summon up the courage and meant to wait until I received 'Aryan' papers." According to Schulz's former student Harry Zeimer, Schulz was given falsified Aryan documents by Tadeusz Wójtowicz, a Polish friend from Drohobycz involved with the resistance movement. "I had to buy the forged papers," Zeimer said. "Schulz was given them for free by members of the Polish resistance, a testament both to the esteem in which he was held and his lack of the necessary money."[84] A survivor from Drohobycz, Emmanuel Weintraub, told Benjamin Geissler: "I don't see Schulz as someone who flees unless someone would have taken him, an Izydor Friedman, or perhaps a Frau [Dziunia] Schmer [a friend of Schulz's], had she said 'now I'm going to Warsaw, I can take you with me.' But she wouldn't have done that because Schulz didn't look very Aryan, he looked like an intellectual."[85]

Finally, Schulz's friends in Warsaw understood that they could no longer count on his innate will to survive. They came up with a couple of plans: to send a Polish Home Army soldier disguised as a Gestapo officer to Drohobycz and, under some pretext, to transport Schulz as a "prisoner" to Warsaw; or to smuggle Schulz from Drohobycz to a remote forester's lodge in the vicinity of Kielce, a city in southern Poland two hundred miles northwest of Drohobycz.

At last startled into wakefulness, no longer insensible to his friends' admonishments, Schulz dispelled his doubts and equivocations and set a date for his escape: November 19, 1942.

Black Thursday
DROHOBYCZ, NOVEMBER 19, 1942

> Death is the Messiah.
>
> —ISAAC BASHEVIS SINGER, *THE FAMILY MOSKAT*

In Schulz's story "The Age of Genius," the boy narrator Joseph imagines that the Messiah arrives by mistake or by distraction, and that his arrival goes unnoticed. And yet this double oblivion seems to condition a new beginning:

> On such a day the Messiah approaches the very edge of the horizon and from there looks down at the earth. And when he sees it so white and silent, with its azures and pensiveness, it can happen that in his eyes it loses its boundary, the bluish bands of clouds lie down to form a passageway, and, not knowing himself what he is doing, he descends to earth. And in its reverie the earth won't even notice the one who has descended onto its paths, and people will awaken from their afternoon naps and remember nothing. The entire story will be as if it had been blotted out, and it will be as it was in primeval times, before history began.[86]

How long could Schulz divorce outer compulsion from interior feeling? The savior that Schulz—at the height of his creative powers—had summoned in his fiction would never arrive in fact.

On Thursday, November 19, 1942, Stalin launched a massive Soviet offensive to retake control of Stalingrad from the German Sixth

Army, which was entrenched in the city, inaugurating one of the bloodiest battles of World War II. On the same day—the very day Schulz had planned to escape the Drohobycz ghetto with forged papers—Schulz awakened early and saw the dawn lending color to women's handkerchiefs that had been strung up to dry, undulating as though interpreting the language of the wind.

That day, as every morning in the Drohobycz ghetto, Jews reappeared on the streets after the end of the nightly curfew. Among them was a Jewish pharmacist named Max Kurtz-Reines who had managed to acquire a pistol. Stopped for a routine check by Karl Hübner, a Gestapo guard, Kurtz-Reines panicked, drew his weapon, and shot the German in the finger.[87] In retaliation, beginning at eight a.m., Gestapo officers were given free rein to shoot any Jew they chanced to encounter in the streets. Ze'ev Fleischer, seventeen at the time, described the Gestapo shooting spree as "open hunting" for Jews. According to a witness, Karl Krell: "Felix Landau was one of the main perpetrators of this action and shot several Jews, flaunting himself in front of Jews." Other witnesses (including Shimon Rand and Jacob Goldsztein) saw Landau gun down Jewish men and women that day. Landau had a submachine gun on his shoulder but preferred to use his revolver. He boasted of shooting a hundred rounds that day, all of them into Jews.

Three and a half years earlier, in the spring of 1939, Schulz had happened to meet a student of his, Andrzej Chciuk. "Do you have some time?" Schulz asked. "Well then, let me show you something." They walked to the Drohobycz courthouse and sat in on a hearing about compensation for someone injured in a car collision. Three witnesses to the accident each gave accounts that differed from one another in ways large and small. Schulz smiled. "See? This is what I'm talking about. None of them lie. Each testifies under oath. And yet in the end very little coincides. There is only one truth: that created by the artist. . . . By deviating from the truth in the usual sense, the artist comprehends some other, greater, more universal truth. To the degree a truth created by the artist takes possession of the reader's imagination, it becomes inviolable."

So it was with the contradictory testimonies of Schulz's last moments.[88] We're left with the polyphony of memory.

VERSION 1

Erwin Schenkelbach told me that not long before "Black Thursday," he had been out walking with his father, Bertold, near the town hall when they encountered SS-Oberscharführer (sergeant first class) Karl Günther. Leopold Lustig described Günther, then thirty-three, as having "a broad face, pockmarked from adolescent acne, and rough workman's hands." Bertold had lent German books to Günther and had instructed him in how to develop film (the German styled himself an amateur photographer); in return, the SS officer gave the Schenkelbach family advance notice of roundups. On this occasion, Günther gave Erwin a benign smile and an avuncular pat on the head. "Oh, what a handsome *knabe* [boy] you have, Bertold!" With deliberate slowness, the German reached into a leather shoulder bag. Improbable as it seems, he withdrew not a pistol, as Erwin feared, but a bar of chocolate in purple wrapping.

Erwin's fears were hardly unfounded. On October 28, 1942, Karl Günther had chanced on three Jewish teenage girls (with the family names Cukierman, Sternbach, and Kupferberg) who had been forced to work as bricklayers and plasterers, mixing chalk and lime. Leon Thorne bore witness to what followed:

> Günther came near them, stood a while and observed them as they labored, and then took out a gun and for no reason at all shot them dead. One girls' father, Kupferberg, was a barber who used to serve Günther, the Gestapo beast. After shooting the three girls, Günther went home and sent for Kupferberg because

he wanted a shave. When the Jew finished his task, Günther looked at him and said, "Kupferberg, half an hour ago I shot your [sixteen-year-old] daughter." Kupferberg fainted.[89]

According to Amalia Buchman, the shooting was accompanied by Günther's "loud rippling laughter." One of the victims, Schenkelbach said, "was my first platonic love, seventeen-year-old Wisia (Lerna) Cukierman."

Earlier in November, Felix Landau had shot Adolf (Dolek) Löw, a Jewish dentist who had been under Günther's "protection."[90] (In return for sexual favors, Günther had extended similar protection to a young Jewish woman, Maria Steczkowska.) "I saw how he went through the clothes of the dentist Löw whom he shot on the street," said a witness named Izydor Badian, "and removed gold from him."

According to several accounts, just before noon on November 19, Karl Günther spotted Schulz at the intersection of Czacki and Mickiewicz Streets, not a hundred yards from the house where Schulz was

The Drohobycz intersection where Schulz was murdered, as it looked before World War II (CREDIT: Polish National Digital Library, public domain)

born. Schulz was wearing dark gray pin-striped pants and his "necessary Jew" band on his right arm, beneath which he had tucked a loaf of
bread. "Jew, halt!" Günther shouted. As Schulz turned, Günther shot
him in the head with a Browning pistol at point-blank range. He was
fifty years old. Günther left his body where it lay in the street, which
descended into an eerie silence. Less than an hour later, the Gestapo
men met in the dining room of Villa Jarosz (named after a former
mayor of Drohobycz). In a stagey voice, Günther told Landau: "You
killed my Jew, I killed yours."[91]

VERSION 2

Eyewitness Julian Holcman remembered the blood running "in
streams on the streets" that Thursday, and the murderers' jubilant
throaty laughter. Josef Gabriel, the *Judenreferent* of the Drohobycz
district (an SS "Jewish expert" who reported to Adolf Eichmann),
pistol in hand, rounded up several Jews, including Holcman. Gabriel
ordered them to fetch a cart and gather up corpses from the streets.

> As he was talking to us, Landau arrived and said laughingly to
> Gabriel: "Gabriel, I shot your friend Professor Schulz." Landau
> boasted that he had started out with a hundred bullets and that
> none remained. Gabriel laughingly replied: "Good for you. I
> shot no fewer Jews. I only regret that Schulz didn't die because
> of a bullet from me."[92]

VERSION 3

Laughter of the most detestable kind also figures in an account given
soon after the war by a young woman who studied in the Leon Sternbach School in Drohobycz:

Bruno Schulz visited us and told the most beautiful stories to my young cousin. He painted portraits of the Germans and was supposedly favored by them. As he walked down the street, two gendarmes stopped Schulz with a smile: "Here comes our court painter." Laughing, one of them shot him from behind.[93]

VERSION 4

According to several witnesses, it was neither Karl Günther nor Felix Landau who shot Schulz but a thirty-four-year-old Austrian-born Gestapo officer named Friedrich (Fritz) Dengg, who bent down over the body and took Schulz's watch from his left wrist.[94]

VERSION 5.

Tadeusz Smolnicki, a chemistry teacher, gave still another account:

Standing on the curb with an armband on his sleeve, Schulz was feeding breadcrumbs to pigeons on the street. Since Jews were only allowed to walk on the street, he provoked a Gestapo man with his disobedience. He died instantly by a bullet.[95]

That day, to borrow a phrase he used in another context, Schulz "instantly crossed over from history to legend as if from one room into the next."[96] Of one thing we can be sure: neither Schulz's artistic achievements nor his formal renunciation, six years earlier, of his belonging to the Jewish community carried any weight for his murderer. Recall Józefina's observation that Schulz saw in every person some resemblance to animals. The end of Schulz's life was determined by people who behaved like predatory beasts.

Between 160 and 230 Jews were killed that day, during a bacchanal of violence that came to be called "Black Thursday." Women and children were not spared. When the groans of agony subsided, a silence descended on Drohobycz like a shroud. Only the joyful perpetrators of the massacre were heard. The murderers, whistling gaily, walked to the Jewish council offices, demanded to be served brandy, and gulped it down fast.[97]

In late November, the young Polish literary critic Artur Sandauer received by return mail a postcard he had sent to Schulz. It bore a stamp from the Drohobycz *Judenrat*: "Addressee unknown."[98] Sandauer, who had known Schulz personally, made the controversial claim (derived not from testimonies but from his own interpretation of Schulz's writing and temperament) that Schulz had deliberately sought death simply by going out into the street when he knew the Nazis were shooting with wild abandon. According to Sandauer, Schulz's murder was in effect the writer's suicide by someone else's hand, driven by a masochistic drive toward "self-annihilation."[99]

Of Bread and Burial

DROHOBYCZ, NOVEMBER 20, 1942

Ze'ev Fleischer, a former student of Schulz's, recalled:

> I waited for the Germans to go away, and then I walked past the dead people. There were dead bodies everywhere. Dead people in the street was an everyday thing. If you saw the dead body of a cat in the street it would have made a bigger impression. I didn't notice that anything special had happened, and I also didn't know who they were. . . .
>
> I saw, from one of the bodies lying on the sidewalk, something like a piece of bread. It was sticking out there, from the pocket of his trench coat. I went over to this dead man, and

I guess I wanted to take his bread. And the dead man turned over. I turned him over, and the way I turned him he was facing me, and I look and see that it's Schulz. It was Schulz's face. . . .

My instinct was to take the bread and run away. And it seems I didn't do that. It seems I didn't do it. Look, a person who doesn't eat—and we, after all, didn't eat, we ate inedible things, we ate soup that was mostly water with some grass or something. . . .

I felt a chill and I felt afraid. . . . You understand by now that he was more than a teacher for me. I felt a special kind of connection with him; he was a spiritual relative in certain respects . . . And suddenly I see him dead. I was about seventeen at the time, and I had already seen many dead, but suddenly—*him*.[100]

Schulz's body lay in the street through the afternoon and night. Abraham Schwarz reported:

The next day, I was among those "chosen" to "clean up" and collect corpses. On Thursday, no one could force us to do so, because the shooting lasted until dusk. . . . Many corpses had already been undressed. We stacked them on those carts like firewood. We hurried and wanted to do everything as quickly as possible because in the end it was an unpleasant activity, and there were a lot of bodies. . . . So, during that "clean-up," I came across Schulz's body. At first, I saw a group of people leaning over a man's body. I told them to disperse so that I could do my duty. And then I heard, "No, leave him; this is Bruno Schulz. Someone will come to pick him up, because he had asked an acquaintance to bury him next to his mother."[101]

War's Embers

DROHOBYCZ, JANUARY 1943–AUGUST 1944

In early 1943, as the Red Army was defeating the Wehrmacht at Stalingrad, Trude Segel and Felix Landau applied for permission to marry. They requested an expedited response to their application so that they could celebrate their union on a special *Volksfest* (a people's festival): Hitler's birthday, April 20.[102] Permission arrived too late, and they married in Drohobycz on May 5, 1943. In March 1944, they would welcome the birth of their only child together, Teja-Udo Landau.

Half a year after Schulz's murder, the Gestapo liquidated the Drohobycz ghetto and killed its remaining twenty-three hundred Jews. Most were trucked to Bronica Forest and shot. One of the few survivors of that massacre was Schulz's former student Fleischer. (About a third of the almost six million Jews killed during the war perished not in the extermination camps but in shootings in forests and killing fields—what some historians call a "Holocaust by bullets.")

On June 30, 1943, Fritz Katzmann submitted his "Final Report on the Solution of the Jewish Question in the District of Galicia" to the SS and Police Chief Friedrich Krüger. Two weeks later, Drohobycz was declared "cleansed of Jews" (*Judenrein*). In a speech to the Ukrainian volunteers who had enthusiastically formed the SS Galicia Division, SS-Reichsführer Heinrich Himmler said: "Your homeland has become so much more beautiful since you have lost—on our initiative, I must say—those residents who were so often a dirty blemish on Galicia's good name, namely the Jews."[103]

Russian bombs struck Drohobycz for the first time on April 10, 1944. Four days later, SS officers led by Friedrich Hildebrand (commandant of the slave labor camp of Drohobycz and Borysław) rounded up 1,022 Jewish forced laborers, including Schulz's students Alfred Schreyer and Leopold Lustig. Most were transported from Drohobycz to the Plaszów concentration camp near Kraków, run by notorious

SS-Untersturmführer (second lieutenant) Amon Göth.[104] (Plaszów is the camp featured in Steven Spielberg's 1993 movie *Schindler's List*.) On June 26, 1944, an American B-17 Flying Fortress from the Eighth Air Force bombed an oil refinery two miles out of Drohobycz.

In 1921, the Polish census had counted 11,883 Jews (more than 40 percent of the town) in Drohobycz. The 1938 census had registered some 17,000 Jewish residents of Drohobycz. Of these, only about 400 survived to see the arrival of the Red Army in August 1944.[105]

Some 130 of those owed their lives to the Hamburg-born Wehrmacht major Eberhard Helmrich and his wife, Donata. The couple employed Jews on an agricultural labor camp called Hyrawka, which provided fresh vegetables for German soldiers. They also sheltered Jews in their own home and smuggled them out of town in an official car.[106]

Two days after Schulz's murder, Metropolitan Andrei Sheptytsky, archbishop of Galicia and Lwów and an influential leader of the Ukrainian Greek Catholic Church, issued a pastoral letter, "Thou Shalt Not Kill," exhorting the faithful not to abet Nazi atrocities. Although the penalty for assisting Jews in German-occupied Poland was death, there were other saviors. A Ukrainian acquaintance of Major Helmrich's, Taras Snyatynsky, would be recognized by Yad Vashem as a Righteous Among the Nations for saving a Jewish mother and her two children in Drohobycz. In return for handsome payment, a Ukrainian factory worker named Ivan Bur hid forty-five Drohobycz Jews, including Alex Haberman (the only survivor from his family) and Bernard Mayer and his family, for eighteen months in a stifling thirty-by-ten-foot bunker under a brick house (59 Boryslawska Street).[107] A Polish family concealed Leon Thorne, a Drohobycz rabbi, under a pigsty. Jan and Zofia Sawinski hid thirteen Jews, including Marcel and Irena Drimmer and their parents, Jacob and Laura, on their small farm from August 1943 to August 1944. Izydor and Jaroslawa Wolosianski hid thirty-nine Jews, including the Herzig family, beneath their house in Drohobycz. Frania Sobkowa, a devoutly Catholic nanny and house-keeper, hid Irene and Pola Bienstock and their mother, Sarah, in her tiny Drohobycz apartment for two and a half years. Leon Wieseltier reports that Izydor Friedman "survived the war by hiding for many months in a small chamber under a pigsty in a barn near an oil well in a hamlet called Schodnica. There were four other people with him in that wretched heaven-sent hole. One of them was my mother."[108] The Polish couple Władysław and Olga Grzegorczyk saved eighteen Jews from the Drohobycz ghetto, including an eleven-year-old girl named Mina Fuchsberg—later known as Shulamit Aloni, a left-wing member of Knesset and the Israeli minister of education. Another survivor: the economist David Horowitz, later the first governor of Israel's central bank.[109]

These were the rarest exceptions. Many Polish neighbors either hardened their hearts with indifference to the fate of people who had lived in their midst for generations or openly rejoiced in the prospect of a Drohobycz without Jews. Some blamed the Jews for dragging Poland into a war with Hitler. Bystanders remained silent or acquiesced to the evil that is indifference to evil.

More common were cases of Poles who turned in Drohobycz Jews for half a pound of sugar. Tadeusz Servatko, eleven years old in 1942, remembers a tiny hideout for Jews on Shevska Street, a narrow lane near the market square. Once a child's hand, holding a cup to catch raindrops to drink, emerged from the hideout's hatch. A neighbor saw this and informed the Germans. The next day, Servatko said, everyone in the hideout was shot, children first. Rubin Schmer-Gartenberg's parents, who built a hideout under their house on Czackiego Street, were betrayed by a Polish neighbor, and taken out in 1943 to be shot in Bronica Forest.

Russian forces retook Drohobycz on August 6, 1944. Bernard Mayer, who as a teenager had hidden in an underground bunker, said, "It was the first time I'd seen daylight in a year and a half, and the light dazzled my eyes. The sight of two Red Army soldiers was the happiest sight in my life." Only in January 1945 would the Red Army reach Warsaw. On May 9, the Germans surrendered to the Soviets.

Shortly before the war's end, Vasily Grossman, then a war correspondent for the Soviet military newspaper, *Red Star*, wrote an essay called "Ukraine Without Jews":

> Stillness. Silence. A people has been murdered. Murdered are elderly artisans . . . murdered are teachers, dressmakers; murdered are grandmothers who could mend stockings and bake delicious bread . . . and murdered are grandmothers who didn't know how to do anything except love their children and grandchildren. . . . This is the death of a people who had lived beside Ukrainian people for centuries, labouring, sinning, performing acts of kindness, and dying alongside them on one and the same earth.[110]

Drohobych had belonged to the Polish-Lithuanian Commonwealth for four hundred years, to Austrian Galicia for almost a hundred and fifty years, and to Poland for twenty-nine years between the wars. The town was now incorporated into the Ukrainian Soviet Socialist Republic—after Russia, the largest republic in the USSR. On Stalin's orders, 810,000 Poles from Galicia were deported west to mainland Poland and 630,000 Ukrainians were deported from Poland to Soviet Ukraine.[111] (The Drohobych "Resettlement Office" was housed at 16 Mickiewicz Street.) As part of "Polonia Irredenta" (historically Polish but under the political control of another state), Schulz's hometown would remain under Soviet rule for the next forty-six years, until Ukraine gained independence in 1991.

CHAPTER 6

AMNESIA IN THE AFTERMATH

1945–2001

Reality is a shadow of the word.

—BRUNO SCHULZ

Erasure: Schulz in Ukraine

At age twenty, Jonathan Safran Foer traveled from Brooklyn to Ukraine in search of his grandparents' origins. His quest for an obliterated past resulted in his first novel, *Everything Is Illuminated* (2002). Years later, the American Jewish writer discovered Bruno Schulz. On Kafka's well-known maxim that "a book must be an ice-axe to break the seas frozen inside us," Foer remarked: "Schulz's two slim books are the sharpest axes I've ever come across." Foer's fascination with Schulz culminated in his 134-page die-cut book *Tree of Codes*, which carves out passages from *The Street of Crocodiles* ("I've never read another book so intensely or so many times," Foer said) to form new phrases and sentences. Excising two-thirds of Schulz's text, Foer created his own narrative from the remaining fragments of the original. This creation by means of redaction, Foer said, was an attempt "to create a die-cut book by erasure."[1]

Selective erasure of a less clear-cut kind conditioned Schulz's

fate in postwar Ukraine. With the acquiescence of Roosevelt and
Churchill, the Yalta Conference, in February 1945, decided that
Drohobycz and Lvov would come under Soviet Ukrainian rule, as
Stalin had urged. The official line in postwar Soviet Ukraine elimi-
nated national and religious identities and submerged the Jewish fate
into the undifferentiated wartime suffering of "all freedom-loving
peoples." Under the slogan "Do Not Divide the Dead," Soviets ruled
out the claim that Jews had been singled out during the Great Patriotic War. One and a half million of Ukraine's Jews had perished by
1945, a quarter of all victims of the Holocaust. Yet Ukrainian historians of World War II tallied their own losses (some three million
Ukrainians were killed by the Nazis) and said precisely nothing about
the Shoah.[2] This was no ordinary forgetfulness. In Eastern Galicia,
the cradle of Ukrainian nationalism, the Jewish past was subject to a
dual forgetting: of the specificity of the illimitable Nazi hatred of the
Jews and of the role of home-grown ultranationalist collaborators in
the murder of Jews.

Drohobycz expunged memory of Jewish absence even in its material traces. The city's old Jewish cemetery, in use from the seventeenth
century, was vandalized during World War II, subsequently demolished, and in the 1950s built over with a Khrushchev-era apartment
block (today 3 Pylypa Orlyka Street). "When digging for the foundation," Alfred Schreyer said, "they extracted bones. . . . Epidemiolo-
gists went to the party's regional committee and told them that less
than ten years had passed since the last burial there. After all, you
cannot build in such places. . . . But the regional committee said that
they should build, because this place is included in the general development plan of Drohobycz."[3] Schulz once said that the headstones there,
"carved in soft sandstone, are worthy of twelfth-century cathedrals,
and show the noblest feeling of a decorative bas-relief surface." It was
the final resting place of Rabbi Asher the Second of Karlin; Rabbi
Eliezer Drohobycz, a disciple of the Seer of Lublin; and Rabbi Eliezer

Nisan Teitelbaum, a son of Moshe Teitelbaum of Ujhely, the author of *Yismakh Moshe*. Down the road (across from 22 Pylypa Orlyka Street), the neglected "new Jewish cemetery," in use between 1853 and the 1970s, is today visible behind a locked iron gate. Many of its four hundred gravestones have been vandalized or demolished or heaped up as rubble. It contains a small memorial to the victims of the November 19, 1942, massacre.

Drohobycz's cultural mosaic—crushed by the might of the Soviet Union, then Nazi Germany, and then Polish and Ukrainian nationalisms—went to wrack and ruin. "It was altogether hard to imagine anything that had happened in Drohobych before Soviet times," writes the Polish journalist Ziemowit Szczerek of his "classic *tour de Schulz*" pilgrimage. "Or even to imagine Galicia."[4] As Schulz's war-numbed native town came under Soviet domination, his legacy, like his half-forgotten murals, lived on only in the memory of his few surviving students. As one empire faded away and another came into being, this Jew who wrote in Polish faded into an apparition, a ghostly absence. His writing seemed to speak in tones discordant to the times. After the maelstroms of the war, in a diminished Drohobycz, Communist guardians of literary standards deemed Schulz's work irrelevant to *Homo sovieticus*—or too fine a clay for the crude mandates of socialist realism. Convinced of the rightness of their views, they excluded Schulz from the new literary canon and suppressed his books as products of bourgeois decadence. It didn't help matters that the Ukrainian nationalistic intelligentsia held Polish-language literature in contempt.

Schulz's Ukrainian translator Yuri Andrukhovych remarked that in 1869, 48 percent of Drohobycz's residents were Jews. By 1970, Ukrainians had come to dominate, and Poles and Jews had each dwindled to 3 percent. He asked, "Can we also assume that Drohobych's loss of its Poles and its Jews corresponds to its loss of Bruno Schulz, whose language was Polish and whose heritage was Jewish?"

"Drohobycz Has Disappeared from My Memory": Trude's Testimonies

VIENNA, OCTOBER 1949

In Austria and Germany, other repressed memories were surfacing. Trude Segel, newly divorced from Felix Landau, had been arrested in Vienna on August 2, 1945, and imprisoned in Glasenbach, Austria, in March 1946. In June 1947, she was taken to the public prosecutor's office in Vienna to face charges of war crimes and murder based on five eyewitness testimonies. There she became one of the thirty-eight thousand people who faced "preliminary investigations" by the "People's Courts" (*Volksgerichte*) run in Vienna from immediately after the war until 1955. The office was led by Wolfgang Lassmann, Austria's observer at the Nuremberg trials, who vehemently opposed notions of collective guilt. Trude Segel conceded to investigators that she had been aware of "the weekly reports on the liquidations" of Jews in Drohobycz but insisted she couldn't remember details.

> I have in the meantime experienced so many things that the time spent in Drohobycz has disappeared from my memory. I myself was only in the ghetto a few times at the beginning to get myself some things sewn. I recall that from time to time transports left Drohobycz for Lemberg [Lwów], from where they were presumably transported to another camp. In response to insistent allegations, I admit that I am aware that "actions" took place in Drohobycz. Questioned about the nature of these "actions," I admit that a number of people—we are talking about Jews—were involved. What happened to them, what the actions were about, I don't know because I was not present. . . . I admit that my husband in part also participated in these "actions."

In October 1949, Lassmann dismissed the eyewitness testimonies to Trude Segel's alleged war crimes as "mere narratives" (*blosse Erzählungen*) and declined to prosecute her.

Straying from Socialist Realism
COMMUNIST POLAND, 1945–56

In December 1922, the first president of the Second Polish Republic, Gabriel Narutowicz, abhorred by far-right critics for sympathizing with Jews, was assassinated at the opening of a contemporary art exhibition in Warsaw. Ever since, Polish attitudes toward Jews past have served as a yardstick for pluralist stances more widely.[5]

A trilogy of short films called *And Europe Will Be Stunned*, made between 2007 and 2011 by the Israeli director Yael Bartana, features a Polish activist who leads a fictional Jewish Renaissance Movement. In a speech delivered to the empty grandstands of Warsaw's Communist-era Decennial Stadium, the young leader, played by Sławomir Sierakowski, declares that a Poland without Jews is a dismembered body:

> We want three million Jews to return to Poland, to live with us again. We need you! Please come back! . . . Return not as shadows of the past, but as a hope for the future. . . . Without you, we cannot even remember. Without you, we will remain locked away in the past.

In the final part of the trilogy, the leader is assassinated. We learn from his followers' eulogies that he was shot at a Warsaw art exhibition as he stood before a painting by Bruno Schulz.[6]

Before the war, more Jews lived in Poland—a polyglot, multiethnic state—than in any other European country. Due to the sanctuary Polish rulers and landed nobles had extended over the centuries to Jews

expelled from Western Europe, more than three million Jews lived in
Poland in 1939 (in a population of thirty-five million). Of those Jews
who stayed under German occupation, 90 percent were murdered. Of
the survivors, many would immigrate to Israel. By 1950, only forty-five
thousand Jews were left. After the war, Poland became a country of
one ethnicity, one language, and one religion—a country transformed
beyond recognition, unable even to remember.[7]

In Communist Poland, Jewish victims of the Nazis were tallied not
as Jews but among the Polish victims of "the Great Patriotic War"; they
were said to have been murdered not as members of a "race," as defined
by the Nuremberg Laws, but as opponents of fascism. "The paradox
of eight hundred years of Jewish presence in these lands," the Polish
photographer Mikołaj Grynberg said of this conflation, "was that they
were only allowed to be Poles once they were dead."[8]

The Polish recovery of Schulz, in particular, could proceed undistracted by the still, small voice of a guilty conscience, since Schulz was
killed by a Nazi, not a Pole. Unlike Germans, Poles didn't see their
postwar reconstruction as founded on a crime. With barely a shud-
der of contrition, many Poles voiced a lachrymose recital of victim-
hood and enjoyed the dubious good fortune of not having to think too
much about the Jewish victims. In this climate of denial, they regarded
Poland as the suffering Christ of Nations, as though transfiguring the
entire Catholic nation into a sacrificial body.[9]

For three years after the war, many Poles resisted the imposition
of a Moscow-backed regime. Beginning in December 1948, however,
Poland became for all intents a Russianized Stalinist state, with cen-
sorious effects on cultural life. At the fourth congress of the Union of
Polish Writers (known by its Polish acronym, ZLP) in Szczecin in January 1949, where Schulz was discussed, delegates were warned against
the bourgeois reactionary art of "the philosophy of catastrophism,
helplessness, mysticism, and irrationalism."[10] Socialist realism, with

its moralistic depictions of class conflict, became the only acceptable literary mode.

In a 1941 letter, Schulz argued that "realism, as the exclusive urge to copy reality, is a fiction. No such thing has ever existed."[11] For more than a decade after the war, Communist authorities confined Schulz's legacy—deemed dangerously decadent and anti-realist—in quarantine.[12] Poland's officially approved high school literature textbook for 1952 antagonistically numbered Schulz (misspelled "Schultz") among writers who represented a "deliberately deformed image of the world" and "created grotesque characters and situations that symbolized their loathing for life. . . . Today the reactionary nature of such views is clear to us." A 1952 book on Polish interwar writers likewise lamented Schulz's "helpless straying from reality."[13]

Midwife of Memory: Jerzy Ficowski

"Poland today is the ironic fulfilment of the dreams nurtured by Polish chauvinists," Czesław Miłosz said in 1956 of his war-shattered country's vassalage to the USSR. "They wanted a homeland cleaned up, stripped of mixtures and minorities—and they have it, but as a dependence of another State."[14]

With Soviet premier Nikita Khrushchev's denunciation of Stalinism in early 1956 and the Gomułka "revolution" in October 1956, Stalinism in Poland collapsed. As Poland's official censorship thawed, Schulz's books could at last reappear.[15] Only then did some dare to say that if Polish literature wished to chart an independent way forward, it would have to find a path back to Schulz. This, in turn, prompted a spate of international translations of his books in the 1960s: French and German (1961);[16] Spanish and Swedish (1962); Hungarian, Italian, and English (1963); Danish and Norwegian (1964); Finnish (1965); and Japanese (1967).

I spoke with two Poles who first encountered Schulz's writing in Polish universities in the late 1950s. Henryk Grynberg, the author of *Drohobycz, Drohobycz*, first heard of Schulz during a university lecture on Kafka in Warsaw:

> The professor, who was Jewish, did not mention that both those authors were ethnically Jewish. I got my Master's degree in 1959 not knowing this. . . . As for Schulz, I bought a book of his collected prose and read it as purely universal writing. His Jewishness I detected years later from his drawings and paintings, not from his prose.

Joanna Rostropowicz-Clark, born in Warsaw in 1939, recalled:

> How did Schulz's Jewishness matter to us? (I say "us," as I was then a typical Polish university student.) A great deal, but somewhat superficially. The same as we felt about Kafka, but with more directness to Schulz, who was murdered *because* he was a Jew. We knew all too well—twenty years after the war was not that long—what had happened to the majority of Polish Jews. Our word for it was *Zagłada*, or annihilation. ("Holocaust" came later.) But we were young and "modernist"; books seem to matter more than reality. We loved Artur Sandauer's phrase about the world of Schulz's fiction: "reality degraded." Degraded, before destroyed.

Schulz owed his post-1956 revival to the single-minded devotion of a single ardent disciple. In 1942, the last year of Schulz's life, Jerzy Ficowski read *Cinammon Shops* and experienced "the incomparable emotion which accompanies a first reading of Schulz's works. . . . I too found the Authentic . . . a book different from all others . . . one for which no rival has ever emerged." Ficowski, then eighteen, sent the author a letter describing his embarrassment that he had not learned earlier about this "greatest writer of our times" and his "gratitude for [Schulz's] existence itself." "I naively wrote that although it might mean nothing to him, he should know that there was someone for whom *Cinnamon Shops* was the source of intense delight and revelation."[17] Schulz would be dead before the letter arrived.

Ficowski had displayed considerable courage both before and during the war. In the 1930s, boys at his school in Warsaw organized a boycott of two Jewish classmates. The Polish boys refused to sit down unless the Jewish students left the classroom. Without hesitation, Jerzy sat down in solidarity beside the two Jewish boys.[18]

During the war, Ficowski had joined the Home Army, Poland's armed resistance. Already in pursuit of Schulziana, Ficowski discovered three letters by Schulz, only later to misplace them somewhere at the University of Warsaw. When the letters were found, he was asked to prove that he was their real owner. It was easy for Ficowski to do so; he knew them so well that he could recite them by heart. The letters were returned to him.[19] In October 1943, he was arrested by the Gestapo and put behind bars in Warsaw's notorious Pawiak prison. After his release, Ficowski took part in the Warsaw Uprising of 1944, and he spent the five years after the war, as he put it, in and out of "the dungeons of secret police, military intelligence, and counter-intelligence." A fervent Catholic, he was also beset by overwhelming guilt. "Because this [the suffering of Jewish people] is my great guilt," he told an interviewer. "The 'guilt' of all those who survived."[20] Rescuing Schulz's legacy became a search for absolution.

As he gained prominence as a poet, Ficowski memorialized in verse the Jewish victims of the Holocaust, particularly in his book *A Reading of Ashes*, illustrated by Marc Chagall.[21] Ficowski also paid homage to Schulz in his poem "My Unsurvivor."[22]

In searching for Schulz, Ficowski had to contend with a fragmentary record. In 1948, he bought ads in *Kuźnica, Przekrój,* and other magazines, asking for anyone with manuscripts, letters, or drawings of Schulz's to notify him. Thus began a search campaign with global reach and the cultivation of an extensive network of correspondents and collaborators.[23]

Ficowski published his first article on Schulz in 1956, and a landmark book, *Regions of the Great Heresy* (the phrase comes from one of Schulz's stories), in 1967 (that book was brought out in an updated edition in English by W. W. Norton in 2003). It is less a biography than the record of a tireless pursuit; it reads in parts like an elaboration of that first worshipful fan letter. Wooed by the tragic shadow of his subject, Ficowski visited Schulz's hometown in 1965. "My findings were meagre," he reported, "but my Drohobycz walks were like a pilgrim's visit to a sacred site—to the cradle of Schulzian myths."[24]

Some criticized the rescuer's one-sided valorization. "Ficowski is not a critic," said Schulz's former student Andrzej Chciuk, "but a reverent hagiographer."[25] And yet, without Ficowski, cradler of the Schulzian myth, we would not know Schulz, just as without Max Brod we would not know Kafka.[26]

Felix Landau on Trial
STUTTGART, GERMANY, FEBRUARY 26, 1962

In late February 1962, two and a half months after Adolf Eichmann was sentenced to death by a special tribunal of the Jerusalem District Court, a parcel with a Munich postmark but no return address unexpectedly landed on the untidy desk of the Stuttgart public prosecutor, Wolfram Koch, as he was drafting his opening statement in the trial of Felix Landau. Koch unsealed it to find a school notebook filled with lines written in light pencil and, to his astonishment, recognized Felix Landau's original wartime journal (with entries from June 1941 to December 1941), long thought lost. On the first day of the trial, Koch presented it with a certain showmanship and moved that it be submitted into evidence. The defendant admitted its authenticity but portrayed himself, without a touch of misgiving or remorse, as a benign functionary in the death machine—as though the Nazi Party had been a sort of limited liability company exempting him of personal responsibility. There were many events from those years of aberration that Landau said he could no longer recall, and he made not even the haziest apologies for those he could.

Recognized in Linz by a former Jewish forced laborer in 1946, Landau had been briefly imprisoned by the Americans in the Camp Marcus W. Orr internment compound near Salzburg. (General Dwight D. Eisenhower visited the camp in October 1946.) Landau escaped in early August 1947 and went into hiding under the name Rudolf Jaschke in Nördlingen, a town in Bavaria, Germany. He had borrowed the name from Franz Jaschke, a deceased Austrian painter and member of the Vienna Secession. (The notorious SS physician Josef Mengele was hiding at the time under a false name at a farm near the Bavarian town Rosenheim.) Shielded by the moral indifference of the few who knew his real identity, Landau passed himself off as a Sudeten ethnic German refugee and confected a new life as an interior designer. Though he feared retribution, he carried from the war no burden of trauma or loss. In fact, his hubris unshaken, he exulted in his good fortune: amid the countless nameless dead, he stood alive; he had deflected death.

Although both the state court in Vienna and the Salzburg police had issued warrants for his arrest, in 1958 Felix Landau registered his real name to authorities in order to remarry. He was arrested in August 1958, and put on trial from February 26 to March 12, 1962, before three judges and six jurors.

Landau's defense attorney, the right-wing extremist and former Nazi Rudolf Aschenauer, accused prosecution witnesses (who were staying together in the Alter Ritter hotel in Stuttgart) of coordinating their testimonies.[27] One of the witnesses was Bruno Schulz's former student Harry Zeimer. During a court recess, Zeimer overheard a group of Germans chatting in the hallway about how they knew nothing about the atrocities carried out by the SS and Gestapo. They said they were shocked to hear such things at Landau's trial. Zeimer interrupted and told them that when he'd fled from Drohobycz to Switzerland in September 1942 with forged papers, he'd traversed the entire breadth of Germany by train.

"During that trip," Zeimer said to them, "I happened to hear a German soldier in SS uniform boast to fellow passengers in the car of how his unit had engaged in mass murders of Jews in the occupied eastern territories. Not a single passenger objected or expressed amazement. On the contrary, an elderly well-dressed German gentleman, a typical bourgeois, piped up: 'Yes, you must continue to carry out your work in haste.'"

One of the German women objected: "But that soldier shouldn't have spoken about such things."

"Precisely," Zeimer replied. "In your view the soldier should be reprimanded not for the murders but for daring to recount them."[28]

On March 16, 1962, the Stuttgart Regional Court handed Landau a double life sentence.[29] He remained still and vacant-eyed as the sentence was read. In June 1963, Germany's Federal Court of Justice (*Bundesgerichtshof*) denied his appeal. In prison, Landau spent a great deal of time painting. He did not serve out his sentence. Ten years later, in June 1973, the German state of Baden-Württemberg commuted his sentence and released him from prison the following month. In November 1982, when his probation expired, Germany formally restored his right to hold public office (*Amtsfähigkeit*). Forgiven by the state, Felix Landau remained unrepentant. He died in Vienna on Hitler's birthday in 1983.

Felix Landau's son Wolf-Dieter claimed he remembered his father's horses in Drohobycz, but not the murals Bruno Schulz painted for his playroom. Jens Carl Ehlers, the director of a film about Schulz (*Republik der Träume*, 1993), told me that Wolf-Dieter reacted "aggressively" when asked about the murals. Wolf-Dieter Landau died in Australia at age sixty-two on July 1, 2001, four months after the rediscovery of those murals.

The original manuscript of Landau's diary disappeared after the trial; only typed copies have survived. Felix Landau and Trude Segel's son, Teja-Udo Landau, raised in Vienna after the war, first brought himself to read his father's diary only in 2001, at age fifty-seven. He could not comprehend his father's gloating over the inhuman crimes he committed. "It took me a while to come to terms with myself," he said, "and say to myself, Okay, you are your father's son, but that doesn't mean you have to be like him." He noticed one malady of his father's mind that persisted more than three decades after the war: a fear of Jewish revenge. More than once, Teja-Udo said, while sitting at a pub with his father, by then a more temperate man, Felix would grow suddenly anxious. "We have to leave," he would say. "They're watching me. They're all Jews."[30] On one occasion, the German filmmaker Benjamin Geissler asked Teja-Udo whether he had any heirlooms from his father. Teja-Udo brought out a small wooden box, its cover inlaid with a woman astride a horse, a ribbon fluttering from the rider's hat. The intricate work had been done by Bruno Schulz.

Exodus
POLAND, 1968

At Israel's birth in 1948, some 40 percent of the country's Jews were of Polish origin. By the end of the 1950s, there were thirty lending libraries of Polish-language books in Israel. Polish newspapers could be perused on wicker racks in Tel Aviv cafés. A Tel Aviv newspaper advertisement from 1954 announced, "Dalia coffee shop: A meeting place for Polish customers. Moderate prices." By then, at least some of those customers knew that Polish anti-Semitism had not evaporated when the German occupiers were defeated; the end of the war had not brought about a "clean break." By then they knew that even after Germany's defeat, Poles had perpetrated deadly pogroms in Rzeszów (June 12, 1945), Kraków (August 11, 1945), and Kielce (July 4, 1946).[31] They knew, too, that in the early 1950s the Polish Communist Party apparatus—while still paying lip service to the abolition of ethnic and religious hatreds—had purged itself of Jews. Yet none of this stopped *Davar*, the newspaper of Israel's ruling Mapai party, from running favorable articles about Poland in the late 1950s. One of them read, "From among the states of the Soviet bloc, Poland is today the only state maintaining friendly relations with Israel. There is a development between the two countries of commercial and cultural relations, of art, science and sport, under the banner of coexistence of nations with different opinions."[32]

After a decade during which permission to leave for Israel was denied, the emigration of Polish Jews began in January 1955, gained momentum when Władysław Gomułka rose to power the next year, and peaked in 1957. But any Polish openness toward the Jewish state chilled when Poland severed diplomatic ties with Israel after the 1967 Six-Day War and anti-Jewish passions of the not-so-distant past returned. Under the guise of anti-Zionism, the Polish United Workers' Party launched an anti-Semitic campaign, cresting in March 1968. First Secretary Gomułka vilified the country's Jews—then numbering only thirty thousand out of a Polish population of thirty-two million—as a "fifth column." Many Polish Jews were purged from their jobs. Over the next three years (1968–71), between twelve and twenty thousand Jews fled the country. The state required them to renounce Polish citizenship and to sign declarations that they were leaving for their "own country" (Israel). The 1968 campaign, historian Lucy S. Dawidowicz wrote, "put the finishing touches to the Final Solution to the Jewish Question which the Germans had so efficiently accomplished for them."[33]

In 1967, the Adam Mickiewicz Museum of Literature, in Warsaw, then headed by Schulz enthusiast Adam Mauersberger, mounted the world's first major exhibition of Schulz's drawings. It included 117 works that, months before he was killed, Schulz had given to his former student Emil Górski, and six prints from his *Booke of Idolatry* that he had given to his patron Zofia Nałkowska in 1933. "After the years of dead silence," said Wojciech Chmurzyński, "when Schulz's name was on the Communist blacklist, the exhibition came as a real shock, especially to the younger generation brought up in an atmosphere of social-realist optimism."[34]

In 1973, the Polish film director Wojciech Has adapted Schulz's stories for the big screen. His movie *The Hourglass Sanatorium*, in which young Joseph travels in time to visit his deceased father in a phantasmagoric sanatorium, won the Jury Prize at the Cannes Film Festival. Dozens of Polish stage productions followed.[35] "What we got from him," a Polish actress told the critic Clive James about Schulz, "was luxury." James agreed, writing, "He was about as far from socialist realism as you could get."[36]

The first conference in Poland dedicated to Bruno Schulz took place in 1974 at the University of Silesia, even as Polish critics continued to assign his work to "the field of psychopathology."[37] Only in the late 1970s, in parallel with renewed interest in Poland in the country's Jewish past, did Polish scholars begin to explore Jewish aspects of Schulz's writing.[38] Until then, Polish historians and writers had by and large treated the country's Jewish heritage in a superficial and fragmentary way.[39] Even afterward, they extended a hand in earnest goodwill to someone who was no longer there.

The Unforgetting: Schulz in America
PRINCETON, NEW JERSEY, OCTOBER 1975

"Under the imaginary table that separates me from my readers," Schulz's narrator asks in "The Book," "don't we secretly clasp each other's hands?" After several false starts, Schulz clasped hands in those years with more readers in America than in his native country.

In the spring of 1962, Arthur Miller spent part of his honeymoon with Inge Morath, an Austrian photographer, in the Lviv area where his father was from (Brody). During the trip, the American playwright met Karol Kuryluk, the Polish ambassador to Austria, in a sanatorium near Vienna. Karol's daughter, Ewa Kuryluk, acted as translator. "My father was an extremely silent and cautious man," Ewa told me, "but that afternoon he became rather talkative. Among other things, he recommended to Miller the writings of Bruno Schulz, and told him how he, as a twenty-three-year-old student, went to Drohobycz [in June 1933 and again in September 1934] to pay tribute to the older and already famous writer."

Arthur Miller would have to wait to take up the recommendation. Schulz's *The Street of Crocodiles* first appeared in English in 1963. The Warsaw-born translator, Celina Wieniewska (née Miliband), had escaped from Nazi-occupied Poland in 1940 via Dresden, Italy, Istanbul, Iraq, and India, and settled in 1941 in London (where she worked for the Polish government-in-exile and the BBC Polish Section). Her Jewish parents remained in the Warsaw ghetto and perished. In 1957, at age forty-eight, she married Peter Janson-Smith, thirty-four, the literary agent of James Bond author Ian Fleming.[40]

At a dinner party in Princeton in October 1975, Philip Roth met Joanna Rostropowicz-Clark, the thirty-five-year-old Warsaw-born wife of Blair Clark, the editor of the *Nation* and an executive at CBS News.

She had emigrated from Poland four years earlier. Gathered around the table: Blair's sister Anne Martindell, a Princeton grande dame; Melvin Tumin, Roth's longtime friend from Newark, the model for the protagonist of Roth's novel *The Human Stain* (2000) and the first Jewish full professor at Princeton University; and Stefan Morawski, a

professor of philosophy who had been expelled from his post in Warsaw during the 1968 anti-Semitic purge that swept through Poland.

Between dinner courses, Rostropowicz-Clark passionately commended Schulz's writing to Roth. The next morning, he found a copy
of Celina Wieniewska's translation in Princeton's Firestone Library.
Roth, like Schulz no stranger to the imperatives of immaturity, "was
instantly taken," Rostropowicz-Clark said. I asked her thoughts on
why Roth felt so drawn to Schulz's fiction. What affinities did he sense?

She offered several: "The image of the father (as important to Roth
as to Kafka): both grotesque and powerful in his undead omnipres-
ent existence. The aspect of blasphemy mingled with awe toward the
Jewish lore. The delirious sensuality of the language and vision—in
contrast to Kafka's delirious asceticism. And, perhaps not quite con-
sciously, the territorial affinity: Roth's family roots. Both grandparents came from that same eastern nook of Galicia, Tarnopol, with
the similar provincial (yet teeming with prospects of change) background."[41] Rostropowicz-Clark later gave Roth fifteen museum reproductions of Schulz's artworks from a 1973 exhibition in Poland. "I
gave Philip reproductions of Schulz's drawings," she told me, "because
I thought that their particular eroticism would add to the appreciation
of Schulz's literary work."

In November 1976, Philip Roth called Isaac Bashevis Singer "and
asked," Roth later related, "if we might get together to talk about
Schulz and about what life had been like for a Jewish writer in Poland
during the decades when they were both coming of age there as artists."
They met in Singer's fifth-floor apartment in the Belnord, a massive
building on West Eighty-Sixth Street off Broadway. Dvorah Menashe
(later Telushkin), Singer's twenty-two-year-old personal assistant,
watched both men fiddling helplessly with the tape recorder before
that conversation. "I had to teach them both: pause, play, record,"
she told me. "Eventually I just managed the recorder—much easier."

With the tape running, Singer told Roth that Schulz "was not really at home, neither at home among the Poles nor at home among the Jews."

"It looks as though Schulz could barely identify himself with reality," Roth interjected, "let alone with the Jews. One is reminded of Kafka's remark on his communal affiliations: 'What have I in common with the Jews? I have hardly anything in common with myself and should stand very quietly in the corner, content that I can breathe.' . . . [Schulz] reimagines bits and pieces of Kafka for his own purposes."

"I would say that between Schulz and Kafka there is something that Goethe calls *Wahlverwandtschaft*," Singer said, "an affinity of souls that you have chosen for yourself." He added: "The more I read Schulz—maybe I shouldn't say it—but when I read him, I said he's better than Kafka."[42]

Despite rave reviews (the *Times Literary Supplement* rhapsodized about its "lavishness of the evocation, fertility of the metaphor"), Celina Wieniewska's finely tuned translation gained wide acclaim only in 1977, when Philip Roth included it in his Penguin series Writers from the Other Europe. "The purpose of this paperback series," Roth said, "is to bring together outstanding and influential works of fiction by Eastern European writers. In many instances they will be writers who, though recognized as powerful forces within their own cultures, are virtually unknown in America."[43] Roth's friend Benjamin Taylor told me that Roth "felt *The Street of Crocodiles* to be the most important volume of the series." (In donating his personal library to the Newark Public Library in 2016, Roth issued a list of the fifteen works of fiction he considered most significant to his life. It included Schulz's *The Street of Crocodiles*.) The cover carried Isaac Bashevis Singer's claim that Schulz "wrote sometimes like Kafka, sometimes like Proust, and at times succeeded in reaching depths that neither of them reached."

V. S. Pritchett called *The Street of Crocodiles* "a masterpiece of comic writing: grave yet demented, domestically plain yet poetic." In her *New York Times* review of the book, Cynthia Ozick called Schulz "one of the most original literary imaginations of modern Europe." Ozick, whose 1987 novel *The Messiah of Stockholm* would enact an homage to Schulz, counted him "among those writers who break our eyes with torches." To round out the year, the *New Yorker* published three of Schulz's stories.[44]

Schulz's second story collection, *Sanatorium Under the Sign of the Hourglass*, also translated by Celina Wieniewska, followed in Roth's series the next year (1978). In a glowing introduction, John Updike names Schulz "one of the great transmogrifiers of the world into words."

In the fall of 1988, a series of events, organized by the American Foundation for Polish-Jewish Studies and the PEN American Center, revived Schulz in New York. Schulz's artworks (sixty drawings) were exhibited for the first time in the United States at the New York Academy of Art. Readings of Schulz's work were performed at the Town Hall, on West Forty-Third Street (where Jerzy Kosinski introduced the readers Czesław Miłosz, Elizabeth Hardwick, and Susan Sontag), and at Saint Peter's Church, on Fifty-Fourth Street (where Lwów-born poet Zbigniew Herbert read in Polish and Sontag delivered the English translations). An audience of a thousand people attended the Town Hall event. At the same time, the Polish American literary celebrity Jerzy Kosinski established the $10,000 Bruno Schulz Prize for a "neglected Eastern European writer." (Its first and only recipient: Zbigniew Herbert.) Three Polish films based on Schulz's works were meanwhile screened at the 57th Street Playhouse, and a play inspired by Schulz's stories (*The Fatal Lack of Color*, by Chris Hariasz and J. Emil Warda) was staged at the Lamb's Theatre, an Off-Broadway venue near Times Square.

Ever since, a whole host of writers in the United States, Canada, Britain, Germany, Czechoslovakia, Romania, Croatia, Serbia, Italy,

Iceland, Chile, Sweden, Israel, and of course Poland have been caught in the gravitational field of Schulz's mythology.[45]

Only in 1989 would Schulz's writing be canonized in Poland's National Library series (equivalent to the Library of America).[46] The first Ukrainian translation of *Cinnamon Shops* (by Ivan Hnatiuk) also appeared in 1989. The following year, the Drohobych city council changed the name of a street in the city center: Darwin gave way to Schulz.

The Unpossessed: Searching for the *Messiah*
1987–PRESENT

> Exegetes of the Book assert that all books aim for the Authentic. . . . Books wane, but the Authentic grows.[47]

—BRUNO SCHULZ

The sacred but hidden urtext—the lost object that bestows sense on the world—appears in various guises in Schulz's fiction. It is the father's ornithological textbook in the story "Birds." It is an old calendar—the book of the year—with a thirteenth month. In "Spring," it takes the form of a stamp album that Joseph venerates as both a thing of blazing beauty ("that burning Book . . . the genuine Book of Radiance") and a "compendium of all knowledge about that which is human."[48] In another story, the precious is hidden in a drawer together with Adela's erotic talismans, her silk dress and shoes. In "The Book," it appears as a yellowed mail-order catalog with advertisements: "a great, rustling Codex, an agitated Bible through whose pages the wind moved."[49] The Father, who has torn pages out to wrap his lunches, says, "The Book is a myth we believe in when we are young, but cease to take seriously when we grow older." He offers his son the Bible instead. For the son, however, the Bible is an inadequate substitute, a clumsy and corrupted copy of the timeless Original. In the end, the authentic Original may never have existed, except in the sense, as Schulz put it, "that the Book is a postulate, that it is a task."[50]

Schulz understands his own writing as an extension of that task, as a re-creation of that sacred text or a merging with it:

> Ah, when writing down these narratives of ours, arranging these stories about my father on the worn margin of its text, am I not surrendering to a secret hope that someday, unnoticed, they will take root among the yellowed pages of this most magnificent, disintegrating book, that they will enter into the great rustling of its pages that will swallow them?[51]

For disciples of Schulz, the authentic Book, the great Original, is the lost novel *Messiah*. In 1987, Jerzy Ficowski received a telephone call from one Alex Schulz, who claimed to be the illegitimate son of Bruno's elder brother. Alex, a plumber living in Los Angeles, was born Eizig Schulz in 1918. His father was from Borysław and his mother from Drohobycz. He told Ficowski he had been contacted by an unnamed man in Lviv seeking a buyer for a two-kilogram (four-and-a-half-pound) packet containing eight drawings by Schulz and the manuscript of *Messiah*. Alex Schulz died of a cerebral hemorrhage before he could pass on the name of his mysterious contact. Still, Ficowski did not desist.

Two years later, Sweden's ambassador to Poland, Jean-Christophe Öberg, relayed to Ficowski a credible report from an official in the Soviet embassy in Stockholm: "Among the millions of documents in one of the Soviet KGB archives, there is a stuffed parcel containing Schulz's literary manuscripts, including, most importantly, the novel *Messiah*." It sounded plausible enough: the Soviet transfer of Gestapo material to Moscow (a case of treasure plundered by the Nazis re-stolen by the Soviets) is well known. Öberg died of a rapidly progressing cancer before he could divulge any additional leads.

Ficowski's quest was further obstructed, he said, by the fact that the manuscripts were not cataloged under Schulz's name. "They were first seized by the SS, then taken over by the Russians and included in the Soviet archives. They arrived in the archives together with the confiscated papers of a man arrested by the SS. No one knows his name." Ficowski acknowledged the irony. "Isn't it a horrifying twist of fate," he remarked, "that if *Messiah* has survived, and I'm convinced it has, if it is ever found, we will owe it to the SS, the same monstrous institution that killed Schulz and all those who were dear to him?"[52]

Cynthia Ozick's *The Messiah of Stockholm*—dedicated to Philip Roth—answers Ficowski's quest. The novel follows a Swedish orphan, Lars, a middle-aged book reviewer for the *Stockholm Morgontörn*, who believes himself to be Schulz's son.[53] Overcome by his obsession and beset by this "anxiety of influence," Lars is a ripe target for a woman named Adela (the femme fatale of Schulz's fictions) who says she has the lost manuscript of *Messiah*. In the end, amid questions about its authenticity, Lars burns the manuscript in a brass amphora.

Ozick calls Schulz's language "dense with disappearances." So was his war-winnowed material legacy. He is an artist without an archive. So much of what he wrote and painted has been destroyed or lost: all of the manuscripts of his works, published and unpublished, except one (a six-page manuscript of the story "A Second Autumn")[54]; notes Schulz made in the Drohobycz ghetto for what he called "a work about the most awful martyrdom in history"; Schulz's letters to his fiancée, Józefina Szelińska (some two hundred, which she called "masterpieces of epistolary art"),[55] to Debora Vogel,[56] and to Zofia Nałkowska; countless prints and drawings (some four hundred, a fraction of his output, survived); and all but one of his paintings. Also lost: the only story Schulz wrote in German, "The Homecoming" ("Die Heimkehr").[57] In 1937, Schulz had sent a thirty-page typescript to Thomas Mann in Zurich, in the hope that the novelist could help secure him a German-speaking readership. That typescript, too, has yet to be found. Schulz's "selected works" were selected not by an editor but by unkind fate. Schulz's grave, too, has never been found. The old Jewish cemetery where he might have been buried was demolished in the Soviet years. Schulz's legacy, so much of it lost, resembles fragmentary murals; we can only guess at what was there, beyond the visible.

If, by filling in the discontinuities, Ozick regarded herself as Schulz's true daughter, Nicole Krauss might have felt a granddaughterly tug. Krauss's novel *The History of Love* (2005) refers to an enigmatic writer named Bruno and to a long-lost manuscript. In Krauss's alternative history, Leopold, a Polish Jewish author who is believed to have died during the war, unexpectedly reappears in New York in possession of that manuscript.[58]

Undeterred to the end, Jerzy Ficowski died in 2006 without knowing whether *Messiah* had long since perished, like its author. The cold case of the missing novel, one of the literary world's greatest unsolved mysteries, continues to fascinate as a symbol of loss.[59]

In her second memoir, the singer-songwriter Patti Smith connects that loss to a cherished misplaced black coat:

> Within my childish mourning, I think of Bruno Schulz, trapped in the Jewish ghetto in Poland, furtively handing over the one precious thing he had left to give to mankind: the manuscript of *The Messiah*. The last work of Bruno Schulz drawn into the swill of World War II, beyond all grasp. Lost things. They claw through the membranes, attempting to summon our attention through an indecipherable mayday.[60]

The Nobel laureate Olga Tokarczuk has said that Poland's history of disappearing and reappearing on the map of Europe has for better or worse lent its literature not only a certain precarity but a tolerance for ambiguity, permeability, and loss—a literature, in other words, that claws through membranes. In 2018, Tokarczuk gathered

ten other writers (including Yuri Andrukhovych) in the newly restored
Choral Synagogue in Drohobych to read stories they'd embroidered
from the legendary first lines of Schulz's *Messiah*. She spoke of the
novel as a metaphor for how irreplaceable loss can release powerful
gusts of inspiration.

Unforgotten Griefs: Józefina
GDAŃSK, POLAND, JULY 1991

On July 11, 1991, a day before what would have been Schulz's ninety-
ninth birthday, Józefina Szelińska swallowed several handfuls of sleeping pills. She died, aged eighty-six. She left a bottle of champagne in
the fridge.

In the half century since Schulz's death, his former fiancée had
remained faithful to his memory. She had never smothered that memory
and had never married. After the war, she had moved to Gdańsk, on the
Baltic coast, as far away from Drohobycz as possible while remaining in
Poland, and never again visited Drohobycz. In 1952, she gave up teaching and created a pedagogical library. ("She locked herself in the world
of words," her biographer Agata Tuszyńska says.) Forced to resign from
her position as its director in April 1968, during the wave of resurgent
anti-Semitism that washed over Poland, she shared with Jerzy Ficowski
her feelings of "emptiness and void" and her desire to escape. "My
today is without tomorrow," she told him. All along she had kept two
dozen of Schulz's artworks on the walls of her apartments in Gdańsk
(on Sienkiewicza Street and then on Kościuszki Street), including two
portraits he had painted of her, one portraying her with an eccentric
yellow hat. She also kept a file of notes, careful correctives to all the
fallacies and fabrications swirling around the Schulz myth. At the same
time, she firmly forbade mention of her relationship with Schulz and
barred Ficowski from publishing her name until after her death.[61]

A month and a half after Józefina Szelińska's suicide, across a newly porous border, the parliament of Ukraine (from the Polish word *ukraina*, "borderland") adopted the Act of Independence. That December, despite political pressures from Moscow, which considered the Ukrainians "Little Russians" (*Malorusy*) rather than members of a separate nationality with its own language and culture, an overwhelming majority of Ukraine's fifty-two million citizens voted for independence.

Two Busts
JERUSALEM, 1992

Only in 1987, after decades of Poles insisting that the slaughter of Polish Jews was solely a matter of German responsibility, would the Polish Catholic intellectual Jan Błoński—who had witnessed the liquidation of the Warsaw ghetto in 1942—declare, "Yes, we are guilty." Only a national soul-searching, he said, could "cleanse our desecrated soil."[62] In September 1990, Warsaw's Umschlagplatz Monument, marking the site from which more than three hundred thousand Jews were deported from the Warsaw ghetto to Nazi extermination camps in the years 1942–43, was defaced (not for the first time) by graffiti: "A good Jew is a dead Jew" (*Dobry żyd to martwy żyd*). "Anti-Semitism is conspicuous on the streets of Polish towns," the historian Szymon Rudnicki observed at the time. "Walls are covered with epithets such as *Jude raus*. The word 'Jew' or the Star-of-David are painted on election posters."[63] That December, Poland's Catholic bishops at last spoke out against the pervasive view of the Jew as a contemptible enemy of Christendom. They issued a condemnation of anti-Semitism as "against the spirit of the Gospel" and expressed "sincere regret over all cases of anti-Semitism which were committed at any time or by anyone on Polish soil."

Against this backdrop, Poland marked the 1992 centenary of Schulz's birth and the fiftieth anniversary of his death. The country issued a postage stamp in his honor and hosted major international conferences, including a three-day symposium at the Jagiellonian University in Kraków.[64]

That year also saw new Ukrainian translations of Schulz's stories and the first conference in Drohobych dedicated to Schulz's work, held in the former high school building where Schulz once taught. Alfred Schreyer shared memories of his teacher; Jerzy Jarzębski came from Kraków to interpret Schulz's metaphor-rich language; and Jerzy Ficowski reported on his "search for the master's lost legacy," including the hunt for *Messiah*. Most Drohobych residents remained unaware of the three-day conference. "It is lamentable that this extraordinary and unique event was not widely advertised in the city," Drohobych resident Leonid Golberg wrote.

That same year, a group of Drohobych survivors living in Israel commissioned two busts of Bruno Schulz financed by Naftali (Tulek) Backenroth—one intended for Drohobych, the other for Yad Vashem. Erwin Schenkelbach told me that the group hired a fifty-seven-year-old sculptor, Peter (Pesach) Flit, who had emigrated from Ukraine to Israel in 1990. To get Schulz's likeness, Flit met in Jerusalem with six people who had known Schulz, over several sessions.

In the end, both busts were declined. Yad Vashem cited a lack of space. A Drohobych city official worried that residents would object to raising a monument to "a stranger." Today, Drohobych features monuments to four Ukrainian writers—Ivan Franko, Taras Shevchenko, Vasyl Stefanyk, and Markian Shashkevich—none of whom died there. Besides a small sidewalk plaque, there is no monument or sculpture for Schulz.

CHAPTER 7
AFTERIMAGES

2001–Present

In old apartments there are rooms that people have forgotten about. Not visited for months at a time, they shrivel in their abandonment between the old walls, and it happens that they withdraw into themselves, become encased in bricks, and, lost to our memory once and for all, slowly lose their own existence, too.[1]

—BRUNO SCHULZ

A Holocaust Heist

VILLA LANDAU, DROHOBYCH, UKRAINE, MAY 19, 2001

On March 29, 2001, the German filmmaker Benjamin Geissler informed Yehudit Shendar at Yad Vashem that the expert restoration work of the murals in Villa Landau, at an estimated cost of 144,000 deutsche marks (about $65,500), "should be completed by the end of September 2001 at the latest."

Unbeknownst to Geissler, earlier that month Yad Vashem archivist Mark Shraberman had traveled to Drohobych at the instructions of Yad Vashem chairman Avner Shalev. Shraberman had emigrated from Ukraine to Israel in the 1990s. According to someone who worked with him there, "Shraberman was widely rumored to be former KGB, and some of our colleagues kept their distance from him." Shraberman

met with Drohobych's mayor, Oleksy Radziyevsky, and the municipality's head of cultural affairs, Mikhail Michatz. According to Yad
Vashem, both officials "expressed willingness to hand over" Schulz's
murals to Yad Vashem. Shraberman persuaded Michatz and deputy
mayor Taras Metyk to arrange a meeting with the owners of the apartment, the Kaluzhni family. (In reply to my inquiries, Mark Shraberman replied, "I have nothing to say to you. Sorry." Avner Shalev, who
retired as Yad Vashem chairman in February 2021, likewise declined
multiple requests to be interviewed for this book.)

Nikolai Kaluzhni described that meeting in a letter he faxed to
Christian Geissler (dated May 17, 2001):

> The Israeli started urging me to sell him the brick wall above
> the [pantry] door frame. For this he promised to pay $2,000 to
> $3,000. I explained to him that you and your son discovered
> the murals and started to restore them, that they belong not to
> me but to history, and that I considered his proposal pointless
> and unacceptable.

On May 19, 2001, as Nadezhda Kaluzhni looked on with a reproving
grimace, three Israeli agents carried black duffel bags bulging with
tools into the apartment on the second floor of Villa Landau. Mark
Shraberman; Joseph "Dodo" Shenhav, a veteran of Israel's 1948 War
of Independence and the head of the restoration laboratories of the
Israel Museum; and Eliyahu (Ilya) Matskin entered the Kaluzhnis' pantry and touched the walls as if to assure themselves of the paintings'
reality. Their mission: to pry Bruno Schulz's murals from the walls and
"repatriate" them to Jerusalem.

The three Israelis were acting under direct orders of Avner Shalev, then sixty-two, a son of immigrants from Poland and a veteran of
the Israel Defense Forces, where he served between 1956 and 1980,
reaching the rank of brigadier general. Shalev still bore wounds he had

incurred in action on the Egyptian front during the 1967 Six-Day War. After retiring from the army, he headed the National Culture and Art Council and the Culture Authority in Israel's Ministry of Education and Culture (which controlled about $50 million a year in government subsidies for the arts). He had served as Yad Vashem chairman since Prime Minister Yitzhak Rabin had appointed him in 1993. "One of the primary takeaways from our experience during the Holocaust," Shalev said, "is that it is essential that we can take care of ourselves, our country, and our Jewish moral values. This is a basic part of our national identity."[2] Shalev got a green light for the Schulz operation from Ariel Sharon, elected prime minister three months earlier, but according to a person with firsthand knowledge of the discussions between Sharon and Shalev, "Shalev took the initiative on his own." However the decision came to be, Joel Rappel told me, "it's clear that Yad Vashem did not pull this off on its own." Rappel, a historian at Bar-Ilan University's Institute of Holocaust Research, had visited Drohobych many times and knew the background to the 2001 operation. "It's my sense—but no one will confirm this for you—that the Mossad carried it out. . . . I don't believe anyone will ever speak of these things." The removal of the murals, Rappel said, was followed by a cover-up operation.

Conservators refer to methods of removing wall paintings—a practice nearly as old as painting on walls—by their Italian terms: *strappo* (literally "tearing" off the paint layer alone with a facing adhesive) and *stacco* (detaching a painting together with its underlying plaster). Using those techniques, murals from Pompeii were detached and sent to the Museum of Portici, and masterpieces of the Italian Renaissance were extracted from the walls of the churches and palaces where they had been painted; they then found their way into private collections and galleries across Europe. After the flooding of the Arno in November 1966, for instance, Taddeo Gaddi's *Last Supper*, a fresco measuring 122 square meters (1300 square feet), was removed in one piece from the refectory of Santa Croce in Florence.[3]

For "Operation Schulz," Shenhav and Matskin chose the *stacco* method. Using thin metal spatulas, they covered parts of the murals with a varnish-like substance. Then they cut deep incisions in the walls (down to the underlying brick) along the edges of the five scenes they wished to take. With rubber mallets and chisels, they pried the fragments of Schulz's murals from the pantry walls, leaving the walls marred and scarred.

In the 1920s, a Jew from Drohobycz had toured Europe with a meticulous model he'd made of the Temple in Jerusalem, a building that hadn't existed for two thousand years.[4] Photographs of the pantry walls when the Israelis were through recalled the Jewish custom, even today, to leave a section of wall unfinished, a mark of incompleteness in memory of the destruction of the Temple.

The three Israelis left behind several scenes on the walls, including Schulz's depiction of two children—a boy and a girl, perhaps Hansel and Gretel; a stooped old woman wearing a headscarf; a velvet-black cat with its tail up; and a tree with a bird. (These remaining fragments would be removed by Ukrainian conservators a year later, in March 2002, and restored in Lviv. They're displayed today in the Drohobych Museum.)

As slivers of stucco splintered and swirled off like snowflakes, the three agents smoothed the chalky plaster on the back of the murals, attached them to boards, wrapped them in protective fabric, shouldered the fragments into crates lined with polyurethane foam, and loaded the crates onto a waiting truck. According to Andriy Pavlyshyn, a Ukrainian scholar and translator of Schulz, local Ukrainian police officers took bribes to escort the truck to the Polish border. Israel's ambassador to Poland, Shevach Weiss, used his diplomatic immunity to bring the murals across the border. (Born in 1935 in Borysław, a town seven miles from Drohobycz, Weiss had served as speaker of the Knesset from 1992 to 1996 and as chairman of the Yad Vashem Council beginning in 2000.) The five fragments were then loaded onto a jet that traveled from Poland to Israel and brought to the basement storerooms of Yad Vashem, where they would remain for more than seven years. The museum sits astride Jerusalem's Mount Herzl, named after the founding father of the Zionist movement, not far from where Theodor Herzl's remains had been reinterred from Vienna fifty years earlier.

If "Operation Schulz," too, was a kind of reinterring—or a kind of forced aliyah (this Hebrew term for immigrating to Israel literally means "ascent")—it was one that defied Ukrainian, Polish, and international laws. Polish law forbids the export of artworks created before 1945. Ukraine, too, requires prior approval from the Ministry of Culture for the export of cultural property created before or during World War II. Ukrainian authorities had listed Schulz's murals in the national registry of cultural artifacts, which protects them from exportation (though it is unclear exactly when the registration took effect). The removal also violated both the Convention on the Means of Prohibiting and Preventing the Illicit Import, Export and Transfer of Ownership of Cultural Property, ratified by 140 countries, including Poland and Ukraine, and accepted standards for the treatment of artistic heritage set forth by ICOM (International Council of Museums, a UNESCO organization founded after the war). According to ICOM guidelines, "detachment and transfer are dangerous, drastic, and irreversible operations that severely affect the physical composition, material structure and aesthetic characteristics of wall paintings. These operations are, therefore, only justifiable in extreme cases when all options of *in situ* treatment are not viable."[5] Some argued that in accordance with the 1998 Washington Principles on Nazi-Confiscated Art (endorsed by Israel), the murals legally belonged not to Yad Vashem but to Bruno Schulz's sole living heir.

Shortly after the removal, Nikolai Kaluzhni called Schulz's former student Alfred Schreyer, who still lived in Drohobych.

"I've given them the frescoes," Kaluzhni said.

"How could you do that?" Schreyer asked. "They probably paid you a lot of money."

"Not a kopeck."

Several days after that call, the Kaluzhnis' daughter Larissa Artemchenkova told a journalist from the *Guardian* that her parents had given away the murals for nothing. "We just wanted to be left in peace. There was talk of making a Schulz museum here, and where would my elderly parents go then?" She then offered to let the journalist see the pantry walls. For a price. "What do you think Jews would charge?" she asked.[6]

As the "fresco fiasco" hit the headlines, Nikolai Kaluzhni issued a lengthy statement:

> I've been living in this apartment with my family for almost forty years, during which time almost no one has approached us or asked about the paintings. In early February 2001, Mr. Alfred Schreyer came to visit us with some other people. I thought he had come to express his condolences over the death of the son we had just buried. But this was not the case. As it turned out, they had completely different intentions and interests. They said that Schulz's paintings were in this apartment and that they wanted to clean them and make a film about them. Polish journalists also arrived. A fight broke out between Mr. Schreyer's people and Polish journalists in our apartment. Needless to say, considering our age and the tragedy that we had just experienced, we found all this very disturbing. The whole day they worked in and argued in our apartment. Afterward they told us that they needed to leave and return in two or three weeks to continue shooting. They also asked us not to share this discovery with anyone and not to allow anyone to take pictures.
>
> After Benjamin and Christian Geissler left, others came to see us, including the Polish consul from Lviv [Krzysztof Sawicki],

Boris Voznytsky [a Ukrainian art historian and the director of the Lviv Art Gallery], and Roman Lubkivsky [a prominent Ukrainian poet, diplomat, and the head of the department of culture of the Lviv Regional State Administration]. Our phone rang off the hook. Everyone wanted to visit and watch. But we refused them all and waited for the Geisslers. We found all this distressing; as elderly people, we wanted peace. Schreyer called us quite often, asking for updates and inquiring whether anyone else had visited. A few days before Mark Shraberman's arrival, he called again to say that "our people" were coming the next day (May 17–18) and that we were to try to receive them well and assist them.

On May 18, Taras Metyk called and said that people from Israel wanted to visit us and see the murals. I told him I already knew from Schreyer that they would come and invited them in the afternoon. Taras Metyk, Mikhail Michatz and another stranger came into our apartment. The third man introduced himself as Mark Shraberman from Israel. It was clear from his conversation that he was well acquainted with all the events. He said that Benjamin Geissler had visited their museum [in Jerusalem] and he recounted his meeting with Boris Voznytsky in Lviv. . . .

Mark asked permission for two more people to enter the apartment in order to inspect everything. I agreed. We conversed with them for a long time about the tragedies that befell the Jews during the war, and about the museum in Jerusalem that honors the victims' memory. (As a war veteran I participated in the battles and saw everything with my own eyes.) Mark asked if I would send some paintings to their museum; he said that they would be stored there, and it would be recorded who had handed them over. After consulting with my wife, and remembering how the Nazis exterminated the Jews, I agreed to donate three paintings to this famous Jewish museum in Jerusalem. I wrote and signed a receipt for them. Shraberman also signed that he received them and thanked us.

Maybe I made a mistake. For the next three months and twenty days, the Geisslers neither visited nor contacted us. They did not leave a forwarding address.

We are not going to leave our apartment and have no desire to move. In my opinion it is immoral to build a museum in this building, where the main fascist of Drohobych [Felix Landau] lived and from which he killed from the balcony.

Reading accusations in the press that city authorities let this happen with their consent, I want to say that neither mayor Oleksy Radziyevsky, nor his deputies Taras Metyk or Mikhail Michatz, nor any other officials contacted me or asked me to do anything. I reaffirm that the transfer of these paintings to a museum in Israel happened without the presence of the authorities and that they have nothing to do with this case.

I believe that there is nothing wrong with the fact that Bruno Schulz's artworks, at my request, are now housed in the world-renowned Yad Vashem. The remaining pictures—due to which we have no peace, day or night—I am ready to transfer to the Drohobych Museum. As a veteran of the Great Patriotic War and an eyewitness to the terrible Nazi crimes, I've no doubt that I am right. I would make the same decision again today.[7]

According to Yad Vashem, "Nikolai Kaluzhni consented to give Yad Vashem all but one of the sketches, pending his written confirmation and signature." Boris Voznytsky, the director of the state-funded Lviv Art Gallery, called the signed document "a dubious and un-notarized gift deed . . . written by a sick person after a stroke." According to Jurko Prochaśko, "the mayor knew Kaluzhni very well and persuaded him to let Yad Vashem do their work. Imagine if the mayor of your city says to you, 'you can trust them.' The mayor was corrupt, not the Kaluzhnis." Prochaśko added, "This is a story of bribery and corruption, of the failure of an expert commission, of greed (including media greed)." Two sources—Krzysztof Sawicki and Drohobych Jewish communal leader Leonid Golberg—independently told me that the alleged bribes amounted to $900,000. Golberg added that he was beaten up by bruisers after publishing a newspaper article that referred to the bribes.

Geissler Sr. and Jr. were meanwhile in Haifa, Tel Aviv, and Jerusalem to film interviews with Schulz's surviving students. The very day the Israelis were removing Schulz's murals from Villa Landau, the Geisslers and their team were invited to a meeting at Yad Vashem. Prochaśko characterized the conversation as "warm and congratulatory."

On the morning of May 24, Benjamin Geissler was in the underground car park across from Jaffa Gate in Jerusalem when he received a call from Wojciech Chmurzyński, the Polish art expert. "They're gone! The murals are gone!"

"It's not possible," Geissler said. "I'm just now coming from a meeting at Yad Vashem."

"But they're the very people who stole them!" Chmurzyński shouted hoarsely.

"They Stole Schulz!"
DROHOBYCH, UKRAINE, JUNE–JULY 2001

The clamor that ensued from the removal of Bruno Schulz's murals to Jerusalem illustrated how the resurrection of forgotten and forsaken paintings made old forms of belonging new again.

At first, Drohobych Mayor Oleksy Radzievsky put up a pretense of law-abidingness. He claimed that he had first learned about the murals from his aides on May 25, denied involvement in the removal of what he called "plaster with paintings," and said that he regarded the affair as a private matter for the residents of the apartment where the murals were found. "Personally, I wasn't impressed by those paintings," he added. (According to Yad Vashem spokesperson Iris Rosenberg, Radziyevsky not only cooperated with the Israelis but "praised the cooperation in a letter to Yad Vashem.") Deputy mayor Taras Metyk went on Ukrainian television to insist the murals had little artistic merit. A local journalist retorted, "Mayor Radziyevsky was first secretary of the Drohobych city committee of the Communist Party [1987–91]. Can people with such a Soviet Communist background and mentality appreciate the true worth of the Schulz frescoes for Drohobych (let alone for Ukraine as a whole)?"[8]

In the ensuing days, public pressure grew. The Ethnology Institute at the National Academy of Sciences of Ukraine issued a statement:

> Feigning concern for the fate of the new find, a group of irresponsible people manipulated the "rescue operation" by desecrating the monument with their brutal actions, dealing a blow to the very name of Bruno Schulz as well as to numerous admirers of his work—both in Ukraine and abroad. It is hard for us to believe that such an inhumane act could be backed by an official Israeli institution, especially one designed to protect the cultural heritage of our compatriots around the world. . . . Schulz's legacy is among the most expressive pages of Galicia's cultural past; any attempt to extract that legacy from its authentic cultural context is savage and futile.

Roman Pastukh, a journalist and local historian, called on the mayor to accept responsibility and resign. "Those guilty of helping to steal the frescoes must admit their guilt," said Mykola Sadokha, the head of Drohobych's Prosvita (a cultural and educational society). Viktor Sokolov, the head of the Drohobych branch of the People's Democratic Party, called for consequences: "Political parties should appeal to the

Bruno Schulz, "Encounter: A Young Jewish Man and Two Women in an Urban Alley," 1920 (Adam Mickiewicz Museum of Literature, Warsaw)

Bruno Schulz, "Bacchanalia," 1920 (National Museum in Wrocław)

Bruno Schulz, "The Booke of Idolatry I," from *The Booke of Idolatry*, 1920s (Adam Mickiewicz Museum of Literature, Warsaw)

Bruno Schulz, "Dedication," from *The Booke of Idolatry*, 1920s (National Museum in Kraków)

Bruno Schulz, "The Enchanted Town II, Drohobycz," from *The Booke of Idolatry*, 1920s (National Museum in Kraków)

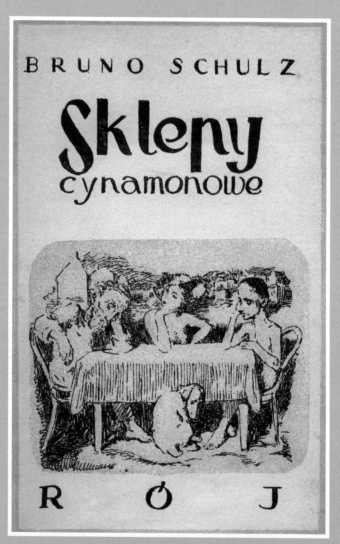

First edition of *Cinnamon Shops* by Bruno Schulz, with the author's cover illustration, 1934

Bruno Schulz, self-portrait, 1933 (Adam Mickiewicz Museum of Literature, Warsaw)

Bruno Schulz, 1935 (University of Warsaw Library/ Karta Center)

Fragment from one of Bruno Schulz's murals, "Carriage Driver (Self-Portrait)," exhibited at Yad Vashem, Jerusalem (Yad Vashem Art Museum)

Discovering the Schulz murals, Drohobych, Ukraine, February 2001 (Benjamin Geissler)

Israeli author David Grossman speaking at the opening of Bruno Schulz exhibition, Yad Vashem, Jerusalem, February 2009 (Gali Tibbon)

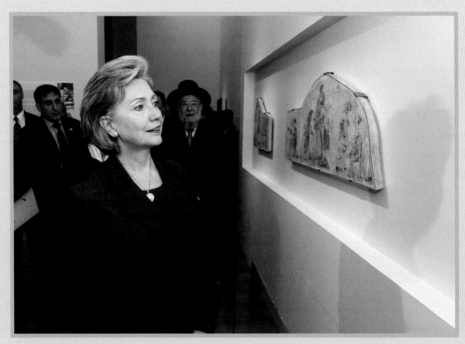

U.S. Secretary of State Hillary Rodham Clinton visits the Bruno Schulz murals, Yad Vashem, Jerusalem, March 3, 2009 (U.S. Dept. of State/Alamy)

voters of Drohobych through the media to seek a vote of no confidence in the mayor and other leaders involved in this crime."

At a contentious meeting of the city council on June 4, Mikhail Michatz, the head of the city council's department of culture and arts, lamented the lack of concern "about preserving the history of our own historical figures, such as Andriy Melnyk [co-founder of the proto-fascist Organization of Ukrainian Nationalists (OUN) in 1929]." The chairman of the Coordination Council, Tymofy Bordulyak, remarked, "Schulz is all well and good. But we have problems with our own culture. . . . The memories of [Ukrainian writers] Les Martovych and Vasyl Stefanyk haven't been perpetuated in the city. And now foreign funds—for a Schulz museum!" The session concluded by requesting Ukraine's Ministry of Foreign Affairs to lodge a formal protest with the Israeli government against the illegal export of Schulz's murals and to demand their return.

Three days later, the chairman of the Association of Drohobych Deputies wrote to the mayor to "demand an extraordinary session of the city council to consider the illegal removal of Bruno Schulz's paintings from the city of Drohobych." The proposed session would summon the head of the culture department of the Lviv Regional State Administration (Roman Lubkivsky), the city prosecutor, a representative of the Security Service of Ukraine (SBU), and representatives of local Jewish organizations.

On June 11, the Polish-Ukrainian commission of experts documented the damage in the Kaluzhnis' pantry and began preparing a formal report for the Polish Ministry of Culture. The next day, Zenovy Mazuryk, chair of Ukraine's Association of Museums and Galleries, expressed a growing anger both with the Israelis' methods in removing the murals and with Ukrainians' lack of interest in the work of Schulz. The murals scandal, he said, reflects Ukraine's "crisis of culture, crisis of values, both in society and among government officials . . . with below-average cultural competence. We believe that for moral and ethical reasons, the mayor of Drohobych, his deputy for humanitarian affairs, and the head of the department of culture should resign with immediate effect."

Along with thirty-five others, Alfred Schreyer signed an open letter, dated June 12, urging Ukraine's President Leonid Kuchma and Prime Minister Anatoliy Kinakh to secure the return to Drohobych of the "illegally exported murals" and to conduct a prompt investigation into the local officials who had let the Israelis violate "the cultural heritage of Ukraine."

Later in June, two Drohobych officials—deputy mayor Taras Metyk and Mikhail Michatz, head of the culture and arts department—acknowledged an "illegal conspiracy" between city officials and Yad Vashem to remove Schulz's murals. They also apologized to Benjamin Geissler and his film crew for slandering them in a Lviv newspaper.

On July 4, the city council passed a resolution requiring the remnants of the Schulz frescoes to be dismantled and transported from Villa Landau to the museum of local history. On July 13, Bohdan Vavryk, head of the Ukrainian Security Service in the Lviv district, announced that an investigation into the circumstances of the disappearance of Bruno Schulz's frescoes had led the SBU to find the Drohobych authorities' actions criminal. The SBU, he said, would recommend that the prosecutor's office in Lviv open a criminal case for abuse of office. Boris Voznytsky said he was interviewed by officers from both the SBU and the prosecutor's office. "I told them all I knew, but I had more questions than I did answers. For example: How were the frescoes smuggled out of Ukraine? These were frescoes, not something you could hide in your glove box."[9]

Months later, the prosecutor's office launched an investigation into alleged corruption on the part of Drohobych officials who had aided the Israelis. Oleksy Radzievsky, having lost face, was defeated in the next mayoral election in April 2002; eight years later he would be reelected for a second term.

The Makings of a Scandal: Reactions in Poland
JUNE–JULY 2001

The discovery in February 2001 of Schulz's murals initially attracted little notice in Poland. The Israeli *removal* of the murals, however, sparked loud laments, keening, and public posturing about the loss of these new national treasures.[10]

On June 6, Polish president Aleksander Kwasniewski denounced the Israeli action as nothing short of furtive cultural vandalism. Poland's minister of culture, Kazimierz Ujazdowski, sent an indignant note of protest to the Israeli embassy in Warsaw. Polish undersecretary of state Stanisław Żurowski, the official within the Ministry of Culture responsible for Polish heritage abroad, added that the murals "are our heritage—the memory of a Polish author of Jewish descent. Schulz wrote in Polish, he had Polish citizenship. He himself felt like a Pole." Przemyslaw Grudzinski, then Polish ambassador to the United States, stressed that Schulz's works "grew in the soil of Drohobych." He noted, "As such, they are an inseparable part of that cultural and historic environment." To transplant them into a different environment, he added, would give them "a lifeless existence." The Polish consul general in Lviv, Krzysztof Sawicki, called on law enforcement agencies of Ukraine, Poland, and Israel to conduct an international investigation. A headline in *Gazeta Wyborcza*, Poland's leading newspaper, exclaimed, "They Stole Schulz!" A cartoon in the Polish daily *Rzeczpospolita* depicted a truck—labeled "Yad Vashem Institute" and driven by bearded Jews with sidelocks—carting away an entire Polish town on its trailer. The Polish essayist Jerzy Pilch expressed a sense of humiliation:

> It's one thing when we (with difficulty and unwillingness) confront ourselves with our own impotence, and it's something entirely different when someone else is assured of our

impotence . . . [it] is doubly painful: first, because they knew
that we couldn't manage with the uncovered treasure of our
own artist, and second—more painfully—because they knew
how easy it would be to take the discovery from us.[11]

The Schulz controversy came at a fraught moment, just when Poles
were convulsed by a rupture in their self-image as blameless victims par
excellence of Nazi atrocities—and in their understandable preoccupation with the Polish nation's own sufferings as a testament to its vir-
tues. That flattering mythology, which for so long structured Poland's
sense of itself, had been dented by the broadcasting on Polish television
of Claude Lanzmann's 1985 documentary film *Shoah*. But a real reckoning with Polish complicity arrived only fifteen years later, after the
fall of the Iron Curtain, in the form of a fiercely debated book by Jan T.
Gross, *Neighbors: The Destruction of the Jewish Community in Jedwabne* (published in Poland in 2000, and in the U.S. in 2001).[12] Gross
documented how Poles—not Germans—had burned and clubbed to
death up to sixteen hundred Jews in July 1941 in Jedwabne, a village
in northeastern Poland.

On July 10, 2001, the sixtieth anniversary of the massacre, Polish
president Aleksander Kwaśniewski spoke at a ceremony in Jedwabne
attended by some three thousand people and broadcast live on Polish
television. "Today, as a man, citizen and president of the Polish republic," he said, "I ask pardon in my own name and in the name of those
Polish people whose consciences are shocked by this crime."

Israel's ambassador to Poland, Shevach Weiss, also addressed the
gathering, saying, "People who lived together with the Jews of Jedwabne, who knew them by name and were friendly with them, these
same people set upon their Jewish neighbors, dragging them to the
local barn before slaughtering them and burning them alive." Weiss,
who grew up in Poland, added that he "was fortunate to get to know
other neighbors. Thanks to these people, my family and I were able to

survive the Holocaust. Thanks to these people, I am standing before
you today."

The primate of Poland's Roman Catholic Church, Jozef Cardinal
Glemp, boycotted the ceremony, as did Yad Vashem, which objected
that the plaque at the site did not explicitly acknowledge that it had
been Poles, not Germans, who had murdered the town's Jews. Yad
Vashem's absence occasioned a joke in some Polish circles:

Q. Why didn't representatives from Yad Vashem make an
    appearance at the Jedwabne commemoration?

A. Because there were no murals to be had.

"That kind of joke wouldn't have happened before," said Konstanty
Gebert, founding editor of the Polish Jewish magazine *Midrazs*,
"because Yad Vashem had huge moral authority." "We feel robbed,"
Gebert said of the removal of Schulz's murals. "A limb of our heritage
was cut off; our pain is indescribable." Schulz, Gebert added, stood
for "a whole galaxy of Jewish Austro-Hungarian intellectuals . . . who
came up with an entirely new idea of identity: identity is not about
realizing what is given to me, but about choosing from the world's
abundance. This idea of identity so terrified Europe that it had to
exterminate them all."[13]

The Memoryscape of Moral Right: Yad Vashem's Defense
SEPTEMBER 2001

In the summer of 2001, Ukraine lodged official complaints both
with the Israeli government and with the International Council of
Museums (ICOM). On September 11, 2001, Avner Shalev, chairman
of Yad Vashem, replied in a letter to ICOM secretary-general Manus
Brinkman:

Yad Vashem received the Schulz sketches, which were in a state
of severe deterioration, with the full backing of the mayor of
Drohobych, the deputy mayor, and the city's culture officer—
who also assisted with the technical aspects of packing and dis-
patch. City officials stated that the works were private property
and had never been registered as national assets—a fact that
was confirmed by the Ukrainian Minister of Culture in July
2001. . . . Furthermore, the mayor of Drohobych sent a letter
to Yad Vashem thanking the institution for its cooperation in
perpetuating the memory of Bruno Schulz.

Regarding the alleged damage to the works, Yad Vashem's
representatives did not cause any impairment; in fact, quite the
contrary is true. Yad Vashem's conservation experts saved the
fragments from further decomposition and carried out eminent
necessary restoration work. The single images, which do not
constitute a thematic total, were in fact on the verge of extinc-
tion, covered with layers of paint, while shelves were nailed to
the plaster. Furthermore, we would like to emphasize that these
works were no more than embellishments created for the Nazi
officer's children's room and are not to be viewed as examples
of Bruno Schulz's artistic endeavors. It was evident to the team
of experts that if action was not taken immediately, then within
a very short period of time the images would have been completely ruined. We would like to add that the Schulz works are
only one example testifying to the neglect of Jewish cultural
assets, which can today be encountered in Drohobych. . . .

Moreover, in spite of the fact that Schulz was hailed as an
author and an artist, the Poles did not make any attempts to save
him from his harsh fate. Schulz's wall paintings, executed under
duress, as forced labor . . . are a powerful and unique testimony
to the annals of the Jews under the Nazi regime; their rightful
place of exhibition is Yad Vashem.

The letter written by the president of the Ukrainian National Committee of ICOM bears an unacceptable tone. In an interview on June 2, 2001, in the *Vysoky Zamok* [High Castle] newspaper, Mr. Boris Voznytsky, director of the Lviv Art Gallery, was himself quoted as saying: "We did not register the paintings in the Ukrainian national registry due to the fact that only fragments were discovered," adding in reference to the artistic quality of the paintings: "Schulz's standing as an artist can be equated with a modern, very mediocre, Lviv artist. The value of the paintings is not in their artistic, but rather historic, merit, for they were painted shortly before Schulz's death." Voznytsky does not refer to the circumstances of Schulz's death at all. It may be deduced that Schulz died a natural death and was not brutally murdered solely because he was a Jew. Furthermore, he does not mention the fact that the sketches were done under duress, and thus may not be judged or compared to a modern Lviv artist of one sort or another.

The authors of the letter rely heavily on allegations made by the German filmmaker Mr. Geissler, who to the best of our knowledge has no official professional training in the museological field and has not yet had a museum planning credit to his claim. It is thus quite problematic as to why Yad Vashem has not been approached on these matters, at a time when Mr. Geissler is accorded with expertise he clearly does not have.

In mounting its defiant defense, Yad Vashem issued a remarkable statement of self-assertion, worth quoting at length. It rests on a simple predicate: Having mourned their dead, commemorated their martyrs, and rebuilt their shattered cities, the Polish people had recovered from the war; Polish Jews—and their thousand-year-old culture—had not. As far as Jews are concerned, Yad Vashem maintained, Poland is a wasteland. Thus the rescue of Schulz's fragments was nothing less than a step in the redemptive overcoming of the Jews' exile and fragmentation. For Yad Vashem—concerned with Schulz's death as a Jew rather than his life as an artist—those fragments are witnesses to the Shoah by one of its countless martyrs. (The Greek word for witness is *martis*, or martyr.)

Yad Vashem states that the sketches from the Drohobycz villa were removed with the full cooperation of the Drohobych municipality. They were in a state of severe deterioration, having been neglected for over 55 years and since their arrival in Jerusalem are undergoing a process of restoration and preservation. Bruno Schulz, a Jewish artist, was forced to illustrate the walls of the villa under duress, and was killed by an SS officer for the sole reason that he was a Jew. As a victim of the Holocaust, we believe that housing the sketches at Yad Vashem, the Holocaust Martyrs' and Heroes' Remembrance Authority is fitting and proper. Here the works will be preserved for generations and may be viewed by the millions of tourists from all over the world that visit Yad Vashem each year. . . .

The removal of the "fragments" of sketches was conducted with the full co-operation of the Drohobych municipality, and it was and still is clear to Yad Vashem that the Drohobych municipality was aware of the laws in its own country. But despite this, Yad Vashem's representative asked the Drohobych municipality if there was any need for a further check to be made with other parties, above and beyond that which had been carried out directly with the Drohobych municipality. The answer given was that the Drohobych municipality is responsible for all issues in its own town. . . .

At the apartment the Yad Vashem restoration specialists found the sketches peeling off the walls and in a most neglected condition. The sketches found were only fragments and not one complete sketch, and Yad Vashem's restoration experts saved the fragments from further decay even carrying out necessary restoration work on one of the fragments left behind in the apartment at the house. . . .

As Bruno Schulz was a Jewish artist—forced to illustrate the walls of the home of a German SS officer with his sketches as a Jewish prisoner during the Holocaust, and killed by an SS officer purely because he was a Jew—the correct and most suitable place to house the drawings he sketched during the Holocaust, is Yad Vashem, the Holocaust Martyrs' and Heroes' Remembrance Authority in Jerusalem. Yad Vashem is not stating that all Bruno Schulz's creations and heritage are the property of any specific country or institution, and dismisses attempts by any country to claim monopoly on an internationally acclaimed artist. Moreover, it has never been checked in what way a major part of Schulz's additional creations now in Poland reached there.

Unfortunately, it is a fact that from the around 3.5 million Jews who lived in Poland before the Shoah, today there are only a few thousand Jewish inhabitants. Despite the fact that today most of the Holocaust survivors live in Israel, the remnants of the vibrant Jewish life and the suffering both of the victims and the survivors are scattered all over Europe. Therefore Yad Vashem has the moral right to the remnants of those fragments sketched by Bruno Schulz.

The elastic assertions of "moral right" echoed Israeli assertions forty years earlier, in May 1960, after the kidnapping of Adolf Eichmann from Argentina to Jerusalem to stand trial for crimes against the Jewish people. (At the time, there was no international criminal court.)[14]

The few Jews remaining in Drohobych were split. Moses (Mojzesz) Weiss, a leader of the Jewish community in Drohobych, believed that Schulz's works would be in good hands in Israel. Alfred Schreyer, a former student of Schulz's and a survivor of several Nazi concentration camps, felt otherwise. "Schulz was born here, he worked here, he lived here, he died here," Schreyer said. "These paintings should remain here."[15]

Dora Katznelson, an eighty-year-old Jewish woman from Drohobych and a retired professor of Polish philology, said that the city's remaining Jews, however diminished in numbers, felt both disregarded by Yad Vashem's assumption that they were not up to the task of looking after their own heritage and slandered by the notion that Drohobych was now nothing more than a ghost-inhabited graveyard—and that Ukraine in general was a home of "anti-Semitism without Jews." While acknowledging "a Communist and post-Communist tradition of irresponsible theft of the valuable heritage of the culture of national minorities," Katznelson insisted that this time-tested tradition in no way legitimized what she called the "robbery" of Schulz's artworks. She intended to take the matter to the European Court of Human Rights in Strasbourg. For now, she contented herself with issuing an open letter:

> Not only Jews and Poles, but Ukrainians as well, reading daily in the Ukrainian papers about the barbaric theft of Schulz's paintings, cry out in amazement: "Yad Vashem? It can't be!" And Jews add, "Israel, our ethical model, our hope? It couldn't do this!"[16]

"The implication from Yad Vashem is that I should leave," a fortysomething Jewish woman who intended to stay told me. "If this place isn't good enough for objects made by the hands of Jews, it's certainly not good enough for living Jews."

American Jews, meanwhile, worried that "Operation Schulz" would backfire. "This action by Yad Vashem was not only arbitrary, uninformed and ill-advised," said Samuel Gruber, the president of the International Survey of Jewish Monuments and one of the world's leading experts on Jewish heritage sites, "but it has the potential of setting back by ten years the progress in protection and preservation of Jewish sites and monuments, including Holocaust sites, mass burials, and others places presumably of concern to Yad Vashem and Holocaust survivors." He added, "By this action, Yad Vashem gives the green light to any number of institutions and individuals that claim a 'moral right' to plunder cultural heritage without consultation and consideration by all concerned parties."[17]

Benjamin Geissler's documentary film chronicling the discovery of Schulz's murals, *Finding Pictures* (2002), put that claim through its paces. (After being invited and then disinvited to screen at the Berlin International Film Festival, the film premiered on November 19, 2002, the sixtieth anniversary of Schulz's death, at the Center for Jewish History in New York.) Using synchronized projections, Geissler has since built a virtual true-to-scale re-creation of the room in which Schulz painted his last murals. The exhibition, called *The Picture Chamber of Bruno Schulz*, has traveled to Luxembourg, Berlin, Hamburg, Freiburg, Zittau, and Paris. The *Frankfurter Allgemeine Zeitung* called it "a moving requiem . . . and a protest against the unauthorized collection of art."[18]

Two Plaques

DROHOBYCH, UKRAINE, NOVEMBER 19, 2006

In November 2006, a small copper plaque (sponsored by the Janusz Palikot Foundation and designed by the Lublin artist Andrzej Antoni Widelski) was placed at the site of Schulz's murder. The inscriptions in Ukrainian and Polish read, "In this place in November 19, 1942, the Great Artist of Drohobych, Bruno Schulz, was killed by a Gestapo agent." At the unveiling ceremony, a performance artist from Lviv, Włodek Kaufman, blew postage stamps from the surface of the plaque and from the pages of an open book in homage to the fantastical stamp album that features in Schulz's fiction.

Even this did not pass without incident. "The seemingly simple matter," Leonid Golberg reported, "caused an outburst of anti-Semitic and anti-Polish sentiments among Drohobych deputies." Wiera Baisa, a politician from the center-right Our Ukraine party, insisted that the Schulz plaque signaled "subservience and a loss of Ukrainian dignity." The editor of a local newspaper called *Tustan* published an article attacking Schulz and lamenting the "Judaization of Ukraine." Drohobych mayor Mykola Huk sought to dampen the controversy. "We are obliged to honor Bruno Schulz," he said, "because he made our town famous throughout Europe. And in general, Drohobych belongs to Ukrainians, Poles, and Jews alike."

The Schulz memorial plaque was pried loose from the pavement in May 2008 and sold as scrap metal. (The thief was a twenty-one-year-old illiterate local who later told the court that he was not aware of the plaque's symbolic meaning. A judge fined him 510 Ukrainian hryvnia—the equivalent of $18—and let him off.) A copy was installed in its place on November 19, 2010.

"Grains of Sugar"

YAD VASHEM, JERUSALEM, FEBRUARY 20, 2009

In 2005, the new $56 million Yad Vashem museum opened in Jerusalem. "By building this kind of museum," said Tom Segev, an Israeli historian and the author of *The Seventh Million*, "Israel is trying to gain back the monopoly on the Holocaust; the Holocaust is ours and ours alone, and no humanistic or universal values should overtake what we feel about the Holocaust."[19]

As the extensive renovations were being completed, heated negotiations ensued about the murals kept out of sight in a basement vault. Zinoviy Bervetsky, the director of the Drohobych Museum, was invited to accompany Ukrainian president Viktor Yushchenko to Jerusalem for the talks. "I flatly refused," Bervetsky said. "Let them first return the illegally exported goods to Drohobych, and then we'll negotiate."

In the end, Bervetsky visited Yad Vashem as part of a Ukrainian delegation including deputy minister of culture Vladyslav Kornienko, ambassador to Israel Ihor Tymofieiev, and a representative of Ukraine's Ministry of Foreign Affairs. Yehudit Inbar, the director of the museum department, and Yehudit Shendar, the director of the arts department, allowed the guests to inspect Schulz's murals. (All these years later, the episode remains a sensitive issue. "I still can't talk about the Schulz murals at Yad Vashem," Inbar told me.)

The Ukrainians admired the artworks' state of preservation. "Our frescoes would not be restored as well as Yad Vashem restored them," Bervetsky said. "I am generally delighted with what I saw there. I also think it would be good if we in Ukraine honored the victims of the Holodomor [the famine and mass starvation that convulsed Soviet Ukraine from 1932 to 1933 as a result of Stalin's policies], for example, in the way Israel honors victims of the Holocaust."

Nearly seven years after the Israeli operation to spirit Schulz's murals to Jerusalem, Israel and Ukraine reached an agreement: the disputed artworks would remain in Yad Vashem "on loan" from Ukraine for twenty years, after which the loan could be renewed every five years. The Israelis pledged to provide Drohobych with facsimile copies of the murals.[20] On February 28, 2008, Pinchas Avivi, deputy director general and head of the Central Europe desk in the Israeli Foreign Ministry, and Ukraine's ambassador to Israel, Ihor Tymofieiev, signed the agreement in the presence of Yad Vashem chairman Avner Shalev and Ukraine's Vice Prime Minister Ivan Vasyunik.

Just over a month later, the Israeli Ministry of Education, the

Jewish Agency, and the Claims Conference brought 450 Jewish tenth-grade students from the former Soviet Union to Schulz's hometown. Uri Ohali, a Jewish Agency staffer who organized the trip, said it was the first of its kind. "Through Bruno Schulz the students understand the complexity of Jewish life in Poland before the war," Ohali said.[21]

A year after the signing, in February 2009, Yad Vashem put Bruno Schulz's murals on public display for the first time. Ihor Tymofieiev and deputy minister of culture Vladyslav Kornienko attended an opening ceremony in the museum's auditorium. "The paintings have artistic, cultural, national and historic significance both to the Jewish people and the Ukrainian people," Kornienko said.

The Israeli novelist David Grossman spoke at the opening about the experience of encountering Schulz's writing. A Polish immigrant to Israel, he said, was a fan of Grossman's book *The Smile of the Lamb* (1983) and told its author, "You obviously are greatly influenced by Bruno Schulz."

> I was young and polite and since it sounded like a compliment I didn't argue with him. The truth is that, up to that moment, I had not read a single story by Schulz. But, after the phone call, I thought I should try to find one of his books. And that very evening, at the home of friends, I happened to come across a Hebrew edition of his collected stories. I borrowed it and read it. I read the whole book in several hours. Even today it is hard for me to describe the jolt that ran through me. . . .
>
> Every one of Schulz's lines is a rebuke—to a world in which, as he put it, all meaningful things are walled up; a protest against evil, banality, routine, against stereotyping of human beings, against the tyranny of the mob, against the shrunken and the simplistic, against whatever lacks daring and is devoid of inspiration and nobility, against whatever has no soul.[22]

Under the force of that rebuke, Grossman felt that "Schulz had given me, for the first time, the key to writing about the Shoah—not about death nor about destruction, but, in truth, about life itself."

> I read Schulz's stories and felt the gush of life. On every page, life was raging, exploding with vitality, suddenly worthy of its name; it was taking place on all layers of consciousness and sub-consciousness, in dreams, in illusions, and in nightmares. I felt the stories' ability to revive me, to carry me beyond the paraly-sis and despair that inevitably gripped me whenever I thought about the Holocaust or came into contact with the aspects of human nature which had ultimately allowed it to happen.

The result was Grossman's acclaimed novel *See Under: Love* (pub-lished in Hebrew in 1986 and in English in 1989). Momik, the novel's narrator, reports that when he was writing about Schulz, it was "as though I could hear him rapping out answers from the opposite side of the page; as though we were two miners tunneling from opposite sides of a mountain." Finally, Momik fantasizes that Schulz was not gunned down in the streets of Drohobycz but survives and travels to Danzig. There Schulz visits an exhibition devoted to the Norwegian painter Edvard Munch, plunges into the sea, and joins a school of salmon (moved, like the Jews, by an instinct to return against the prevailing currents to the place of their birth).[23]

Grossman closed the ceremony with an anecdote from Schulz's childhood:

> Once, when Schulz was a boy, on a melancholy evening, his mother Henrietta walked into his room and found him feeding grains of sugar to the last houseflies to have survived the cold autumn.

"Bruno," she asked, "why are you doing that?"

"So they will have strength for the winter," he said.

In recent years I've been going back more or less once a year to the stories of Bruno Schulz. For me, it's sort of annual tune-up, a strengthening of the antidotes against the temptations of apathy and withdrawal. Every time I open his books, I'm amazed anew to discover how this writer, a single human being who very rarely left his hometown, created for us an entire world, an alternate dimension of reality, and how he continues even now, so many years after his death, to feed us grains of sugar so that we may somehow make it through the long endless winter.

Two weeks after the exhibit's opening, U.S. Secretary of State Hillary Rodham Clinton was introduced to Schulz's murals during her visit to Yad Vashem. The day after her visit, Yehudit Shendar wrote to Schulz's last living descendant, Marek Podstolski: "Bruno received 'stately recognition' with Secretary Clinton at Yad Vashem yesterday. This is his triumph!" Benjamin Geissler took a less enthusiastic view; he believed that Yad Vashem had used Clinton "to cover up and legitimize the destruction."

Finding Undula
LVIV, UKRAINE, 2019

Like William Blake, Bruno Schulz thought as much in images as in words. Schulz's stories are word paintings, and his drawings are stories encapsulated in a scene. Whether rendered visually or verbally, his characters are bathed in the same mythological light. But was his pen more prudish than his brush?

A Polish Jewish journalist asked Schulz just that. "I noticed long ago that you find an outlet for your spirituality in writing, and for your

sexuality in drawing." "So it is," Schulz said. "I could not write a masochistic novel. Anyway, I'd be ashamed."[24] "A drawing sets narrower
limits by its material than prose does," Schulz remarked elsewhere.
"That is why I feel I have expressed myself more fully in my writing."[25]

In late 2019, a Ukrainian researcher, Lesya Khomych, was leaf-
ing through a set of editions of an old Polish oil industry newspaper
at the Stefanyk National Scientific Library of Ukraine in Lviv.[26] As
evidenced by the uncut pages, the set had never been read. In the fifth
issue, she noticed a report on a previously unknown art exhibition of
Bruno Schulz's work in Borysław. Some days later, she made an astonishing find in a January 1922 edition: a short story titled "Undula,"
under the pseudonym Marceli Weron. (It is the only piece in all the
surviving copies of the newspaper accompanied by an editorial note
forbidding republication without permission.) She was familiar with
the sultry Undula figure from the sexual mythology of Schulz's *Booke
of Idolatry*, which features cliché-verre works titled "Undula at Night"
and "Undula, the Eternal Ideal." Her first thought, Lesya told me, was:
"This is Schulz!"

> This thought literally did not give me peace. I had a feeling of
> incredible discovery, but at the same time doubts and hesita-
> tion. Could this be possible? Nineteen twenty-two? Why Mar-
> celi Weron? I reread the story again and again. The motifs and
> images so characteristic of his work were obvious. I confess that
> I pondered whether anyone could have written this story under
> the influence of Schulz's graphic works. But the convergence
> seemed too clear. The possibility that someone was imitating
> Schulz was ruled out, because at that time his literary work was
> still unknown.

The story follows a first-person narrator, confined to his room.
The story's opening sentence: "It must've been weeks now, months,

Bruno Schulz, "Undula and the Artists," from *The Booke of Idolatry,* 1920s
(CREDIT: Biblioteka Jagiellońska, public domain)

since I've been locked up in isolation. Over and over I sink into slumber
and rouse myself anew, and real-life phantoms get jumbled up, blurring into drowsy figments." As time itself slackens through "a handful
of pale squandered nights," he see his family's former maid, Adela,
wearing a "black unfastened gown" and admires "her slender legs
with their swanlike silhouette." Finally, amid the skulking shadows,
Schulz's dreamer conjures images of Undula "deliciously swooning and
careening . . . in black gauze and lingerie." He fantasizes about lower-
ing himself before her:

> Through you, in the warm shiver of pleasure, I've come to know
> my misery and ugliness in the light of your perfection. How
> sweet it was to read from a single glance the verdict condemn-
> ing me forevermore, with the most profound humility to sub-

Bruno Schulz, "Undula at Night," from *The Booke of Idolatry*, 1920s (CREDIT: Biblioteka Jagiellońska, public domain)

mit to the flick of your hand that cast me from your banquet tables. I would've doubted your perfection should you have done otherwise.[27]

Lesya Khomych had stumbled across a previously unknown short story that Schulz had published at age twenty-nine, nearly twelve years before he made his literary debut under his own name. (He likely adopted a pseudonym to protect his respectable brother, Izydor.) Seventy-seven years after the author's death, she had discovered a missing link between the two parts of Schulz's creative life, the point where the crafts of the artist and the writer intersect.

See Under: Schulzology
DROHOBYCH, UKRAINE, NOVEMBER 2020

In November 2020, I traveled from my home in Jerusalem to Drohobych, where I'd been invited to take part in the Bruno Schulz Festival. There I met the discoverer of "Undula" and a loose but loyal confederation of pilgrims (known as Schulzoids) following in his faint footsteps; scholarly stalwarts (known as Schulzologists); creative writers who have adopted him as their patron saint; and translators of his fiction. (Several of those translators, including his Finnish translator and his translator into Chinese, the Taiwanese poet Wei-Yun Lin-Górecka, learned Polish just to translate Schulz's works from the original.) My flight from Tel Aviv carried pilgrims of a different sort: religious Jews on their way to visit the grave in Uman, Ukraine, of the revered Rebbe Nachman, the charismatic founder of the Breslov Hasidic dynasty.

I learned that the first Schulz Festival, in July 2004, had been precipitated by the Israeli removal of Schulz's murals. In the late 1990s, the newly fledged literary scholars Igor and Wiera Meniok hit on the idea of reviving the memory of Schulz in his hometown. In 2001, the Ukrainian couple vociferously protested what they saw as Israel's theft of that memory. Wiera Meniok told me, "When [Israeli Holocaust historian] Yehuda Bauer said, 'Who in Drohobych cares about Schulz?,' we said, 'We do!'" SchulzFest (as it is informally called) has since been held in Drohobych every two years, with funding from the Polish Ministry of Culture, the Book Institute in Kraków, the Ministry of Foreign Affairs of the Republic of Poland, the Polish Institute in Kyiv, the Polish Consulate General in Lviv, and the Drohobych municipality.

After her husband, Igor, died in 2005, at age thirty-two, Wiera Meniok, the head of the Polish Studies Center at the University of Drohobych, enlisted Grzegorz Józefczuk, the chair of the Bruno Schulz Society in Lublin and a well-known Polish journalist, as the festival's artistic director. Together they staged the second Schulz Festival in

November 2006. Until the murals scandal in 2001 brought Schulz's memory into the present and into the Ukrainian field of vision, Józef-czuk told me, "Schulz was in fact a stranger, dissonant with nationalist tendencies, and we aimed with the festival precisely in changing that, in rooting Schulz here. . . . Schulz's legacy is not just a dusty book on the shelf of a home library. On the contrary, it is a book to which you can constantly return and find something new, something that allows us to better understand modernity, our hopes and doubts, our dreams and failures."[28]

In 2012, the Supreme Council of Ukraine adopted a resolution to celebrate the one hundred and twentieth anniversary of Schulz's birth and the seventieth anniversary of his death. The text of the resolution expressed the hope that these celebrations would "foster the strengthening of friendly relations between Poland and Ukraine." That year Yuri Andrukhovych published a new Ukrainian translation of Schulz's complete fiction—"not the first translation," a SchulzFest participant told me, "but the first *good* translation."[29] Andrukhovych said that he thought of himself as a conductor, and that if Schulz's "melody of expressions" were transformed into music, it would sound like klezmer composed by Alban Berg or Arnold Schoenberg.

Not to be outdone by their Ukrainian counterparts, the Polish Senate declared November 2012 "Bruno Schulz Month" and proposed that "the figure of Schulz and his works might stand as a point of departure for conversations about Polish-Jewish-Ukrainian relations." Since 2012, when the rights to Schulz's works entered the public domain, those works have inspired Polish operas and ballads,[30] rock bands,[31] calendars,[32] and internet games.[33]

I was welcomed in Drohobych by my interpreter, a bright Ukrainian university student born and raised in the city. "To be honest," he said, "I never heard of the Schulz Festival until I was asked to serve as your interpreter." Indeed, says the Ukrainian literary scholar Oksana Weretiuk, "it is still difficult to find Schulz's books in the bookshops of

Drohobych. We can still hear occasional discordant voices of zealous Ukrainian patriots who say: 'Schulz was implanted in us by foreigners. Big deal! One has to remember about an anniversary of [the Ukrainian writer Ivan] Franko [who was born near Drohobycz and went to school there]. We need to care about ours.' . . . The nationalistic Ukrainians do not care about the Polish-Jewish-Ukrainian writer."[34] This pertains as much to the writing as to the writer. The Cambridge University Schulzologist Stanley Bill explained why at his talk at the 2014 Schulz-Fest: "The Ukrainian element of the city's social and cultural tapestry is entirely absent from Schulz's writings. . . . This absence remains a challenge for Ukrainian scholars and artists seeking to revive Schulz's memory in today's Drohobych, as it is almost impossible to reconcile his work with the prevailing national narratives."[35]

Asked whether there's a growing interest in Schulz's writing among Ukrainians, the Schulz scholar Andriy Pavlyshyn said, "Ukraine is not a literature-centric culture, unlike Poland and Russia, where they go crazy over the written word. . . . In Ukraine, even the most inventive books sell hardly a thousand copies."[36] Drohobych resident Leonid Golberg quoted the Italian psychiatrist and criminologist Cesare Lambroso, who, in his book *The Man of Genius*, wrote: "There are countries where the level of education is very low, and in which not only geniuses but also talented people are treated with contempt." Golberg commented, "I don't know about the country at large, but in Drohobych today they treat their spiritual heritage with a kind of willful ignorance."[37]

These days, visitors to the city are greeted with a sign bearing the slogan "Glory to Ukraine!" (*Slava Ukraini!*), a salute that had been banned by Soviet authorities after the war. My first stop was Schulz's former home on Floriańska Street. Today, a trilingual plaque (in Ukrainian, Polish, and Hebrew) adorns the house where Schulz lived from 1910 to 1941. It memorializes him in black marble as "a renowned Jewish artist and distinguished author, a master of the

Polish word." This plaque, installed in 2002, replaced an earlier bilingual one in Ukrainian and Polish, affixed in 1989, that had referred to Schulz as "a magician of the Polish language" but neglected to mention that the magician was Jewish.[38] I'd asked my interpreter to call the home's owners, Natalia Glazkina and Anton Malchenko, a Ukrainian couple in their thirties. Natalia had inherited the place from her grandmother Alexandra. Anton was kind enough to invite us inside. Parts of the house have remained unchanged since Schulz's day: the dim raftered attic, the creaky planked floors, the frosted-glass interior windows, the lilac bushes in the garden. The rooms are small, conducive to intimacy. On the way out, I asked Anton whether he had read Schulz's books. "I haven't," he replied, "but I think my wife has."

The following day, four of us found Leonid Golberg, the sixty-four-year-old key keeper of the Choral Synagogue and one of only ninety Jews still living in Drohobych today. It was at this synagogue in May 1939, he told us, that Menachem Begin, the future prime minister of Israeli, married Aliza Arnold, born in Drohobycz to a family in the oil business. The Germans had turned the synagogue into a horse stable, Golberg said, and the Soviets used it as a salt warehouse. From the 1960s until the late 1980s it served as a furniture warehouse. He remembers buying sofas there. "Where the *aron hakodesh* [holy ark] was," Golberg said, "they made an iron gate, and the truck brought furniture right into the former prayer hall." When the warehouse closed, the soot-stained synagogue was patronized as a public lavatory by stall keepers at the nearby market.

The city's other synagogues fared no better. The Old Beit Midrash next door (built in the 1740s) became a bakery. The synagogue on 32 Rynek Square, built at the end of the nineteenth century, was converted into apartments. The Oseh Chessed (Progressive) synagogue (on the corner of Mazepa Street, formerly Stryjska Street), built in 1909, was gutted and leased to the Spartacus boxing club. When I visited it, a

"For Sale" sign was visible on a façade crafted in the fashionable style of Vienna Secession.

The ruined Choral Synagogue was the target of four firebombing attacks in the 1990s. After a mysterious fire in 1998 caused extensive damage, the synagogue was given a new roof and partially repaired in 2004 with a $100,000 donation from American philanthropist George Rohr. About a decade later, the Ukrainian-born billionaire oligarch Viktor Vekselberg, the founder and chairman of the Renova Group, a Russian energy conglomerate, funded a complete restoration. Vekselberg was a major donor to the Tate Modern, in London, and to Lincoln Center and Carnegie Hall, in New York, and from 2013 to 2018 was a member of the board of trustees of MIT, where he established a scholarship in his name. His father, Felix Vekselberg, born in Drohobycz in 1922, had been a student of Schulz's (same class as Alfred Schreyer). The holy ark was restored by a graduate of the Stryi art school, Yuriy Onisko, who worked from a rare photograph from the early 1920s. After five years, at a cost of about $1 million, the synagogue had regained its former splendor and was inaugurated in 2018. But for whom?

Weeks before the dedication ceremony, vandals smashed several of the synagogue's windows. "Apparently," Vekselberg said, "the fact that the town now has an active Jewish synagogue that was rebuilt with the money donated by a Russian businessperson made some unhappy." (In April 2018, following the Russian occupation of Crimea, the U.S. Treasury froze some of Vekselberg's assets. In March 2022, the United States issued a new round of sanctions targeting Kremlin-linked elites, including Vekselberg, who "supported Russian President Vladimir Putin's brutal and illegal invasion of Ukraine.")

After our visit to the synagogue, as the evening sank into dusk, we joined a torchlight procession. At each of twelve stations throughout the town—a local version of Jerusalem's Via Dolorosa—festival participants read a passage from Schulz's stories.

Kaddish

DROHOBYCH, UKRAINE, NOVEMBER 19, 2020

The next morning, we took a short bus ride through pastureland to Bronica Forest. The sky was sullen and low. We silently walked toward the mass graves. These were marked by thirteen immense concrete slabs and surrounded by linden trees, their leaves fallen on the rain-sodden ground, and by pine trees standing like watchful sentries. No birdsong was heard overhead. I remembered a scene in Henryk Grynberg's book *Drohobycz, Drohobycz*. The narrator quotes Schulz's former student Leopold Lustig:

> I have never been back to Drohobycz, and I don't want to. Wilek Tepper flew there to say good-bye and laid a plaque on one of those large graves in Bronica. And what happened? In broad daylight, people came with a bulldozer looking for gold and unearthed the bones.

The simple concrete commemorative slabs were installed over the mass graves here in the 1970s with funds donated by Tepper, a survivor from Drohobych. Until lately, locals came to enjoy a nearby barbecue and picnic spot. "No one cared about this place," said Joseph Karpin, a leader of what remains of the Drohobych Jewish community. The Ukrainian government has contributed not a cent to its upkeep. Today the memorial site is maintained with funds from Viktor Vekselberg, who lost sixteen family members here.[39] Karpin donned a silk *tallit* around his shoulders, and with a gentle dip of his face toward the pages of a prayer book in his hands, he broke the vast silence with a recitation of Kaddish and a prayer for the dead, "El Male Rachamim" ("Merciful God"), in Hebrew and Ukrainian.

The festival concluded on November 19, the date of Schulz's murder, with an ecumenical service on the sidewalk where Schulz was shot.[40] We clustered in the cold, in a hushed semicircle around the memorial plaque (the copy). Our backs were to the two-story *Judenrat* building, still standing, church towers peeping up behind it. As if in reply to a nagging awareness that "commemorating" Schulz is no substitute for reading him, a passage of his story "A Second Autumn" was read aloud in Polish and Ukrainian. It included this line: "Beauty is an illness, my father taught, it is a type of shivering caused by a mysterious infection, a dark portent of decay."[41]

During the reading, I noticed a martial statue standing atop a high pedestal in the adjacent park, within the area of the former Jewish ghetto, a stone's throw from where we stood. It depicted the proto-fascist Ukrainian hero Stepan Bandera, whose followers took part in the ethnic cleansing of Poles and Jews during World War II. Bandera's grandson had spoken at the unveiling ceremony of this monument in October 1999.[42] (Drohobych is also home to a Bandera car wash.) A day before, I'd met a Ukrainian historian at his university office; he'd told me that by 1939, Bandera was already collaborating with the Gestapo and with the Abwehr (German military intelligence) in the hopes that the Nazis could defeat both enemies of Ukrainian nationalists—the Poles and the Soviets. He mentioned that shortly before leaving office in 2010, President Viktor Yushchenko conferred on Bandera the highest state honor, "Hero of Ukraine," a recognition condemned by the European Union, the chief rabbi of Ukraine, and the president of Poland.

After the reading, Karpin stood beside the memorial plaque in the sidewalk and recited Kaddish for Schulz, at once calling to the dead and recalling him. I couldn't help imagining the statue's legs buckling a little at the sound of it. A few passersby walked through, hands plunged into the pockets of their thick coats, eyes averted, in brisk indifference to the threnody.

EPILOGUE

The word disintegrates into elements and dissolves, returns to its etymology, enters again into its depths, into its dark root.[1]

—BRUNO SCHULZ

History's Hostage

One night, not long after I stood before his murals in a seldom-visited corner of Yad Vashem's art wing, Bruno Schulz appeared to me in a dream. He was giving an informal reading in Polish in a wood-paneled café that seemed to float outside time, a room unweighted by its own obsolescence. A gray jacket was draped over the back of his chair. Bewildered to find myself there, I looked into his triangular face, with its tentative smile and wide, furrowed forehead and deep-set eyes that still bore traces of the boy. ("To express physiognomy in words," he once wrote, "to convey it completely, to exhaust the world it contains—that's what attracts me: the human face as a starting point of a novel.")[2] Though I couldn't understand the words, I heard a solicitude in his voice that reminded me of the voices of my grandparents, born, like him, in Galicia. I sensed that in his unassuming way, he was describing his art—the works of his words and his brush, two talents so rarely entrusted to a single soul.

At this distance, we can fathom why Schulz's murals—and his

literary legacy—have become a palimpsest of competing myths. There
are at least as many answers to the question "Who was Bruno Schulz?"
as there are versions of his death, and each answer touches on the question "To which nation or country or cartography does Schulz belong?"
Does Schulz's legacy belong to Poland, Ukraine, Israel, or to cultural
heritage as such? Or to things that by their nature cannot be owned?
Is it folly to enlist artists into "national" schools?

On one level, the murals are physical objects, cultural capital subject both to commodification and to legal claims. But they also invite
not just rhetorical sallies but broader perplexities, each grappling on
the back of another: Was the 2001 "Operation Schulz" a clandestine
rescue—a homecoming to a home Schulz could not have envisioned—
or a usurpation? An emancipation or a theft? Where would Schulz's
murals, beautiful even in their damaged and decayed state, speak more
eloquently: in Yad Vashem, which draws about one million visitors a
year, or in situ in the town where Schulz spent his entire life and where
he set his stories but which since his death has relegated him to near
oblivion? (An artwork's accent, after all, falls differently in one setting
than another.) Who has the right to curate the murals and to construe
their meanings? How does Schulz's orphaned art figure in the politics
of erasure and elision?

Parochialism and Prejudice: Belonging to World Culture

In conversation with Johann Peter Eckermann, perhaps on one of their
strolls on the Ettersberg hill, near Weimar (later the site of the Buchenwald concentration camp), Goethe said that the age of national literatures had ended and the era of world literature had begun. But is
there such a thing as "world literature"?

Many of his friends insisted that Schulz's aesthetic achievement
transcended the petty parochialism of national claims. Schulz's friend
Gombrowicz called him "the most European writer, with the right to

take his place amongst the greatest intellectual and artistic aristocracy of Europe."³ On reading *Sanatorium Under the Sign of the Hourglass*, Rachel Auerbach wrote to Schulz:

> I'm strongly convinced that your writing could become a revelation on a universal scale, and since you don't write in the language of the Jews and you don't belong to the milieu from which you have sprung, then you must at least belong to the world.⁴

More recent tribunes of a free-floating universalism attempted retroactively to serve up a universal Schulz, as though he belonged to a cosmopolitan European humanism, as though he was killed not as a Jew but as a human being, and as though his masters were guilty not of crimes against Jews but of crimes against humanity. Twenty-four art historians took the universalist line in a letter to the *New York Review of Books*: "The work of Bruno Schulz, after all, reminds us that this region was long one of unique cultural richness and diversity; an effort by any single group to monopolize his memory erases this history of pluralism." (That the Nazis had laid waste to that pluralism goes unmentioned.) The writers deplored "this effort to wrest Schulz and his work out of any context but one."⁵ For others, Yad Vashem's removal of the murals, and its "ethnocentric drive to attribute Schulz's work entirely to Jewish culture," confirmed that Israel engaged in "post-Holocaust cultural colonization."⁶

The murals' discoverer, Benjamin Geissler, described the removal as "a violent postmortem attack" and published an open letter demanding that "Schulz's frescoes must be restored in their entirety at their place of origin." He elaborated:

> The work of Bruno Schulz belongs to the cultural heritage of eastern Central Europe, a region which has experienced a kaleidoscopic and often dramatic history. Schulz is now a symbolic

figure, who embodies both the multicultural and multilingual features so characteristic of his surroundings as well as the horrors of the Holocaust.

Signatories to Geissler's letter included Nobel laureate Günter Grass, Jerzy Ficowski, Marek Podstolski, and Alfred Schreyer.

Yad Vashem's "repatriation" or "rescue" of Schulz's artworks assumed that even the most acculturated European Jew belongs to Israel because he was murdered as a Jew. This, too, was hotly contested. Some questioned whether Yad Vashem had used the memory of the most heinous crime of the twentieth century to justify an unscrupulous pilfering in the twenty-first.[7] John Czaplicka, a cultural historian affiliated with the Ukrainian Research Institute at Harvard University, asked, "Are these German, Austrian and Polish Jews who contributed to their various European cultures ex post facto automatically Israelis?"

> If we follow the absurd logic of "returning" the frescoes to Israel, then perhaps the Mossad should now start spiriting away artworks painted by Jews in German and Austrian museums or carving out the walls wherever a "Jewish" painter left her/his mark. . . . Does Israel have the "God-given" right to all cultural goods produced by Jews? Do all the works created by Holocaust victims belong to and in Israel?

According to the Israeli dissident poet Yitzhak Laor, a son of refugees from the Shoah, "Hebrew readers knew nothing about Schulz until 1979." That was the year *Cinnamon Shops* first appeared in Hebrew, in the edition translated by Uri Orlev (a survivor of the Warsaw ghetto and the Bergen-Belsen concentration camp), Rachel Kleiman, and Yoram Brunovski.[8] "The act of deceit was necessary because of something that was obscured here, something no true common sense can explain, and which certainly does not fall within the sphere of international law," Laor wrote, "namely that the work of an artist who was a victim of the Holocaust belongs to Israel, because the Holocaust is 'ours.'"[9]

Since a majority of Polish Jewish survivors had found refuge in Israel, retorted Israel Gutman, a Warsaw-born academic adviser to Yad Vashem, "the decisive and unremittingly painful fact is that the Holocaust really is 'ours,' even if Laor refuses to accept that."[10]

Marek Podstolski, Schulz's grandnephew and the unpropitiated heir of the Schulz estate, replied in turn to Gutman: "Your statement that the Holocaust is yours is correct, but at the same time, as an executor to Bruno Schulz's estate, I maintain that Bruno Schulz is still mine. . . . As to the argument to whom Bruno Schulz belongs, I say: Bruno Schulz is simply part of world literature."[11]

Ingathering: Belonging in Jerusalem

Schulz never sought to be universal in his art; he expressed no desire to be at home everywhere. "There is no international novel," Isaac Bashevis Singer once said. "Art is, in its essence, national. It is deeply connected with a land, a locality, a group. . . . It must have an address."[12] "Operation Schulz," in 2001, was not the first time Israelis had assigned European artworks a Jerusalem address. The idea of *kinnus*, or ingathering, of Jewish cultural artifacts had long informed the Zionist imperative to construct a collective memory and find cultural continuity with the Jewish past.[13] That project, inaugurated in the nineteenth century, reached peak urgency in the post-Holocaust period. In those years, several venerable figures traveled to Europe to rescue "heirless" cultural treasures and bring them to the newborn Jewish state, a state that saw itself as heir to the property of Jews who had perished.

One of these rescuers was Mordecai Narkiss, the Polish-born director of the Bezalel Museum in Jerusalem and the founder, during the war, of the Schatz Fund for the Salvage of Jewish Art Remnants. In September 1948, on returning from one such trip, Narkiss wrote, "In general, it is the same in all countries. The Jewish communities and the government are indifferent to the condition of these remnants. This atmosphere changes when one comes to claim the objects—then they both get interested." Narkiss cited a Talmudic prediction: in the messianic future, the synagogues and the study halls will be transported from Babylonian exile to the Land of Israel. That legend, Narkiss said, symbolized the imperative "to do our utmost to bring select examples of the remnants of our artistic culture from each land . . . to salvage these captives and bring them to Israel."[14]

Under the pressure of that imperative, Israel's parliament passed the 1953 Martyrs and Heroes Remembrance Law, which instructs Yad Vashem "to gather in to the homeland material regarding all those members of the Jewish people who laid down their lives, who fought and rebelled against the Nazi enemy and his collaborators." Some dissenters acted as though Israel and Yad Vashem were synonyms. In the weeks of debate leading to the Knesset's approval of that law, critics of the creation of Yad Vashem argued that the state itself, and the rebirth it signaled, was a sufficient memorial to the annihilated diaspora; there could be no better monument than Israel.[15]

In January 1990, the Israel Museum, in Jerusalem, mounted a major exhibition of Schulz's drawings, culled from the collection of two hundred works in the Adam Mickiewicz Museum of Literature, in Warsaw. It was curated by Yona Fischer, Nella Cassouto, and Wojciech Chmurzyński.[16] (Cassouto told me about her unfeigned delight in watching God-fearing ultra-Orthodox Israelis gazing at Schulz's masochistic scenes.) That April, days after the Schulz exhibition closed, Jerusalem mayor Teddy Kollek took 103 works by Marc Chagall, packed into five suitcases, from Paris to Jerusalem for the Israel Museum. He had been given the works (drawings, gouaches, a painting, and sketches of the three large Chagall tapestries that adorn the walls of the Knesset)

by Ida Chagall, the artist's daughter. But Kollek had obtained no permits to take what were regarded as French artistic heritage. (French
regulations on the export of artworks apply to both public and private
collections.) The Israel Museum claimed that Kollek, intending no sub-
terfuge, had acted "spontaneously." The ensuing uproar required three
months of negotiations, including the personal interventions of French
prime minister Michel Rocard and minister of culture Jack Lang. The
Chagall works remain in Jerusalem to this day.

"Operation Schulz" was not the first time Israel's intelligence
agency had helped "repatriate" cultural treasures. In 1957, Israeli
agents aided in the smuggling of the tenth-century Aleppo Codex—the
oldest and most authoritative copy of the Hebrew Bible—from Syria
to the Ben Zvi Institute, in Jerusalem. In 1993, the Mossad worked
with Rabbi Abraham Hamra, the last leader of the Damascus Jewish
community, to bring nine rare medieval Hebrew manuscripts—known
as the Crowns of Damascus—from Syria to Israel's National Library,
in Jerusalem. "We got them from the Mossad on condition that we
would keep it a complete secret," said Raphi Weiser, then director of
the library's manuscripts division.[17]

In keeping with the project of *kinnus*, Yehuda Bauer, the dean of
Israeli Holocaust scholars, joined other writers in insisting that Schulz's
artworks reflect not cultural pluralism but barbarity that tramples on
pluralism; that Schulz was enslaved and murdered because he was a
Jew, not because he was "a symbol of universal artistic genius."[18] The
cause of Schulz's death, Bauer told me, is not far to seek:

> I do recognize the legitimacy of the Polish struggle for keeping
> the artwork of Schulz. But Schulz was murdered because he was
> a Jew, not because of his Polish citizenship. In the eyes of his Pol-
> ish contemporaries, he was a Jew, not a Pole, whatever his own
> views may have been. . . . I think that as he was killed for his
> Jewishness, there is every justification for his work to be kept by

Yad Vashem, an institution set up to commemorate Jews killed
because they were Jews, whatever their formal citizenship.

I also asked Cynthia Ozick, the author of *The Messiah of Stockholm*,
for her thoughts on what I had called "the justice of this ingathering of
fragments." She answered, "My instinct, (more primitive than moon-
ings over 'justice') insists that Europe has never deserved, and never
will deserve, the presence of Jews, or the work of their hands and their
minds." Others, elated by the "ingathering" of the work of Schulz's
hands, drew analogies to another homecoming: the bold rescue of
Israeli hostages from Entebbe, Uganda, in 1976.[19]

Of course, to say that Schulz was a Jew is not to say that he regarded
Zion as a place of inevitable return, nor that retrievable fragments of
his legacy should necessarily be brought to Israel (as posthumous ben-
eficiaries of the Law of Return). Precisely because Schulz was a product
of exilic Jewishness, it could be said, those fragments should remain
in the diaspora.

But if the Israeli removal of Schulz's murals was an act of interpretation, of understanding Schulz less as an artist than as a victim
of the Shoah, it rested on an unspoken premise: not just that Schulz's
murals would get better curatorial care—and more prominent public
display—at Yad Vashem, but that Israel today acts as the standard-
bearer of Shoah memory.

Whatever the merits or demerits of such a premise, it is no fault of
Israel that Schulz's homeland no longer exists except in Schulz's prose,
that the multiethnic patchwork called Galicia has long since ceased to
be. "With Schulz's death in 1942 as a victim of the Holocaust," writes
Hungarian-born American historian István Deák, "there disappeared
the last illusion about a country called Galicia in which Poles, Ukrainians, Jews, Germans, and others lived, if not in harmony, at least with
some respect for the rights and passions of the others."[20] But as far
as Israel is concerned, if Schulz's "patria" no longer exists, the ethics

of repatriation bend toward the Jewish state—and thus toward Yad Vashem. What endures of Polish Jewish memory after the Holocaust? In the view of Yad Vashem: only what can be salvaged from Europe and brought to the Jewish state.

Mother Tongue and Fatherland:
Belonging to the Polish Language

Small nations, those that cannot take their existence for granted, often place exaggerated emphasis on recruiting their artists and writers to the national struggle. The Jewish people, Milan Kundera remarks, are "*the* small nation par excellence."[21] But so, by that measure, are the Poles, whose national anthem, a mazurka, begins with the words "Poland has not yet perished."

Books of enduring value beget commentaries. Innumerably more words have been written about Schulz than he penned himself. Among his readers and commentators, Schulz's fiction has become a Rorschach for personal and national predilections both. Polish Schulzologists have invented a Schulz in their own image, variously ventriloquizing him as a kabbalist;[22] a Hasidic storyteller who "places the avant-garde in a new light, by transplanting it into the culture of a Jewish *shtetl*";[23] a gnostic;[24] an existentialist; a disciple of Henri Bergson's; a Nietzschean; a magical realist à la Gabriel García Márquez; and simply as "a shy philosopher incognito." The sensuous density of his prose has been described as surrealist, symbolist, Chagallesque, and as realizing "a postmodern aesthetics of the sublime dissolution of form."[25] And that's only half the harvest. (Many of these recondite debates and polemical passions play out in the journal *Schulz/Forum*, founded in Gdańsk, Poland, in 2012.) Though the convolutions of Schulzology keep multiplying, vinelike, until interpretations have overgrown the stories, in the end Schulz eludes his exegetes. He refuses to be cut down to comprehensible size. "In order to understand," Schulz wrote, "man is obliged to reduce. . . . This is how pettiness gnaws its way through greatness."[26]

If Schulz's Polish commentators have anything in common, it is the view that the best in his writing no longer belongs to any individual, perhaps no longer even to the author, but to the Polish language itself. For them, Schulz's choice to use the Polish language, not German or Yiddish, is dispositive: by his language shall ye know him. "He was born in Poland, he died in Poland," the poet Czesław Miłosz concludes, "and the most salient characteristic of Schulz as a writer is his intimacy with the Polish language." Having achieved a cult status in ways he never could have hallucinated, Schulz is today revered as a high priest of Polish modernism, as though his prose were an emanation of the national soul. In doing him homage, the Polish novelist Olga Tokarczuk, the 2018 Nobel laureate in literature, said that Schulz's "beautiful, sensitive, meaningful stories raised the Polish language to a completely different level. I love him but I also hate him because there's no way to compete with him. He's the genius of the Polish language."[27]

Others who saw Schulz's choice of Polish as decisive regarded that choice as a kind of self-enslavement. Schulz's contemporary Chaim Löw, a Polish Zionist critic, wrote in the 1930s of Jewish authors "who have given themselves entirely into the slavery of Polish culture, Polish language, and soon the Polish nation—though it is true they are forced now and again to recognize that sweet slavery of theirs."[28]

In the 1931 Polish census, over 80 percent of the country's more than three million Jews declared Yiddish as their native tongue; most of them conducted their entire lives exclusively in Yiddish. (Austro-Hungarian censuses, which did not recognize Yiddish as a language, subsumed Yiddish speakers under the category "German-speaking." Citizens were subject to fine or arrest for listing Yiddish as their mother tongue on census forms.)[29] According to Isaac Bashevis Singer, twelve years younger than Schulz: "There were hundreds of thousands of Jews in Poland to whom Polish was as unfamiliar as Turkish."[30] A smaller number moved amphibiously, like Debora Vogel, between Yiddish and Polish.

Marek Podstolski, the executor of Schulz's estate, noted that his great-uncle, by contrast, maintained only the most tenuous connections with Jewish languages. "In the home of my great-grandparents . . . Polish and German were spoken because it was Galicia. Neither Bruno Schulz, nor his brother—my grandfather—spoke Hebrew or Yiddish."[31] In his view, to cast Schulz as a Jewish writer is at best a misreading and at worst a larceny. "Although he was a Jew," the scholar Wiesław Budzyński told *Rzeczpospolita* newspaper, "he wrote and dreamed in Polish. Schulz was a member of the Union of Polish—not Jewish—Writers."[32] For many Poles, then, it is only fitting that most of Schulz's material legacy—manuscripts, letters, and drawings—remains in Warsaw.

Yet Schulz has been subjected to a certain double-entry accounting of Jews and Poles. In the early days of perestroika, reports Harvard professor James R. Russell, a Polish colleague asked him whether he had read much modern Polish literature. "When I replied that I had been reading the stories of Bruno Schulz, he interrupted impatiently that he meant books by Poles, not Jews." From this Russell derived an understanding of the ways Schulz's "life and art are exploited by opportunists for whom he has become suddenly a Polish writer whose Jewish identity is relevant only to the manner of his murder."[33]

If we put the murder aside, can we appreciate Schulz's deep affinities for—and surrenders to—the Polish language without conflating them with national allegiances?

Schulz's Last Crypt: Belonging in Drohobych

Wherever he traveled—Vienna, Warsaw, Paris—Schulz always returned to the burrow of Drohobycz, to the outward and inward landscape he coveted. Whenever he left Drohobycz, he felt himself a stranger.[34] Philip Roth suggested that this half-remembered, half-mythologized place became the wellspring of Schulz's creative energies—and there-fore inextricable from his art. "It may only have been in Drohobycz that Schulz's imagination fermented," Roth remarked.[35]

The Drohobycz that consoled and consumed Schulz, that was his lifelong address, no longer exists, except in the eyes of a wistful few who regard themselves as its heirs. "We inherited the small homeland of Schulz," said Ukrainian writer and Schulz translator Yuri Andruk-hovych. "It's part of Ukraine, so we bear a serious responsibility for Schulz and his legacy."[36] "This was his small homeland," Jerzy Ficowski said, "the only world where he could breathe and work, as he himself has said." Elsewhere Ficowski insisted that "even in his most phantasmagoric visions Schulz never severed this fragile umbilical cord connecting his artistic vision with his birthplace."[37]

The playroom—now pantry—in Villa Landau was haunted by the spirit of Schulz. "There exists no other grave which contains his ashes," Ficowski said. "And now even his last crypt has been violated, while he himself has been deported, banished to other lands, ones foreign to him." He feared that the most lasting consequence of the discovery and exhumation of Schulz's murals would be "a xenophobia revived in no small measure by Yad Vashem."[38]

Some regarded the former children's room almost as a temple, and the removal of its murals as a kind of profanation. (The Latin *profa-nus* literally means "outside the temple.") Nick Sawicki, a historian of early-twentieth-century European modernist art, has studied Schulz since 1999, when a research fellowship brought him to Warsaw and Lviv. He, too, decried the Israeli-sanctioned "plunder" and "annexa-tion" of Schulz's murals: "I can't help but feel that by removing the fragments from their place, we have become gravediggers of a sort, turning over headstones and agitating the last work of a great artist and writer."

Even some locals acknowledged that Drohobych, with its

obliterated Jewish past and its underfunded museums, would make a less than ideal home for Schulz's treasures. Zinoviy Bervetsky, the director of the Drohobych Museum, said, "I would like to instruct Ukrainians to learn from Jews how to treat their culture."

In voicing skepticism about Ukrainian custodianship of Schulz's traces, Jewish survivors from Drohobych invoked tropes about locals too ignorant to appreciate and protect their own cultural heritage. "Yad Vashem is definitely right," Henryk Grynberg told me, "that no one in Drohobych was interested in the murals behind the closet until they landed in Jewish hands." "The Ukrainians had Schulz's works for fifty-eight years and did nothing to maintain them," said a survivor named George Oscar Lee, "and if we look at the tragic remnants of Jewish culture in Drohobych, it is hard not to be persuaded that it is bad and will become even worse."[39]

The director Jens Carl Ehlers visited the city in the winter of 1990 to research his film about Schulz (*Republik der Träume*, 1993). "I've never felt so lost as I felt in Drohobych," he told me. "A former cultural melting pot turned into a wasteland." "If memory is the central issue, then the place of memory is preeminently Yad Vashem, and it belongs there," said Yosef H. Yerushalmi, a professor of Jewish studies at Columbia University. "The town of Drohobych is not a place of memory. A few tours might go by to see the flat, and that would be it."[40]

Quite apart from Schulz, visitors might have wished to see a museum to Jewish art and culture in Drohobych with exhibits devoted to locally nourished talents: the painter Maurycy Gottlieb;[41] the virtuoso pianist Paula Szalit; the pianist Ignace Tiegerman, teacher of Edward Said; the actress Elisabeth Bergner, a star of 1920s German theater;[42] Diana Reiter, a prominent architect; and the Hebrew-language poet Shin Shalom (pseudonym of Shalom Joseph Shapira). Ukrainians never conceived of such a museum, let alone built and furbished it.

Which, then, rings hollower: Ukrainian and Polish protests against

what was regarded as Yad Vashem's Jewish ethnocentrism and lar-
cenous seizure of Schulz's murals or Israeli claims that the murals
should remain in Jerusalem because such heritage is either untended or
endangered in Ukraine? The Israeli claims have gained urgency during
Russia's recent invasion of Ukraine, the largest military mobilization
in Europe since World War II, with its endangerment of cultural heritage. (According to Adam Michnik, editor in chief of *Gazeta Wyborcza*, Russian president Vladimir Putin had years earlier jokingly told
former Polish prime minister and European Council president Donald
Tusk, "We are taking Kyiv, Donbas, Kharkiv, Odessa, and you take
what once belonged to you: Lwów, Drohobycz, Stanisławów.")[43] In
February 2022, twenty-five paintings by the Ukrainian artist Maria
Primachenko (much admired by Pablo Picasso), went up in flames during clashes in the town of Ivankiv, northwest of Kyiv. In Mariupol, a
Ukrainian city on the Black Sea that saw some of the worst devasta-
tion, city council members alleged that Russian soldiers had stolen
hundreds of artifacts from museums, including valuable Torah scrolls.
In May 2022, after Russian shelling destroyed the historic home and
museum of the Ukrainian poet and philosopher Hryhorii Skovoroda,
Ukraine's president, Volodymyr Zelensky (who is Jewish and lost relatives in the Holocaust), said that Russian forces had so far destroyed
nearly two hundred heritage sites. Later that month, Yaakov Hagoel,
the chairman of the World Zionist Organization and a member of
the Yad Vashem Council, gave Russia's ambassador to Israel, Anatoly
Viktorov, a list of Jewish heritage sites in Ukraine, in the hopes that
Moscow would avoid targeting them. "Ukraine is home to some of
the most important and sensitive heritage sites for the Jewish people,
including Holocaust memorials and monuments, ancient Jewish cem-
eteries, tombs of the righteous that serve as a pilgrimage site for many
Jews, and more," Hagoel said. "We must do everything in our power
to preserve these sites for future generations, especially in light of the
risks created in the area due to the ongoing fighting."

A Jew in Hindsight

One of the first mentions of Schulz in print after the war appeared in the form of a caption. In a 1948 edition of the Polish weekly magazine *Odrodzenie* (Revival), a single sentence ran beneath a portrait of Schulz by S. I. Witkiewicz: "Six years ago, Schulz perished in Drohobycz, murdered by Nazis." Ever since, some of Schulz's most ardent admirers, like the keepers of his murals at Yad Vashem, have had the tragic circumstances of his death a little too much in mind, as if his end were somehow inscribed in his beginnings, as if his fate were foreordained. Though Schulz's murder inevitably colors our view of his literary position, this myopic hindsight, what the French call a *déformation professionnelle*, diminishes and flattens his life. Needless to say, that life was not synonymous with his harrowing fate, with what his murderer turned him into.[44] Schulz may have been under the sway of certain forebodings, but he neither foresaw the *khurbn* ("catastrophe" in Yiddish) nor plowed dread of annihilation into his writing. His fictions, however inflected by beauty's "dark portent of decay," are untroubled by premonitions or inklings of the terrors to come. Though he bore many indignities under Nazi rule and created his last paintings under Nazi coercion, the Shoah was incidental to his art.

Was Jewishness any more relevant to his writing? Though Schulz regularly published in Jewish Polish-language papers and magazines,[45] he had never belonged to the shtetl's insular Yiddish-speaking traditionalists. He had no moorings in their rituals or liturgies. He made his own liturgy, more daring and more exalted than any he heard when he sat with his father once a year, on Yom Kippur, in the pews of the Choral Synagogue. Schulz neither acquired a religious education nor delved into Judaism to give sense and substance to his life. His fiction seldom makes explicit reference to Jews. He on occasion compares the Father to his biblical namesake Jacob[46] and to Moses,[47] but, like Kafka, he strips his stories of most ethnic and historical markers.

Such blanks have tempted critics to tease out Jewish and biblical allusions in Schulz's work, to show how his stories "retain the *essence* of Jewish mythology if not the realism of everyday Jewish life,"[48] as one scholar puts it, or to find evidence of his Jewishness in his passion for interpretation—in short, to ascribe Schulz's literary peculiarities to the Jewishness that freighted his fiction. "Jewishness was the background, the very substance of his phantasmagoria," Rachel Auerbach avowed.[49] Hermann Sternbach, a writer from Drohobycz, commended Schulz's "visionary powers" and called *Cinnamon Shops* "true and fascinating in its Jewishness. . . . With this, his debut, the author has secured himself a leading position within Polish letters, and virtually the first place among Polish-Jewish writers whose themes are drawn from Jewish life."[50]

By virtue of that "first place," no single figure in Poland's literary history more insistently confronts us with questions about the stewardship of suffering, about demands for validation of Jewish and non-Jewish grief over the Shoah.

"Verbal Homeland"

In the last decade of Bruno Schulz's life, as he matured to immaturity, National Socialism regressed into atavistic mythic unreason, into dark fantasies of "Blood and Soil" (*Blut und Boden*). The Nazis manipulated primitive myth for political use. "Henceforth," wrote the German philosopher Ernst Cassirer, "myths can be manufactured in the same sense and according to the same methods as any other modern weapon—as machine guns or airplanes."[51] Amid and against that manufacture, Schulz irrigated the soil of his creative life with myth—the kind of myth, he said, that "murmurs in our blood, is tangled in the depths of phylogeny, branches out into the metaphysical night."[52]

Schulz's favorite novel was Thomas Mann's *Joseph and His Brothers*. (In Schulz's story "Spring," the narrator Joseph confesses,

"I committed an unconscious plagiarism of another Joseph.") In his open letter to S. I. Witkiewicz, Schulz dwells on his fellowship with the German novelist:

> Mann shows that beneath all human events, when the chaff of time and individual variation is blown away, certain primeval patterns, "stories," are found, by which these events form and re-form in great repeating pulses. For Mann, these are the biblical tales, the timeless myths of Babylon and Egypt. On my more modest scale I have attempted to uncover my own private mythology, my own "stories," my own mythic family tree. Just as the ancients traced their ancestry from mythical unions with gods, so I undertook to establish for myself some mythical generation of forebears, a fictitious family from which I trace my true descent. . . . I have always felt that the roots of the individual spirit, traced far enough down, would be lost in some matrix of myth."[53]

In 1936, Schulz published an essay called "The Mythologizing of Reality" in the short-lived Polish magazine *Studio*, edited by Zofia Nałkowska. It was the summa of his religion of art, the closest he would ever come to articulating a literary credo. Everyday words, Schulz asserts, encode the grammar of shadow-rimmed myths:

> We usually regard the word as the shadow of reality, its symbol. The reverse of this statement would be more correct: reality is the shadow of the word. Philosophy is actually philology, the deep, creative exploration of the word.
>
> The old cosmogonies expressed this with the statement, "in the beginning was the word." . . . The isolated word as a mosaic piece is a late product, an early result of technology. The primeval word was a shimmering aura circling around the sense

of the world, was a great universal whole. The word in its common usage today is only a fragment, a remnant of some former
all-embracing, integral mythology. That is why it possesses a
tendency to grow back, to regenerate and complete itself in full
meaning. The life of the word consists in tensing and stretching
itself towards a thousand connections, like the cut-up snake in
the legend whose pieces search for each other in the dark. This
thousand-formed but integral organism of the word was torn
apart into syllables, sounds, everyday speech; and in these new
forms, adapted to practical needs, it was handed down to us as
a handy code of communication.[54]

The word's longing to disperse the dark, Schulz concludes, to become
complete again, and "to return to its verbal homeland, we call poetry."

What remains of this artist's voyages into the Republic of Dreams,
where "nothing happens in vain"?[55] Or to modulate the question into
the future tense: What will endure of his cartography of that imagined
territory, of the surveyor's map he spread out before us? Somewhere
along the line, in the truceless contest between peoples and in the
struggle to shape their afflicted and unappeased pasts, our admission
into Schulz's own mythmaking has become occluded. But if we strive
beyond the prosaic facts of history, maybe we'll see that a poetry also
thrums in the longing to restore Bruno Schulz to his homeland, wherever that might be.

ACKNOWLEDGMENTS

Let your last thinks all be thanks.

—W. H. AUDEN

My profound thanks to those who allowed me to ply them with questions and who generously shared their knowledge in person, by phone, or by email: Yehuda Bauer, Stanley Bill, Maxim Biller, Nella Cassouto, Joanna Rostropowicz Clark, Jens Carl Ehlers, Benjamin Geissler, Leonid Golberg, David Goldfarb, Henryk Grynberg, Joseph Hertz, Dierdre Janson-Smith, Jerzy Jarzębski, Grzegorz Józefczuk, Ariko Kato, Lesya Khomych, Ewa Kuryluk, Adam Lipszyc, Yaacov Lozowick, Anastasiya Lyubas, Barłomiej Michałowski, Cynthia Ozick, Piotr Paziński, Jurko Prochaśko, Joel Rappel, Theodosia Robertson, Krzysztof Sawicki, Erwin Schenkelbach, Helen Maryles Shankman, Nancy Sinkoff, Martin Stern, Devorah Telushkin, Agata Tuszyńska, Leon Wieseltier, and two members of the Yad Vashem staff who have chosen, no doubt wisely, to go unnamed.

I thank Bayla Pasikov at the Van Leer Institute library, my base in Jerusalem; Andreas Weigl at the Wien Stadt- und Landesarchiv for help with locating the Felix Landau and Gertrude Segel files; Randol Schoenberg for sharing documents pertaining to the Altmann case; Elisha S. Baskin for her meticulous photo research; Susan Kennedy for her translations of archival documents from the German; and Kateryna Gladka for her translations from the Ukrainian.

Special salutes to literary agents Deborah Harris and George Eltman, whose belief in this book never flagged or faltered; to Matti Friedman, Jessica Kasmer-Jacobs, Paul Mendes-Flohr, and Kathrine Tschemerinsky for their discerning comments on drafts of the manuscript; to George Rohr and his colleagues at the Sami Rohr Jewish Literary Institute for their gracious support; and to Wiera Meniok and Grzegorz Józefczuk for inviting me to take part in the 2020 Bruno Schulz Festival in Drohobych.

I'm indebted to Jerzy Ficowski's invaluable *Regions of the Great Heresy: Bruno Schulz, a Biographical Portrait* (W. W. Norton, 2003) and to Anna Kaszuba-Dębska's Polish-language biography of Schulz (Znak, 2020), itself indebted to Ficowski's labors. "Without Ficowski," she has justly said, "Schulz would have disappeared without a trace."

This book has benefited immeasurably from the expert editing of John Glusman, Helen Thomaides, and Dassi Zeidel at W. W. Norton, and from the attentive copyediting of Bonnie Thompson.

Last and first: the inflections of Karina Korecky's intelligence— and sustaining love—are everywhere between these lines.

NOTES

PROLOGUE

1. Bruno Schulz, *Letters and Drawings of Bruno Schulz with Selected Prose,* ed. Jerzy Ficowski, trans. Walter Arndt and Victoria Nelson (Harper & Row, 1989) (hereafter *Letters and Drawings*), 110; *The Collected Works of Bruno Schulz,* ed. Jerzy Ficowski (Picador, 1998) (hereafter *Collected Works*), 367. Originally published as S. I. Witkiewicz, "Interview with Bruno Schulz," *Tygodnik Illustrowany* 17 (1935).
2. Schulz to Wacław Czarski (editor of the weekly *Tygodnik Ilustrowany*), winter 1934–35; *Letters and Drawings*, 98.
3. The Quay Brothers created *Street of Crocodiles* (1986), a twenty-one-minute-long stop-motion animation based on the blurring of the animate and inanimate in Schulz's fiction. "We could make films around Bruno Schulz for the rest of our lives," the filmmakers said, "and still try and grasp, apprehend his universe." (Andre Habib, "Through a Glass Darkly: Interview with the Quay Brothers," *Senses of Cinema*, March-April 2002.) See also Suzanne H. Buchan, "The Quay Brothers: Choreographed Chiaroscuro, Enigmatic and Sublime," *Film Quarterly* 51, no. 3 (Spring 1998): 2–15. Another stop-action animated film, based on Schulz's story "Loneliness," was directed by Betina Bożek and Igor Kawecki (2017). Théâtre de Complicité dramatized Schulz's *The Street of Crocodiles* in a co-production (directed by Simon McBurney, written by Mark Wheatley) with the National Theatre in London. Reviewing it, Ben Brantley wrote: "Schulz's work, like that of Proust and Kafka, shakes readers free of the blinkers of habitual perception." ("A Haunting Vision Untainted by Order or Logic," *New York Times*, July 18, 1998.) See also Anna Suwalska-Kołecka, "Schulz According to Complicité: Instability, Metamorphosis, and Fluidity," *CzasKultury* 1 (2014).
4. Schulz, review of Maria Kuncewicz's 1936 novel, *The Stranger* [*Cudzoziemka*], *Letters and Drawings*, 89. Originally published as Schulz, "Aneksja podświadomości (Uwagi o *Cudzoziemce* Kuncewiczowej)" [The annexation of the subconscious (Observations on Kuncewicz's *The Stranger*")], *Pion* 17 (1936); reprinted in *Opowiadania: Wybór esejów i listów,* ed. Jerzy Jarzębski (Zakład Narodowy im. Ossolińskich [Biblioteka narodowa series 1, no. 264], 1989), 368–79.

CHAPTER 1: MUROMANCY

1. "An Essay for S. I. Witkiewicz," *Letters and Drawings*, 113.
2. Christian Geissler's novel appeared in English in 1962, translated by James Kirkup. On the life of Christian Geissler, see the autobiographical novel by his wife, Sabine Peters, *Feuerfreund* (Wallstein Verlag, 2010).
3. Irena Subbotej, "Music Saved Me from Death: An Interview with Alfred Schreyer," *Kurier Galicyjski*, May 17–30, 2013. The Nazis murdered Schreyer's father (in Belzec) and mother (in the Bronica Forest outside Drohobycz). Schreyer corresponded extensively with Schulz biographer Jerzy Ficowski (twenty-eight letters between 1988 and 2001). See also the 2011 film *The Last Jew from Drohobycz* (dir. Paul Rosdy); the 2010 film *Alfred Schreyer z Drohobycza* [Alfred Schreyer from Drohobycz], (dir. Marcin Gizycki); and the 1995 film *Gdzież jesteście przyjaciele moi . . .* [Where are you, my friends . . .], (dir. Mariusz Kobzdej).
4. Chajes, born in Drohobycz in 1894, died in Kraków in 1969. His wife, Róza, was shot in Bronica Forest outside of Drohobycz in 1943. See Marla Raucher Osborn, "Artwork as Witness to History: Destruction of a Drohobycz Family," JewishGen, Feb. 2016.
5. According to the provenance researcher Nawojka Cieślińska-Lobkowicz, "Ella and Jakub Schulz—the lawful heirs of Bruno Schulz—were not only completely passed over, they were also never even informed [of the 1986 sale]." (Cieślińska-Lobkowicz, "Who Owns Bruno Schulz? The Changing Postwar Fortunes of Works of Art by Jewish Artists Murdered in Nazi-Occupied Poland," paper presented at the international conference of the Documentation Centre for Property Transfers of Cultural Assets of WWII, Prague, Oct. 21–22, 2015.)
6. Schulz gave *Encounter* to his close friend Stanisław Weingarten for his thirtieth birthday. The painting made its way after the war to the antiquarian Henryk Maszewski. On the sensational circumstances of that purchase, see Wojciech Chmurzyński, "Bruno Schulz i pieniądze," *Gazeta Wyborcza* 84 (1992): 11. Art historian Carol Zemel writes, "Schulz's picture may recall Sigmund Freud's account of childhood shame when, walking with his father, the elder Freud told his own story of a youthful walk and how he silently deferred to non-Jews who knocked his (phallic) hat into the gutter. . . . Both Freud's tale and Schulz's picture convey a sense of Jewish otherness and anxiety in that Eastern European diaspora." (Zemel, *Looking Jewish: Visual Culture and Modern Diaspora* [Indiana University Press, 2015], 58.)
7. Voznytsky died in 2012; Chmurzyński died in 2019.
8. "A Treatise on Mannequins; or, The Second Book of Genesis," Bruno Schulz, *Collected Stories*, trans. Madeline G. Levine (Northwestern University Press, 2018) [hereafter *Collected Stories*], 25.
9. Andrew Meier, "Whose Art Is It Anyway?," *Time*, July 16, 2001.
10. In 1973, Yad Vashem recognized Berthold Beitz as a Righteous Among the Nations. "The Jews that he rescued from deportation," Yad Vashem stated, "included many unqualified workers, often in poor physical condition, who could not by any stretch of the imagination be described as 'professionals' or indispensable to the oil industry." Else Beitz was accorded the same honor in 2006. In parallel, Roman Lubkivsky, a prominent Ukrainian poet, diplomat, and head of the department of culture of the Lviv Regional State Administration, also wrote to Beitz in support of creating a Schulz museum in Villa Landau.

11. "Uproar continues over Yad Vashem murals," *JTA*, June 26, 2001. "For whom, then, do we need the Schulz reconciliation center in Drohobych," asked the Lviv-based Ukrainian writer Yaryna Borenko, "for tourists or for us?" ("Schulzgate," *New Horizons*, Dec. 2002, 49–50.)

12. *Słownik schulzowski* [Schulz Dictionary], ed. Włodzimierz Bolecki, Jerzy Jarzębski, and Stanisław Rosiek (Gdańsk: Słowo/obraz terytoria, 2003).

13. Schulz, "An Essay for S. I. Witkiewicz," *Letters and Drawings*, 111.

CHAPTER 2: THE REPUBLIC OF DREAMS

1. Schulz to Romana Halpern, Dec. 5, 1936; *Collected Works*, 402.

2. On the story of how Jews in the Austrian provinces of Galicia and Bukovina, like the Schulz family, adopted German family names, see Johannes Czakai, *Nochems neue Namen: Die Juden Galiziens und der Bukowina und die Einführung deutscher Vor- und Familiennamen, 1772–1820* (Wallstein, 2021).

3. The "idolatrously loved" quote is from Polish-born Holocaust survivor and historian Arno Lustiger, "Wirklichkeit ist ein Schatten des Wortes," *Die Welt*, March 29, 2008. The "shaken" quote comes from Schulz, "An Essay for S. I. Witkiewicz," *Letters and Drawings*, 111.

4. "August," *Collected Stories*, 4.

5. Schulz to Andrzej Pleśniewicz, March 4, 1936; quoted in Ficowski, *Regions of the Great Heresy*, 157. For the original Polish, see Bruno Schulz, *Księga listów* [Book of letters], ed. Jerzy Ficowski (Słowo / Obraz Terytoria, 2008) [hereafter *Księga listów*], 113–14. "The yearning for lost childhood is as old as art itself," his biographer Jerzy Ficowski notes. "But none before Schulz had made it into the very essence of his creativity or used it to such literary perfection." (Ficowski, "On the Cross-roads of Three Cultures: The Life and Work of Bruno Schulz," *Jewish Quarterly* 27, no. 1 [Spring 1979].)

6. Schulz, "List do Stanisława Ignacego Witkiewicza" [A letter to Stanisław Ignacy Witkiewicz], *Księga listów*, 101; quoted in Jerzy Ficowski's introduction to Schulz, *The Street of Crocodiles*, trans. Celina Wieniewska (Penguin, 1977), 19.

7. Schulz to Stefan Szuman, July 24, 1932, *Letters and Drawings*, 37; *Księga listów*, 34–35. Schulz met Szuman (a specialist in child psychology and a professor at Jagiellonian University, in Kraków, who published poetry under the pseudonym Łukasz Flis) in Żywiec, Poland, in the summer of 1932. It was Szuman who suggested to Schulz the title *Cinnamon Shops* for his first book.

Schulz's colleague Aleksy Kuszczak also recalled Schulz's "fear of the loss of reproductive power by castration. Once, Bruno unexpectedly told me that he considered castration to be the worst fate that could befall a human being." (Kuszczak to Jerzy Ficowski, 1965; quoted in Anna Kaszuba-Dębska, *Bruno: Epoka genialna* (Znak, 2020) [hereafter *Bruno: Epoka genialna*], 490).

8. One version of Adela's story is included in Salomon Buber's *Anshei Shem* ([Kraków, 1895], 19). I. L. Peretz, the Yiddish-language writer who dominated Jewish literary life in Warsaw until his death in 1915, adapted Adela's tragedy in his short story "Three Gifts," *The I. L. Peretz Reader*, ed. Ruth R. Wisse (Yale University Press, 2002), 222–30.

9. The Galician Jewish writer Karl Emil Franzos published a collection of short stories called *Aus halb-Asien* [From Half-Asia, 1876], in which he portrayed Galicia as an exotic, half-Asian land. In a 1910 study, a Polish scholar of Galicia called

the province's Jews an "ignorant, superstitious population." (Stanisław Gruiński, *Materyały do kwestyi żydowskiej w Galicyi* [Lwów: Wydział Krajowy, 1910], 35; quoted in Omer Bartov, *Tales from the Borderlands: Making and Unmaking the Galician Past* [Yale University Press, 2022], 233.) Sigmund Freud's son Martin referred to Galician Jews as possessing "little grace and no manners. . . . They were highly emotional and easily carried away by their feelings." Both of Sigmund Freud's parents came from Galicia. (Martin Freud, *Sigmund Freud: Man and Father* [Vanguard, 1958], 11.) Galician Jews strenuously countered such negative stereotypes. In his 1934 book *Medinah va-chakhameha* [A land and its scholars], Gershom Bader listed accomplished Galician-born authors, artists, scholars, and so on.

10. *Dreyssig Briefe über Galizien: Oder Beobachtungen eines unpartheyischen Mannes, der sich mehr, als nur ein paar Monate in diesem Königreiche umgesehen hat* [Thirty letters about Galicia: or, Observations of a nonpartisan man who has looked around the Kingdom for more than a mere few months] (Vienna: Wucherer und Beer, 1787), 117; quoted in Larry Wolff, "Inventing Galicia: Messianic Josephinism and the Recasting of Partitioned Poland," *Slavic Review* 63, no. 4 (Winter 2004).

11. Roth, "Journey Through Galicia," *The Hotel Years: Wanderings in Europe Between the Wars*, trans. Michael Hofmann (Granta, 2015), 70. "What is so special about Galician towns?" Isaac Babel asked when he rode through in 1920. "That mixture of the dirty and sluggish East (Byzantium and the Jews) with the beery German West." (Babel, *1920 Diary*, ed. Carol J. Avins, trans. H. T. Willetts [Yale University Press, 2002], 77.) The best studies of Galicia are Omer Bartov, *Erased: Vanishing Traces of Jewish Galicia in Present-Day Ukraine* (Princeton University Press, 2007); Omer Bartov, *Tales from the Borderlands: Making and Unmaking the Galician Past* (Yale University Press, 2022); and Larry Wolff, *The Idea of Galicia: History and Fantasy in Habsburg Political Culture* (Stanford University Press, 2010). See also Andrei S. Markovits and Frank E. Sysyn, eds., *Nationbuilding and the Politics of Nationalism: Essays on Austrian Galicia* (Harvard University Press, 1982). For studies of Schulz's place in Galicia, see Bohdan Budurowycz, "Galicia in the Work of Bruno Schulz," *Canadian Slavonic Papers* 28 (1986): 359–68 (reprinted in *Bruno Schulz, in Memoriam, 1892–1942*, ed. Małgorzata Kitowska-Łysiak, trans. Monika Adamczyk-Grabowska (Lublin: Wydawnictwo Fis, [1992]); Eugenia Prokop-Janiec, "Schulz and the Galician Melting Pot of Cultures," trans. Valerie Laken, *Periphery* 3 (1997): 84–88; and Karen Underhill, *Bruno Schulz and Galician Jewish Modernity* (Indiana University Press, forthcoming in 2023).

12. For detailed accounts of the rapid development of the petroleum industry in Galicia, see Alison Fleig Frank, *Oil Empire: Visions of Prosperity in Austrian Galicia* (Harvard University Press, 2005); and Valerie Schatzker, *The Jewish Oil Magnates of Galicia* (McGill-Queen's University Press, 2015). The second part of the latter book features the first English translation of a 1954 Yiddish novel by Julian Hirszhaut, *The Jewish Oil Magnates* (trans. Miriam Dashkin Beckerman).

13. Schulz, "The Street of Crocodiles," *Collected Stories*, 55.

14. See *William Faulkner and Bruno Schulz: A Comparative Study*, by Zbigniew Maszewski (Lodz University Press, 2003).

15. *Letters and Drawings*, 217.

16. Schulz, "The Republic of Dreams," *Collected Stories*, 245; originally published as "Republika marzeń," *Tygodnik Ilustrowany* 29 (1936).

17. Izabela Czermakowa, "Wspomnienie o Schulzu" [A Remembrance of Schulz], *Schulz/Forum* 4 (2014): 103–08; originally published as Czermakowa, "Bruno Schulz," *Twórczość* 21, no. 10 (Oct. 1965): 99–102. The first sentence is quoted in Ficowski, *Regions of the Great Heresy*, 83. Czermakowa (born Hermanowa), who hosted a salon in Lwów for artists and writers, translated works by Stefan Zweig, Arthur Schnitzler, and Gottfried Keller into Polish.

18. Schulz, "E. M. Lilien," *Schulz/Forum* 6 (2015). Schulz's previously unknown essay on Ephraim Moses Lilien was based on three public talks on Lilien to the Drohobycz chapter of the Women's International Zionist Organization (WIZO) in December 1937, February 1938, and April 1938. It originally appeared during 1937–38 in eight installments in a petroleum industry newsletter called the *Subcarpathian Review* (*Przegląd Podkarpacie*). See Karen Underhill, "Bruno Schulz's Galician Diasporism: On the 1937 Essay 'E. M. Lilien' and Rokhl Korn's Review of *Cinnamon Shops*," *Jewish Social Studies* 24, no. 1 (Fall 2018). For the story of the essay's rediscovery in 2015 by Bohdan Lazorak and Piotr Sitkiewicz, see Piotr Sitkiewicz, "Ocalony przez mit: Schulz i Lilien," *Schulz/Forum* 6 (2015): 97–104.

19. Schulz, *Z listów odnalezionych*, ed. Jerzy Ficowski (Chimera, 1993), 21; quoted in Luiza Bialasiewicz, "Back to Galicia Felix?," in *Galicia: A Multicultured Land*, ed. Christopher Hann and Paul Robert Magocsi (University of Toronto Press, 2005), 169.

20. Bruno Schulz, "An Essay for S. I. Witkiewicz" ["Do Stanisława Ignacego Witkiewicza"], *Tygodnik Illustrowany* 17 (1935).

21. Schulz, "Tragic Freedom," in Czesław Prokopczyk, ed., *Bruno Schulz: New Documents and Interpretations* (Peter Lang, 1999), 44.

22. See the letter from the Zion society in Drohobycz to *Die Welt* with Theodor Herzl's corrections, 1898, Central Zionist Archives, Jerusalem (file H1\3196). See also Ezra Mendelsohn, *Zionism in Poland: The Formative Years, 1915–1926* (Yale University Press, 1981); Kenneth B. Moss, *An Unchosen People: Jewish Political Reckoning in Interwar Poland* (Harvard University Press, 2021); Joshua Shanes, *Diaspora Nationalism and Jewish Identity in Habsburg Galicia* (Cambridge University Press, 2012); and Shanes, "Neither Germans nor Poles: Jewish Nationalism in Galicia Before Herzl, 1883–1897," *Austrian History Yearbook* 34 (2003): 191–213.

23. The founding circle of Drohobycz *maskilim* included Asher Zelig Lauterbach, the co-owner of a large oil refinery and co-founder of the local branch of the Alliance Israelite Universelle; Shmuel Avraham (Abel) Apfel; Alexander Haim Shor; and Aron Hirsh Żupnik.

24. Hasidism was founded in Galicia by a teacher named Baal Shem Tov in the early eighteenth century. The Drohobycz Hasidic community was led until World War I by Rabbi Haim Meir Yehiel Shapira. His grandson was the Hebrew poet Shin Shalom, who would become a close friend of Max Brod's. "In his Hebrew poetry," writes the Polish poet Anna Banasiak, "Shin Shalom comes back to Drohobycz, the Promised Land and the city of his grandfathers. For this peace visionary, Drohobycz is the center of the Hasidic movement in Eastern Europe." ("Shin Shalom's Republic of Dreams," *Times of Israel*, June 5, 2016.) Avraham Yaakov Shapira, known as "the Rebbe Painter," born in 1884, was the last of the Drohobycz

Hasidic dynasty. He moved from Drohobycz to Palestine in 1922. Hasidic leaders who settled in Drohobycz include Eliezer, the son of Todros of Nemirow from the Belz dynasty; Eliezer Rubin, from the Rufshits dynasty; Moshe of Stanislaw, from the Karlin-Ludmir dynasty; Avraham Heshel of Stanislav, from the Zbaraz dynasty; Israel David Rokeach and his son Efraim Arie, from Kotov; and Nisan Haim from the Przemysl-Nedvorna dynasty.

25. The most prominent were Yaakov Feuerstein, a deputy mayor of Drohobycz, and Nathan Löwenstein, elected to the Austrian Reichsrat in 1907 and 1911.

26. Mieczysław Orłowicz, *Ilustrowany przewodnik po Europie: Europa Wschodnia i Środkowa (Rosya, Austro-Węgry, Niemcy, Szwajcarya)*, 1914. According to Austrian censuses, 9,181 Jews (50 percent of the town's population) lived in Drohobycz in 1880, and 15,313 Jews (44 percent) in 1910. The term "one and a half cities" was coined by the Jewish Lwów-born poet and songwriter Marian Hemar (né Marian Hescheles). "The Jews were the 'tone setters' in matters of culture, education and good taste," a contemporary of Schulz's recalled. (Rivka Shapira, "My Memories of Drohobycz," trans. from the Hebrew by Anita Harband, in *Sefer zikaron le-Drohobycz, Boryslaw ve-ha-seviva* [Memorial to the Jews of Drohobycz, Borysław, and surroundings], ed. N. M. Gelber [Tel Aviv, 1959].) See also Rubin Schmer-Gartenberg, "My Return Home," *Galitzianer* 13, no. 3 (May 2006).

27. Alfred Döblin, *Journey to Poland*, trans. Joachim Neugroschel (Paragon House, 1991), 177–78. Yiddish writers who wrote travelogues or dispatches from Galicia in the 1920s include Chone Gottesfeld, Yoel Mastboym, Nachman Meisel, and Israel Joshua Singer. For modern Galician travelogues in German, see Martin Pollack's *Nach Galizien* (1984) and Verena Dohrn's *Reise nach Galizien* (1991).

28. "The Night of the Great Season," *Collected Stories*, 77–78.

29. These included the Great or Choral Synagogue; the Sadhora synagogue on Jagiellońska Street; the Lan-Kloiz synagogue (Hasidic); Yishrei Lev on 22 Rynek Square (Zionist); and Beit Yehudah on Grunwaldska Street (Zionist). Reform temples included the Osei Hesed synagogue on Stryiska Street and the temple in the building of the old-age home on Mickewicz Street. See Vladimir Levin, "Synagogues in Drohobycz," Center for Jewish Art, Hebrew University of Jerusalem, 2000.

30. In his travelogue *Reise in Polen*, Alfred Döblin writes of his visit to Drohobycz: "A big, freshly whitewashed house shines, horrible, in the midst of this woe. . . . It's the synagogue. It too was ruinous, but then it was renovated. And I can't help thinking that it shouldn't have been renovated." (Döblin, *Journey to Poland*, trans. Joachim Neugroschel [Paragon House, 1991], 176.)

31. Yaakov Avigdor was appointed chief rabbi of Drohobycz in 1920, wrote a doctoral dissertation on "Jewish metaphysics" at the University in Lwów, and published books in Hebrew, Polish, and Yiddish. At the outbreak of war, he hid in the attic of the Yishrei Lev synagogue in Drohobycz and in a bunker on the "Aryan" side of town. After his capture, he survived the Buchenwald concentration camp. See the biography written by his son, Rabbi Isaac C. Avigdor: *Faith After the Flames: The Life of Rabbi Dr. Yaakov Avigdor* (New Haven: Rodgiva), 2005.

32. Michał Chajes to Jerzy Ficowski, 1948, quoted in *Bruno: Epoka genialna*, 144. A young woman acquainted with Schulz called his hands "dazzlingly beautiful." (Maria Budratzka to Jerzy Ficowski, 1977, quoted in *Bruno: Epoka genialna*, 319.)

33. A. Brun, "Bruno Schulz—i co dalej?," *Chwila*, Sept. 14, 1935, 9.

34. Edmund (Lewandowski) Löwenthal to Jerzy Ficowski, 1948; *Bruno Schulz: Listy, fragmenty, wspomnienia o pisarzu*, ed. Ficowski (Wydawnictwo Literackie, 1984), 56–57; quoted in *Bruno: Epoka genialna*, 71.

35. On the career of Izydor Schulz, see Bohdan Łazorak, "Wpływowy brat Izydor (Baruch, Izrael) Schulz" [The influential brother: Izydor (Baruch, Israel) Schulz], *Schulz/Forum* 3 (2013): 89–104. On Bruno Schulz and cinema, see Paweł Sitkiewicz, "Fantasmagorie: Rozważania o filmowej wyobraźni Brunona Schulza" [Phantasmagoria: Reflections on Bruno Schulz's cinematic imagination], *Schulz/Forum* 1 (2012): 35–46.

36. Quoted in *Bruno: Epoka genialna*, 286.

37. For a detailed account of the election-day massacre, see Joshua Shanes, "The 'Bloody Election' in Drohobycz: Violence, Urban Politics, and National Memory in an Imperial Borderland," *Austrian History Yearbook* (2022): 1–29, and "Blutige Wahlexcesse in Galizien" [Bloody electoral excesses in Galicia], *Die Neue Zeitung*, June 21, 1911. Although some of the victims were Ukrainian, Shanes writes, Zionists and Jewish socialists "tried to use the moment to enflame popular passion against the 'assimilationist' establishment" (22). The Breiter speech is quoted in Shanes, 28. A plaque commemorating the massacre in Ukrainian was placed at the site in 1969 and remains there today.

38. Andrzej Chciuk, *Ziemia księżycowa: Druga opowieść o Księstwie Bałaku*, 2nd ed (1989), 91; quoted in Wiesław Budzyński, *Schulz pod kluczem* [Schulz under lock and key] (2013), 41. See also Chciuk's poem "Poemat o Brunonie Schulzu" [An elegy for Bruno Schulz]. Chciuk escaped Nazi-occupied Poland as a twenty-year-old in 1940.

39. Schulz to Tadeusz Wojciechowski, Sept. 28, 1940; quoted in Prokopczyk, *Bruno Schulz: New Documents and Interpretations*, 34.

40. See Bruno Schulz's review of Lachowicz's work in *Przeglądzie Podkarpacia* [Subcarpathian review], Dec. 2, 1934, and the album of Lachowicz's work *Drohobycz Feliksa Lachowicza*, eds. Beata Długajczyk, Romuald Kołudzki-Stobbe, and Jerzy M. Pilecki (BOSZ, 2008).

41. *Im Epizentrum des Zusammenbruchs: Wien im Ersten Weltkrieg*, eds. Alfred Pfoser and Andreas Weigl (2013), 668. See also David Rechter, "Galicia in Vienna: Jewish Refugees in the First World War," *Austrian History Yearbook* 28 (1997): 113–30, and "Galizien in Wien," *Mythos Galizien*, eds. Jacek Purchla, Wolfgang Kos, Żanna Komar, Monika Rydiger, and Werner Michael Schwarz (2015). Our knowledge of Schulz's years in Vienna is indebted to the archival research of Paolo Caneppele, who presented his findings at the Bruno Schulz International Symposium in Trieste in 2000 (later published in Polish in *W ułamkach zwierciadła: Bruno Schulz w 110. rocznicę urodzin i 60 rocznicę śmierci*, eds. Władysław Panas and Małgorzata Kitowska-Łysiak (2003).

42. "Cockroaches," *Collected Stories*, 62.

43. *Neue Freie Presse*, Dec. 11, 1918. Two weeks earlier, on November 27, the paper reported, "The full misery of unleashed unrestraint broke over Lemberg only when the country's own children turned their weapons upon one another, when Poles and Ukrainians struggled over the possession of this city with grim hatred, a centuries-old national rivalry. Last Friday the Poles succeeded in mastering their adversaries and hoisting the red and white flag upon the towers of Lemberg. This victory was celebrated by a three-day pogrom against the Jews."

44. Anonymous, "Drohobycz Under Ukrainian Authority (Memories)," trans. Sara Mages, in Gelber, *Sefer zikaron le-Drohobycz, Boryslaw ve-ha-seviva* [Memorial to the Jews of Drohobycz, Borysław, and surroundings], 102.

45. On September 8, 1919, the *New York Times* reported on an American commission sent by President Woodrow Wilson to investigate the pogroms in Ukraine, where "127,000 Jews have been killed and 6,000,000 are in peril." Besides Lwów, pogroms took place in Ukrainian towns including Cherkasy (more than 600 Jews killed), Zhytomyr, Dubovo (1,200 Jews murdered or chased out), Fastiv (almost 2,000 killed), Proskuriv (between 900 and 1,200 killed), and Trostyanets (between 350 and 650 killed). See Jeffrey Veidlinger, *In the Midst of Civilized Europe: The Pogroms of 1918–1921 and the Onset of the Holocaust* (Metropolitan Books, 2021); Elissa Bemporad, *Legacy of Blood: Jews, Pogroms, and Ritual Murder in the Lands of the Soviets* (Oxford University Press, 2019); and William Hagen, "The Moral Economy of Popular Violence: The Pogrom in Lwow, 1918," in *Antisemitism and Its Opponents in Modern Poland*, ed. Robert Blobaum (Cornell University Press, 2005).

46. Jan Lechoń, *Poezje*, ed. Matylda Wełna (Wydawnictwo Lubelskie, 1989), 30.

CHAPTER 3: THE SENSUOUS SAINT

1. Bruno Schulz, "An Essay for S. I. Witkiewicz," *Letters and Drawings*, 112.

2. Its members included Klemens Funkenstein, a journalist and editor; Michał Friedländer, a teacher and writer; Emmanuel (Mundek) Pilpel, a law student and connoisseur of literature and art; artist Maria Budratzka-Tempele, daughter of the president of Moriah, an organization of Zionist women; Schulz's cousin Tinka Kupferberg; Michał Chajes, a former schoolmate of Schulz's; Stanisław Weingarten, an engineer in the oil company Galicia and an admirer of Schulz's artworks; Simon Lustig; and Otokar Jawrower, a conductor of chamber music, patron of the arts, and close friend of Schulz's. See Maria Budratzka-Tempele in Ficowski, *Bruno Schulz: Listy, fragmenty, wspomnienia o pisarzu*, 42. For an interpretation of Kalleia as a cipher for Schulz's private mythology, see Jan Gondowicz, *Trans-Autentyk: Nie-czyste formy Brunona Schulza* [Trans-Authentic: Bruno Schulz's impure forms] (Warsaw: PIW), 2014.

3. Maria Budratzka to Jerzy Ficowski, 1977, quoted in *Bruno: Epoka genialna*, 329–31.

4. Bruno Schulz to Ostap Ortwin (pseudonym of Oskar Katzenellenbogen), *Księga listów*, 32. Katzenellenbogen, a journalist and literary critic, was murdered by Nazis in the spring of 1942 in Lwów.

5. Compare this with a scene from Schulz's story "Spring": "She sits opposite me on the bench beside her governess, both of them reading. Her white dress . . . lies like an open flower on the bench. Her slender, dusky legs are crossed with ineffable charm" (*Collected Stories*, 127).

6. Irena added: "When I was in eighth grade Mother showed me a folder of Schulz's drawings. There were thirteen of them: pen drawings, etchings, and copperplate engravings, tormented and tortured, thirteen steps to hell. They expressed loneliness and despair. The women were monstrous, cruel and contemptuous. Even the drawings of houses and streets seemed full of dark secrets. Mum asked: 'Now do you understand how unhappy he is?' " ("Wspomnienie Ireny Kejlin-Mitelman," Ficowski, *Bruno Schulz: Listy, fragmenty, wspomnienia o pisarzu*, 47–48; also

quoted in *Bruno: Epoka genialna*, 360–67.) None of Schulz's portraits of the Kejlin family have survived.

7. When Schulz studied there, the school had been named after the Austrian emperor Franz Joseph. By the time he began teaching there, it had taken the name of Władysław Jagiełło, a former king of Poland. By 1934, his teaching salary was 265 złotys.

8. *Letters and Drawings*, 100.

9. Schulz to Andrzej Pleśniewicz, March 4, 1936, *Księga listów*, 68. Pleśniewicz, a literary critic who knew both Schulz and Gombrowicz, would be killed in a Luftwaffe raid in early 1945.

10. Schulz to Romana Halpern, June 1939, *Księga listów*, 177.

11. "An Essay for S. I. Witkiewicz," *Letters and Drawings*, 114.

12. *Letters and Drawings*, 37.

13. Schulz to Romana Halpern, Oct. 29, 1938; *Letters and Drawings*, 190; *Księga listów*, 174.

14. Schulz to Wacław Czarski, editor of *Tygodnik Illustrowany*, winter 1934–35; *Letters and Drawings*, 98–99; *Księga listów*, 93–94. "My official duties fill me with fear and loathing," Schulz wrote to Romana Halpern, "and cast gloom over any *joie de vivre*." (Nov. 15, 1936; *Letters and Drawings*, 140; *Księga listów*, 134.)

15. Schulz to Tadeusz Breza, Dec. 2, 1934; *Letters and Drawings*, 55–56. "My nervous system has a delicacy and fastidiousness that are not up the demands of a life not sanctioned by art," Schulz wrote to Romana Halpern on August 30, 1937. "I'm afraid this school year may kill me." (*Letters and Drawings*, 151.)

16. Henryk Grynberg, *Drohobycz, Drohobycz and Other Stories: True Tales from the Holocaust and Life After*, trans. Alicia Nitecki (Penguin, 2002), 10.

17. Tadeusz Wójtowicz, "Portret Brunona Schulza z rejestrem klasowym w ręku," *Teksty Drugie* 5 (1992): 125.

18. Aleksy Kuszczak to Jerzy Ficowski, 1965; quoted in *Bruno: Epoka genialna*, 468.

19. Leopold (Paul) Lustig as told to Henryk Grynberg, "Life and Deaths: Interview with Alan Adelson," PEN America, Jan. 19, 2007; https://pen.org/life-and-deaths/.

20. Irena Subbotej, "Music Saved Me from Death: An Interview with Alfred Schreyer," *Kurier Galicyjski*, May 17–30, 2013.

21. Andrzej Chciuk, "Wspomnienie o Brunonie Schulzu," *Kultura* 7, no. 141, and 8, no. 142 (1959).

22. Emil Górski, in Ficowski, *Bruno Schulz: Listy, fragmenty, wspomnienia o pisarzu*, 70.

23. David Grossman, "The Age of Genius," trans. Stuart Schoffman, *New Yorker*, June 8–15, 2009.

24. Chaim Winter to Jerzy Ficowski, 1981; quoted in *Bruno: Epoka genialna*, 370–71.

25. Joanna Nestel, "I was a Pupil of Bruno Schulz," video interview, https://vod.tvp .pl/video/notacje,joanna-nestel-bylam-uczennica-brunona-schulza,11746006.

26. Harry Zeimer to Benjamin Geissler, Jerusalem, May 26, 2001. See also Tadeusz Linder, as told to Wiesław Budzyński: "'Sit down for a moment,' he said, and folded my hands. I posed for fifteen, maybe twenty minutes. Then he gave me this drawing: 'You have a souvenir.'" (Budzyński, *Schulz pod kluczem*, 106.)

27. Józef Sieradzki and Leon Cieślik, "Wspomnienia o Brunonie Schulzu," *Nowa Kultura* 45 (1957); quoted in *Bruno: Epoka genialna*, 371–72.

28. Regina Silberner, *Strzępy wspomnień: Przyczynek do biografii zewnętrznej Brunona Schulza* (London, 1984), 12.

29. Ibid., 11. After the war, Regina Silberner took two of Schulz's portraits of Mundek in pencil from Drohobycz to Geneva, to Princeton, and ultimately to Jerusalem.
30. Andrzej Chciuk, *Ziemia księżycowa: Druga opowieść o Księstwie Bałaku* (1989), 78–79. "The professor told us to kick him," a student named Lydia Burstin said. "He wanted us to kick him, but we were really just nudging him with our feet . . . very delicately." (Burstin as told to Krzysztof Miklaszewski, *Zatracenie się w Schulzu: Historia pewnej fascynacji* [Państwowy Instytut Wydawniczy, 2009], 193.) See also Henry J. Węgrocki, "Masochistic Motives in the Literary and Graphic Art of Bruno Schulz," *Psychoanalytic Review* (Jan. 1946), 160. Narcissism, Schulz wrote to one of his female correspondents, "is a quality that never fails to fascinate me in a woman, as an expression of a fundamental otherness, a harmony and self-affirmation that are for me unattainable. That is what will forever remain alien to me, therefore alluring and yearned after." (Schulz to Romana Halpern, Dec. 5, 1936, *Letters and Drawings*, 143.)
31. Tadeusz Lubowiecki (Izydor Friedman) to Jerzy Ficowski, 1948; quoted in *Bruno: Epoka genialna*, 381.
32. *Collected Stories*, 196.
33. "The Age of Genius," *Collected Stories*, 96.
34. Ibid., 102.
35. Letter from Michał Chajes to Jerzy Ficowski, 1948; quoted in *Bruno: Epoka genialna*, 75. In 2022, Kordegarda: The Gallery of the National Centre for Culture in Warsaw mounted an exhibition on the kinship of Lucas Cranach the Elder and Bruno Schulz. According to the curator, Katarzyna Haber, Cranach's "Eves, Judiths, and Venuses are the embodiment of beauty and cruelty. . . . Their strong, confident posture, alluring bodies, and cold glances anticipate Schulz's obsessions."
36. These included portraits of his mother, his close friend Stanislaw (Staszek) Weingarten, Stefania Czarnecka (a friend of Józefina Szelińska's later arrested by the Gestapo for "anti-German sentiments" [see United States Holocaust Memorial Museum Archives, Records of the Gestapo in Łódź, RG-15.002M, Accession Number 1991.A.0037, file 300]), Stanisława Szczepańska (an intern at the Drohobycz high school, 1934–36), Walery Brach, Emil Zegadlowicz, and Emmanuel (Mundek) Pilpel.
37. Schulz, "Review of Maria Kuncewicz's *The Foreigner*," *Letters and Drawings*, 90.
38. Overtly or obliquely, Schulz alluded to women in his life and gave some members of his gynocracy the features of friends, including Mila Lustig, Tinka Kupferberg, Dziunia Schmer (a younger sister of Naftali Backenroth's), Frederika Wegner, and a Ms. Kuziw (the daughter of a Ukrainian lawyer). As S. I. Witkiewicz put it,

    For Schulz, the female instrument of oppression over males is the leg. . . . With their legs Schulz's females stamp on, torture, and drive to desperate, helpless fury his dwarfish, humiliated and sex-tormented male-freaks, who find in their own degradation the highest form of agonized bliss. (Quoted in Stanislaw I. Witkiewicz, *Beelzebub Sonata: Plays, Essays and Documents*, ed. and trans. Daniel Gerould and Jadwiga Kosicka [1980], 144, and in Polish in Jan Gondowicz, *Bruno Schulz [1892–1942]* [Edipresse Polska, 2006], 59.)
39. See Michała Kuny, *Perypetie Schulzowskie: Ekslibrisy Brunona Schulza* [Schulz's

adventures: bookplates by Bruno Schulz], ed. Grzegorz Matusza and Roman Nowoszewski (Łódź: Łódzkie Towarzystwo Przyjaciół Książki, 2013). Goldstein, a collector of Jewish antiquities and a distinguished specialist in Jewish folk art, directed the Jewish Museum in Lwów during the Soviet occupation. He was killed in December 1942 in the Janowska concentration camp on the outskirts of Lwów.

40. Schulz to Zenon Waśniewski, April 24, 1934, *Letters and Drawings*, 73; *Księga listów*, 64. According to Schulz expert Ariko Kato, "Some cliché-verre works of Schulz identically imitated compositions of images reprinted in the double-volume book of masochistic images, *Die Weiberherrschaft in der Geschichte der Menschheit* [Female domination in the history of mankind], edited by Eduard Fuchs, a renowned art collector." See Ariko Kato, "The Early Graphic Works of Bruno Schulz and Sacher-Masoch's *Venus in Furs*," in *(Un)masking Bruno Schulz: New Combinations, Further Fragmentations, Ultimate Reintegrations*, ed. Kris Van Heuckelom and Dieter De Bruyn, (2009), 219–49, and Ariko Kato, "Eduard Fuchs i Bruno Schulz," *Schulz/Forum* 7 (2017), 240–44.

41. In August 1942, as Erwin Schenkelbach hid beneath a pile of rags under the stairs, Bertold Schenkelbach and his Vienna-born wife, Edda Hauser, were seized from their home by three Gestapo officers and deported to Belzec. Schulz's oil painting of Erwin's sister Tusia, which adorned the Schenkelbachs' apartment on Bednarska Street, has been lost. Bertold Schenkelbach's negatives, kept in his home, were destroyed. Five decades later, some thirty of his prints were discovered in New York. Erwin Schenkelbach emigrated from Warsaw to Israel in 1963. See Erwin Schenkelbach's book *The First Night with Satan* [*Pierwsza noc u Szatana*] (Kraków: Austeria, 2005) and his testimony in the Jewish Historical Institute (Warsaw) archive, record group 301, number 5900.

42. Schulz, "Review of Witold Gombrowicz's *Ferdydurke*," *Letters and Drawings*, 159–60. See also Kris Van Heuckelom, "Artistic Crossover in Polish Modernism: The Case of Bruno Schulz's *Xięga Bałwochwalcza* (The Idolatrous Booke)," *Image & Narrative*, Nov. 2006.

43. Maria Chazen to Jerzy Ficowski, quoted in *Bruno: Epoka genialna*, 74. "He uses his art to dwell on his own debasement," says Polish painter Ewa Kuryluk. "This makes contact with his work embarrassing and painful. It's like listening to a confession one does not want to hear." (Kuryluk, "The Caterpillar Car, or Bruno Schulz's Drive into the Future of the Past," *The Drawings of Bruno Schulz*, ed. Jerzy Ficowski [Northwestern University Press, 1990].)

44. Philip Roth, *Shop Talk: A Writer and His Colleagues and Their Work* (Houghton Mifflin, 2001), 82.

45. Witold Gombrowicz, "On Bruno Schulz," *New York Review of Books*, April 13, 1989. Gombrowicz achieved fame in 1938 with his novel *Ferdydurke*, which Schulz praised as "an extraordinary manifestation of literary talent, a new and revolutionary novelistic method and form. . . . Gombrowicz has demonstrated . . . that life can get along very well without endorsement from above; that it thrives better under five crushing fathoms of abomination and shame than on the heights of sublimation." (Schulz, *"Ferdydurke,"* *Skamander* 96–98 [July–Sept., 1938], trans. Paul Coates, based on Schulz's January 1938 talk on *Ferdydurke* at the Polish Writers' Union in Warsaw.) After his murder, says one critic, "Bruno Schulz became Gombrowicz's intimate double . . . his dybbuk." (Jean-Pierre Salgas, "Gombrowicz-Schulz, du duel au double" [Gombrowicz-Schulz, from duel to double], *L'infini*, Spring 2015.) See also Dorota Głowacka, "The Heresiarchs

of Form: Gombrowicz and Schulz," in *Gombrowicz's Grimaces: Modernism, Gender, Nationality*, ed. Ewa Płonowska Ziarek (State University of New York Press, 1998), 65–88, and Jan Kott, "On Gombrowicz and Schulz," trans. Jadwiga Kosicka, in *Memory of the Body: Essays on Theater and Death* (Northwestern University Press, 1992).

46. Leopold von Sacher-Masoch—the writer from whose name the German sexologist Richard von Krafft-Ebing, in his monumental 1886 taxonomy of sexual perversions, derived the term "masochism"—was both a product of Galicia himself and an amateur ethnographer of Galician character types, as evidenced in his first work of fiction, "A Galician Tale" (1858). Bohdan Budurowycz writes: "Just as Sacher-Masoch gained immortality when the term derived from his surname was added to the dictionary of sexual aberrations, so Schulz acquired renown on account of his masochistic tendencies." Although masochism, he adds, "cannot be solely tied to a given place or region, its Galician pedigree remains indisputable." ("Galicja w twórczości Brunona Schulza" [Galicia in the works of Bruno Schulz], in *Bruno Schulz: In Memoriam 1892–1942*, ed. Małgorzata Kitowska-Łysiak, trans. Monika Adamczyk-Grabowska, 1992.)

47. For a review of the 1922 exhibition, see A. Bienenstock, "Z wystawy wiosennej: Prace graficzne Brunona Schulza" [From the spring exhibition: Graphic works by Bruno Schulz], *Chwila* 1213 (1922). For a review of the December 1935 group exhibition in Lwów, see Karol Kuryluk, "Życie kulturalne we Lwowie" [Cultural life in Lwów], *Tygodnik Illustrowany* 77, no. 5 (Feb. 2, 1936): 96.

48. Juliusz Flaszen, quoted in *Letters and Drawings*, 67; and quoted in John Updike, "The Visionary of Drohobycz," *New York Times*, Oct. 30, 1988.

49. Schulz to Romana Halpern, March 20, 1938, *Letters and Drawings*, 179; *Księga listów*, 162.

50. Juliusz Flaszen to Jerzy Ficowski, June 1, 1948, *Letters and Drawings*, 67.

51. Artur Lauterbach writing in *Chwila* in 1929; quoted in Bruno Schulz, *The Booke of Idolatry*, ed. Jerzy Ficowski (Interpress, 1989), 12.

52. Both quoted in Jerzy Ficowski, "Bruno Schulz and His Drawings," *Drawings of Bruno Schulz* (Israel Museum, 1990), 12. See also Debora Vogel's review of that exhibition: "Bruno Schulz," *Judisk Tidskrift* 3 (1930): 224–26.

53. S. I. Witkiewicz, "Interview with Bruno Schulz," *Letters and Drawings*, 107–09; originally published in *Tygodnik Ilustrowany*, 76, no. 17 (1935).

CHAPTER 4: THE WRITER DISCOVERED

1. Schulz to Romana Halpern, Dec. 5, 1936.

2. On February 20, 1940, representatives of the Soviet NKVD and the Gestapo met for a week in Zakopane to coordinate the pacification of resistance in Poland. The German delegation was led by Adolf Eichmann, the Soviet team by Grigoriy Litvinov. There they planned the wholesale murder of Polish intelligentsia and of Polish officers held by the Soviet Union as prisoners of war.

3. Schulz to Witkiewicz, April 12, 1934, *Księga listów*, 104; Prokopczyk, *Bruno Schulz: New Documents and Interpretations*, 24; first published in *Twórczości*, June 1982.

4. Debora Vogel's letters to her uncle Rabbi Marcus Ehrenpreis are preserved in the Ehrenpreis archives (E1:3–E1:28), housed in the Archives of the Jewish Community Stockholm.

5. Debora Vogel was the author of two volumes of poetry, *Day Figures* (1930, illustrated by Henryk Streng) and *Mannequins* (1934), and the prose montage *Acacias Bloom* (1935). Jurko Prochaśko, mentioned in chapter 1, translated all three books into Ukrainian (2015, 2018). *Acacias Bloom* appeared in Polish as *Akacje kwitną* (Austeria, 2006). For Vogel's writing in English, see *Blooming Spaces: The Collected Poetry, Prose, Critical Writing, and Letters of Debora Vogel*, ed. Anastasiya Lyubas (Academic Studies Press, 2020). Lyubas's volume follows a 2016 German edition of Vogel's writing, *Die Geometrie des Verzichts* (The geometry of renunciation), edited and translated by Anna Maja Misiak, the first edition of Vogel's work in any language to include all her prose and poetry. Adrienne Rich translated Vogel's poem "On Longing" for *A Treasury of Yiddish Literature*, ed. Irving Howe and Eliezer Greenberg (Schocken, 1969).

   In his memoir *My Century* (W. W. Norton, 1988, trans. Richard Lourie), the Polish poet Aleksander Wat credits Vogel ("a very intelligent woman, a subtle critic") for his survival of a Soviet prison during World War II. Vogel was murdered—along with her mother; her husband, Szulim Barenblüth; and their six-year-old son, Asher—in the Lwów ghetto in August 1942.

   On the relationship between Vogel and Schulz, see Annette Werberger, "Nur eine Muse? Die jiddische Schriftstellerin Debora Vogel und Bruno Schulz," in *Ins Wort gesetzt, ins Bild gesetzt: Gender in Wissenschaft, Kunst und Literatur*, eds. Ingrid Hotz-Davies and Schamma Schahadat (Transcript Verlag, 2009), 257–86. For Vogel's views on S. I. Witkiewicz, see Debora Vogel, "Pozycja Stanisława Ignacego Witkiewicza we współczesnej kulturze polskiej" [Stanisław Ignacy Witkiewicz's position in contemporary Polish culture], *Pomost* 1 (1931), and Janusz Degler, "Debora Vogel i Witkacy," *Ogród* 17 (1994): 208–12. Witkiewicz recounts his conversations with Vogel in his 1932 novel *Narkotyki*, published in English as *Narcotics*, trans. Soren Gauger (Twisted Spoon Press, 2018). On Vogel's pedagogical practices, see Maks Schaff, "The Publication of the Home for Orphans in Lwów, Zborowska 8," in *For the Good of the Nation: Institutions for Jewish Children in Interwar Poland; A Documentary History*, ed. S. Martin (Academic Studies Press, 2017), 64–71, and Anna Maja Misiak, "Reading as the Shaping Force of Life: Debora Vogel's Contributions to Education," *In geveb*, Oct. 2021. See also Irena Kossowska, "In Search for Cultural Identity: Bruno Schulz, Debora Vogel and Giorgio de Chirico," in *Art in Jewish Society*, ed. Jerzy Malinowski, Renata Piątkowska, Małgorzata Stolarska-Fronia, and Tamara Sztyma (Polish Institute of World Art Studies/ Tako Publishing House, 2016), 161–170.

6. "Dwojre Fogel," in Melekh Ravitch, *Majn leksikon* (Montreal: Aroysgegebn fun a Komitet, 1945; in Yiddish); quoted in Karolina Szymaniak, *Być agentem wiecznej idei* (Universitas, 2006), 33 (in Polish).

7. Debora Vogel to Schulz, Dec. 7, 1938, *Księga listów*, 245; also quoted in Anna Maja Misiak, "Im Schatten von Bruno Schulz," *Neue Zürcher Zeitung*, Aug. 8, 2008.

8. Schulz to Romana Halpern, Nov. 29, 1936, *Letters and Drawings*, 142.

9. This according to Ella Schulz-Podstolska, daughter of Izydor and Regina Schulz, in a letter to Jerzy Ficowski (June 16, 1992). Ernestina Kupferberg survived the war and lived in Düsseldorf into her nineties.

10. Quoted in Szymaniak, *Być agentem wiecznej idei*, 45.

11. Schulz to Andrzej Pleśniewicz, March 4, 1936, *Letters and Drawings*, 125.

12. Walter Benjamin, "Theses on the Philosophy of History," *Illuminations* (Schocken,

1968). For a comparison of Schulz's *Cinnamon Shops* with Walter Benjamin's *Berlin Childhood Around 1900*, see Jurko Prochaśko, "Sfinks w labiryncie: Walter Benjamin i Bruno Schulz w poszukiwaniach utraconego dzieciństwa," *Konteksty* 2019 (1–2): 147–52.

13. Schulz, "The Book," *Collected Stories*, 92.

14. Vogel and Auerbach met in a philosophy seminar in 1928, and the next year cofounded the Yiddish-language literary journal *Tsushtayer* (Contribution), which published both Eastern European and North American writers. (The Yiddish verb *tsushtayern* connotes "reaching the shore.") For more on the journal *Tsushtayer*, see Adam Stepnowski, "Debora Vogel w galicyjskim jidyszlandzie: Czasopismo *Cusztajer*" [Debora Vogel in Galician Yiddishland: The *Tsushtayer* journal], *Schulz/Forum* 16 (2020): 176–90. After moving from Galicia to Warsaw in 1933, Auerbach worked for the Jewish-Polish newspaper *Nowe Słowo* and became the companion of prominent Yiddish poet Itzik Manger. During the war, she was active in the underground Oyneg Shabes archive led by Emanuel Ringelblum in the Warsaw ghetto. (See Samuel D. Kassow, *Who Will Write Our History? Emanuel Ringelblum, the Warsaw Ghetto, and the Oyneg Shabes Archive* (Indiana University Press, 2007), and David G. Roskies, *Voices from the Warsaw Ghetto* (Yale University Press, 2019). After three years in the ghetto, she wrote "Yizker," a powerful elegy for Warsaw's Jews (translated from Yiddish into English in *The Literature of Destruction: Jewish Responses to Catastrophe*, ed. David Roskies, 1988). One of only three survivors of the Oyneg Shabbes group, she immigrated to Israel in 1950, where she vehemently rejected the German reparations agreement in the early 1950s. Starting in 1954, she served as the first director of Yad Vashem's Department for the Collection of Witness Testimony. In May 1961, she testified at the Eichmann trial in Jerusalem. Auerbach died in Tel Aviv in 1976. Her personal archive is housed in thirty-eight boxes at Yad Vashem. See Boaz Cohen, "Rachel Auerbach, Yad Vashem, and Israeli Holocaust Memory," *Polin: Studies in Polish Jewry* 20 (2008): 197–221, and Karolina Szymaniak, "On the Ice Floe: Rachel Auerbach," in *Catastrophe and Utopia*, ed. Ferenc Laczo and Joachim von Puttkamer (De Gruyter, 2017), 304–52. For Auerbach's recollections of Vogel and Schulz, see her articles "Nisht oysgeshpunene fedem" [Unfinished weaving] in *Di goldene keyt* [The golden shackle] 50 (1964): 131–43 (Yiddish); "Comment est mort Bruno Schulz," *Les lettres nouvelles*, Oct.–Nov. 1966 (French); and "The Polish Kafka: Memories of Bruno Schulz," *Haaretz*, Dec. 28, 2012 (Hebrew).

15. Schulz read Proust's *In Search of Lost Time* in the Polish translation by Tadeusz Boy-Zelenrski. Schulz reviewed Aragon's novel *Bells of Basel* in 1936. Schulz sent Joseph Roth, a fellow Galician writer then living in Paris, a dedicated copy of *Cinnamon Shops* in 1934, praising works of Roth's he had read: *Radetzky-marsch* (1932), *Zipper und sein Vater* (1928), and *Rechts und Links* (1929).

16. Regina Silberner, *Strzępy wspomnień*, 12. As Pilpel was dying of lung cancer in 1936, Schulz visited him daily. "During this painfully protracted disease," Silberner reports, "Schulz faithfully visited his friend. But as my father later told me, Mundek [Pilpel] could stand his presence less and less, once throwing out Schulz. He explained to my father that Bruno seemed to be inspired by this atmosphere, that he liked that stench" (Silberner, 20). The papers of Regina and Edmund Silberner are housed at the National Library of Israel (ARC. 4* 1629).

17. "An Essay for S. I. Witkiewicz," *Letters and Drawings*, 114.

18. Schulz to Stefan Szuman, July 24, 1932, *Letters and Drawings*, 36.

19. Zofia Nałkowska's best-known novel, *Boundary*, was translated into English by Ursula Phillips (Northern Illinois University Press, 2016). Czesław Miłosz called it "one of the milestones of the 'somber thirties.'" In her short book *Medallions* (1946), she wrote about the horrors of World War II in Poland; the work was based on her participation in the Commission for Investigating Nazi Crimes. See also Schulz's essay "Zofia Nałkowska na tle swojej nowej powieści" ["Zofia Nałkowska against the backdrop of her new novel"], *Skamander*, April 1939, and Ewa Kraskowska, "Nałkowska i Schulz, Schulz i Nałkowska," *Teksty Drugie* (1999): 211–27.

    Rój, founded in 1924 by Marian Kister and co-owned by Melchior Wańkowicz, also published books by the young Polish writers Julian Tuwim and Witold Gombrowicz, and Polish translations of books by Marcel Proust, Thomas Mann, Aldous Huxley, Sinclair Lewis, Bertrand Russell, and John Steinbeck. During World War II, Marian Kister reestablished the firm in New York as Roy Publishers.

20. This account, related by Alicia Giangrande, is quoted in Jerzy Ficowski, *Regions of the Great Heresy*, 63–64. Alicia Giangrande (previously known as Jakarda Goldblum) gave her account in a letter to Ficowski (April 16, 1985). In 1939, Alicia escaped from Poland to Brazil before settling in Buenos Aires, Argentina. See also the recollections Paweł Zieliński, Magdalena Gross's husband, shared with Ficowski in 1948: "Wspomnienie Pawła Zielińskiego," in Ficowski, *Bruno Schulz: Listy, fragmenty, wspomnienia o pisarzu*, 63–66. According to Zieliński, the "copious correspondence" between Schulz and Magdalena Gross was lost during World War II. See also Zdzisław Bau, "Wspomnienie Alicji Giangrande," *Gombrowicz w Argentynie: Świadectwa i dokumenty 1939–1963* [Gombrowicz in Argentina: testimonies and documents 1939–1963], 2004.

21. In September 1933, Nałkowska wrote, "I'm no longer in love with Miroslav Krleža, only Bruno Schulz. I saw him in August for two days in Warsaw and here in [Wołomin] Górki [her hilltop estate east of Warsaw]. I'm surrounded by his letters, which help me come to terms with myself. And his pictures! They do not express great joy, but rather a secret, sad happiness." (Zofia Nałkowska, *Dzienniki IV 1930–1939: Część 1 (1930–1934)*, ed. Hanna Kirchner [Warsaw, 1988], 388.) In 1934, Nałkowska began a love affair with a much younger man named Bogusław Kuczyński, who refused to allow her to meet Schulz alone; in a fit of jealousy, he destroyed a hand-illustrated copy of *Cinnamon Shops* that Schulz had bound in brown silk and inscribed to her. For her recollections on Schulz, see also Zofia Nałkowska, "Z Dzienników Bruno Schulz," *Twórczość* 12 (1974): 66–80.

22. See Zofia Nałkowska's diary entry, March 2, 1934, *Dzienniki IV 1930–1939: Część 1 (1930–1934)*, 416.

23. Schulz's description of *Cinnamon Shops* (*Letters and Drawings*, 153) was discovered in Buenos Aires in 1973, thirty-seven years after he wrote it.

24. "Spring," *Collected Stories*, 109.

25. Ibid., 113.

26. "Cockroaches," *Collected Stories*, 62. In the story "Mannequins," the father appears as a kind of magus: "In contact with that unusual man, all things somehow retreated to the root of their being . . . returned to some extent to the primal idea, in order to betray it at that point and incline toward those dubious, risky, and ambiguous regions that we shall refer to, in short, as the regions of the great heresy." (*Collected Stories*, 24.)

27. "A Visitation," *Collected Stories*, 11.

28. "Mannequins," *Collected Stories*, 20.
29. *Letters and Drawings*, 154. The mother remains on the periphery of the narrator's imagination: "That was a very long time ago. Mother was not there yet. I spent my days alone with Father in our room, which was then as great as the world." ("The Book," *Collected Stories*, 84.) For commentary on this passage, see Russell E. Brown, "Bruno Schulz: The Myth of Origins," *Russian Literature* 22 (1987): 200–01.
30. "A Treatise on Mannequins; or, The Second Book of Genesis," *Collected Stories*, 25.
31. According to Jerzy Ficowski, "Spared by his mother, who never raised her hand against him, Bruno was often punished by his nanny when his parents were not at home. He never complained about this, and only many years later did he confide to someone close to him that probably those dim and apparently minor incidents were the cause of his masochistic tendencies, which in time developed and intensified." (Ficowski, *Regions of the Great Heresy*, 40.)
32. "Birds," *Collected Stories*, 17.
33. "A Treatise on Mannequins; or, The Second Book of Genesis," *Collected Stories*, 28. In Schulz's story "The Age of Genius," a thief just released from jail contemplates Adela's shoe with great seriousness before stealing it:

> And lifting Adela's slender slipper with horror, he spoke as if spellbound by the glossy, ironic eloquence of that empty lacquer shell. "Do you understand the monstrous cynicism of this symbol on a woman's foot, the provocation of her dissolute tread on these ingenious heels? How could I leave you under the power of this symbol? God forbid that I would do this . . ." ("The Age of Genius," *Collected Stories*, 102–03.)

34. Tadeusz Breza, "Sobowtór zwykłej rzeczywistości," *Kurier Poranny* 3 (1934). Schulz had reviewed Breza's debut novel, *Adam Grywald* (1936).
35. Stanisław Ignacy Witkiewicz, March 1, 1934, *Listy do żony (1932–1935)*, ed. Anna Micińska and Janusz Degler (Warsaw, 2010), 198. "This debut," raved *A Portrait of Contemporary Polish Literature*, "is in its art so completely different, unprecedented, and mature, that it does not appear to have any precursors; here we have an enormously unique literary event." (Kazimierz Czachowski, *Obraz współczesnej literatury polskiej, 1884–1933 [A portrait of contemporary Polish literature, 1884–1933]*, 3 vols. (Lwów: Państwowe Wydawnictwo Książek Szkolnych, 1934–36.) See Antoni Gronowicz, "Letter to the editor," *Polish Review* 22, no. 1 (1977): 66.
36. Czesław Miłosz, "A Few Words on Bruno Schulz," *New Republic*, Jan. 2, 1989.
37. Włodzimierz Bolecki, "Three Modernists: Witkacy–Schulz–Gombrowicz," trans. David Malcolm, *Tekstualia* (January 2014): 11. "The great trinity of Witold Gombrowicz, Bruno Schulz, and Stanisław Witkiewicz," adds Milan Kundera, "anticipated the European modernism of the 1950s." (Kundera, "The Tragedy of Central Europe [1984]," in *Re: Thinking Europe: Thoughts on Europe; Past, Present and Future* [Amsterdam University Press, 2016], 199.) See also Jerzy Jarzębski, "Witkacy, Schulz, and Gombrowicz Versus the Avant-Garde," in *The Slavic Literatures and Modernism: A Nobel Symposium (August 5–8, 1985)*, ed. Nils Åke Nilsson (Stockholm: Almqvist & Wiksell International, 1987), 151–65, and Alexander Emanuely, "Die drei Musketiere in der toten Klasse: Gombrowicz, Schulz, Witkacy, Kantor," *Context* 21, nos. 4–5 (2004).

38. Rokhl Korn, "'Tzimring gevelber' fun Bruno Schulz," *Literarishe Bleter*, April 20, 1934; trans. Karen Underhill. Born to a family of Jewish farmers in Galicia, Korn published her first volume of Yiddish poems, *Dorf*, in 1927.

39. Kornelja Grafowa, "Jedna dziwna książka" ["One strange book"], *Chwila*, Feb. 1934, 11–12.

40. Ignacy Fik, "Literatura choromaniaków," quoted in Dieter De Bruyn and Kris Van Heuckelom, "Introduction: Seven Decades of Schulzology," *(Un)masking Bruno Schulz*, 10.

41. Zofia Nałkowska, *Diaries*, Jan. 16, 1934.

42. Zofia Nałkowska, *Dzienniki IV 1930–1939: Część 1 (1930–1934)*, 448.

43. Schulz to Zenon Waśniewski, April 24, 1934, *Letters and Drawings*, 77; *Księga listów*, 63.

44. Schulz to Zenon Waśniewski, Nov. 7, 1934, *Księga listów*, 74.

45. Izabela Czermakowa, "Wspomnienie o Schulzu" ["A remembrance of Schulz"], *Schulz/Forum* 4 (2014): 103–08; originally published as "Bruno Schulz," *Twórczość* 19 (1965): 99–102.

46. Quoted in David Grossman, "The Age of Genius," *New Yorker*, June 8–15, 2009.

47. Emmanuel Weintraub to Benjamin Geissler, Paris, Sept. 28, 2001.

48. "Letters and Applications to Regional and National School Authorities, 1924–1938," trans. Dorota Glowacka, Prokopczyk, *Bruno Schulz: New Documents and Interpretations*, 11–13, 17–18. In 1987, Iwan Łoziński discovered eighteen letters Schulz had sent to regional school authorities to request leaves of absence in the Central Historical Archive in Lwów. See Iwan Łoziński, "Nieznane listy Brunona Schulza," *Literatura Radziecka* 7 (1987): 155–68.

49. "Spring," *Collected Stories*, 147.

50. Józefina Szelińska to Jerzy Ficowski, Sept. 5, 1967, quoted in *Bruno: Epoka genialna*, 414–15. See also Aleksy Kuszczak's letter to Ficowski, July 30, 1965.

51. Józefina Szelińska to Jerzy Ficowski, 1965; quoted in Ficowski, *Regiony wielkiej herezji i okolice*, 2002, 325.

52. Ibid.

53. Ibid.

54. Schulz to Maria Kasprowiczowa, Jan. 25, 1934, *Listy Brunona Schulza*, http://www.brunoschulz.org/kasprowiczowej.htm (trans. Timothy Williams). This letter, discovered in 1992 by Roman Loth in the Jan Kasprowicz archives, was published in *Polityka i kultura* 11 (1992).

55. Schulz to Zenon Waśniewski, Jan. 28, 1935, *Księga listów*, 78.

56. Andrzej Chciuk's letter to Jerzy Ficowski, April 13, 1966.

57. Schulz to Romana Halpern [undated, likely early Nov. 1936], *Letters and Drawings*, 138; *Księga listów*, 132.

58. Schulz to Romana Halpern, Sept. 19, 1936, *Letters and Drawings*, 134; *Księga listów*, 127.

59. Schulz to Romana Halpern, Sept. 30, 1936, *Księga listów*, 130.

60. Still, Jerzy Ficowski says, "his being a Jew posed a problem. To non-Jews, even those that were not prejudiced, this very fact created a symbolic ghetto around him. . . . One could say that he removed himself from the ritual of the synagogue to the temple of the arts. Nevertheless, he always remained fascinated by the magic of Jewish ritual and was peculiarly sensitive to it. On High Holidays, and especially on Yom Kippur, he used to go to the synagogue in Drohobycz. There, as one of a congregation immersed in prayer, he would be moved not only by being

at one with the mystery of his ancestry, but also experienced that which was one of the mainsprings of his own creativity: the moulding of a day-like-any-other into something sacred and mythical." (Ficowski, "On the Cross-roads of Three Cultures: The Life and Work of Bruno Schulz," *Jewish Quarterly*, Spring 1979.) "His ties with his own genealogy," Ficowski writes elsewhere, "marginal in the present, mainly had to do with prehistory, with the mythic ancestors in the mythic Bible of his own devising." (Ficowski, introduction to *The Street of Crocodiles*, by Bruno Schulz, trans. Celina Wieniewska [Penguin, 1977], 22.) The account of Schulz's visit to the Zaddik is from Schulz's niece, Ella Schulz-Podstolska.

61. Hanna Mortkowicz-Olczakowa, "Bruno Schulz: Wspomnienie" [Bruno Schulz: A reminiscence], *Przekrój* 67 (March 23, 1958): 22.

62. Letter from Józefina Szelińska to Jerzy Ficowski, 1967; quoted in *Bruno: Epoka genialna*, 473. The translation was issued by the Zdrój publishing house in Warsaw; it would be reprinted in 1957. Apart from *The Trial*, Szelińska also translated two of Kafka's story fragments: "The Bucket Rider" (1921) and "The Hunter Gracchus" (1931). Wanda Kragen, herself a distinguished translator from German into Polish, called Schulz "Kafka's predestined translator" (Wanda Kragen, "Twórczość Franciszka Kafki," *Chwila*, Aug. 1936). Kafka's writing, banned in Poland after World War II, reappeared only in October 1956, when "The Penal Colony," translated by Witold Wirpsza, was published in the literary magazine *Twórczość*.

63. *Letters and Drawings*, 88; *Collected Works*, 349.

64. Schulz, "Tragic Freedom," in Prokopczyk, *Bruno Schulz: New Documents and Interpretations*, 48. A German critic called Schulz's *Cinnamon Shops* "a modern version of Ovid's *Metamorphoses*, albeit with a pessimistic twist." (Stefanie Peter, "Diese Wirklichkeit ist dünn wie Papier," *Frankfurter Allgemeine Zeitung*, March 27, 2008.)

65. "An Essay for S. I. Witkiewicz," *Letters and Drawings*, 113; *Collected Works*, 369.

66. "Cockroaches," *Collected Stories*, 65. One reviewer of *Sanatorium Under the Sign of the Hourglass* said the author inhabited "the same mental climate" as Franz Kafka. (Marian Promiński, "Nowości literackie," *Sygnały* 40 [1938].) Yet for most critics the divergences run deeper than the affinities. "They both are Jews and come from the Austro-Hungarian Empire," Artur Sandauer wrote, "they both combine the biblical tradition with that of German culture, they both transcend from reality into myth. . . . There is, however, one basic difference: Kafka's world is bound to goodness, while Schulz's succumbs to a fascination with evil." (Sandauer, "Présentation de Bruno Schulz I," *Lettres nouvelles*, July 8, 1959.) Jerzy Ficowski likewise insisted on the dissimilarities: "Schulz was a metaphysician garbed in all the wealth of color; Kafka was a mystic in a hair shirt of worldly denials." (*Regions of the Great Heresy*, 101.) Schulz's world, writes the British literary critic John Bayley, "does not in the least resemble Kafka's. There is no quest, no terrible unknown compulsions, no anguish before the law." (Bayley, "The Power of Delight," *New York Review of Books*, April 13, 1989.) The Polish artist and art historian Ewa Kuryluk writes, "Franz Kafka and Bruno Schulz are two outstanding citizens of 'The Republic of Dreams,' to use Schulz's beautiful metaphor, capable of transmuting acute observation into prophecy by circumscribing reveries and nightmares as precisely as if they were facts of life." Although both writers exhibit a preoccupation with male degradation, Kuryluk

notes, "Kafka renders debasement in a dry, hard-edged German with a deliberately bureaucratic and rabbinic touch," while Schulz registers it "in an overheated, poetic Polish of a grotesque visual artist inspired by the sensuality, irony, and wit of Hasidic storytelling." (Ewa Kuryluk, "The Caterpillar Car, or Bruno Schulz's Drive into the Future of the Past," *Drawings of Bruno Schulz*, ed. Jerzy Ficowski [Northwestern University Press, 1990], 38, 42.)

For more comparisons of Schulz and Kafka, see: Paul Coates, "Bruno Schulz and Franz Kafka," *Canadian Slavonic Papers* 3, no. 4 (1989); Paul Coates, "Transformation and Oblivion: Bruno Schulz and Franz Kafka," *The Double and the Other: Identity as Ideology in Post-Romantic Fiction* (Macmillan, 1988); Paul Kruntorad, "Bruno Schulz: Ein Vergleich mit Franz Kafka," *Wort in der Zeit* 3 (March 1965): 9–19 (German); Leonard Orr, "The 'Kafkaesque' Fantastic in the Fiction of Kafka and Bruno Schulz," *Newsletter of the Kafka Society of America* 6, nos. 1–2 (June–Dec. 1982): 34–40; Margarita Pazi, "Bruno Schulz— Ähnlichkeit mit Kafka?," in *Galizien als gemeinsame Literaturlandschaft*, eds. Fridrun Rinner and Klaus Zerinschek (Innsbruck: Institut für Sprachwissenschaften, 1988), 95–104 (German); Margarita Pazi, "Bruno Schulz v'Kafka: HaYesh Beynehem Min HaDimyon?" [Bruno Schulz and Kafka: Are there similarities?], *Ravkol*, 1989 (Hebrew); Marcel Reich-Ranicki, "Bruno Schulz: Ein polnischer Kafka?," in *Erst leben, dann spielen: Über polnische Literatur* (Wallstein Verlag, 2002), 75–78 (German); Beate Sommerfeld, *Kafka-Nachwirkungen in der polnischen Literatur: unter besonderer Berücksichtigung der achtziger und neunziger Jahre des zwanzigsten Jahrhunderts*, Peter Lang Publishing, 2007 (German); Johanne Villeneuve, "Le livre animé: Bruno Schulz et Frank Kafka," *Textimage: Revue d'étude du dialogue texte-image*, Summer 2014 (French); and Andrzej Wirth, "Nachwort zur ersten deutschen Ausgabe," in Bruno Schulz, *Die Republik der Träume*, ed. Mikołaj Dutsch (Hanser, 1967), 336–42 (German).

67. "The Night of the Great Season," *Collected Stories*, 72.

68. Regina Silberner, *Strzępy wspomnień*, 21.

69. "In my imagination," Schulz wrote to Romana Halpern, "I've already been fired from my job and plunged into abject poverty. When I see the town idiots and the ragged beggars, the thought springs to mind that I may look like that soon." (Schulz to Halpern, Nov. 15, 1936, *Letters and Drawings*, 140; *Księga listów*, 133–34.) For his fiancée's observations of Schulz's feeling for fatherhood and family, see Józefina Szelińska to Jerzy Ficowski, 1965, quoted in *Bruno: Epoka genialna*, 425. For her recollection of his beggar image, see Szelińska to Ficowski, 1968, quoted in *Bruno: Epoka genialna*, 581. "Himself sunk in poverty," Ficowski writes, "he never refused alms to a beggar." (Ficowski, *Regions of the Great Heresy*, 53.) One Polish scholar writes, "Schulz is the writer of destitution and longing: a destitution which is found by no means only in external circumstances, but seethes deep down inside his characters." (Czesława Samojlik, "Groteska—pisarstwo wszechstronnie banalne . . . Sprawa prozy Brunona Schulza," in *Z problemów literatury polskiej XX wieku*, vol. 2, ed. Alina Brodzka and Zbigniew Żabicki [Państwowy Instytut Wydawniczy, 1965], 295.)

70. Józefina Szelińska to Jerzy Ficowski, Sept. 5, 1967 (private letter, unpublished).

71. Bruno Schulz to Tadeusz and Zofia Breza, June 8, 1937; *Letters and Drawings*, 65; *Księga listów*, 57. In a letter to Kazimierz Truchanowski of April 11, 1936, Schulz refers to "the undermining of my union with a loving, brave, unusual woman because of my material circumstances" (*Letters and Drawings*, 106).

72. After learning of Schulz's murder, Józefina Szelińska fled Warsaw and found refuge working in the Laski Catholic orphanage and school for the blind, which had been turned into a makeshift hospital. She later reported that during the war she had left a package of about two hundred letters from Schulz to her in the attic under the rafters of her family home in Janów. They were presumed destroyed. Elżbieta Ficowska, the wife of Schulz biographer Jerzy Ficowski, gave Agata Tuszyńska seventy-nine letters and postcards Józefina Szelińska sent to Ficowski beginning in 1948. See Agata Tuszyńska, *La fiancée de Bruno Schulz*, trans. Isabelle Jannès-Kalinowski (Grasset, 2015), in French; originally published in Polish as *Narzeczona Schulza* (Wydawnictwo Literackie, 2015).

73. Agata Tuszyńska, "About Bruno Schulz and His Fiancée, Józefina Szelińska," talk delivered in Cleveland, May 3, 2019 (unpublished).

74. Schulz to Zenon Waśniewski, June 2, 1937, *Księga listów*, 84–85.

75. Schulz to Andrzej Plesniewicz, Nov. 29, 1936, *Letters and Drawings*, 127; *Księga listów*, 74.

76. Schulz to Romana Halpern, Aug. 16, 1936, *Letters and Drawings*, 133. In 1989, Romana Halpern's son, who on immigrating to Los Angeles had taken the name Stephen J. Howard, gave the Adam Mickiewicz Museum thirty-eight letters from Schulz to Romana Halpern.

77. Sept. 30, 1936, *Letters and Drawings*, 136; *Księga listów*, 129. In August 1937, Schulz wrote to Romana Halpern, "What I lack is not so much faith in my own gifts but something more pervasive: trust in life, confident acquiescence in a personal destiny, faith in the ultimate benevolence of existence." (*Letters and Drawings*, 148.)

78. Schulz to Romana Halpern, Nov. 29, 1936, *Letters and Drawings*, 142; *Księga listów*, 136. Schulz expressed a similar sentiment two days later in a letter to Andrzej Pleśniewicz, in which he ascribed his "meager production" to "a lack of discipline or of the technique of living, an inability to arrange my day. I surrender to the prejudice that creative work may begin only when . . . all difficulties are dealt with, nothing threatens me, and a breath of cheerfulness hovers over the 'reassured' soul." (Schulz to Andrzej Pleśniewicz, Dec. 1, 1936, *Księga listów*, 116.)

79. Schulz to Romana Halpern, Sept. 30, 1936, *Letters and Drawings*, 136; *Księga listów*, 129.

80. Schulz to Romana Halpern, April 30, 1937, and July 24, 1937, *Letters and Drawings*, 144–45; *Księga listów*, 139, 147. After the first great "liquidation action" in July 1942, Romana Halpern escaped from the Warsaw ghetto to Kraków (where she lived under a false name, Janina Sokołowska). She was shot by the Gestapo in late 1944. The location of her grave is unknown.

81. Schulz to Romana Halpern, Aug. 20–26, 1937, *Letters and Drawings*, 149.

82. The contract added, "Rój purchases from Mr. Bruno Schulz his text entitled *Sanatorium Under the Sign of the Hourglass*, of which it will publish 1,000 numbered copies. . . . As payment, the Author will receive 15 percent of the gross price of the book, which shall be established in the amount between 6 and 10 polish złotys. The Author will receive half of the payment before the book is published; and the other half in three equal monthly installments after the book is printed. The Author will receive 15 complimentary copies of his book."

83. Schulz to Romana Halpern, Aug. 16, 1937, *Letters and Drawings*, 147; *Księga listów*, 142.

84. *Letters and Drawings*, 146.
85. Quoted in Celina Wieniewska, "Translator's Preface," *The Complete Fiction of Bruno Schulz* (Walker, 1989), xi. In his review, Emil Breiter praised the way Schulz's exuberant, almost euphoric writing blurred the real and the unreal while retaining an "intrinsic outward logic." (*Wiadomości Literackie* [Literary news], May 29, 1938.) For Schulz's ambivalence about *Sanatorium*, see his letter to Zenon Waśniewski, June 2, 1937: "I'm not pleased with the book." (*Księga listów*, 85.) "Your words about the book have given me a lot of pleasure," Schulz wrote to Romana Halpern. "It's very good that you like it. I nearly stopped believing in it. Nobody apart from you has said something good about it to me." (Schulz to Halpern, Jan. 23, 1938, *Księga listów*, 154.)
86. Ludwik Fryde, "O *Ferdydurke* Gombrowicza," *Pióro* 1 (1938). See also Barbara Lewitówna, "Proza Brunona Schulza," *Ster* 5 (1938): 7, in which the reviewer says that Schulz's prose, however enriching its dreamlike distortions of reality, "is not intended for the general public."
87. Stefan Napierski and Kazimierz Wyka, "Dwugłos o Schulzu," *Ateneum*, Jan. 1939. For a full discussion of this review, see Maciej Urbanowski, "Ja rozpisałem się bardzo, bo żółć mnie zalała," *Schulz/Forum* 8 (2016): 143–50, and the letter from Stefan Napierski to Kazimierz Wyka (Nov. 15, 1938), published in the same issue of *Schulz/Forum*. On the contemporaneous reception of Schulz's fiction in Poland, see Włodzimierz Bolecki, *Poetycki model prozy w dwudziestoleciu międzywojennym: Witkacy, Gombrowicz, Schulz i inni* [A poetic model of interwar fiction: Witkacy, Gombrowicz, Schulz, and others] (Universitas, 1996).
88. Bruno Schulz to Tadeusz Breza (culture editor of *Kurier poranny*), June 21, 1934, *Letters and Drawings*, 54.
89. Jerzy Pomianowski, *To proste: Opowieści Jerzego Pomianowskiego nagrane przez Joannę Szwedowską dla Programu II Polskiego Radia* ["It's simple: Jerzy Pomianowski's stories as recorded by Joanna Szwedowska for Program II of Polish Radio"], ed. Elżbieta Jogałła (Austeria, 2015), 216.
90. Alicja Mondschein-Dryszkiewicz's recollections are quoted in Stanisław Rosiek, "Odcięcie. Siedem fragmentów" [Cutting off: seven fragments], *Schulz/Forum* 7 (2016): 25–64, and in Jerzy Pomianowski, *To proste*, 216–17. Mondschein-Dryszkiewicz described her acquaintance with Schulz in a letter to Henryk Bereza (Oct. 15, 1992). See Magdalena Wasąg, "Miasteczko wyobrażone: Schulz w liście Alicji Mondschein-Dryszkiewicz do Henryka Berezy" [The imaginary townlet: Schulz in Alicja Mondschein-Dryszkiewicz's letter to Henryk Bereza], *Konteksty* 324, nos. 1–2 (2019): 283–86.
91. Full quote: "Let us put it bluntly: the fatal flaw of this quarter is that nothing in it is ever realized, nothing reaches its *definitivum*, all movements that are initiated hang in the air, all gestures are exhausted prematurely and cannot proceed beyond a certain dead end. . . . Nowhere do we feel as threatened by possibilities as here, as shocked by the closeness of fulfillment, as pale and powerless before the exquisite terror of consummation." ("The Street of Crocodiles," *Collected Stories*, 60.)
92. Witold Gombrowicz described Schulz as "a tiny gnome with an enormous head, appearing too scared to dare exist; he was rejected by life and slouched along its peripheries. . . . No, he was not made to dominate! . . . We often discussed various moral and social issues but behind everything he said crouched the passivity of someone brought to ruin." (Witold Gombrowicz, *Diary*, ed. Jan Kott, trans. Lillian Vallee, vol. 3 [Northwestern University Press, 1993], 6–7.)

93. Ola Watowa, *Wszystko co najważniejsze* (Czytelnik, 1990), 13–14; quoted in Marci Shore, *Caviar and Ashes: A Warsaw Generation's Life and Death in Marxism, 1918–1968* (Yale University Press, 2006), 90.

94. Henry J. Węgrocki, "Masochistic Motives in the Literary and Graphic Art of Bruno Schulz," *Psychoanalytic Review* 33 (1946), 164.

95. Artur Sandauer writes, "In Schulz's work [masochism] is more than an erotic perversion. When the father falls to his knees in front of the slayer of fantastic birds he breeds, the mundane Adela, it is not only a demonstration of a masochist. It is a bow from nineteenth-century poetry to the brutal reality of the new age; the bow of Schulz's Arcadian childhood to the experiences of his manhood." (Sandauer, *Rzeczywistość Zdegradowana: Rzecz o Brunonie Schulzu* [Degraded reality: On Bruno Schulz] [Wydawnictwo Literackie, 1957].)

96. "The Book," *Collected Stories*, 89–90.

97. "Spring," *Collected Stories*, 142.

98. Ozjasz Thon, "Introduction," *Żydzi w Polsce Odrodzonej*, ed. Ignacy Schiper, Arieh Tartakower, and Aleksander Hafftka, vol. 1 (Warsaw: Wydnawnictwo Żydzi w Polsce Odrodzonej, 1932), 17–18; quoted in Antony Polonsky, "Writing the History of the Jews of Poland and Russia," *European Judaism* 46, no. 2 (Autumn 2013): 7.

99. Schulz, "The Formation of Legends: Commemorating the Death of Józef Piłsudski, Marshal of Poland, on May 12, 1935," *Letters and Drawings*, 59. Schulz writes elsewhere: "He [Piłsudski] emerged from the underground of history, from graves, from the past. . . . He dragged history behind him, as a coat for all of Poland." (Schulz, *Powstają legendy: Trzy szkice wokół Piłsudskiego*, ed. Stanisław Rosiek [Oficyna Literacka 1993], 25.) For a student's recollections of Schulz's portrait of Piłsudski, see Bogusław Marszal, "Kiedy śni mi się Drohobycz . . ." [When I dream of Drohobycz . . .], an interview with A. Goszczyńska-Górska, *Dekada Literacka* 2 (1984): 4–5. For a survey of letters Polish Jews sent to Piłsudski, see Natalia Aleksiun, "Regards from My 'Shtetl,' " *Polish Review* 56, nos. 1–2 (2011).

100. Stanisław Rosiek, "Schulz poza czasem" [Schulz out of time], *Schulz/Forum* 10 (2017): 6. "Schulz's mythologization of Piłsudski," writes Stanley Bill, "might even suggest a nostalgic view of lost stability akin to [Joseph] Roth's elegiac vision of the Austro-Hungarian Empire." (Stanley Bill, "History and Myth: Bruno Schulz's *Spring*," *The Routledge World Companion to Polish Literature*, ed. Tomasz Bilczewski, Stanley Bill, and Magdalena Popiel (Routledge, 2022,) 247.)

101. See Adam Penkalla, "The 'Przytyk Incidents' of 9 March 1936 from Archival Documents," *Polin* 5 (1990): 326–359, and Emanuel Melzer, *No Way Out: The Politics of Polish Jewry, 1935–1939* (Hebrew Union College Press, 1997). "During the post-Piłsudski years," writes Ezra Mendelsohn, "the government's attitude toward the Jewish question was fairly clear. In the short run, the Jews' role in the Polish economy and in all other walks of life was to be drastically reduced. In the long run, emigration was the only solution." (Mendelsohn, *The Jews of East and Central Europe Between the World Wars* [Indiana University Press, 1983].)

102. Czesław Miłosz, foreword to Aleksander Hertz, *The Jews in Polish Culture*, trans. Richard Lourie (Northwestern University Press, 1988), ix.

103. Quoted in Anna Landau-Czajka, "Image of the Jew in the Catholic Press," in *Jews in Independent Poland 1918–1939*, ed. Antony Polonsky et al. (London: Littman Library, 1994), 165–66. For Tadeusz Borowski's attack in 1947 on Zofia Kossak and her Auschwitz novel *Z otchłani* [From the abyss], see Dariusz Kulesza,

Dwie prawdy: Zofia Kossak i Tadeusz Borowski wobec obrazu wojny w polskiej prozie lat 1944–1948 (Trans Humana, 2006). In September 1942, Zofia Kossak recanted somewhat and authored a passionate appeal calling upon the Poles to help save Jews. "Whoever remains silent in the face of murder," she wrote, "becomes an accomplice to that murder."

104. "Theses on the Jewish Question," quoted in Edward D. Wynot Jr., " 'A Necessary Cruelty': The Emergence of Official Anti-Semitism in Poland, 1936–39," *American Historical Review* (Oct. 1971): 1048.

105. Schulz to Romana Halpern, March 3, 1938, *Letters and Drawings*, 175; *Księga listów*, 160.

106. Schulz to Romana Halpern, March 20, 1938, *Księga listów*, 162–63.

107. Schulz to Zenon Waśniewski, April 24, 1938, *Księga listów*, 87.

108. Schulz, "E. M. Lilien," *Schulz/Forum* 6 (2015), trans. Stanley Bill.

109. Another of Schulz's students, Benio Löffelstiel, shared a similar memory: "Schulz went to the old Jewish center next to the synagogue with his easel and made various drawings. Someone asked him, 'What are you doing there?' And he replied that he was a prophet: 'I'm doing this because I know that it won't be standing forever.' " (Benjamin Geissler, ed., *Exhibition Catalogue: The Picture Chamber of Bruno Schulz* [Geissler Filmproduktion, 2012], 18.)

110. Egga van Haardt, born in 1912 in Lwów to a Dutch-Polish family, exhibited her paintings and pastels in 1937 in Warsaw, Munich, Katowice, and Kraków, and in 1938 at the Galerie Zak in Saint-Germain-des-Prés, Paris. See Małgorzata Kitowska-Łysiak, "Kim była Eggo?" ["Who were you, Egga?"], *Schulzowskie marginalia* (2007): 69–90.

111. For his deliberations about furnishing his own room, see Schulz's letters to Romana Halpern of March 10, March 31, and April 17, 1938.

112. *Księga listów*, 102.

113. Maria Chazen to Schulz, July 26, 1938, *Księga listów*, 277.

114. Kazimiera Rychterówna to Schulz, July 20, 1938, *Księga listów*, 283. Her young nephew Marian Eile attempted to organize an exhibition of Schulz's drawings at the Zodiak café in Warsaw to help fund Schulz's trip.

115. See Ariko Kato, "Schulz i Lille," *Schulz/Forum* 3 (2013): 127–34.

116. I'm indebted to Stanisław Rosiek for this find. See Stanisław Rosiek, "Schulz poza czasem" [Schulz out of time], *Schulz/Forum* 10 (2017): 20.

117. *Księga listów*, 320.

118. Schulz to Romana Halpern, Aug. 29, 1938, *Letters and Drawings*, 188; *Księga listów*, 171. For more on Schulz's time in Paris, see Dominique Hérody, *À Paris, égaré: Bruno Schulz, août 1938* [Phb Editions, 2019].

119. Schulz to Wacław Czarski, Aug. 10, 1938, *Księga listów*, 100; Prokopczyk, *Bruno Schulz: New Documents and Interpretations*, 29.

120. *Księga listów*, 123.

121. Schulz to Romana Halpern, Feb. 21, 1938, *Księga listów*, 158.

122. Schulz to Romana Halpern, Oct. 29, 1938, *Księga listów*, 174.

123. Schulz to Romana Halpern, June 1939, *Letters and Drawings*, 193.

CHAPTER 5: THE ARTIST ENSLAVED

1. "An Essay for S. I. Witkiewicz," *Letters and Drawings*, 114.

2. Mauricy Weiss (Schulz's cousin and student) to Benjamin Geissler, Drohobycz, Feb. 6, 2001. Unpublished.

3. Artur Sandauer, *Byłem* ... (1991), 24; accessible at https://www.sandauer.pl/obrazki/file/bylem-artur-sandauer.pdf.

4. Grynberg, *Drohobycz, Drohobycz*, 17–18. In February 1940, Jan Karski, a hero of the Polish wartime resistance, reported: "Polish opinion considers that Jewish attitudes to the Bolsheviks are favorable. It is universally believed that the Jews betrayed Poland and the Poles, that they are all communists at heart, and that they went over to the Bolsheviks with flags waving. Indeed, in most towns, the Jews *did* welcome the Bolsheviks with bouquets, with speeches and with declarations of allegiance and so on." (Karski, "The Situation of the Jews on Territories Occupied by the USSR," Hoover Archival Documentary Series, Stanford, Mikolajczyk Collection, box 12, file titled "The Jews in Occupied Poland, 1939–1945.")

5. Jerzy Ficowski, *Regiony wielkiej herezji i okolice*, 416.

6. Schulz to Anna Płockier, Nov. 15, 1940, *Księga listów*, 191; also quoted in Marci Shore, *The Taste of Ashes: The Afterlife of Totalitarianism in Eastern Europe* (Crown, 2013), 178.

7. Quoted in Jerzy Ficowski, *Regions of the Great Heresy*, 130. Schulz's story was either about a Bolshevik commissar who betrayed his artistic vocation or about a "misshapen son of a shoemaker." (Artur Sandauer, *Byłem* ... , 25; quoted in Agnieszka Cieślikowa, *Prasa okupowanego Lwowa* [Wydawnictwo Neriton, 1997], 93.) See also Adam Ważyk's account in Ficowski, *Bruno Schulz: Listy, fragmenty, wspomnienia o pisarzu*, and in Adam Ważyk, "Spotkanie w Zakopanem" [Meeting in Zakopane], *Życie Literackie*, Nov. 28, 1965. Ważyk (pseudonym of Ajzyk [Isaac] Wagman), born in Warsaw in 1905, met Schulz in Zakopane in the mid-1920s.

8. Interview with Sandauer conducted by Ryszard Pietrzak, "Świat Brunona Schulz" [The world of Bruno Schulz], *Trybuna Ludu* 281 (Nov. 27–28, 1982).

9. Andrzej Chciuk, "Wspomnienie o Brunonie Schulzu," *Kultura* 7, no. 141, and 8, no. 142 (1959): 28. See Stanley Bill, "Propaganda on the Margins: Bruno Schulz's Soviet Illustrations, 1940–41," *Slavonic and East European Review* 96, no. 3 (2018): 432–68.

10. Schulz to Tadeusz Wojciechowski, Oct. 4, 1940; Prokopczyk, *Bruno Schulz: New Documents and Interpretations*, 32.

11. Marcel Drimmer, then seven years old, remembers: "On July 1, hordes of peasants from the nearby villages entered Jewish homes, robbing, beating, and killing the Jews. They killed about eighty Jews and wounded about two hundred. (Marcel Drimer [originally Drimmer], "The First Few Days," *Echoes of Memory*, United States Holocaust Memorial Museum, Nov. 1, 2015.) According to survivor Leon Thorne: "Until the Germans came, the Ukrainians had not indulged in any pogroms because there were so many Jews that it was dangerous for them to invite unnecessary trouble. The Ukrainians who lived in the area welcomed the Germans with great joy; however, the Jews were tense when the district changed hands. During the celebrations, a rumor was started that many imprisoned Ukrainians had been shot by the departing Russians. It later developed that the victims were Zionists. ... But at this time the Ukrainians thought that their own people had been massacred and they started a pogrom against the Jews." (Thorne, *Out of the Ashes* [Bloch, 1976], 100.)

At the same time, in late June and July 1941, Ukrainian nationalists and

German death squads (*Einsatzgruppen*) perpetrated a series of pogroms in the nearby city of Lwów, where Jews made up a third of the population. At the 2020 SchulzFest in Drohobych, I attended the opening of an exhibition called *Mutilated Myth*, by the acclaimed young Ukrainian artist Nikita Kadan, who recombined Schulz's masochistic etchings with drawings based on photographs from the Lwów pogroms (including a German man whipping a nude Jewish woman in the street). In Kadan's explanation:

> Schulz's works are weirdly similar to some of the photographs from the Lwów pogroms. In both cases we see naked or half-naked women in the streets; furthermore, these are often undressed women wearing nothing but black stockings. And next to them—some sort of expressly monstrous-looking men. Except, while the men in the pogrom photos are pulling faces, having fun and showing in every way that they are the masters of the situation, it is the other way around in Schulz's pictures—they are humiliating themselves and clowning around to entertain these dominating women. . . . These are scenes in which Schulz, to some extent influenced by Goya, renounces realistic lighting to create his own masochistic theatre. I make replicas of the Lwów pogrom photos and replicas of Schulz's works in such a way as to invoke a coherent visual register, so that these images could almost be mistaken for each other. (Galina Rymbu, "Interview with Nikita Kadan," *Arterritory*, Oct. 17, 2019.)

See also Grzegorz Józefczuk, "Schulz i Kadan: Awangarda, rewolucja, pogrom i Sąd Ostateczny" [Schulz and Kadan: Avant-garde, revolution, pogrom, and the Last Judgment], *Konteksty* 4 (2021): 32–37.

12. Amalia Buchman (née Shönfeld), *The Holocaust of the Jews of Drohobycz: Memoirs*, trans. Eli Buchman, Yad Vashem testimony 13119 (Sept. 1943), 21. Another survivor of the Drohobycz pogrom recounted: "With my own eyes I saw a Ukrainian youth wrench a seven-month-old baby from his mother's arms, Lea Eidelman, tear him into two, and throw each half to a different side. Victims who were lying on the ground and showed signs of life were treated with blows and kicks until their souls departed." (Quoted in Amalia Buchman, 22.)

13. See Marcel Drimer, "Hiding," *Echoes of Memory*, United States Holocaust Memorial Museum, Nov. 1, 2013, and Wojciech W. Kowalski, *The Machinery of Nazi Art Looting: The Nazi Law on the Confiscation of Cultural Property in Poland* (Institute of Art and Law, 2000).

14. On the Jewish councils, see Raul Hilberg, "The Judenrat: Conscious or Unconscious 'Tool,'" in *Patterns of Jewish Leadership in Nazi Europe, 1933–1945: Proceedings of the Third Yad Vashem International Historical Conference*, ed. Y. Gutman and C. J. Haft (Yad Vashem, 1979), and Dan Michman, "Judenrat," in *The Holocaust Encyclopedia*, ed. Walter Laqueur (Yale University Press, 2001), 370–77.

15. Hans Frank would be captured by American soldiers in Bavaria in May 1945, tried for war crimes before the International Military Tribunal in Nuremberg in November 1945, and hanged in October 1946. Lasch was arrested on January 24, 1942, on charges of corruption and trade in foreign currency, convicted in May, and died in prison in June. Fritz Katzmann escaped justice and lived in Darmstadt, Germany, under a false name, Bruno Albrecht, until his death in September 1957. Friedrich Hildebrand, a favorite of Fritz Katzmann's, served as commandant of

the slave labor camps of Drohobycz and Borysław beginning in July 1942. He would be tried in Bremen in 1953, sentenced to life imprisonment, pardoned in December 1955, rearrested in March 1965, again sentenced to life imprisonment, and released from prison on health grounds in 1974 (see the Wiener Holocaust Library, London, archive reference 1185/9; Landesgericht Bremen files 29 Ks 1/66; and Justiz und NS-Verbrechen files JuNSV 355 and JuNSV 653). In September 1946, the Polish government requested that Otto Wächter be put on trial for "mass murder, shooting and executions. Under his command of District Galicia more than one hundred thousand Polish citizens lost their lives." Wächter evaded arrest and in April 1949 was given refuge in Rome by a pro-Nazi Austrian bishop in the Vatican. He died there that July, aged forty-eight. See *The Ratline: Love, Lies and Justice on the Trail of a Nazi Fugitive*, by Philippe Sands (Knopf, 2020). Jedamzik later served in Einsatzkommando 10b, part of Einsatzgruppe D, was exonerated by a German *Spruchkammergericht* [court of appeal] in September 1948, and died in 1966. See Thomas Sandkühler, *"Endlösung" in Galizien: Der Judenmord in Ostpolen und die Rettungsinitiativen von Berthold Beitz, 1941–1944*, (Dietz, 1996), 454.

16. Marian Jachimowicz, "Wspomnienie Brunona Schulza," *Schulz/Forum* 14 (2019), 191 [written May 7, 1946]. See also Marian Jachimowicz, "Bruno Schulz," *Poezja* 4 (1966). Jachimowicz—a poet and painter who became acquainted with Schulz in 1938—began corresponding with Ficowski on June 10, 1948.
17. Letter from Józef Kossowski to Jerzy Ficowski, 1948; quoted in *Bruno: Epoka genialna*, 540.
18. Quoted in *Bruno: Epoka genialna*, 572.
19. Schulz to Anna Płockier, June 19, 1941, *Letters and Drawings*, 206; *Księga listów*, 196. Schulz met Płockier at a cultural salon in Borysław. Schulz came to these meetings from Drohobycz with his friends Laura Wurzberg, a writer; the poet Juliusz Wit; and Alina Dawidowiczowa, a young mathematics teacher. Płockier later married the visionary theater director Marek Zwillich. Eighteen letters from Schulz to Płockier were rescued by their common friend Marian Jachimowicz.
20. Schulz to Płockier, Sept. 23, 1941, *Letters and Drawings*, 208.
21. See Thomas Sandkühler, *"Endlösung" in Galizien*, 318.
22. See the description of the Drohobycz ghetto in Amalia Buchman, 42; Thorne, *Out of the Ashes*, 100–94; and the eyewitness account by Michael Rudorfer of the Drohobycz ghetto and forced labor (Jan. 28, 1954), Wiener Holocaust Library, London, archive reference number 1656/3/8/691.
23. Thorne, *Out of the Ashes*, 131.
24. Samuel Rothenberg, "List o zagładzie Żydów w Drohobyczu" [A letter on the extermination of Jews in Drohobycz], *Biuletyn SPZD* 21 (2017); originally published as a pamphlet edited by Edmund Silberner (London: Poets and Painters Press, 1984).
25. In an agonized letter to Zenon Waśniewski (April 24, 1934), Schulz described the "insurmountable resistance" he felt to writing anything (*Księga listów*, 67). See also Schulz's letter to the novelist Kazimierz Truchanowski, Oct. 10, 1935, in which Schulz reported, "*Messiah* grows, little by little" (*Letters and Drawings*, 103; *Collected Works*, 362.)
26. Jerzy Ficowski noted that Schulz's drawings "reflect the specific atmosphere of pious waiting in the Diaspora and the joyful arrival of the Messiah—the

consummation of ancient prophecies." (Ficowski, introduction to *The Drawings of Bruno Schulz* [Northwestern University Press, 1990], 17.)

27. "Rozmowa z autorem *Sklepów cynamonowych* (Wywiad z Brunonem Schulzem)," *Nowy Kurier* 7 (Jan. 11, 1938): 4–5.

28. The two archives are the Military Historical Archive and the Special Collections at the State Archive of the Russian Federation (known by its acronym GARF). The latter is the successor to the Central State Archive of the October Revolution and the Central State Archive of the Russian Soviet Federative Socialist Republic.

29. Amalia Buchman, 37.

30. Joseph Weissman, Yad Vashem oral testimony, O.3 2744, recorded on Dec. 28, 1964. Weissman worked with Nazi-hunter Simon Wiesenthal from 1946 to 1949.

31. Quoted in David Grossman, "The Age of Genius," *New Yorker*, June 8–15, 2009.

32. Letter from Tadeusz Lubowiecki (Izydor Friedman) to Jerzy Ficowski, Aug. 26, 1948.

33. Oral account by Michał Mirski to Jerzy Ficowski, 1948; quoted in *Bruno: Epoka genialna*, 583.

34. Schulz, "Loneliness," *Collected Stories*, 231; originally published in *Przegląd Podkarpacie*, Sept. 1937.

35. Aleksy Kuszczak to Jerzy Ficowski, 1965; quoted in *Bruno: Epoka genialna*, 565–66.

36. Amalia Buchman, 37.

37. Christian Wirth was killed in May 1944 by Yugoslav partisans and was buried with full military honors. His successor, Gottlieb Hering, served as commandant from June 1942 until the camp was liquidated in June 1943; he died in October 1945. Only one perpetrator was convicted of crimes committed at Belzec: Josef Oberhauser, Wirth's adjutant. On January 21, 1965, the Munich Regional Court found Oberhauser guilty of aiding and abetting the murders of three hundred thousand people. His total sentence: four and a half years in prison. Oberhauser was released on July 31, 1966, and died in Munich, a free man, in 1979. For details of the deportation of one thousand to fifteen hundred Jews from Drohobycz to the Belzec extermination camp in March 1942, see Thomas Sandkühler, *"Endlösung" in Galizien*, 324. For an eyewitness account of the gassing operations at Belzec, see the testimony by Kurt Gerstein, former head of the "disinfection service" of the Waffen SS, cited in the "Judgment in the Trial of Adolf Eichmann," part 14, section 124 (dated May 5, 1945).

38. Quoted in Amalia Buchman, 20. Samuel Rothenberg corroborated this account in *Brief über die Vernichtung der Juden in Drohobycz* [A letter on the extermination of Jews in Drohobycz], trans. Naomi Silberner-Becker (1992), in German, and in *List o zagładzie Żydów w Drohobyczu* (London: Poets and Painters Press, 1984), in Polish. (There's a copy in the Central Zionist Archives, Jerusalem, K14\298.)

39. "Wspomnienie Emila Górskiego," in Ficowski, *Bruno Schulz: Listy, fragmenty, wspomnienia o pisarzu*, 67. In 1965, Górski sold these works to the Adam Mickiewicz Museum in Warsaw, where they remain today.

40. *The Street of Crocodiles and Other Stories*, trans. Celina Wieniewska (Penguin, 2008), 318–19.

41. Emil Górski, "Wspomnienia o Brunonie Schulzu" [Memories of Bruno Schulz], in Ficowski, *Bruno Schulz: Listy, fragmenty, wspomnienia o pisarzu*, 79.

42. Zbigniew Moroń to Jerzy Ficowski, 1965; quoted in *Bruno: Epoka genialna*, 566.

43. Harry Zeimer, interview with Benjamin Geissler, Jerusalem, May 26, 2001.

44. Grynberg, *Drohobycz, Drohobycz*, 23. According to Schulz's former student Leopold Lustig: "Schulz was seen for weeks on end on the scaffolding in the hall of the Arbeitsamt [in the former Jewish orphanage] lying on his back under the ceiling like Michelangelo and painting at Landau's command. He also painted in the Reithalle. He painted horses because Landau loved horses."

45. See the interview with Artur Klinghoffer, Aug. 2, 1996, USC Shoah Foundation Institute Visual History Archive. Klinghoffer's diary (Aug. 1943–Aug. 1944), in Polish, is available online: www.drohobycz-boryslaw.org/images/families/drohobycz/klinghuper-zseler/dazgar-compressd-3.pdf.

46. Grynberg, *Drohobycz, Drohobycz*, 23. Henryk Grynberg told me the background: "Leopold Lustig was just a reader of my books. One day he called me from Newton (a suburb of Boston) to tell me that his school friend from Drohobycz, the historian Karol Gruenberg, a friend of mine from Poland, had sent him copies of protocols from the debates in prewar Polish Sejm and Senate pertaining to Jewish matters, as well as clippings from Polish press of those days, and they both thought that I might be interested in reading those documents. Of course, I was interested. Lustig's voice sounded so emotional, as if he has been personally involved, and so I asked him a few questions about himself, and we both came to the conclusion that he had a story to tell me, starting with his Drohobycz school where Schulz was his teacher. He invited me to his home. . . . He did have a specific voice and I had an ear for it. It was a perfect partnership." After the war, Lustig lived in the Landsberg DP camp, and immigrated to the United States in 1949.

47. Clive James, "The Iron Capital of Bruno Schulz," in *The Meaning of Recognition* (Picador, 2005).

48. See Anne-Marie O'Connor, *The Lady in Gold: The Extraordinary Tale of Gustav Klimt's Masterpiece* (Knopf, 2012).

49. The Nazi-era records of the Dorotheum were destroyed in the 1970s. See Hubertus Czernin, *Die Fälschung: Der Fall Bloch-Bauer und das Werk Gustav Klimts* (Czernin Verlag, 1999), 311.

50. The *Einsatzkommando zum besonderen Verwendung* (for special assignments), operating from the end of June to September 1941, was led by SS-Brigadeführer (brigadier general) Karl-Eberhardt Schöngarth. His staff included: SS-Sturmbannführer Kurt Sawitzki, SS-Hauptsturmführer Hans Krüger, SS-Untersturmführer Walter Kutschmann, and SS-Hauptscharführer Felix Landau.

   As a peripheral region of the "Third Reich," Galicia had been neglected until the 1990s, when historians gave it belated attention. See Thomas Sandkühler, "Anti-Jewish Policy and the Murder of the Jews in the District of Galicia, 1941–1942," in *National-Socialist Extermination Policies: Contemporary German Perspectives and Controversies*, ed. Ulrich Herbert (Berghahn, 2000), 104–27 (2nd ed.: Yad Vashem, 2001, 125–50); originally published in German as "Judenpolitik und Judenmord im Distrikt Galizien, 1941–1942," in *Nationalsozialistische Vernichtungspolitik, 1939–1945: Neue Forschungen und Kontroversen*, ed. Ulrich Herbert (S. Fischer, 1998), 122–47. See also Dieter Pohl, *Nationalsozialistische Judenverfolgung in Ostgalizien, 1941–1944* (De Gruyter Oldenbourg, 1996); Wolfgang Curilla, *Die deutsche Ordnungspolizei und der Holocaust* (Schöningh/ Paderborn, 2006), especially the section on East Galicia, 770–89; Thomas Geldmacher, *"Wir als Wiener waren ja bei der Bevölkerung beliebt": Österreichische Schutzpolizisten und die Judenvernichtung in Ostgalizien,*

1941–1944 (Mandelbaum Verlag, 2002); and Jan T. Gross, *Polish Society Under German Occupation: The Generalgouvernement, 1939–1944* (Princeton University Press, 2019).

51. Thomas Sandkühler, *"Endlösung"in Galizien*, 305. In his diary, Felix Landau calls Tolle "Dolte." In October 1941, Tolle was replaced by SS-Hauptsturmführer (captain) Franz Karl Wenzel as chief of the Gestapo Drohobycz. The town's SiPo (Security Police) was commanded by Helmut Tanzmann.

52. Ernst Klee, Willi Dressen, and Volker Riess, eds., *Those Were the Days: The Holocaust Through the Eyes of the Perpetrators and Bystanders* (Hamish Hamilton, 1991), 93.

53. Koch to Benjamin Geissler, Stuttgart, Oct. 1, 2001.

54. *Those Were the Days*, 96–98.

55. Thomas Sandkühler, *"Endlösung" in Galizien*, 308.

56. After the war, Naftali Backenroth was imprisoned by Ukrainian officials for four months for being on friendly terms with the Germans, immigrated to Paris, and changed his name to Bronicki. For more on Backenroth (1905–1993), see Mordecai Paldiel, *Saving One's Own: Jewish Rescuers During the Holocaust* (University of Nebraska Press, 2017), and Leon Thorne, *It Will Yet Be Heard: A Polish Rabbi's Witness of the Shoah and Survival* (Rutgers University Press, 2018); originally published as *Out of the Ashes: The Story of a Survivor* (Bloch, 1976).

57. "The Sanatorium Under the Hourglass," *Collected Stories*, 200.

58. Oral history interview with Anna Lustman, May 9, 2000, United States Holocaust Memorial Museum (RG-50.407.0207).

59. Quoted in Hagai Chitron, "Bruno Schulz Treasure Revealed," *Achbar Ha-ir*, Feb. 26, 2009 (in Hebrew). During the war, Marela Schwarz (later Birman), born in 1930, had served as a babysitter for Felix Landau's young children and remembered Schulz's murals in the children's room. She immigrated with her parents to Israel in July 1950.

60. *Those Were the Days*, 101–02.

61. Ibid., 105.

62. Omer Bartov writes of Felix Landau's diary: "It is impossible to understand the nature of the Holocaust without such a document, for it is only in this manner that we can see it . . . perceived by its perpetrators as part of their normal routine . . . a professional duty that must in no way interfere with the normal course of their lives." (Omer Bartov, ed., *The Holocaust: Origins, Implementation, Aftermath* [Routledge, 2000], 8; pages 185–203 feature excerpts from Landau's diary.) The original diary was lost after Landau's trial, but typed copies survived. In 1963, a Hebrew translation by Tuviah Friedmann appeared under the title *Diary of SS-Hauptscharführer F. Landau About His Activities in Drohobycz, 1941–44*. An English translation was made in 1987 by the Institute of Documentation in Israel for the Investigation of Nazi War Crimes. Copies of the diary are held in the German Federal Archives in Ludwigsburg (inventory B 162 no. 21164) and in the U.S. Holocaust Memorial Museum in Washington (accession number 1997.A.0146). See also Robert Stieber, *Vom eigenen Tagebuch überführt: Der Wiener NS-Täter Felix Landau* (Grin Verlag, 2016).

63. *Those Were the Days*, 89–90. See also Bogdan Musial, *Konterrevolutionäre Elemente sind zu erschiessen: Die Brutalisierung des deutsch-sowjetischen Krieges im Sommer 1941* (Propyläen Verlag, 2000), 255.

64. Diary entry July 9, 1941, *Those Were the Days*, 94–95.
65. Diary entry July 30, 1941, *Those Were the Days*, 103.
66. *Die Tagebücher von Joseph Goebbels*, part 2, entry for December 13, 1941 (Munich: Saur, 1993–98), 498.
67. Secretaries like Segel, the historian Wendy Lower writes, "were not ordinary office workers. If they passed the SS examiners' test in physical appearance, genealogy, and character, these young women in Himmler's headquarters in Berlin and Vienna could fully envision themselves as members of an emerging elite. The route to success could involve service in the East, and many volunteered to be posted in Poland, the Baltics, and Ukraine." (Wendy Lower, *Hitler's Furies: German Women in the Nazi Killing Fields* [Houghton Mifflin Harcourt, 2013], 60.)
68. Quoted in Walter Mossmann, "Der Maler und seine Mörder," *Badische Zeitung*, June 8, 2002, and "Kontroverse um entwendete Wandbilder," *Wochen Zeitung*, June 7, 2002.
69. Wendy Lower, *Hitler's Furies: German Women in the Nazi Killing Fields*, 139.
70. Salo Weiss, Jan. 13, 1948, witness statement in legal proceedings against Gertrude Landau (Wien Stadtarchiv, VG 8514/46).
71. Yaffa Eliach, *Hasidic Tales of the Holocaust* (Oxford University Press, 1982), 227; based on interviews Eliach conducted with Stella Wieseltier, née Backenroth, June 17 and 22, 1981. Stella Backenroth's mother and brother were murdered in Bronica Forest on May 8, 1943; her father was shot there on July 23. After the liquidation of the Drohobycz ghetto, she survived for nine months by hiding in a cellar under a stable.
72. This section draws on my research in the following archival files: Felix Landau statement (Aug. 7, 1947): Abschrift in Wien Stadtarchiv, VG 8514/46, and Landesgericht Wien VG 3b VR 734/47 (gegen Felix Landau u.a.). Gertrude Segel Landau statements (May 29, June 2, and June 17, 1947, and Feb. 17 and Feb. 27, 1948): Wien Stadtarchiv, VG 8514/46; VR 7658/47. "The incident which my wife describes is not accurate," Felix Landau insisted during his interrogation in July 1947. "It is probably right that I often shot at birds with my Flobert rifle, but under no circumstances did I shoot at people." The Vienna Landesgerichte archives holds the report of Osias Weidmann, then fifty years old, who was working alongside others in the garden: "I personally knew Gertrude Segel very well; in my capacity as a gardener, I brought vegetables and fruit to her apartment almost daily. As far as I know, Segel, then Landau's lover, was under the influence of Landau; I can say with certainty that she also sometimes feared him. I am not aware that Segel ever treated us Jews with any kind of human dignity. . . . I would like to make it known that I witnessed perfectly how Gertrude Segel, holding the rifle atop the balcony parapet, seated and aiming precisely, fired the final shot." Marian Beninski (né Bernfeld), a member of the Drohobycz Judenrat, saw the Fliegner shooting from the window of his apartment. He said he could not ascertain who fired the fatal shot, "but I saw that both Landaus shot from the weapon, and I expressly saw a weapon in the hand of Frau [Trude] Landau." On March 24, 1960, Hans Joachim Badian, a concentration camp survivor from Drohobycz, testified against Felix Landau in a hearing at the German embassy in London (unpublished protocol of Badian testimony, 5).
73. Thorne, *Out of the Ashes*, 105. See also witness statement of Marjan Nadel, Aug. 18, 1959; quoted in Tuvia Friedmann, ed., *Die Tätigkeit der Schutzpolizei, Gestapo und Ukrainische Miliz in Drohobycz, 1941–1944* (Institute of

Documentation in Israel, 1995), and in Irene Sagel-Grande, H. H. Fuchs, and C. F. Rüter, ed., *Justiz und NS-Verbrechen: Sammlung deutscher Strafurteile wegen nationalsozialistischer Tötungesverbrechen, 1945–1966* (University Press Amsterdam, 1978), 18: 364–65. According to Amalia Buchman, Ruhrberg "was later murdered by the Germans when he was caught for not fulfilling orders. He was tied to a horse-drawn carriage and dragged through the streets of the city until he died." (Buchman, 26.)

74. Schulz to Tadeusz Breza, June 21, 1934, *Letters and Drawings*, 54; *Księga listów*, 48.

75. Małgorzata Kitowska-Łysiak, quoted in *Schulzowskie marginalia* (2007), 161.

76. Emil Górski, quoted in Ficowski, *Regions of the Great Heresy*, 166–67; "Wspomnienia o Brunonie Schulzu," in Ficowski, *Bruno Schulz: Listy, fragmenty, wspomnienia o pisarzu.*

77. Artworks by Haas and Lurie are featured in *Last Portrait: Painting for Posterity,* ed. Eliad Moreh-Rosenberg (Yad Vashem, 2012).

78. See Aldo Carpi's memoirs, *Diario di Gusen* (Einaudi, 1993).

79. In 1973, several portraits of Dina Babbitt (née Gottliebova) were found by the Auschwitz-Birkenau Memorial and State Museum. Her request to have the works returned to her was denied. See the short animated film *The Last Outrage: The Dina Babbitt Story*, created by Neal Adams, Joe Kubert, and Rafael Medoff (Disney Educational Productions, 2009), and Lidia Ostałowska, *Farby wodne* (Wołowiec: Wydawnictwo Czarne, 2011); published in English as *Watercolours: A Story from Auschwitz*, trans. Sean Gasper Bye (Zubaan Books, 2016).

80. "The Age of Genius," *Collected Stories*, 94.

81. See Sandkühler, *"Endlösung" in Galizien*, 356.

82. "Father's Final Escape," *Collected Stories*, 236.

83. Ficowski, *Regions of the Great Heresy*, 134.

84. Zeimer's fourteen-page testimony about Drohobycz and Schulz, given to Yad Vashem on October 14, 1964 (O.3 2718), and his videotaped oral testimony (V.T/334). See also Annę Grupińską, "Interview with Harry Zeimer," *Czasie Kultury* 13–14 (1990); reprinted as "Śmierć Brunona Schulza: O 'czarnym czwartku' w Drohobyczu opowiada Harry Zeimer—uczeń i przyjaciel Schulza," *Życie* 98 (2001): 14. Born in Vienna in 1921, Zeimer moved with his parents to Drohobycz in 1928, escaped to Switzerland with forged papers in September 1942, settled in Paris after the war, and immigrated to Israel in 1960. According to Anna Kaszuba-Dębska, Aryan documents were sent to Schulz by Ryszard Matuszewski (*Bruno: Epoka genialna*, 582). The Polish artist Ewa Kuryluk told me: "My [Galicia-born] father Karol Kuryluk —founder and editor in chief of the anti-fascist Lwów magazine *Signals*, to which Schulz contributed—told me that there was effort to get Schulz out of Drohobycz. In that provincial nest, hiding him was impossible, so they wanted to bring him to Lwów and then to Warsaw, where Zofia Nałkowska might have been able to find him a hiding place."

85. Emmanuel (Manek) Weintraub to Benjamin Geissler, Paris, Sept. 28, 2001. After fleeing to France, Weintraub served as interpreter for French president Charles de Gaulle's 1961 meetings with German chancellor Konrad Adenauer, as head of the translation service of the Organization for Economic Cooperation and Development (OECD) in Paris, as chairman of the French section of the World Jewish Congress, and finally as vice president of the French Jewish umbrella body CRIF. He died in 2012.

86. "The Age of Genius," *Collected Stories*, 101.
87. See the Archive of the Jewish Historical Institute, Warsaw (Archiwum Żydowskiego Instytutu Historycznego), file 301/4920.
88. For attempts to resolve the inconsistencies between the versions see Wiesław Budzyński, *Schulz pod kluczem*, 10–32, and Jakub Orzeszek, "Schulz i żałoba: O drugim ciele pisarza" ["Schulz and mourning: On the writer's second body"], *Schulz/ Forum* 14 (2019). In a chapter of her 2020 biography of Schulz called "The Many Deaths of Bruno Schulz," Anna Kaszuba-Dębska collects thirteen versions of the artist's murder.
89. Thorne, *Out of the Ashes*, 105. In an unpublished letter to Jerzy Ficowski of June 16, 1992, Ella Schulz-Podstolska relays the recollection of this incident by ninety-three-year-old Ernestyna Juańska, then living in Düsseldorf.
90. For more on Löw, see Samuel Rothenberg, *List o zagładzie Żydów w Drohobyczu* [A letter on the extermination of Jews in Drohobycz] (Poets and Painters Press, 1984), 13; Wiesław Budzyński, *Uczniowie Schulza* [Schulz's students] (Państwowy Instytut Wydawniczy, 2011), 139; and a letter from Regina Silberner to Jerzy Ficowski, dated Jerusalem, Aug. 17, 1992. Abraham Schwarz suggested another reason for the rivalry between the two SS officers. The Gestapo had forced Jews to build a greenhouse and plant nursery opposite Villa Landau. "One day," Schwarz reported, "[Landau] went out on his balcony and saw a couple of girls resting (they had been plastering the walls there). He went into his room, took a rifle, and shot them both. Günther was responsible for the work at the greenhouse. It's possible that after that the antagonism between him and Landau arose, which led to the death of Schulz. Eventually, Günther began to hunt for Schulz." (Małgorzata Kitowska-Łysiak, "Requiem: Alfred Schreyer and Abraham Schwarz Talk About the Death of Bruno Schultz," *Schultzowskie marginalia* (Wydawnictwo KUL, 2007), 143–52.) The same story is recounted in the documentary film *Bruno Schulz* (dir. Adam Sikora, Studio Largo, 2014).
91. In German: "Du hast meinen Juden erschossen, da habe ich deinen Juden erschossen." The phrase echoes an old German saying, "If you beat my Jew, I'll beat your Jew" ("Haust du meinen Juden, hau ich deinen Juden"). See, for example, the comedy *Der Datterich*, by Ernst Elias Niebergall, act 1, scene 6. The phrase is also attributed to Johann Peter Hebel, a Protestant clergyman best remembered for his dialect poems, published as *Alemannische Gedichte* in 1802. See the oral account by Zeev Händler to Jerzy Ficowski, 1993; quoted in *Bruno: Epoka genialna*, 592. According to Michał Ambros, the phrase was "I shot down your Schulz" ("Ich habe deinen Schulz niedergeschossen"). (Letter from Michał Ambros to Jerzy Ficowski, 1974, quoted in *Bruno: Epoka genialna*, 593.) According to Hersz Betman, a witness named Izydor Badian (later shot dead) related the conversation this way: Günther: "Guess who I shot today. Your artist, that Schulz." Landau: "Shame, I still needed him." Günther: "That's why I shot him." Other testimonies that identify Günther as Schulz's killer include those by Emil Górski, Izydor Friedman, Leopold Lustig, Alfred Schreyer, and Abraham Schwarz. In an essay called "The Messiah on Vacation in Truskavets," the Polish writer Włodzimierz Paźniewski told this version of Schulz's murders as a Passion play: Schulz in the role of Christ, Felix Landau as Pontius Pilate, and Karl Günther as Judas. (Włodzimierz Paźniewski, *Życie i inne zajęcia* [Państwowy Instytut Wydawniczy, 1982].) Karl Günther escaped justice; he never stood trial for his murders of Jews

in Drohobycz or other crimes (including complicity in the massacre of several hundred Jews in the nearby town of Turka).

92. Josef Gabriel was tried by jury in Vienna in March 1959 for atrocities he committed in Drohobycz, Borysław, Stryj, and Sambor. Though sentenced to life in prison, he was conditionally released in December 1968 (LG Wien 20 Vr 1077/57).

93. "Testimony of an anonymous female pupil in the Leon Sternbach School in Drohobycz, Poland," Yad Vashem archives, O.62 340. Her testimony was given to the Polish Jewish writer Michał Maksymilian Borwicz, who led the Jewish Historical Commission (Zydowska Komisja Historyczna) in Kraków from 1945 to 1947.

94. The witnesses were: Chaim (Ignacy) Patrich, born 1922, a former pupil of Schulz's who had been forced to work for a local SD officer; Moses Marcus Weidmann, born 1923, a forced laborer in Drohobycz, who gave his testimony on September 30, 1946; Theodora Reifler, born 1922, who testified on January 21, 1947; and Josef Weissman, born 1912, who gave his testimony on December 4, 1957. Copies of the protocols of these testimonies, part of Jerzy Ficowski's archive, became the property of the Polish National Library in 2014. One source for the watch-removal story is Bohdan Odynak, twelve years old at the time. Dengg is mentioned as "scharführer Denk" in Małgorzata Kitowska-Łysiak, "Requiem: Alfred Schreyer i Abraham Schwarz rozmawiają o śmierci Brunona Schulza" ["Requiem: Alfred Schreyer and Abraham Schwarz talk about the death of Bruno Schulz"], Kresy 14 (Spring 1993): 78–82; reprinted in Schultzowskie marginalia (Lublin: Wydawnictwo KUL, 2007), 143–52. Abraham Schwarz was "Dengg's Jew," much as Schulz was Landau's. According to the testimony of Chaim Patrich, Dengg used to dress in civilian clothes and hunt Jews using Aryan papers. See "Protokół przesłuchania Patrycha Chaima," Żydzi z Drohobycza—protokoły relacji z Zagłady [Jews from Drohobycz—Reports from the Holocaust], trans. Tadeusz Zatorski, Schulz/ Forum 10 (2017), and Wiener Stadt- und Landesarchiv, file LG Vg 8e Vr 654/55. Two years after Schulz's death, Dengg was awarded Germany's Military Cross of Merit for participating in the "resettlement" of Jews in Galicia.

95. Edwin Śmiłek, "Przyczynki do Schulza: 12.07.1892–12.07.1992," Tygodnik Powszechny 30 (1992).

96. Schulz, "Tragic Freedom," in Prokopczyk, Bruno Schulz: New Documents and Interpretations, 43.

97. Thorne, Out of the Ashes, 112.

98. Artur Sandauer, Zebrane pisma krytyczne (Państwowy Instytut Wydawniczy, 1981), 1:580.

99. Artur Sandauer, "Rzeczywistość zdegradowana" [Degraded reality] (1957), in Zebrane pisma krytyczne, 1:578, and O sytuacji pisarza polskiego pochodzenia żydowskiego w XX wieku [On the situation of a writer of Polish Jewish descent in the twentieth century] (Czytelnik, 1982), 36–37. Sandauer repeated this theory at a talk he gave in November 1962 to the Association of Polish Writers in Warsaw on the twentieth anniversary of Schulz's death. Schulz, Witold Gombrowicz had said, "sought his own annihilation—not that he wanted to commit suicide; he merely 'strove' for nonbeing with all his might." (Witold Gombrowicz, Diary, ed. Jan Kott, trans. Lillian Vallee, vol. 3 [Northwestern University Press, 1993], 7.) Later in his diary, Gombrowicz contrasts himself to Schulz: "He wanted annihilation. I wanted realization. He was born to be a slave. I was born to be a master. He wanted denigration." (Diary, trans. Lillian Vallee [Yale University Press,

2012], 522). In a short story about Schulz, the Israeli writer Amir Gutfreund has the narrator say, "You, so skilled at pleading, at sinking under a commanding hand—how did you surrender? In the final moment were you filled with desire for a submission more profound, more decisive? For the pleasure of sprawling below without rising?" ("Trieste," trans. Jessica Cohen, from the collection of stories *Shoreline Mansions* [Toby Press, 2013]).

100. Fleischer, born in Drohobycz in 1925, studied at the Sternbach Gymnasium there. Together with his parents and fifteen other Jews, he survived the war by hiding for thirteen months in a bunker under his family's iron-casting factory. In 1950, Fleischer emigrated from Poland to Israel, where he died in November 2019.

101. Małgorzata Kitowska-Łysiak, "Requiem: Alfred Schreyer and Abraham Schwarz talk about the death of Bruno Schultz," 143–52. Schulz's friend Izydor Friedman reported: "During the night, I found his body, searched his pockets, and gave his documents and some notes I found there to his nephew [Zygmunt] Hoffman— who lost his life a month later. Toward morning, I buried him in the Jewish cemetery." "Trzy listy Tadeusza Lubowieckiego (Izydora Friedmana) do Jerzego Ficowskiego z 1948 roku" [Three letters from Tadeusz Lubowiecki (Izydor Friedman) to Jerzy Ficowski from 1948], *Schulz/Forum* 7 (2016).

102. Marriage application of Felix Landau, Bundesarchiv/German Federal Archives (SS-Rasse-und-Siedlungs-Hauptamt [RuSHA], marriage file BArch RS D490.

103. Tadeusz Piotrowski, *Poland's Holocaust: Ethnic Strife, Collaboration with Occupying Forces and Genocide in the Second Republic, 1918–1947* (McFarland, 1998), 231. Together with Vladimir Kubiyovich (Volodymyr Kubijovyč), head of the Ukrainian Central Committee (UCC), Otto Wächter, Nazi governor of the Galicia district, forged Ukrainian volunteers into the SS Galicia Division in 1943. This force, writes Abraham Brumberg, "was so popular with Ukrainians that it couldn't accommodate everyone who wanted to join it." (Brumberg, "Not So Free At Last," *New York Review of Books*, Oct. 22, 1992.) John Armstrong, in *Ukrainian Nationalism* (Ukrainian Academic Press, 1990), writes that the SS Galicia Division enjoyed "almost universal support" among Stepan Bandera's followers. See also P. A. Rudling, "'They Defended Ukraine': The 14. Waffen Grenadier-Division der SS Revisited," *Journal of Slavic Military Studies* 25, no. 3 (2012): 329–68, and the *Deschenes Commission Report*, Canadian Commission of Enquiry on War Crimes, (1986), chapters 1–8.

104. For a typewritten list of Jewish forced laborers deported on April 14, 1944, from Drohobycz and Borysław (777 men and 245 women), see "Liste der am 14.4.44 aus Drohobycz und Borysław überstellten jüdischen Häftlinge," World Jewish Congress Collection, U.S. Holocaust Memorial Museum archives, file RG-67.035.

105. A list of Jews who survived the German occupation in Drohobycz is held in the archives of Centralna Żydowska Komisja Historyczna przy Centralnym Komitecie Żydów w Polsce [Central Jewish Historical Commission at the Central Committee of the Jews in Poland], Sygn. 303/XX, 1944-1947, RG-15.182M, files 238 and 607.

106. In December 1965, Eberhard Helmrich became one of the first Germans to be recognized by Yad Vashem as a Righteous Among the Nations. In June 2016, a memorial plaque to Eberhard and Donata Helmrich was unveiled at their former house in Drohobych, in tribute to their heroism during the Holocaust. See the book about them by their daughter, the German politician Cornelia Schmalz-Jacobsen, *Zwei Bäume in Jerusalem* (Metropol, 2013); published in English as

Two Trees in Jerusalem (Humanity in Action Press, 2015). Seven decades after the war, Ukrainian tenants of that house, the Pavlenko family, discovered documents during repairs of their roof and attic: passports and birth certificates that had belonged to Jews rescued by Helmrich.

107. Bernard Mayer, quoted in Joan Fleischer, "Secret Survivors," *South Florida Sun-Sentinel*, Sept. 14, 1997.

108. Leon Wieseltier, "A Footnote," *New Republic*, July 1, 2009. After the war Friedman lived in Gliwice, in southern Poland.

109. Horowitz was born in Drohobycz in 1899. See his memoir *My Yesterday* (Schocken, 1970); published in Hebrew as *Ha-Etmol Sheli*.

110. Vasily Grossman, "Ukraine Without Jews," trans. Polly Zavadivker, *Jewish Quarterly* 58, no. 1 (2011): 12–18. The essay first appeared in abbreviated form in Yiddish ("Ukraina on Yidn," *Einikayt*, Nov. 25, 1943, and Dec. 2, 1943).

111. Bohdan Kordan, "Making Borders Stick: Population Transfer and Resettlement in the Trans-Curzon Territories, 1944–1949," *International Migration Review* 31, no. 3 (Sept. 1997): 705.

CHAPTER 6: AMNESIA IN THE AFTERMATH

1. "Often, while working on this book, I had the strong sensation that *The Street of Crocodiles* must have, itself, been the product of a similar act of exhumation . . . that there must have existed some yet larger book from which *The Street of Crocodiles* was taken." (Foer, *Tree of Codes* [Visual Editions, 2010], 138–39.) *Tree of Codes* was adapted into a ballet by the British choreographer Wayne McGregor, and into an opera by the Australian composer Liza Lim. See also Heather Wagner, "Jonathan Safran Foer Talks *Tree of Codes* and Conceptual Art," *Vanity Fair*, Nov. 2010, and Kseniya Tsiulia, "Defamiliaryzacja w *Sklepach cynamonowych* Brunona Schulza i *Tree of Codes* Jonathana Safrana Foera," *Schulz/Forum* 15 (2020): 94–108.

2. See Bohdan Vitvitsky, "Slavs and Jews: Consistent and Inconsistent Perspectives on the Holocaust," in *A Mosaic of Victims—Non-Jews Persecuted and Murdered by the Nazis*, ed. Michael Berenbaum (New York University Press, 1990), 106.

3. Małgorzata Kitowska-Łysiak, "Requiem: Alfred Schreyer and Abraham Schwarz talk about the death of Bruno Schulz," *Schultzowskie marginalia* (Lublin: Wydawnictwo KUL, 2007), 152.

4. Ziemowit Szczerek, "Bruno Schulz's Suicide," trans. Scotia Gilroy, *Asymptote*, Jan. 2017.

5. "Whenever the shadow of anti-Semitism arose in Polish public life," said Polish dissident Adam Michnik, "it was an unmistakable signal that people with anti-democratic, intolerant views were on the political offensive." (Michnik, "Poland and the Jews," *New York Review of Books*, May 30, 1991.)

6. Yael Bartana, *And Europe Will Be Stunned: Nightmare* (2007, 11 min.); *Wall and Tower* (2009, 15 min.); and *Assassination* (2011, 39 min.).

7. In the decades after the war, the novelist and Solidarity activist Andrzej Szczypiorski said that Poles were "unaware that they have been crippled, and that without the Jews they are no longer the Poles they once were and should have remained forever." Andrzej Szczypiorski, *Poczatek* (Instytut Literacki, 1989), 37; published in English as *The Beautiful Mrs. Seidenman*, trans. Klara Glowczewska (Grove, 1990).

8. Mikołaj Grynberg, "Forgetting, Again: Poland's Conflict with History," *Jewish Quarterly* (May 2021): 30.

9. "Only in Poland," writes Abraham Brumberg, a scholar of Eastern Europe, "have the political authorities and most of the country's intellectual leaders been reluctant to examine themselves and their past critically. One reason that has been adduced for this reluctance is Poland's self-image as a victim of History, since a victim often resents the idea that he may himself also victimize others and may develop a propensity for self-righteousness and martyrology." (Brumberg, "Poland, the Polish Intelligentsia and Antisemitism," *Soviet Jewish Affairs* 20, nos. 2–3 (1990): 21.)

10. For a program of that conference, see "Program Zjazdu Literatów w Szczecinie," *Trybuna Ludu*, Jan. 20, 1949.

11. Schulz to Anna Płockier, Nov. 6, 1941; *Księga listów*, 197.

12. One of the rare exceptions: In 1949, the Warsaw Zionist magazine *Opinia* ran the first article about Schulz in postwar Poland, accompanied by two illustrations by Schulz; see Ernestyna Podhorizer-Zajkin, "Pamięci Brunona Schulza, literata i artysty malarza" [In memory of Bruno Schulz, writer and painter], *Opinia* 50 (1949).

13. The textbook is Ewa Korzeniewska, *Zarys literatury polskiej dla klasy XI wraz z antologią poezji i publicystyki, cz. II: 1918–1950* [An outline of Polish literature for the 11th grade with an anthology of poetry and journalism, part II: 1918–1950] (Warsaw, 1952). Quoted in Katarzyna Warska, "W granicach psychopatologii? Szkolna recepcja Brunona Schulza w okresie stalinowskim," *Schulz/Forum* 10 (2017): 111–24.

14. Czesław Miłosz, "The Real Mickiewicz," *Encounter*, Feb. 1956, 23.

15. A volume of Schulz's *Cinnamon Shops* and *Sanatorium Under the Sign of the Hourglass*, with an introduction by Artur Sandauer, was published in Poland in 1957 (Wydawnictwo Literackie).

16. In French: *Traite des mannequins*, trans. Suzanne Arlet, Allan Kosko, Jerzy Lisowski, and Georges Sidre (Julliard, 1961). In German: *Die Zimtläden*, trans. Josef Hahn, separately published in West Germany (Hanser Verlag, 1966, and Suhrkamp Verlag, 1974) and in East Germany (Verlag Volk und Welt, 1970; 2nd ed. 1982). See also *Gesammelte Werke in zwei Banden*, trans. Josef Hahn and Mikolaj Dutsch, vol. 1, *Die Zimtladen und alle anderen Erzahlungen*; vol. 2, *Die Wirklichkeit ist Schatten des Wortes: Aufsatze und Briefe* (Hanser, 1992). After forty-five years during which Josef Hahn's translations cornered the German market, new German translations, by Doreen Daume, appeared in 2008 (*Die Zimtläden*) and 2011 (*Das Sanatorium zur Sanduhr*). Schulz's works were later translated into Spanish (1972, by Salvador Puig) and Greek (1980, 1982, by Spiros Tsaknias). Schulz's writing first appeared in Russia in 1985, when the samizdat magazine *Mitin żurnal* published his story "Loneliness," translated by Olga Abramowicz. *Cinnamon Shops* first appeared in Russian in 1993, translated by Asar Eppel.

   In 1939, Joseph Roth had tried in vain to cajole Saul Frishman (Fryszman), son of the great Hebrew and Yiddish writer and editor David Frishman, to translate *Cinnamon Shops* into German. Dorota Wygard translated several chapters of that book into German to Schulz's satisfaction, but they were never published. Despite his hopes, no translations of Schulz's works appeared in his lifetime. Over the years, Józefina Szelińska had asked Jerzy Ficowski to send her "editions of

Bruno's books in Norwegian, Japanese, Hebrew, Swedish, French, and English. She lived to see his literary dreams come true." (Agata Tuszyńska, "About Bruno Schulz and His Fiancée, Józefina Szelińska," talk delivered in Cleveland, May 3, 2019 [unpublished].)

17. Ficowski, *Regions of the Great Heresy*, 25–27.

18. Krzysztof Czyżewski, "Inny świat Jerzego Ficowskiego," *Gazeta Świąteczna*, May 13–14, 2006.

19. Ficowski tells this anecdote in his book *Okolice sklepów cynamonowych* (Wydawnictwo Literackie, 1986), 82.

20. "Please put this guilt in inverted commas," Ficowski added. "Please do not take it literally. It is not my sin or my guilt in a literal sense or, even less so, my wrongdoing. But I feel that if I was destined to survive, this means that I am guilty." (Ficowski, "Nie pogardzam nawet najmizerniejszą wizją," interview with Malwina Wapińska, *Dziennik* 18 [2006].) In an earlier interview, Ficowski had insisted, "I don't want my fascination for Schulz to be interpreted as the reflection of a subconscious sense of guilt, anxiety of conscience and so on." ("Pomylona chronologia: Z Jerzym Ficowskim rozmawia Anna Grupińska," *Wcielenia Jerzego Ficowskiego*, ed. Piotr Sommer (Wydawnictwo Pogranicze, 2010), 603; originally published in the journal *Czas Kultury* 20 [1990].)

21. *A Reading of Ashes* [*Odczytanie popiołów*], one of Ficowski's twenty volumes of poetry, was first published in London (1979). It appeared in English in 1981 (Menard Press) and later in Yiddish, Hebrew, German, and other languages. In his foreword to that book, the Polish poet Zbigniew Herbert writes:

> To describe the unparalleled Nazi crime against Polish Jews is a task beyond the scope of any epic, any novel, even any documentary account. High statistics do not appeal to the imagination. In his *A Reading of Ashes* Ficowski has achieved something that would have seemed impossible: he has given artistically convincing shape to what cannot be embraced by words; he has restored to the faceless their human face, their individual human suffering, that is to say, their dignity. In the teeth of hypocritical indifference and a conspiracy of silence, he has once more meted out justice before the visible world.

A collection of reviews and interviews with Ficowski from the years 1956–2007, edited by Piotr Sommer, appeared in Polish as *Wcielenia Jerzego Ficowskiego* (Pogranicze Sejny, 2010). See also Marta Baron, *Grzebanie grzebania: Archeolog i grabarz w twórczości Jerzego Ficowskiego* (Wydawnictwo Pasaże, 2016).

22. "My Unsurvivor," *Everything I Don't Know: The Selected Poems of Jerzy Ficowski*, trans. Jennifer Grotz and Piotr Sommer (World Poetry Books, 2020).

23. Ficowski's correspondents included Schulz's former students Mieczysław Łobodycz (Warsaw), Bogusław Marszal (Gdańsk), Edward Alojzy Lewicki (Mikołów, in southern Poland), Marek Spaet (Copenhagen), Irena Mitelman (Tel Aviv), Ida Rubinstein (Haifa), and Feiwel Schreier (Kiryat Ono, Israel). He also corresponded with scholars who did not know Schulz, including Natan Gross, Shalom Lindenbaum, Simon Schochet, and Lucjan Dobroszycki (a historian at the YIVO Institute for Jewish Research and a professor at Yeshiva University). This section is indebted to the work of Jerzy Kandziora, a scholar at Institute of Literary Research (Instytut Badań Literackich Polskiej Akademii Nauk) in Warsaw. See Kandziora, "Ukryci świadkowie, czyli co pozostało w książce Ficowskiego i w realnym świecie po dwóch kolegach Brunona Schulza," *Konteksty* no. 1–2

(2019): 335–40, and Kandziora, "Przestrzenie pamięci, przestrzenie rozposzenia (Składanie biografii Brunona Schulza)," *Przestrzenie geo(bio)graficzne w literaturze,* ed. Elżbieta Konończuk and Elżbieta Sidoruk (Wydawnictwo Uniwersytetu Białostockiego, 2015), 245–65.

24. Ficowski, *Regions of the Great Heresy,* 30. See also Ficowski, "Przypomnienie Brunona Schulza," *Życie Literackie,* Feb. 5, 1956, 6–7.

25. Andrzej Chciuk, "Pierwsza książka o Schulzu," *Kultura* 4 (1968). "Schulzology was born of rapture," the scholar Stanisław Rosiek has said, and Ficowski "was able as no one else to turn his rapture into scholarship." (Rosiek, "Zachwyt Ficowskiego," *Schulz/Forum* 3 (2014): 3.) See also Marcin Romanowski, "Jerzy Ficowski and the Biographical Affect," *Les grandes figures historiques dans les lettres et les arts* 6 (2017): 11–30.

26. See Jaroslaw Anders, "Bruno Schulz: The Prisoner of Myth," *Between Fire and Sleep: Essays on Modern Polish Poetry and Prose* (Yale University Press, 2009). Unlike Max Brod, of course, Ficowski never received instructions to destroy the author's unpublished works. Jerzy Jarzębski writes that Ficowski "is the most classical of [Schulz's] researchers and exegetes. He does not impose his interpretation upon others—he is more like a guardian of the letter, defending the integrity of the Schulzian message against all those who would like to dumb it down, trivialize or reduce it to their own needs or ideological assumptions." (Jarzębski, "Krytyk miłujący: Jerzy Ficowski jako badacz twórczości Schulza," in *Prowincja centru: Przypisy do Schulza* [Wydawnictwo Literackie Kraków, 2005].)

27. Aschenauer had joined the Nazi Party in May 1937 and the Wehrmacht in April 1941. After being classified in July 1947 as "exonerated" in the de-Nazification process, he was admitted to the bar and defended accused Nazi war criminals, including Otto Ohlendorf in the 1947 *Einsatzgruppen* trial, Werner Hersmann at the 1958 Ulm *Einsatzgruppen* trial, Walther Funk during his detention in Spandau, and Wilhelm Boger in the 1965 Auschwitz trial. In 1949, Aschenauer contacted the then largely unknown U.S. senator Joseph McCarthy and claimed that the convictions of seventy-three Waffen-SS soldiers in the Malmedy massacre trial (*U.S. v. Valentin Bersin et al.*) had been obtained by confessions extorted through torture. McCarthy repeated these allegations in a May 1949 Senate hearing.

28. Harry Zeimer, Yad Vashem testimony, Oct. 14, 1964 (Yad Vashem archives O.3 2718, p. 4).

29. Judgment of the Stuttgart Regional Court, March 16, 1962, published in *Justiz und NS-Verbrechen,* 18: 364–65. Witnesses included David Backenroth, Naftali Backenroth (Paris), Hans Joachim Badian (London), Hersz Betman, Jacob Goldsztein (Haifa), Wolf Herz (then living in Beersheva, Israel), Markus Kleiner, Artur Klinghoffer, Albert Kolpenicki, Chaim Krater, Gustav and Johanna Kreisler, Günter Mülberger, Chaim Patrich, Shimon Rand, Ida Rubinstein (Haifa), Leonard Seif, Rudolf Sokoll, Schachne Weissmann (Haifa), Franz Wenzel (former head of the German police department in Drohobycz), and Harry Zeimer (or Cajmer, then living in Jerusalem). Archival sources: Preliminary investigation of Felix Landau and records of the Staatsanwaltschaft Stuttgart: 11 208 AR-Z 60a/1959, BAL/3380. Indictment of Felix Landau (April 20, 1961): 14 Js 3808/58, BAL 162/3380, and Staatsarchiv Hamburg Az 147 Js 7/69. In February 1963, the Vienna court closed proceedings against Landau regarding his participation in the 1934 July Putsch in accordance with a 1957 amnesty (LG Vg 8e Vr 654/55).

30. Interview with Teja-Udo Landau, *Vater, Mutter, Hitler—Vier Tagebücher und eine Spurensuche* (dir. Tom Ockers, ECO Media, 2016).

31. See Jan T. Gross, *Fear: Anti-Semitism in Poland After Auschwitz* (Random House, 2006).

32. *Davar*, Aug. 3, 1960.

33. Lucy S. Dawidowicz, *The Holocaust and the Historians* (Harvard University Press, 1981), 124. See also Bożena Szaynok, "Israel in the Events of March 1968," in *1968: Forty Years After*, ed. Leszek W. Głuchowski and Antony Polonsky (Littman Library of Jewish Civilization, 2009), 150–58.

34. Wojciech Chmurzyński, ed., *Bruno Schulz, 1892–1942: Rysunki i archiwalia ze zbiorów Muzeum Literatury im. Adama Mickiewicza w Warszawie* (Warsaw: Adam Mickiewicz Museum of Literature, 1992), 13.

35. Among others: *Cinnamon Shops*, dir. Ryszard Major, 1976; *The Republic of Dreams*, dir. Rudolf Zioła, 1987; *Sanatorium Under the Hourglass*, dir. Jan Peszek, 1994; *The Last Escape*, dir. Aleksander Maksymiak, 2004; *Schulz: Scraps*, dir. Konrad Dworakowski; *Jakub's Room*, dir. Robert Stępniewski. Tadeusz Kantor, Poland's most outstanding avant-garde theater director, was inspired by Schulz (especially the use of mannequins) in plays like *The Dead Class* (1975). The Polish director and screenwriter Janusz Majewski has also expressed his indebtedness to Schulz's imagination.

36. Clive James, "The Iron Capital of Bruno Schulz," in *The Meaning of Recognition* (Picador, 2005). James does not give the actress's name.

37. Julian Krzyzanowski, *A History of Polish Literature* (Polish Scientific Publishers, 1978).

38. The renewed interest in Poland's Jewish history was led by Jerzy Tomaszewski, Zenon Guldon, Jerzy Holzer, and Piotr Wróbel, following tracks first laid in 1956 by the literary critic Artur Sandauer. A classical philologist educated in Lwów, Artur Sandauer taught at the Hebrew high school in Kraków. After escaping from the Sambor ghetto, he survived World War II on the Aryan side of the city.

39. See Andrzej Chojnowski, "The Jewish Community of the Second Republic in Polish Historiography of the 1980s," *Polin* 1 (1986); and Marcin Wodziński, "Jewish Studies in Poland," *Journal of Modern Jewish Studies* 10 (2011). Schulz's English translator Madeline G. Levine adds: "From 1948 into the 1980s the overwhelming majority of Polish works of fiction (not counting works by Jewish authors) represented Jews—if they did so at all—only *en masse*, as pitiful victims of the Holocaust, or, if individually, as superficially delineated minor characters." (Madeline G. Levine, "Wrestling with Ghosts: Poles and Jews Today," *East European Studies Occasional Papers* 36 (1998): 11.) What changed in Poland in the 1980s, said Marek Edelman in 1987, was that "interest in the Jewish problem can be interpreted as a mark of opposition to the idea of Communism. If the Commies are against the Jews then I'm for them!" (Marek Edelman, "Poland's 'Jewish Problem,'" *Harper's*, Aug. 1987.)

40. Besides Schulz, Celina Wieniewska's translations into English include Czesław Miłosz's novels *The Usurpers* and *The Seizure of Power*, Leszek Kolakowski's *The Key to Heaven and Conversations with the Devil*, and Henryk Grynberg's *Child of the Shadows*. Wieniewska's stepdaughter Deirdre Janson-Smith told me, "I know Celina and my father were very proud indeed of her work on Schulz and in later life he defended her work against criticism." Isaac Bashevis Singer reviewed her translation in the *Herald Tribune*: "Another translator might have tried to

make the author easier to read, by cutting his long and complicated sentences or even reducing the number of his adjectives. Miss Wieniewska has sensed that such editing would ruin Schulz's style. An almost literal translation, which in another case might be detrimental, is the only appropriate method here" (December 22, 1963). Nobel laureate J. M. Coetzee praised Wieniewska's English translation for its "rare richness, grace, and unity of style" but cited "numerous instances where Wieniewska cuts Schulz's prose to make it less florid, or universalizes specifically Jewish allusions." (Coetzee, "Bruno Schulz," *Inner Workings: Literary Essays 2000–2005* [Vintage, 2008], 65–78; first published as "Sweet Persuasions of the Dark" *New York Review of Books*, Feb. 27, 2003.) See also Zofia Ziemann, "The Inner and Outer Workings of Translation Reception: Coetzee on (Wieniewska's) Schulz," in *Travelling Texts: J. M. Coetzee and Other Writers*, ed. B. Kucała and R. Kusek (Peter Lang, 2014), 79–91. Coetzee was not the first to take such a view. Harry M. Geduld remarked in his 1965 review of *The Street of Crocodiles*: "Schulz was not really a Polish writer but a Jew who chose to write in Polish. . . . Wieniewska's translation succeeds in suggesting the burning colors, the richly sensuous 'tactile' evocations of a painter's prose, though a translator saturated in The Song of Solomon and Revelations might also have found ways of conveying Schulz's fundamental Hebraism" (*Studies in Short Fiction* 2, no 4 [1965]: 380).

In 2018, a new translation of Schulz's fiction into English, by Madeline G. Levine, met with acclaim. "Levine's translation is not only exquisitely composed and fastidiously accurate," Benjamin Paloff wrote in the *TLS*, "but it cleaves so tightly to the original that it is easy to imagine that these are the words that Schulz would have written in his own hand had he written in English." (Paloff, "Real Fantasist," *TLS*, April 6, 2018.)

For detailed looks at English translations of Schulz, see Zofia Ziemann, "The Good Bad Translator: Celina Wieniewska and her Bruno Schulz," *Asymptote*, Sept. 20, 2017; Ziemann, "Polish Literature and/or World Literature: Bruno Schulz in English," in *Polish Literature as World Literature*, ed. Piotr Florczyk and K. A. Wisniewski (Bloomsbury Academic, 2022); and Ziemann, "Translating Polish Jewishness: Bruno Schulz in English," *TranslatoLogica: A Journal of Translation, Language, and Literature* 1 (2017): 209–29.

41. In *The Prague Orgy* (1985), Philip Roth brings his narrator, Nathan Zuckerman, to Prague in search of two hundred unpublished stories by a Schulz-like writer. Schulz also features in Roth's *Operation Shylock* (p. 55) in a conversation between the Roth character and the Holocaust-haunted Israeli writer Aharon Appelfeld. Joanna Rostropowicz-Clark would write about Schulz in her dissertation, "Jews and Judaism in Polish Romantic Literature" (PhD diss., University of Pennsylvania, 1990).

42. "Roth and Singer on Bruno Schulz," *New York Times*, Feb. 13, 1977; reprinted in Philip Roth, *Shop Talk*. On another occasion, Roth described Schulz as "a batty writer on the order of, yes, Kafka, but batty about his Jewish father in his own sinister Polish way." (Quoted in Blake Bailey, *Philip Roth: The Biography* [W. W. Norton, 2021], 386.) On affinities between Singer and Schulz, see Caroline Rody, "The Magical Book Within the Book: I. B. Singer, Bruno Schulz, and Contemporary Jewish Post-Holocaust Fiction," in *The Palgrave Handbook of Magical Realism in the Twenty-First Century*, ed. Richard Perez and Victoria Chevalier (Palgrave, 2020), 347–48, and Chone Shmeruk, "Isaac Bashevis Singer on Bruno Schulz," trans. Anna Pekal, *Polish Review* 36, no. 2 (1991): 161–67.

43. The seventeen-volume collection of writing from behind the Iron Curtain, which Roth edited from 1974 through 1989, also introduced English-speaking readers to Milan Kundera's *Laughable Loves* (1975) and *The Book of Laughter and Forgetting* (1980); Tadeusz Borowski, *This Way for the Gas, Ladies and Gentlemen* (1976); Danilo Kiš, *A Tomb for Boris Davidovich* (1989); Jerzy Andrzejewski, *Ashes and Diamonds* (1980); and Witold Gombrowicz, *Ferdydurke* (1983). Ilan Stavans remarked of the authors in Roth's series: "He introduced them to the West, and they were a revelation, a shock, a sentimental education. Without them the present is inconceivable—without Schulz, Kiš, Kundera, and the others." (Stavans, "Lies, Disguises, Exile: A Conversation with Norman Manea," *Salmagundi* [Winter 1997]: 96.).

44. "Loneliness," Nov. 14, 1977; "Sanatorium Under the Sign of the Hourglass," Dec. 12, 1977; and "Father's Last Escape," Jan. 2, 1978.

45. These disciples of Schulz's include the American authors Helen Maryles Shankman (*In the Land of Armadillos*, 2016) and Reif Larsen (see Menachem Kaiser, "What Are You Reading, Reif Larsen?," *New Yorker*, June 24, 2009); Canadian author Norman Ravvin (*Café des Westens*, [Red Deer College Press, 1991]); Italian writers Marko Ercolani (*Il mese dopo l'ultimo*, 1999) and Ugo Ricarelli (*Un uomo che forse si chiamava Schulz*, 2000); Icelandic writer Sjón; Chilean writers Roberto Bolaño and Alejandro Zambra ("Alejandro Zambra Reads Bruno Schulz," *New Yorker* fiction podcast, Feb. 1, 2022); Swedish writer Tom Sandqvist (*At Home in Drohobycz*, 2021); Israeli novelist Amir Gutfreund (*Last Bullet Calls It*, published in Hebrew as *The Legend of Bruno and Adele*, 2017, and the short story "Trieste" from the collection *Shoreline Mansions*, trans. Jessica Cohen, 2013); Polish novelist Magdalena Tulli; French writers Hubert Nyssen and Pierre Pachet; British writers Colin Insole and Nadeem Aslam; Prague-born Berlin-based novelist Maxim Biller (*Inside the Head of Bruno Schulz*, trans. Anthea Bell [Pushkin Press, 2015]; German artist Dieter Jüdt (*Heimsuchung: Und andere Erzählungen von Bruno Schulz*, 1995); Czech writer Bohumil Hrabal; Croatian writer Dubravka Ugrešić; and Serbian writers Mirko Demić (*Cilibar, med, oskorusa* [Amber, honey, and sorb-apple], 2011), Milorad Pavić (*Dictionary of the Khazars*, 1988), and Danilo Kiš, especially in his novels *Garden, Ashes* (1965, trans. William J. Hannaher) and *Hourglass* (1972, trans. Ralph Manheim). On the affinities between Kiš and Schulz, see Alfred Gall, "Mythopoetic Traditions and Inserted Treatises: Bruno Schulz and Danilo Kiš," in De Bruyn and Van Heuckelom, *(Un)masking Bruno Schulz*, 153–72, and Jörg Schulte, *Eine Poetik der Offenbarung: Isaak Babel, Bruno Schulz, Danilo Kiš* [Harrassowitz Verlag, 2004]. In Polish, see Alla Tatarenko, *Pisanie Ojca. "Gen schulzowski" w prozie Danila Kiša* [Writing the father: The "Schulzean gene" in the fiction of Danilo Kiš], *Schulz/Forum* 8 (2016): 65–76.

46. Bruno Schulz, *Opowiadania. Wybór esejów i listów*, ed. Jerzy Jarzębski, Biblioteka narodowa series 1, no. 264 (Zakład Narodowy im. Ossolińskich, 1989); rev. ed. 1998.

47. "The Book," *Collected Stories*, 90.

48. The Polish critic Władysław Panas identified Schulz's reference in the story "Spring" to the true Book of Radiance (in Polish *prawdziwa księga blasku*) with the Zohar, the classic text of Kabbalah. "Schulz not only speaks of *tikkun*," Panas concludes, "but also treats his own narrative art as a work of restitution—as a part of the messianic process" (trans. Karen Underhill). See *Księga blasku: Traktat*

o kabale w prozie Brunona Schulza [The Book of Splendor: A tractate on the Kabbalah in Bruno Schulz's prose] (Lublin: Towarzystwo Naukowe Katolickiego Uniwersytetu Lubelskiego, 1997), 221, and Piotr Drozdowski, "Bruno Schulz and the Myth of the Book," *Indiana Slavic Studies* 5 (1990): 23–30. Michał Paweł Markowski argued that Panas's kabbalistic interpretation is "one-sided and blind to other readings. Above all, it is based on one fundamental assumption, drawn from the Lurianic Kabbalah: that matter is evil and everything should be done to redeem it." (Markowski, *Powszechna rozwiązłość: Schulz, egzystencja, literatura* [Kraków: Jagiellonian University Press, 2012], 89; trans. Zofia Ziemann.) The Polish writer Piotr Paziński told me:

> I think what Panas did at the time is brilliant and inspiring, but still an over-interpretation. . . . Schulz never read the Zohar or Chaim Vital's treatises, never studied in a *yeshiva*. . . . To present him as a kabbalist is to misinterpret his upbringing: assimilation in the Austro-Hungarian style. . . . Still, Panas's work was an important step forward, from Schulz almost entirely stripped of his Jewish identity to Schulz full of Jewishness, however heterodox.

John Updike suggested that Schulz's style reflects "a personal experience taken cabalistically." (Introduction to *Sanatorium Under the Sign of the Hourglass*, trans. Celina Wieniewska [Penguin, 1979].) Bożena Shallcross, a professor of Polish literature at the University of Chicago, argues that Schulz "ingeniously retextualized kabbalistic myths." (Shallcross, "Fragments of a Broken Mirror: Bruno Schulz's Retextualization of the Kabbalah," *East European Politics and Societies* 11, no. 2 [1997]: 272.)

49. "The Book," *Collected Stories*, 85.
50. "The Book," *Collected Stories*, 85. See Piotr J. Drozdowski, "Bruno Schulz and the Myth of the Book," *Indiana Slavic Studies* 5 (1990): 23–30.
51. "The Night of the Great Season," *Collected Stories*, 71.
52. Dorota Głowacka's interview with Jerzy Ficowski, "Interview in Warsaw, July 3, 1993," in Prokopczyk, *Bruno Schulz: New Documents and Interpretations*, 56, 59. See also Mikołaj Gliński, "In Search of 'The Messiah': Bruno Schulz & His Detective," Culture.pl, Oct. 2, 2019.
53. In a letter of July 19, 1987, Saul Bellow wrote to Cynthia Ozick about *The Messiah of Stockholm*:

> About Bruno Schulz I feel very much as you do. . . . But I was puzzled by your "Messiah." I puzzled myself over it. I liked the Hans Christian Andersen charm of your poor earnest young man in a Scandinavian capital, who is quixotic, deluded, fanatical, who lives on a borrowed Jewishness, leads a hydroponic existence and tries so touchingly to design his own selfhood. But when he is challenged by reality, we see the worst of him . . . because he is not the one and only authentic Schulz interpreter, he becomes a mere literary pro, that is, a nonentity. I read your book on the plane to Israel, and in Haifa gave my copy to A. B. Yehoshua. [Yehoshua gave an epigraph by Schulz to his novel *A Late Divorce*.—BB] He wanted it, and I urged him to read it. (Bellow, "Among Writers," *New Yorker*, April 26, 2010.)

54. Jerzy Ficowski discovered the manuscript in the papers of Zenon Waśniewski (a former classmate of Schulz's in the Lwów Polytechnic and co-editor of the

Chełm-based magazine *Kamena*), to whom Schulz had sent it in 1934. Half a century later, *Kamena* would republish Schulz's story "Spring" (Sept. 25–Oct. 8, 1983).

55. Józefina Szelińska to Jerzy Ficowski, April 4, 1964. Also lost: Schulz's letters to the Polish artist Stefania Dretler-Flin. In a 1956 interview, she said, "In the years 1927–32, and perhaps later, [Schulz] wrote to me two or three times a week. The letters were long, sometimes eight pages . . . several hundred of them. They filled the desk drawer to the brim." (Jan Kurczab, "Cień *Xięgi Bałwochwalczej*," *Życie Literackie* 44 [1956]: 5.)

56. In 1965, in search of Schulz's letters to Vogel, Jerzy Ficowski visited the apartment Vogel had shared with her husband on Leśna Street in Lwów. The building's Ukrainian caretaker told Ficowski that he had recently burned all the papers ("superfluous trash," as he called them) left by the former tenants. (Ficowski, "W poszukiwaniu śladów Brunona Schulza," *Współczesność* 25–26 (1965): 6.) Tomasz Różycki, whose father and grandparents lived on that small street until the war, related to me "a hypothesis (I hope not true) that Bruno had deposited the manuscript of his lost novel, *Messiah*, at Debora's place."

57. "The [German] language poses no serious difficulty for me," Schulz wrote to Romana Halpern. "I move in it with almost perfect freedom." (Schulz to Halpern, Sept. 29, 1937; *Letters and Drawings*, 152.) Schulz's manuscript was couriered to Thomas Mann by Aniela Kierska, the mother of Schulz's friend Jerzy Brodnicki. The Polish scholar Monika Szyszka vel Syska reports a rumor "that Mann stole Schulz's text and included it in *Doctor Faustus*." (Szyszka vel Syska, "Creator's Freedom: Schulz's Late Projects," *Acta Universitatis Lodziensis/Folia Litteraria Polonica* [2017]: 83–112.)

58. Nicole Krauss said, "His writing is so dense, and there's no real narrative to speak of. There's just atmosphere and incredible event. . . . There are all these flights of fantasy, and there are all these amazing possibilities, and crazy things happen—things that, if you tried to describe them outside of Schulz's language, sound absurd, but in his language sound perfectly natural." (*New Yorker* podcast, Feb. 17, 2012.)

59. In his novel *See Under: Love*, David Grossman writes, "I've come across a number of theories concerning his lost novel, *The Messiah*: that it's about how Bruno lures the Messiah into the Drohobycz Ghetto with his spellbinding prose, or that it's about the Holocaust and Bruno's last years under the Nazi Occupation" (p. 98). Schulz's lost manuscript forms the basis of the Polish writer Wojciech Żmudziński's surreal 2012 novel, *Messiah* and is one of eight lost manuscripts featured in Giorgio van Straten's *In Search of Lost Books: The Forgotten Stories of Eight Mythical Volumes*, translated from the Italian by Simon Carnell and Erica Segre (Pushkin Press, 2018). "Some maintain that the typescript was buried in a garden," van Straten writes, "others that it was hidden inside a wall; still others insist that it was concealed beneath the tiles of a floor" (p. 61). For more on the search for Schulz's lost manuscript, see Jerzy Ficowski, "W oczekiwaniu na mesjasza" [Awaiting the Messiah], *Polityka*, Nov. 19, 1992; Helena Zaworska, "Czekanie na 'Mesjasza,'" *Gazeta Wyborcza*, 1993; and Mikołaj Gliński, "In Search of 'The Messiah': Bruno Schulz & His Detective," Culture.pl, Oct. 2, 2019.

60. Patti Smith, *M Train* (Knopf, 2015), 128.

61. According to the poet and essayist Anna Frajlich, Ficowski "suffered tremendously when an American publishing house declined to honor this chivalrous code

in the case of the identity of Schulz's fiancée." (Frajlich, "The Lifelong Passion of Jerzy Ficowski," *The Ghost of Shakespeare: Collected Essays* [Academic Studies Press, 2020], 119.)

62. Jan Błoński, "Biedni Polacy patrzą na getto" [A poor Pole looks at the ghetto], *Tygodnik Powszechny* 41, no. 2 (Jan. 11, 1987). The title echoes that of a well-known Czesław Miłosz poem, "A Poor Christian Looks at the Ghetto."

63. Szymon Rudnicki, "Transformations in Poland and Polish-Jewish Relations in the Last Decade," quoted in Abraham Brumberg, "Poland, the Polish Intelligentsia and Antisemitism," *Soviet Jewish Affairs* 20, nos. 2–3 (1990): 6.

64. Two conferences yielded published proceedings: *Bruno Schulz: In Memoriam, 1982–1992*, ed. M. Kitowska-Łysiak (Wydawnictwo FIS, 1992), and *Czytanie Schulza* [Reading Schulz], ed. Jerzy Jarzębski (Instytut Filologii Polskiej Uniwersytetu Jagiellonskiego, 1992).

CHAPTER 7: AFTERIMAGES

1. "A Treatise on Mannequins, Conclusion," *Collected Stories*, 32.

2. Alan Rosenbaum, "Yad Vashem Chair Avner Shalev Recalls Achievements, Challenges," *Jerusalem Post*, Dec. 30, 2020.

3. The Roman architect Vitruvius records that in Sparta, "paintings have been taken out of certain walls by cutting through the bricks, enclosed in wooden frames, and brought to the Comitium" (Vitruvius Pollio, *De architectura*, book 2, chapter 8). Pliny the Elder reports that the first-century Roman emperor Caligula "inflamed with lustfulness," attempted to have a painting of Atalanta and Helena removed from a wall in Lanuvium (modern-day Lanuvio, Italy), "but the nature of the plaster would not admit of it" (Pliny the Elder, *Natural History* 35:6). For exhibitions devoted to detached murals and frescoes, see the three exhibitions, and related catalogs, held in Florence at the Forte di Belvedere in 1957, 1958, and 1959, each entitled *Mostra di affreschi stacatti*; also see *The Charm of the Fresco: Detached Masterpieces from Pompeii to Giotto, from Correggio to Tiepolo* at the Ravenna Museum of Art (curated by Claudio Spadoni and Luca Ciancabilla, 2014) and the two-volume catalog of the same name.

4. "Somewhat to one side, a stranger was sitting on the ottoman. In his lap he was holding a model of the Temple of Solomon, made of pinewood, papier-mâché, and gold paint. Frohmann, from Drohobycz, he said, bowing slightly, going on to explain that it had taken him seven years to build the temple, from the biblical description, and that he was now travelling from ghetto to ghetto exhibiting the model." (W. G. Sebald, *The Emigrants*, trans. Michael Hulse [New Directions, 1996], 167.)

   "Herr L. Schwarzbach, who hails not from Ophir [a port, famous for its wealth, mentioned in the Bible] but from distant Drohobycz, has undertaken to rebuild the Temple of Solomon, 'in miniature, of course,' as he says in his advertisement, on a scale of 1 to 70. . . . Idiosyncratic battlements teeter aloft like little jokes of God, at the expense of this building in His praise." (Joseph Roth, "Solomon's Temple in Berlin," *What I Saw: Reports from Berlin, 1920–1933*, trans. Michael Hofmann [W. W. Norton, 2003], 42.)

5. "ICOMOS Principles for the Preservation and Conservation-Restoration of Wall Paintings," Article 6, ratified by the ICOMOS 14th General Assembly in Victoria Falls, Zimbabwe, in 2003. "Even countries like Israel and Poland that follow the

rule of law," writes Polish-American historian John Radzilowski, "appear willing to exempt themselves from norms of international conduct in taking or keeping art, in particular cases when it suits them." (John Radzilowski, "Thieves Stealing from Thieves, Victims from Victims: The Culture, Morality, and Politics of Stolen Art in Twentieth Century Poland, *Polish Review* 61, no. 4 [2016]: 3–17.)

6. Ian Traynor, "Murals Illuminate Holocaust Legacy Row," *Guardian*, July 2, 2001.

7. Statement of Nikolai Kaluzhni, June 12, 2001.

8. Anatoly Vlasiuk, "Bruno Schulz's Biography, Part of the Holocaust," *The Day* (Kyiv), July 10, 2001.

9. Yury Kril, "The Return of Bruno Schulz," *The Day* (Kyiv), July 23, 2002. Voznytsky had earlier said, "The wall paintings are valuable because they were created by Bruno Schulz in the last days of his life before he was shot. The artwork is more like a memorial than a creative monument. But of course it should be part of Ukraine's national property." Jemmy Dombrowska, *Vysoky zamok* 119 (June 2–3, 2001).

10. "The frescoes only became a story," one observer noted, "when they could be fit into resonant narrative frameworks—of Poles as tragic, misunderstood victims; Jews as outsiders, hostile to the Poles." (Denise V. Powers, "Fresco Fiasco: Narratives of National Identity and the Bruno Schulz Murals of Drogobych," *East European Politics and Societies* 17, no. 4 [Fall 2003]: 645.)

11. Jerzy Pilch, "Męczeństwo państwa Kałużnych z Drohobycza," *Polityka*, June 16, 2001.

12. See also Antony Polonsky and Joanna Michlic, eds., *The Neighbors Respond* (Princeton University Press, 2004), and Geneviève Zubrzycki, "Jan Gross's *Neighbors* and Poland's Narrative Shock," *Jewish Quarterly Review* 112, no. 2 (Spring 2022): 234–38.

13. Gebert, *Almanach Festiwal im. Brunona Schulza 2012* (EMG Publishing), 26. For a discussion of Schulz as a representative of Central European and Austro-Hungarian culture, see Błażej Szymankiewicz, "Bruno Schulz: Pisarz środkowoeuropejski?" [Bruno Schulz: A Central European writer?], *Zeszyty Naukowe Towarzystwa Doktorantów Uniwersytetu Jagiellońskiego: Nauki Humanistyczne* 15, no. 4 (2016): 7–23.

14. Israeli prime minister David Ben-Gurion wrote to Argentine president Arturo Frondizi: "I do not underestimate the seriousness of the formal violation of Argentine law committed by those who found Eichmann, but I am convinced that very few people anywhere can fail to understand their feelings and appreciate the supreme moral validity of their act. . . . I am convinced that Your Excellency will give full weight to the transcendental moral force of these motivations" (June 3, 1960). Joachim Prinz, president of the American Jewish Congress, added that Israel "has not only legal grounds to try Eichmann, but also a great moral right and responsibility for bringing him to justice." See Deborah Lipstadt, *The Eichmann Trial* (Schocken/ Nextbook, 2011), chapter 2.

15. Ian Traynor, "Murals Illuminate Holocaust Legacy Row," *Guardian*, July 2, 2001.

16. Quoted in Ficowski, *Regions of the Great Heresy*, 170, 172.

17. "Uproar That Yad Vashem Took Schulz Murals," *JTA*, June 21, 2001. Gale Stokes, a specialist in the history of Eastern Europe and a professor at Rice University,

added: "It is incomprehensible that someone can claim that stealing art is an ethical act, doubly so when the work is as intimately connected with its location as a mural." (Yad Vashem deputy director Yehudit Shendar and senior art curator Eliad Moreh-Rosenberg insisted that even in their original setting, Schulz's murals were "discontinuous fragments.") Michael Berenbaum, past president of Steven Spielberg's Survivors of the Shoah Visual History Foundation, agreed. "Museums may mumble under their breath, 'All this is about power and the ability to possess. Look what you Jews did when you had the opportunity.'" (Nacha Cattan, "Murals' Grab by Memorial Stirs a Debate in Arts World," *Forward*, July 13, 2001.)

18. Regina Mönch, "Die Märchen im Spielzimmer der SS," *Frankfurter Allgemeine Zeitung*, May 13, 2013. The National Book Award–winning American novelist Jaimy Gordon wrote that Geissler's documentary film "degenerates into a polemic against Yad Vashem: now the powerful Jews of Israel have become the oppressors, and the tiny Jewish remnant of Drohobych the oppressed and disinherited, whose last hope is snatched from them with Schulz's paintings." See also the installation catalog for *The Picture Chamber of Bruno Schulz*: Benjamin Geissler, *Fundstücke und die virtuelle Rekonstruktion der Bilderkammer mit den Wandmalereien des Bruno Schulz* (Berlin: Umwelt Bibliothek Grosshennersdorf, 2012).

19. Chris McGreal, "This Is Ours and Ours Alone," *Guardian*, March 15, 2005.

20. Grzegorz Józefczuk, "Finał awantury o freski Schulza," *Gazeta Wyborcza*, Dec. 31, 2007.

21. Anshel Pfeffer, "In Search of Bruno Schulz," *Haaretz*, April 7, 2008.

22. Grossman used a similar expression in his talk at the 92nd Street Y, New York City, May 4, 2009: "Every story by Schulz is a protest—full of humor and irony but a protest—against oblivion and boredom and banality, against the stereotypical approach to the human being, against tyranny and simplicity and narrow-mindedness, against everything that has no daring and no inspiration and no soul."

23. "When I wrote the 'Bruno' chapter of my book," Grossman says, "and described an imaginary scenario in which Bruno flees the failure of civilization, the perfidious language of humans, and joins a school of salmon, I felt that I was very close to touching the root of life itself, the primal, naked impulse of life, which salmon seem to sketch in their long journey, and which the real Schulz wrote about in his books, and for which he yearned in every one of his stories: the longed-for realm that he called the Age of Genius." (David Grossman, "The Age of Genius," *New Yorker*, June 8–15, 2009.) See also Katarzyna Szurmiak, "Grossman's White Room and Schulzian Empty Spaces," *See Under: Shoah*, ed. Marc De Kesel, Bettine Siertsema, and Katarzyna Szurmiak (Brill, 2014), 59–73, and Naomi Sokoloff, "Reinventing Bruno Schulz: Cynthia Ozick's *The Messiah of Stockholm* and David Grossman's *See Under: Love*," *AJS Review* 13, nos. 1–2 (Spring–Autumn 1988): 171–99.

24. Józef Nacht, "Wywiad drastyczny" [A drastic interview], *Nasza Opinia* 77 (1939).

25. Schulz, "An Essay for S. I. Witkiewicz," *Letters and Drawings*, 112; originally published in *Tygodnik Ilustrowany* 17 (1935).

26. *Dawn: The Journal of Petroleum Officials in Borysław* [*Świt. Organ urzędników naftowych w Borysławiu*], Jan. 15, 1922. The paper, published twice a month, was edited at the time by Klemens Funkenstein, a leader of Kalleia, an arts and

culture salon in Drohobycz that Schulz had joined after World War I. The rediscovered "Undula" was published in *Schulz/Forum* 14 (2019): 5–8. See also Lesia Chomycz, "Wokół wystawy w Borysławiu: O dwóch debiutach Brunona Schulza," trans. Adam Pomorski, *Schulz/Forum* 14 (2019): 13–32, and Ariko Kato, "Is Marceli Weron Bruno Schulz? The Newly Discovered Short Story 'Undula,'" *Polish Review* 66, no. 4 (2021): 106–14. On the centenary of its publication, "Undula" was translated into Ukrainian from the Polish by Svetlana Breslavska, *Zbruč*, Jan. 15, 2022. Stanley Bill, a scholar of twentieth-century Polish literature at Cambridge University, writes: "The discovery of what is probably Schulz's earliest published story opens the tantalizing possibility that he might have published other works under pseudonyms. Polish and Ukrainian researchers are currently combing through archives in both countries for further traces. Almost eighty years after his murder in the Holocaust, the image of Bruno Schulz's life and work could be very far from complete. With the revelation of a new deity in 'Undula,' there may yet be hope for those still waiting for *The Messiah*." (Stanley Bill, "'Undula': A Newly Discovered Story by Bruno Schulz," *Notes from Poland*, July 11, 2020.) Other discoveries continue. In March 2021, a previously unknown pencil drawing by Schulz, "Figures Outdoors" (1935), which had belonged to the Israeli art critic Haim Gamzu, sold at an Israeli auction for $18,880.

27. Bruno Schulz, *Undula*, trans. Frank Garrett (Sublunary Editions, 2020), 9.

28. A Lviv newspaper reported that the Schulz Festival "reminded the people of Drohobych in what celebrated town they live. How the land of chimerical Bruno attracts people from different places: from Stockholm to Melbourne, from Chicago to Tokyo. Step-by-step, the ordinary people and government representing their interests start realizing that every fruit grown in this land is a part of 'our' common cultural heritage, an element of both modern Ukrainian and world process." (Quoted in Oksana Weretiuk, "The Ukrainian Reception of Bruno Schulz's Writings: Paradox or Norm?" in De Bruyn and Van Heuckelom, *(Un)masking Bruno Schulz*, 428.) "During the Schulz festival," Karen Underhill writes, "for those who take part, Drohobych becomes a better world—the kind of world, the kind of Ukraine, the kind of Galicia, the kind of Drohobych, that they would like to live in, and perhaps (as the festival implies, insists) that *could have been*. . . . The figure of Schulz himself becomes during this week at one and the same time the patron saint and the Hasidic *tzaddik* of that imagined world." (Karen Underhill, "Next Year in Drohobycz: On the Uses of Jewish Absence," *East European Politics and Societies* 25, no. 3 [Aug. 2011]: 590.)

29. Andrukhovych's translation was supported by Grzegorz Gauden, director of the Polish Book Institute (Instytut Książki) and backer of the Schulz Festival in Drohobycz. The first Ukrainian translation of *Sanatorium Under the Sign of the Hourglass* (by Andriy Pavlyshyn) followed in 2002. Previous Ukrainian translations of Schulz's stories included those by Mykola Yakovyna, Taras Wozniak, and Andriy Shkrabyuk. In 2012, Schulz's letters and his essays were translated into Ukrainian, the former by Pavlyshyn and the latter by Wiera Meniok. The first Ukrainian biography of Schulz (also by Pavlyshyn) appeared in 2020. In 2022, a bilingual Polish-Ukrainian book, *I'm from Drohobycz* (edited by Piotr Prokopiak and Switłana Bresławska), collected the recently discovered Schulz story "Undula" and poems devoted to Schulz's memory by Jerzy Ficowski, Tadeusz Różewicz, and others.

30. Two operas based on Schulz's prose are Juliusz Łuciuk's *Demiurgos* and Zbigniew Rudziński's *Mannequins*. The Kraków Klezmer Band, together with John Zorn, recorded the album *Sanatorium Under the Sign of the Hourglass*. The Warsaw-born singer and poet Jacek Kleyff wrote a ballad called "On the Death of Bruno Schulz in November '42."

31. A Polish rock band, based in Lodz, took the name Bruno Schulz. Its lead singer, Karol Stolarek, said that encountering Schulz's drawings at age fourteen "was like a revelation."

32. In 2012, the well-known Wrocław artist Mira Żelechower-Aleksiun created a cycle of thirteen paintings titled *The Calendar of Remembrance by Bruno Schulz*. She called it "my tribute to the artist and the entire generation of Jews murdered in the Holocaust, including my father."

33. In 2013, Mariusz Pisarski and Marcin Bylak designed a hypertextual internet game based on Schulz's prose called *Idol* (*Bałwochwał*). See Mariusz Pisarski, "Bruno Schulz—Digitally: The Internet Gamebook *Idol* and the Future of Schulz Adaptations on the Computer Screen," *CzasKultury* 1 (2014).

34. Oksana Weretiuk, "The Ukrainian Reception of Bruno Schulz's Writings: Paradox or Norm?," 429–30. The high school where Schulz taught is today a pedagogical college named after Ivan Franko. According to the first Ukrainian book about Drohobycz and Schulz (2006): "Drohobycz as depicted by Schulz lives as if separated from its inhabitants. The citizens of Drohobycz, as depicted by the Polish author, are simply people, whereas Franko grasps an absolutely different aspect of the problem: their sociopolitical and to some extent, nationalistic features. The same characters (the Roman Catholic Church, the sun, the clock on town hall) perform different functions. In Schulz's writing they take on mythological proportions, while as described by Franko, these characters are concrete and realistic." (Quoted in Weretiuk, 430.)

35. Stanley Bill, "Bruno Schulz and the Vanishing Border," Schulz Festival, Drohobych, May 27, 2014 (unpublished talk).

36. Interview with Yuriy Martynovych, Espreso.tv, July 12, 2021.

37. There are exceptions. The writer and photographer Marianna Maksymova, a participant in the 2020 festival, said, "Immersed in Schulz's prose, I realized that Drohobycz is the city I want to be in. I used to want to leave here, because, obviously, there are more beautiful and comfortable, more promising places. . . . After reading Schulz's works, this city became a much deeper place for me than the way I had seen it before." ("Lan Was Here, Bruno Schulz Lived Here: An Interview with Anna Zolotnyuk," *Tyktor*, Nov. 25, 2021.)

38. Also in 1989, Jerzy Ficowski proposed that a symbolic tombstone for Schulz be placed in Warsaw. The design—by the Warsaw sculptor Marek Tomza—consisted of two *matzevot* ("headstones" in Hebrew), white and black, facing and reflecting each other. It was never carried out. (Ficowski, "Pomnik Brunona Schulza," *Życie Warszawy* 14 [1989].)

39. Salomon, Ruzya, Gilda, Maks, and Gusta Vekselberg; Pepa, Telya, and Bronya Korn; Cilya and Eda Galleman; Adolf and Ruzya Klinghoffer; Zigmund, Lelya, Karol, and Alfred Gausman.

40. "His individual murder—or martyrdom, as it is seen—at the hands of the Nazis further raises the commemoration of his figure to the level of a new religious ritual," Karen Underhill writes. (Karen Underhill, "Next Year in Drohobych: On the Uses of Jewish Absence," *East European Politics and Societies* [Aug. 2011]: 590.)

41. "A Second Autumn," *Collected Stories*, 168.
42. "Stephen Bandera molodym postav v drohobyts'komu skveri," *Za vil'nu Ukrainu*, Oct. 16, 1999.

EPILOGUE

1. "Spring," *Collected Stories*, 120.
2. Schulz to Maria Kasprowiczowa, Jan. 25, 1934.
3. More recently, Karen Underhill has written that Schulz can be seen "as a writer who goes to some length to de-ethnicize and de-contextualize his writing, seeking his entry into a non-marked community of European letters." (Underhill, "Ecstasy and Heresy: Martin Buber, Bruno Schulz, and Jewish Modernity," in De Bruyn and Van Heuckelom, *(Un)masking Bruno Schulz*, 30.) Elsewhere Underhill argues that Schulz sought "to develop a distinctly Jewish modernist aesthetic, shaped by and drawing upon the world of east European Jewish literary, hermeneutic and narrative tradition, while at the same time choosing to actively encrypt, downplay or universalize that Jewish content." (Cited by Zofia Ziemann, "Translating Polish Jewishness: Bruno Schulz in English," *TranslatoLogica: A Journal of Translation, Language, and Literature* 1 [2017]: 216, from a lecture Underhill gave at the Jagiellonian University in June 2016.) For an argument that Schulz downplayed Jewish motifs in his fiction, see Stefan Chwin, "Dlaczego Bruno Schulz nie chciał być pisarzem żydowskim (o 'wymazywaniu' żydowskości w *Sanatorium pod Klepsydrą* i *Sklepach cynamonowych*" [Why Bruno Schulz did not want to be a Jewish writer (on "erasing" Jewishness in *Sanatorium Under the Sign of the Hourglass* and *The Street of Crocodiles*)], *Schulz/Forum* 4 (2014): 5–21.
4. Rachel Auerbach to Schulz, July 25, 1938, *Księga listów*, 294.
5. *New York Review of Books*, Nov. 29, 2001; signed by Padraic Kenney, István Deák, John Connelly, Hugo Lane, Brian Porter, Gale Stokes, et al. In replying to a response to that letter, they shift to a language of predation: "We can agree about the deplorable state of Drohobych, and perhaps the whole of Ukraine. . . . But surely the time has long past when yet another load of Elgin marbles could be carted off to civilization. All over the world, museums are reevaluating their collecting practices, and are sometimes returning works of art long ago looted from private collections or entire communities. This is not the time to embark on a new wave of predatory collecting." (*New York Review of Books*, May 23, 2002.) For another example, among many, of this line of thinking: "As a secularized Jew from Ukraine who spoke Polish and engaged with Catholicism," Callum Goetz writes, "Schulz doesn't easily fit the common ethno-national markers of his readers. A more fitting legacy for Schulz is that of a borderless paragon, a hero of many banners." ("The Fabrication of Bruno Schulz," *Antithesis Journal*, Nov. 23, 2021.) "Schulz is now celebrated by Polish literati, Israeli Zionists, and West Ukrainians," writes Omer Bartov, a historian at Brown University whose mother came from Galicia. "Once disowned by all, now everyone wants a part of him: the Poles his language and art, the Ukrainians his local color, the Zionists his Jewishness." (Bartov, *Tales from the Borderlands: Making and Unmaking the Galician Past* [Yale University Press, 2022], 187.)
6. Arkadiusz Kalin, "The Afterlife of Schulzology: What Is It Good For?," *Czas Kultury*, Jan. 2014. Erica Lehrer similarly classes Yad Vashem's treatment of Schulz's murals among "projects of reclamation [that] retrench ethno-nationalism." Lehrer,

NOTES TO PAGES 210–211

"Material Kin: 'Communities of Implication' in Post-Colonial, Post-Holocaust Polish Ethnographic Collections." In *Across Anthropology: Troubling Colonial Legacies, Museums, and the Curatorial*, edited by Margareta von Oswald and Jonas Tinius, 308.

7. Indeed, even those who saw good reason for Schulz's murals to be at Yad Vashem objected to the underhanded way they got there. The Kraków-born artist Ewa Kuryluk told me, "Every decent person knows, I guess, that paying somebody for getting the Schulz murals out of Drohobych wasn't an admirable deed. And arguing that his work has to be in Jerusalem because of him being Jewish is a bit ludicrous, isn't it? On the other hand, the murals may be safer in Yad Vashem, as are the Greek marbles at the British Museum."

8. The 1979 Hebrew translation of Schulz's fiction (reprinted in 1983 and 1986) was dedicated to Rachel Auerbach, who had died three years earlier. Auerbach had shared with translator Yoram Brunovsky her recollections of Schulz and had shown him Schulz's drawings. (Brunovsky had earlier translated part of Schulz's story "The Age of Genius" into Hebrew: *Haaretz*, March 4, 1977.) Co-translator Uri Orlev (born Jerzy Henryk Orłowski) called it "the most difficult literary work I've ever undertaken. Schulz's Polish simply derailed my Hebrew with its vital force." (*Almanach Festiwal im. Brunona Schulza 2012* [EMG Publishing], 21, 61.) See also Uri Orlev, "Translating Bruno Schulz," *Haaretz*, April 13, 2009 (in Hebrew). An excellent new Hebrew translation by Miri Paz appeared in 2018 (published by Hakibbutz Hameuchad).

9. Yitzhak Laor, "The East Is Ours," *Haaretz*, May 25, 2007.

10. Israel Gutman, "The Holocaust Is Ours," *Haaretz*, June 3, 2007.

11. Letter to the editor, *Haaretz*, June 20, 2007. Only two members of Bruno Schulz's family survived the Shoah: his nephew and niece, the children of his elder brother, Izydor. Bruno's nephew Jakub (Kuba) Schulz escaped to London via the south of France and Portugal. The filmmaker Jens Carl Ehlers told me that Kuba "looked quite similar to Bruno, and as a former businessman he was rather interested in art and the way we (the Quay Brothers and I) were working on his uncle's heritage." In January 1942, Bruno Schulz's niece, Ella Schulz-Podstolska, and her husband, Joseph, fled Lwów with false documents and hid in the mountains around Zakopane. After the war they lived with their son, Marek (born 1945), in Zakopane; they left Poland in 1963 and eventually settled in Düsseldorf, Germany. Ella quit her job as a bank telephone operator and returned to her original love: painting. Jakub and Ella Schulz died in the 1990s. Marek Podstolski died in 2020. He and his wife, Ewa, had no children.

As if to underscore his claim that Schulz "is still mine," Marek Podstolski put seven of Schulz's drawings up for auction at Sotheby's in New York in December 2012: "A Street Scene" sold for $50,000; "Joseph, Jacob, and Fighters" for $47,500; "Jacob, Joseph, and the Photographer" for $46,875; "Bianca with Her Father in the Carriage" for $40,000; "Schoolgirls Taking a Walk" for $40,000; "Four People Sitting at a Table: A Double-Sided Drawing" for $17,500; and "Double Portrait of Mrs. Bartischan" for $11,250.

12. *Old Truths and New Clichés: Essays by Isaac Bashevis Singer*, ed. David Stromberg (Princeton University Press, 2022), 49.

13. See Israel Bartal, "The Kinnus Project: Wissenschaft des Judentums and the Fashioning of a 'National Culture' in Palestine," in *Transmitting Jewish Traditions:*

Orality, Textuality and Cultural Diffusion, ed. Yaakov Elman and Israel Gershoni (Yale University Press, 2000), 310–23.

14. Narkiss, *On the Question of the Salvage of Art Remnants* (Sept. 1948), 3; cited in Shir Kochavi, "Salvage to Restitution: 'Heirless' Jewish Cultural Property in Post–World War II," PhD diss., University of Leeds, 2017, 104. The passage cited by Narkiss is Talmud Bavli, Megillah 29a. Israeli cultural figures involved in the rescue of European Jewish heritage included Gershom Scholem of the Hebrew University, who beginning in 1946 made a number of trips to Germany on behalf of the Commission for Jewish Cultural Reconstruction; Holocaust survivor Miriam Novitch of the Ghetto Fighters' House Museum; Chaim Gamzu, art critic and director of the Tel Aviv Museum of Art; and Chaim Atar (Apteker), a Ukrainian-born Israeli painter and founder of the Mishkan Museum of Art in Kibbutz Ein-Harod. See Miriam Novitch, *Spiritual Resistance: Art from Concentration Camps, 1940–1945* (Jewish Publication Society, 1981).

15. In an article about the Schulz murals, Israeli journalist Tali Lipkin-Shahak wrote, "Seeing today's Polish Jews as if they were a thriving Jewish community raising its collective Jewish voice is an illusion. The State of Israel and Yad Vashem, its agent in Holocaust matters, together constitute the living memorial to the cultural and artistic life of the Eastern European Jews who chose not to die and be buried there after the war. . . . On the most essential, fundamental, and basic, existential level, Israel is the final home of living Jews, while Yad Vashem is the final home of the murdered Jews—and their memory." ("Whose Holocaust Was It, Anyway?," *Jerusalem Post*, July 27, 2001.)

16. See the exhibition catalog: Wojciech Chmurzyński, Yona Fischer, and Bozena Kolodziejczak, eds., *The Drawings of Bruno Schulz: From the Collection of the Adam Mickiewicz Museum of Literature, Warsaw* (Israel Museum, 1990).

17. See Matti Friedman, *The Aleppo Codex* (Algonquin, 2012). After a quarter century of legal battles concerning the Crowns of Damascus, Judge David Gidoni of the Jerusalem District Court ruled in August 2020 that as "treasures of the Jewish people" bearing "historic, religious and national importance," the manuscripts belonged under public trust at the National Library of Israel. Israel's attorney general, Avichai Mandelblit, had told the court that the manuscripts were "cultural property of a public and national nature, which are ascribed historic, religious and national importance of the highest order."

18. "Bruno Schulz's Wall Paintings," *New York Review of Books*, May 23, 2002; the piece was signed by Aharon Appelfeld, Shlomo Avineri, Omer Bartov, Yehuda Bauer, Dina Porat, Hanna Yablonka, A. B. Yehoshua, and seventeen other scholars.

19. Daphne Merkin was as "elated" by Yad Vashem's removal of Schulz's murals as by Entebbe. "My visceral response," she said, "was 'Good for them!' This was an Entebbe-like action." (Quoted in Dinitia Smith, "Debating Who Controls Holocaust Artifacts," *New York Times*, July 18, 2001.) "It boggles my imagination to be discussing the rights of the Polish community and of the [Drohobych] Jewish community of four hundred," Merkin said elsewhere. "If they're that interested, let them to come to Israel" to see the murals. ("After Yad Vashem's Mural 'Rescue,' Questions and Recriminations Linger," *JTA*, July 18, 2001.) The critic Clive James likewise called the Israeli recovery of Schulz's murals "a cultural version of the raid on Entebbe."

20. István Deák, "Review of *The Idea of Galicia* by Larry Wolff," *Slavic Review* 70, no. 2 (Summer 2011): 424.

21. Milan Kundera, "Three Contexts of Art: From Nation to World," *Cross Currents* 12 (1993): 7–8.

22. "When [Władysław Panas] lectures on kabbala in Schulz," Jerzy Ficowski said, "he is so inspired by the supernatural that he almost levitates fifteen centimeters above the ground and doesn't know what is going on around him." (Interview with Ficowski, July 3, 1993, in Prokopczyk, *Bruno Schulz: New Documents and Interpretations*, 69.) The Polish-born literary scholar and Auschwitz survivor Shalom Lindenbaum took a line of interpretation similar to Panas's: "It is not coincidental that the story 'Treatise on Tailors' Dummies' has a subtitle: 'The Second Book of Genesis.' We are dealing here with a 'second creation,' connected in these stories with the arrival of the Messiah, and which, according to the Kabbalah, symbolizes the 'renewal of the world.'" ("Schulz's Messianic Vision and Its Mystical Undercurrents," American Association for Polish-Jewish Studies, undated.) See also Shalom Lindenbaum, "Wizja Mesjanistyczna Schulza i jej podłoże mistyczne," in *Czytanie Schulza* [Reading Schulz], ed. Jerzy Jarzębski (Instytut Filologii Polskiej Uniwersytetu Jagiellonskiego, 1992), 33–67. In the interview quoted at the start of this note, Ficowski dismissed Lindenbaum's view as "a far-fetched exaggeration." (Dorota Głowacka's interview with Jerzy Ficowski, "Interview in Warsaw, July 3, 1993," in Czeslaw Z. Prokopczyk, ed., *Bruno Schulz: New Documents and Interpretations*, p. 69.)

23. Alfred Sproede, "Between Avant-Garde and Hasidic Redemption," in De Bruyn and Van Heuckelom, *(Un)masking Bruno Schulz*, 495. In the last decades, many scholars have searched out Hasidic sources in Schulz's writing. Four examples will suffice. First, Alfred Sproede writes, "Schulz is indebted to the Hasidic tradition not only for his tone of enthusiasm and the illuminated gestures celebrating God's ubiquity. His familiarity with Hasidism reaches well beyond a broad perception of piety and of its expressive manifestations." (Sproede, 480. See also Alfred Sproede, "Eine verlorene Art jüdischen Erzählens: Zur Prosa von Bruno Schulz," in *Jüdische Autoren Ostmitteleuropas im 20. Jahrhundert*, ed. Hans Henning Hahn and Jens Stüben (Peter Lang, 2000), 253–75.) Second, Andrea Meyer-Fraatz adds, "Although he was not religious, his literary work proves his knowledge of the rabbinic tradition. . . . Schulz uses Hasidic elements to expose or rather stage himself as a Jewish avant-garde author." (Meyer-Fraatz, "Exposing and Concealing Jewish Origin: Bruno Schulz and Bolesław Leśmian," in De Bruyn and Van Heuckelom, *(Un)masking Bruno Schulz*, 57.) Third, Karen Underhill sees Schulz's writing "as a point of intersection and conversation between German Jewish and Polish Jewish, or eastern and western Jewish, intellectual trends. . . . Such echoes and borrowings from Hasidic and kabbalistic tradition were integral to Schulz's modernist aesthetic experiments. . . . [He] represents a combination of profound engagement with Jewish tradition and stubborn commitment to a cosmopolitan, universalist vision of art." (Underhill, "Bruno Schulz's Galician Diasporism," 4, 7, 25.) Elsewhere, Underhill writes that for Schulz, as for Martin Buber, "the relationship with myth is simultaneously a relationship to Jewish tradition of the Galician region." (Underhill, "Ecstasy and Heresy: Martin Buber, Bruno Schulz, and Jewish Modernity," in De Bruyn and Van Heuckelom, *(Un)masking Bruno Schulz*, 28–29.) Finally, David A. Goldfarb writes, "Schulz probably did not have intimate direct knowledge of Zohar or Talmud or Maimonides in Hebrew and Aramaic, but he could have read them in German, and it would have been difficult to avoid absorbing their style and fragments of their substance from

the conversation of Orthodox and Hasidic Jews in Galicia at the time of Schulz's youth." (Goldfarb, "The Vortex and the Labyrinth: Bruno Schulz and the Objective Correlative," *East European Politics and Societies* 11, no. 1 [1997]: 265.)

24. Artur Jocz, *The Gnostic Worlds of Bruno Schulz* (Wydawnictwo Nauk Społecznych i Humanistycznych UAM, 2021).

25. Schulz has been read as an existentialist (Michał Paweł Markowski); a disciple of Henri Bergson's (Czesław Karkowski); a Nietzschean (Włodzimierz Bolecki and Barbara Sienkiewicz; the latter writes, "Schulz, like Nietzsche, rejects the Hegelian philosophy of history"); a proto-Heidegger (Krystyna Lipińska-Iłłakowicz); a magical realist (Dorota Wojda); "a shy philosopher incognito" (Arnold Słucki); and as a purveyor of "a postmodern aesthetics of the sublime dissolution of form" (Dorota Glowacka). On how the multitudes of interpretations impede direct contact with Schulz's work, see Grzegorz Józefczuk, "Ha! Schulz? Miejsce zmyślenia i urwanie głowy z mitem miejsca," *Konteksty* 1–2 (2019): 117–22, and Małgorzata Kitowska-Łysiak, ed., *Białe plamy w schulzologii* [Schulzology's blind spots] (Catholic University of Lublin, 2010).

26. Schulz, "The Formation of Legends," *Letters and Drawings*, 59.

27. Olga Tokarczuk, "Books That Made Me," *Guardian*, August 24, 2018.

28. Chaim Löw (pseudonym of Leon Przemski), "Żydzi w poezji odrodzonej polski" [Jews in Polish poetry], *Miesięcznik Żydowski* 3, no. 2 (1933): 27–35; cited in Karen Underhill, "Bruno Schulz's Galician Diasporism," 17. "Schulz is one of those artists who do not choose their subject matter," writes the literary critic Jan Gondowicz. "The subject chooses them. One can even say: he was its slave and was well aware of that enslavement." (Gondowicz, *Bruno Schulz [1892–1942]* (Edipresse Polska, 2006), 11.)

29. "Drohobycz appeared prominently in reports of Jews fined or jailed for answering 'Yiddish,'" Joshua Shanes writes. "One thousand two hundred census sheets indicating 'Yiddish' were later discovered as trash in a cellar there." (Shanes, "The 'Bloody Election' in Drohobycz: Violence, Urban Politics, and National Memory in an Imperial Borderland," *Austrian History Yearbook* [2022]: 7.)

30. Singer [Iccok Warszawski], "Jews and Poles Lived Together for 800 Years but Were Not Integrated," *Forverts*, Sept. 17, 1944; quoted in Chone Shmeruk, "Isaac Bashevis Singer and Bruno Schulz," *Polish Review* 36 (1991). See also Shmeruk, "Hebrew-Yiddish-Polish: A Trilingual Jewish Culture" in *The Jews of Poland Between Two World Wars*, ed. Ysrael Gutman, Ezra Mendelsohn, Jehuda Reinharz, and Chone Shmeruk (University Press of New England, 1989), 285–311. Elsewhere Singer adds, "Though my ancestors had lived in Poland for six hundred years, we were still strangers." (*Old Truths and New Clichés: Essays by Isaac Bashevis Singer*, ed. David Stromberg [Princeton University Press, 2022], 160.)

31. Joanna Szczesna, "Spadkobierca—Interview with Marek Podstolski," *Gazeta Wyborcza*, June 4, 2001. Marek, the grandson of Bruno's brother, Izydor Schulz, and the son of Bruno's niece, Ella Schulz-Podstolska, died in April 2020 at age seventy-five.

32. Wiesław Budzyński, "Czuł się Żydem, śnił po polsku," *Rzeczpospolita*, June 7, 2001.

33. James R. Russell, "Harvard Death Fugue: On the Exploitation of Bruno Schulz," *Zeek: A Jewish Journal of Thought and Culture*, Jan. 2004.

34. Zagajewski, "Preface," *Letters and Drawings*, 14. Schulz gave up, as Cynthia Ozick puts it, "larger places, minds, and lives for the sake of Drogobych—or,

rather, for the sake of the gargoylish and astonishing map his imagination had
learned to draw of an invisible Drogobych contrived entirely out of language."
(Ozick, "The Phantasmagoria of Bruno Schulz," *Art and Ardor: Essays* [Knopf,
1983].) "From childhood, Schulz was in love with Drohobycz," writes the Polish
historian Bohdan Budurowycz, "the hub of his universe, the town which never
ceased to amaze and fascinate him as a living anachronism. . . . Schulz's native
town became a port of embarkation for his frequent journeys into the realm of his
imagination. . . . Schulz felt instinctively that his art would become sterile without the invigorating and vitalizing influence of his native soil, to which his whole
being was inextricably bound and from which alone his creative juices flow."
(Budurowycz, "Galicia in the Work of Bruno Schulz," *Canadian Slavonic Papers*
28, no. 4 (Dec. 1986): 359–68.) For comparison with another fictional rendering
of Drohobycz, see Stanisław Antoni Mueller's novel *Henryk Flis*, published in
Poland in 1908 (reissued by Wydawnictwo Literackie in 1976).
35. Roth, *Shop Talk*, 86.
36. Natalia Tkachik, "Interview with Yuri Andrukhovych," *Нова Польща* [New
Poland], May 21, 2021. The leading Ukrainian literary critic Yevhen Nakhlik
similarly argued that while Schulz "belongs to three nations, Polish, Jewish,
and Ukrainian . . . he is also our national artist who created in Ukraine and,
in particular, for Ukraine." (Yevhen Nakhlik, "Бруно Шульц – незвичайний
і впізнаваний" [Bruno Schulz—unusual and recognizable], *Zbruč*, July 14, 2022.)
37. The first sentence comes from Celestine Bohlen, "Artwork by Holocaust Victim
Is Focus of Dispute," *New York Times*, June 20, 2001. The second comes from
Dorota Głowacka's interview with Jerzy Ficowski, "Interview in Warsaw, July
3, 1993," in Prokopczyk, *Bruno Schulz: New Documents and Interpretations*,
62–63.
38. Ficowski, *Regions of the Great Heresy*, 171. Nathan Goldman, an editor at *Jewish Currents*, writes along similar lines: "The transportation of Schulz's murals
from the city that was his home and muse . . . to the so-called eternal capital of the
Jewish people is an attempt to complete Schulz's work. But that work is essentially
incomplete, and it refuses to understand incompletion as anything other than pro-
foundly generative. . . . It is no one's place to bring his fragmentary wanderings to
an end." (Goldman, "The Diasporist of Drohobycz," *New Inquiry*, May 7, 2018.)
39. George Oscar Lee, "Nostalgia, Drohobycz, Schulz i ja" [Nostalgia, Drohobycz,
Schulz, and me], *Gazeta.Pl Forum*, Feb. 22, 2003. According to a 2009 report by
the Conference on Jewish Material Claims Against Germany (Claims Conference):

> In the 1990's the "National Commission on the Restitution of Cultural Trea-
> sures to Ukraine under the Cabinet of Ministers" was established, which
> primarily deals with Ukrainian losses and does not deal with Jewish cultural
> and religious property currently held in Ukrainian institutions. Although
> attempts have been made at creating a restitution law, to date nothing con-
> crete has materialized. . . . Although there has recently been some restitution
> of Torah scrolls to the Jewish communities of Ukraine, there are no known
> cases of restitution of artworks or other cultural property that originally
> belonged to Jews.

40. Quoted in Celestine Bohlen, "From a Mural, New Life in a Debate over Memory,"
New York Times, June 24, 2001. "Judging by the state of other remnants of
Jewish life in Western Ukraine," writes the Israeli-born historian Omer Bartov,

"one would be justified in expressing skepticism about the willingness of the local municipality to preserve and exhibit the murals." (Bartov, *Erased: Vanishing Traces of Jewish Galicia in Present-Day Ukraine* [Princeton University Press, 2007], 56.)

41. See Ezra Mendelsohn, *Painting a People: Maurycy Gottlieb and Jewish Art* (Brandeis University Press, 2002).

42. Born Elżbieta Ettel in 1897, Bergner was nominated for an Academy Award for Best Actress for *Escape Me Never* (1935) and starred opposite Laurence Olivier in the 1936 film *As You Like It*. The midwife who delivered her, Gittel Wagner, had brought Bruno Schulz into the world five years earlier. In 1949, Bergner stayed for three months in the nascent Jewish state and gave seventy performances and readings.

43. Irena Grudzińska-Gross, "Putin's Historic Blunder: An Interview with Adam Michnik," *Project Syndicate*, June 3, 2022; published in Polish as "Adam Michnik: To nie Czajkowski i Dostojewski niszczą Ukrainę," *Gazeta Wyborcza*, June 1, 2022.

44. For a persuasive argument against this kind of retrospective reading, see *Foregone Conclusions: Against Apocalyptic History*, by Michael André Bernstein. Some who write about Schulz refuse even to name Felix Landau. "I will not write much of Schulz's death or name his killer," the Irish writer David Hayden remarked. "Schulz's work deserves to live alone, above and beyond his end (his murderer is undeserving even of his portion of infamy in the history of death)." (Hayden, "Best Book of 1934: Bruno Schulz's *Cinnamon Shops*," *Granta* online, Dec. 21, 2018.)

45. Including *Chwila* (Moment), co-founded in 1919 by Gershon Zipper (a leader of the Zionist movement in Galicia and the first organizer of the Jewish National Fund in Poland) and Henryk Rosmarin (a Zionist activist, member of the Polish parliament, and Polish consul general in Tel Aviv during World War II). Its editor in chief from 1920 to 1939 was Henryk Hescheles. See Barbara Letocha, "*Chwila*, the Largest Polish-Language Jewish Daily," *Kesher* 20 (1996): 128–36 (in Hebrew).

46. "The man with the black beard lay on top of Father like the Angel on top of Jacob. . . . They wrestled in their mortal sweat. . . . The next day, Father was limping slightly" ("The Dead Season," *Collected Stories*, 184).

47. For example: "His hands outstretched prophetically in the clouds" as "down below, at the feet of this Sinai that had risen up from Father's anger, the people were gesticulating, cursing, and worshipping Baal . . ." only to find him "thundering from on high at the idolators with his mighty word" ("The Night of the Great Season," *Collected Stories*, 76). "The "Great Season" of the title is likely a reference to the High Holy Days of the Jewish calendar. "In the mornings, leaning on his tall walking stick, Father wandered like a shepherd among that blind, woolen flock . . . delaying the moment when he would lift up all his people and move out into the noisy night like that oppressed, teeming, hundredfold Israel" ("The Dead Season," *Collected Stories*, 181). See David A. Goldfarb, "A Living Schulz: 'The Night of the Great Season,'" *Prooftexts: A Journal of Jewish Literary History* 14, no. 1 (1994): 25–47.

48. Lauren A. Benjamin, "The Lost Cause of Poetry: Resistance and Re-creation in Bruno Schulz's 'Traktat o Manekinach,'" *New Zealand Slavonic Journal*, 45, no. 1 (2011): 45–55.

49. Quoted in *Bruno: Epoka genialna*, 401. "Even without faith one can experience

the world theologically," Jan Błoński adds, "in the categories appropriate to religion. This, I believe, was the case for Schulz." (Błoński, "On the Jewish Sources of Bruno Schulz," *Cross Currents* 12 [1993]: 59.)

50. Hermann Sternbach, "Sklepy cynamonowe," *Miesięcznik Żydowski* 4, no. 1 (April 1934); translated by and cited in Karen Underhill, "Bruno Schulz's Galician Diasporism," 20. Sternbach was the author of several collections of poetry in German; a collection of short stories about the Russian occupation of Galicia during World War I, *Wenn die Schakale feiern* (1917); and a drama about the horrors of that war and the hypocrisy of those who unleashed it, *Tag der Mütter* (1929). Sternbach and his wife, Anna, were murdered in the Lwów ghetto in 1942. The journal *Miesięcznik Żydowski*, edited by Zygmunt Ellenberg, appeared in Warsaw between 1930 and 1935. See Zofia Borzymińska, "Miesięcznik Żydowski: W 50 rocznicę wydania pierwszego numeru," *Biuletyn Żydowskiego Instytutu Historycznego* 117 (1981): 63–75 (in Polish).

51. Cassirer, *The Myth of the State* (Yale University Press, 1946), 355. See also Cassirer, "Judaism and the Modern Political Myths," *Contemporary Jewish Record* 7 (1944): 115–26, where he writes that the Jewish people brought into being certain "ethical ideals" that are required "to break the power of the modern political myths."

52. Schulz to Julian Tuwim, Jan. 26, 1934, *Letters and Drawings*, 52. Schulz met Tuwim at a tumultuous reading Tuwim gave in Drohobycz in October 1923.

53. Schulz, *Collected Works*, 370; *Letters and Drawings*, 114; originally published in *Tygodnik Illustrowany* [Illustrated Weekly], April 28, 1935. On Schulz's treatment of myth in his story "Spring," see Stanley Bill, "History and Myth: Bruno Schulz's *Spring*," in *The Routledge World Companion to Polish Literature*, ed. Tomasz Bilczewski, Stanley Bill, and Magdalena Popiel (Routledge, 2022). On Schulz's "mythic family tree," see Ewa Świąc, "Historie rodzinne w prozie Brunona Schulza," in *Literatura i różne historie. Szkice o literaturze XX i XXI wieku*, ed. Barbara Gutkowska and Agnieszka Nęcka (Wydawnictwo Uniwersytetu Śląskiego, 2011). On Schulz and Thomas Mann, see Schulz's essay on Zofia Nałkowska, where he remarks that in Mann's biblical trilogy "the lives of several generations of men are only material in which eternal stories are realized." ("Zofia Nałkowska na tle swojej nowej powieści," *Skamander*, April 1939, trans. Bożena Shallcross.) "Schulz's admiration for Mann's *Joseph und seine Bruder* knew no bounds," Jerzy Ficowski writes, "And tributes to it occurred frequently in his conversations and letters. Schulz regarded Mann as the greatest writer among his contemporaries and knew his works from many readings in the original" (*Collected Works*, 475). See also Elisabeth Goślicki-Baur, "Mann i Schulz," *Teksty* 41, no. 5 (1978): 65–84.

54. Schulz, "The Mythologizing of Reality," *Letters and Drawings*, 115–17; *Collected Works*, 371.

55. Schulz, "The Republic of Dreams," *Collected Stories*, 245.

WORKS BY BRUNO SCHULZ IN ENGLISH

IN CHRONOLOGICAL ORDER OF PUBLICATION

"My Father Joins the Fire Brigade." Translated by Stanley Moss and Zofia Tarnowska. In *Contemporary Polish Stories*, edited by Edmund Ordon, 116–25. Detroit: Wayne State University Press, 1958. (Originally published in *Wiadomości Literackie* 5 [Feb. 1935].)

"A Treatise on Mannequins, or the Second Book of Genesis" and "Birds." Translated by Jenny Rodzinska. *Poland Illustrated Magazine* 10 (1958). (Reprinted in *Introduction to Modern Polish Literature: An Anthology of Fiction and Poetry*, edited by Adam Gillon and Ludwik Krzyzanowski [1964]: 258–61, 266–74.)

Cinnamon Shops and Other Stories. Translated by Celina Wieniewska. London: MacGibbon & Kee, 1963.

The Street of Crocodiles. Translated by Celina Wieniewska. New York: Walker, 1963; New York: Penguin, 1977; Viking Press, 1995; New York: Penguin Classics, 2008 (with an introduction by David A. Goldfarb and a foreword by Jonathan Safran Foer).

"Cinnamon Shops" and "Sanatorium Under the Water Clock" (excerpts). Translated by Christina Cenkalska. *Poland Illustrated Magazine* 12 (1965).

Sanatorium Under the Sign of the Hourglass. Translated by Celina Wieniewska. New York: Walker, 1978; New York: Penguin, 1979; London: Picador, 1980; Boston: Houghton Mifflin, 1997. (Three stories—"Sanatorium Under the Sign of the Hourglass," "Loneliness," and "Father's Last Escape"—appeared in the *New Yorker* in 1978.)

"Dead Season." Translated by Celina Wieniewska. *Partisan Review* 45, no. 1 (1978): 66–79. Originally published in *Wiadomości Literackie* 53–54 (Dec. 1936).

Birds. Translated by Celina Wieniewska. Illustrated by Janet Morgan. Madison, WI: Rara Avis, 1980.

"Mythization of Reality." Translated by Lou Weiss, *Manhattan Review* 2, no. 1 (1981).

"Autumn" and "The Homeland." Translated by Lou Weiss. *Formations* 2, no. 3 (Winter 1986): 64–67, 68–71.

"Prose by Bruno Schulz." Translated by Louis Iribane. *Cross Currents* 6 (1987): 179–94. (Includes "Autumn," "The Republic of Dreams," "An Interview with Bruno Schulz," and "Letter to Anna Plockier.")

The Booke of Idolatry. Edited by Jerzy Ficowski. Translated by Bogna Piotrowska. Warsaw: Interpress, 1989.

The Complete Fiction of Bruno Schulz. Translated by Celina Wieniewska. Afterword by Jerzy Ficowski. New York: Walker, 1989.

Letters and Drawings of Bruno Schulz with Selected Prose. Edited by Jerzy Ficowski. Translated by Walter Arndt and Victoria Nelson. New York: Harper & Row, 1989.

The Drawings of Bruno Schulz: From the Collection of the Adam Mickiewicz Museum of Literature, Warsaw. Edited by Wojciech Chmurzyński, Yona Fischer, and Bozena Kolodziejczak. Jerusalem: Israel Museum, 1990.

The Drawings of Bruno Schulz. Edited by Jerzy Ficowski. With an essay by Ewa Kuryluk. Evanston, IL: Northwestern University Press, 1990.

"An Essay for S. I. Witkiewicz" and "Afterword to Kafka's *The Trial.*" Translated by Walter Arndt. In *Four Decades of Polish Essays*, edited by Jan Kott, 106–14. Evanston, IL: Northwestern University Press, 1990.

"Father Floating over the Lamp" and "Untitled." *Parnassus* 16, no. 2 (1991).

"Father's Experiments." Translated by Wiesiek Powaga. In *The Dedalus Book of Polish Fantasy*, edited by Wiesiek Powaga, 257–67. New York: Dedalus / Hippocrene, 1996.

The Collected Works of Bruno Schulz. Edited by Jerzy Ficowski. Foreword by David Grossman. London: Picador, 1998.

"The Street of Crocodiles." In *The Oxford Book of Jewish Stories*, edited by Ilan Stavans. New York: Oxford University Press, 1998.

Collected Stories. Translated by Madeline G. Levine. Evanston, IL: Northwestern University Press, 2018.

Undula. Translated by Frank Garrett. Seattle: Sublunary Editions, 2020.

Nocturnal Reveries: Essential Stories. London: Pushkin Press, 2022.

BIBLIOGRAPHY

Adams, Jenni. "Intertextuality and the Trace of the Other: Specters of Bruno Schulz." *Symbolism* 12/13 (2013): 49–68.

Anders, Jaroslaw. "Bruno Schulz: The Prisoner of Myth." In *Between Fire and Sleep: Essays on Modern Polish Poetry and Prose*. Yale University Press, 2009. Originally published in the *New Republic*, Nov. 25, 2002.

Appelfeld, Aharon, et al. "Bruno Schulz's Wall Paintings." *New York Review of Books*, May 23, 2002.

Augsberger, Janis. "Ein anti-analythisches Bedürfnis: Bruno Schulz im Grenzbereich zwischen Poetik und Politik." In *Politische Mythen im 19. und 20. Jahrhundert in Mittel- und Osteuropa*, edited by Heidi Hein-Kircher and Hans Hahn, 25–44. Marburg: Herder Institut, 2006.

———. *Masochismen: Mythologisierung als Krisen-Ästhetik bei Bruno Schulz*. Wehrhahn Verlag, 2008.

Balint, Benjamin. "And the Heart Is Forever Broken." Review of *Undula* by Bruno Schulz and *Blooming Spaces: The Collected Poetry, Prose, Critical Writing, and Letters of Debora Vogel*. Translated by Anastasiya Lyubas. *Jewish Review of Books* (Spring 2021).

Banks, Brian R. *Muse & Messiah: The Life, Imagination & Legacy of Bruno Schulz*. InkerMen Press, 2006 (2nd. ed. 2009).

Banner, Gillian. *Holocaust Literature: Schulz, Levi, Spiegelman and the Memory of the Offence*. Vallentine Mitchell, 2000.

Baran-Szołtys, Magdalena. *Galizien als Archiv. Reisen im postgalizischen Raum in der Gegenwartsliteratur* [Galicia as archive: Travels in the post-Galician space in contemporary literature]. Vienna University Press, 2021.

Baranczak, Stanislaw. "The Faces of Mastery." Review of *Letters and Drawings of Bruno Schulz*. New Republic, Jan. 2, 1989: 28–29.

Bartosik, Marta. *Bruno Schulz jako krytyk* [Bruno Schulz as critic]. Kraków: Towarzystwo Autorów i Wydawców Prac Naukowych Universitas, 2000.

Bayley, John. "Pioneers and Phantoms." *New York Review of Books*, July 20, 1978.

———. "The Power of Delight." *New York Review of Books*, April 13, 1989.

Benešová, Michala. *Ve světle kabaly: Židovská mystika v polské literatuře meziválečného období (Aleksander Wat, Bruno Schulz, Bolesław Leśmian)* [In the Light of Kabbalah: Jewish mystics in Polish interwar literature (Aleksander Wat, Bruno Schulz, Bolesław Leśmian). 2017.

Bielik-Robson, Agata. "The Edges of the World: Diasporic Metaphysics of Bruno Schulz." *Eidos: A Journal for Philosophy of Culture* , vol. 6, no. 1 (2022): 49–64.

Bieniek, Beata A. *Bruno Schulz' Mythopoesie der Geschlechteridentitäten: Der Götzenblick im Gender-Spiegel.* Peter Lang, 2011.

Biller, Maxim. *Inside the Head of Bruno Schulz.* Translated by Anthea Bell. Pushkin Press, 2015. Originally published as *Im Kopf von Bruno Schulz.* S. Fischer Verlag, 2013.

Blatman, Daniel, Frank Fox, Henryk Grynberg, Stanislaw Krajewski, Claire Rosenson, and Joanna Wiszniewicz. "Towards a New Jewish and Polish Memory—Reponses to Diana Pinto's essay 'Fifty Years After the Holocaust: Building a New Jewish and Polish Memory.'" *East European Jewish Affairs* 27 (1997).

Błoński, Jan. "On the Jewish Sources of Bruno Schulz." Translated by Michael C. Steinlauf. *Cross Currents* 12 (1993): 54–68.

Bohlen, Celestine. "Artwork by Holocaust Victim Is Focus of Dispute." *New York Times,* June 20, 2001.

Brandt, Hannes. "Liminality and Desire in Bruno Schulz's Short Prose." *Euro-Facta* 2 (2010): 281–87.

Breysach, Barbara. "Kunstobjekt und Metapher: das Buch in Bruno Schulz' Ästhetik der Grenzüberschreitung." In *Schriften der Gesellschaft für europäisch-jüdische Literaturstudien.* Vol. 5 (2012): 134–150.

Bronner, Ethan. "Behind Fairy Tale Drawings, Walls Talk of Unspeakable Cruelty." *New York Times,* Feb. 27, 2009.

Brown, Russell E. "Bruno Schulz and Franz Kafka: Servant Girls and Other Temptations." *Germano-Slavica* 6 (1988): 29–47.

———. "Bruno Schulz Bibliography." *Polish Review* 39, no. 2 (1994): 231–53.

———. "Bruno Schulz: The Myth of Origins." *Russian Literature* 22 (1987): 195–220.

———. "Metamorphosis in Bruno Schulz." *Polish Review* 30 (1985): 373–80.

———. *Myths and Relatives: Seven Essays on Bruno Schulz.* Munich: Verlag Otto Sagner, 1991.

———. "Philip Roth and Bruno Schulz." *ANQ* 6, no. 4 (1993): 211–14.

———. "Schulz and World Literature." *Slavic and East European Journal* 34, no. 2 (1990): 224–46.

Bruncevic, Merima. "The Lost Murals of Bruno Schulz: A Critical Legal Perspective on Control, Access to and Ownership of Art." *Law and Critique* 22, no. 1 (Jan. 2011): 79–96.

Budzyński, Wiesław. *Miasto Schulza* [Schulz's city]. Warsaw: Prószyński I S-ka, 2005.

———. *Schulz pod kluczem* [Schulz under lock and key]. Rev. ed. Warsaw: Świat Książki, 2013.

Caneppele, Paolo. *Die Republik der Träume: Bruno Schulz und seine Bilderwelt.* Graz: Clio, 2010.

Cassouto, Nella. " 'She Walked Up to Father with a Smile and Flipped Him on the Nose': Schulz and the Wars of the Sexes." Translated by Vivianne Barsky. In *The Drawings of Bruno Schulz: From the Collection of the Adam Mickiewicz Museum of Literature, Warsaw,* edited by Wojciech Chmurzyński, Yona Fischer, and Bozena Kolodziejczak, 22–27. Jerusalem: Israel Museum, 1990.

Cattan, Nacha. "Murals' Grab by Memorial Stirs a Debate in Arts World." *Forward,* July 13, 2001.

Chciuk, Andrzej. *Atlantyda* [Atlantis]. Warsaw: LTW, 2002.

Chmurzyński, Wojciech, ed. *Bruno Schulz, 1892–1942: Rysunki i archiwalia ze zbiorów Muzeum Literatury im. Adama Mickiewicza w Warszawie* [Drawings and documents from the collection of the Adam Mickiewicz Museum in Warsaw]. Muzeum Literatury im. Adama Mickiewicza w Warszawie, 1992.

Chrostowska, S. D. " 'Masochistic Art of Fantasy': The Literary Works of Bruno Schulz in the Context of Modern Masochism." *Russian Literature* 55, no. 4 (2004): 469–501.

Cieślińska-Lobkowicz, Nawojka. "Who Owns Bruno Schulz? The Changing Postwar Fortunes of Works of Art by Jewish Artists Murdered in Nazi-Occupied Poland." Paper presented at the international conference of the Documentation Centre for Property Transfers of Cultural Assets of WWII, Prague, Oct. 21–22, 2015.

Coadou, François. *Bruno Schulz: L'inquiétude de la matière.* Paris: Semiose Éditions, 2007.

Coetzee, J. M. "Sweet Persuasions of the Dark." *New York Review of Books*, Feb. 27, 2003. (Republished in *Inner Workings: Literary Essays 2000–2005*, 65–78. London: Vintage, 2008.)

Couturier, Brice. "Bruno Schulz: 'Gnome minuscule' et géant de la littérature." *Esprit* 310, no. 12 (Dec. 2004): 74–83.

Crugten, Alain van. *Bruno Schulz ou La grande hérésie.* Les Editions du CEP (Créations-Europe-Perspectives), 2015.

Czermakowa, Izabela. "Wspomnienie o Schulzu" [A remembrance of Schulz]. *Schulz/Forum* 4 (2014): 103–08. Originally published as Czermakowa, "Bruno Schulz," *Twórczość* 21, no. 10 (Oct. 1965): 99–102.

Davies, Norman. *God's Playground: A History of Poland.* 2 vols. Oxford University Press, 2005.

Davies, Norman, and Antony Polonsky, eds. *Jews in Eastern Poland and the USSR, 1939–46.* New York: St. Martin's, 1991.

De Bruyn, Dieter, and Kris Van Heuckelom, eds. *(Un)masking Bruno Schulz: New Combinations, Further Fragmentations, Ultimate Reintegrations.* Rodopi, 2009.

Durkalewicz, Wiktoria. "On Bruno Schulz's Demythologization of Reality." *Roczniki Humanistyczne* 67, no. 1 (2019): 83–111.

Fauchereau, Serge. "Balthus devant Schulz, Klossowski, Jouve et quelques autres." *Cahiers du Musée National d'Art Moderne* 12 (1983): 225–43.

Fauchereau, Serge, et al. *Bruno Schulz: La république des rêves; Le catalogue de l'exposition.* Paris: Musée d'Art et d'Histoire de Judaïsme / Denoël, 2004.

Fern, William H. *Brief History of the Jews of Drohobycz and Borysław.* Drohobycz-Borysław Reunion, South Fallsburg, NY, May 3–5, 1985.

Ficowski, Jerzy. *The Drawings of Bruno Schulz.* Northwestern University Press, 1990.

———. "On the Cross-roads of Three Cultures: The Life and Work of Bruno Schulz." *Jewish Quarterly* 27, no. 1 (Spring 1979).

———. *Regions of the Great Heresy: Bruno Schulz, a Biographical Portrait.* Translated by Theodosia Robertson. W. W. Norton, 2003. (In Polish: *Regiony wielkiej herezji i okolice: Bruno Schulz i jego mitologia* Sejny: Fundacja Pogranicze, 2002.)

———. "The Schulzian Tense, or the Mythic Path to Freedom." *Polish Perspectives* 10 (1967): 44–53.

Foer, Jonathan Safran. Foreword to *Street of Crocodiles and Other Stories*, by Bruno Schulz. Penguin Classics, 2008.

———. *Tree of Codes.* Visual Editions, 2010.

Frajlich, Anna. "Bruno Schulz: Mythmaker and Legend." *The Ghost of Shakespeare: Collected Essays.* Academic Studies Press, 2020.

Franklin, Ruth. "The Lost: Searching for Bruno Schulz." *New Yorker*, Dec. 8, 2002.
Friedman, Tuvyah. *Die Tätigkeit der Schutzpolizei: Gestapo und Ukrainische Miliz in Drohobycz, 1941–1944*. Haifa, 1989.
Gamdzyk-Kluźniak, Maria, ed. *Archiwum Jerzego Ficowskiego* [Catalog of Jerzy Ficowski Archive]. Polish National Library, 2019.
Gansert, Ulrich. *Erlebnis Ukraine: Auf den Spuren von Joseph Conrad: Bruno Schulz und Joseph Roth*. Loecker Erhard Verlag, 2019.
Gawryś, Cezary. "Yad Vashem i freski Schulza." *Więź* 7 (2001): 9–11.
Geduld, H. M. Review of *The Street of Crocodiles*. *Studies in Short Fiction* 2, no. 4 (1965): 379–81.
Geissler, Benjamin. *Finding Pictures (Bilder Finden)*. Germany, 2002. Documentary film, 107 min., 35mm.
———. "Finds and the Virtual Reconstruction of the Picture Chamber with the Bruno Schulz Murals" ("Fundstücke und die virtuelle Rekonstruktion der Bilderkammer mit den Wandmalereien des Bruno Schulz"). Unpublished text dated Sept. 26, 2011.
Geissler, Christian. "Bilder Finden." *Freitag*, March 16, 2001.
———. "In den Zwillingsgassen des Bruno Schulz." *Die Aktion: Zeitschrift für Politik, Literature, Kunst* 205 (2002).
Gelber, N. M., ed. *Sefer zikaron le-Drohobycz, Boryslaw ve-ha-seviva* [Memorial to the Jews of Drohobycz, Borysław, and surroundings]. Tel Aviv: Association of Former Residents of Drohobycz, Borysław, and Surroundings, 1959.
Głuchowska, Lidia, ed. *Bruno Schulz—Klisza Werk—Transgresiones*. Wrocław: OKIS: Center for Culture and Art, 2013.
Goldfarb, David A. "Appropriations of Bruno Schulz." *Jewish Quarterly* 218 (Summer 2011): 42–47.
———. Introduction to *The Street of Crocodiles and Other Stories*, by Bruno Schulz. Translated by Celina Wieniewska and Walter Arndt. New York: Penguin, 2008.
———. "Light on a Dark Field: Ekaterina Slonova and Bruno Schulz's Sanatorium." Preface to *Sanatorium pod klepsydrą*, by Bruno Schulz. Illustrated by Ekaterina Slonova. Meridian Czernowitz, 2016.
———. "*Pałuby* in Bruno Schulz's Workshop." In *Bruno Schulz: New Readings, New Meanings*, edited by Stanisław Latek, 85–94. Kraków: Polska Akademia Umiejętności, 2009.
———. "Schulz, Dante and Beatrice." In *Bruno Schulz jako filozof i teoretyk literatury: Materiały V Międzynarodowego Festiwalu Brunona Schulza w Drohobyczu*, edited by Wiera Meniok, 454–65. Drohobycz: Koło, 2014.
———. "The Vortex and the Labyrinth: Bruno Schulz and the Objective Correlative." *East European Politics and Societies* 11, no. 2 (1997): 257–69.
Golomb, Jacob. "The Metaphysical Solitude of Bruno Schulz." *Moznaim* 63 (1986): 63–68.
Gombrowicz, Witold. *Diary*. Edited by Jan Kott. Translated by Lillian Vallee. 3 vols. Northwestern University Press, 1988–89.
———. "On Bruno Schulz." Translated by Lillian Vallee. *New York Review of Books*, April 13, 1989.
Gondowicz, Jan. *Trans-Autentyk. Nie-czyste formy Brunona Schulza*. Warsaw, 2014.
Gordon, Jaimy. "The Strange Afterlife of Bruno Schulz." *Michigan Quarterly Review* (Winter 2004): 1–36.
Goslicki-Baur, Elisabeth. *Die Prosa von Bruno Schulz*. Bern: Slavica Helvetica, 1975. (German.)

Grabowski, Jan, and Barbara Engelking, eds. *Night Without End: The Fate of Jews in German-Occupied Poland*. Indiana University Press, 2022.

Grossman, David. "The Age of Genius." Translated by Stuart Schoffman. *New Yorker*, June 8–15, 2009, 66–77.

———. *See Under: Love*. Translated by Betsy Rosenberg. New York: Farrar Straus Giroux, 1989. Originally published in Hebrew as *Ayen Erech: Ahava*. Jerusalem: Hakibbutz Hameuchad, 1986.

Grynberg, Henryk. *Drohobycz, Drohobycz and Other Stories: True Tales from the Holocaust and Life After*. Translated by Alicia Nitecki. New York: Penguin, 2002.

Gutfreund, Amir. *Last Bullet Calls It*. Amazon Crossing, 2017. Originally published in Hebrew as *The Legend of Bruno and Adele*.

Hyde, George. "State of Arrest: The Short Stories of Bruno Schulz." In *New Perspectives on Twentieth-Century Polish Literature*, edited by Stanislaw Eile and Ursula Phillips, 47–67. Macmillan, 1992.

Iribarne, Louis. "On Bruno Schulz." *Cross Currents* 6 (1987): 173–77.

James, Clive. "The Iron Capital of Bruno Schulz." In *The Meaning of Recognition*. Picador, 2005. Originally published in the *Los Angeles Times Book Review*, Nov. 3, 2002.

Janicka, Elżbieta, and Tomasz Żukowski. *Philo-Semitic Violence: Poland's Jewish Past in New Polish Narratives*. Lexington Books, 2021.

Jarrett, David. "Bruno Schulz and the Map of Poland." *Chicago Review* 40, no. 1 (1994): 73–84.

Jarzębski, Jerzy. *Schulz: A to Polska właśnie*. Wrocław: Wydawnictwo Dolnoslaskie, 1999.

Josipovici, Gabriel. "Unrelieved Magic." *Listener*, March 8, 1979, 362–63.

Jüdt, Dieter. *Heimsuchung: Und andere Erzählungen von Bruno Schulz*. Stuttgart: Ehapa, 1995.

Juraschek, Anna. *Die Rettung des Bildes im Wort: Bruno Schulz' Bild-Idee in seinem prosaischen und bildnerischen Werk*. V&R Academic, 2016.

Kalin, Arkadiusz. "The Afterlife of Schulz, or Schulzology: What Is It Good For?" Translated by Timothy Williams. *Czas Kultury* (2014): 4–27.

Karageorgos, Sotirios. "Niepokój religijny w twórczości Brunona Schulza." In *(Nie) pokój w tekstach kultury XIX–XXI wieku*, edited by Barbary Zwolińskiej and Krystiana Macieja Tomali, 138–147. Wydawnictwo Uniwersytetu Gdańskiego, 2021.

Kaszuba-Dębska, Anna. *Bruno: Epoka genialna* [Bruno: The age of genius]. Znak, 2020.

Kijowska, Marta. "Die Infantinnen und ihr Zwerg: Die Frauen im Leben des Schriftstellers Bruno Schulz." *Neue Zürcher Zeitung Online*, Sept. 22, 2001.

Kitowska-Łysiak, Małgorzata. "Xięga Bałwochwalcza: Grafiki oryginalne Brunona Schulza." *Biuletyn Historii Sztuki* (1981): 401–10.

Klee, Ernst, Willi Dressen, and Volker Riess, eds. *Those Were the Days: The Holocaust Through the Eyes of the Perpetrators and Bystanders*. London: Hamish Hamilton, 1991; New York: Free Press, 1991. Originally published in German as *"Schöne Zeiten": Judenmord aus der Sicht der Täter und Gaffer*. Frankfurt: S. Fischer Verlag, 1988.

Knafo, Danielle. "Bruno Schulz: Desire's Impossible Object." With Rocco Lo Bosco. In *Dancing with the Unconscious: The Art of Psychoanalysis and the Psychoanalysis of Art*, 191–216. Routledge, 2012.

Krauss, Nicole. *The History of Love*. Viking, 2005.

Kuny, Michała. *Perypetie Schulzowskie: Ekslibrisy Brunona Schulza* [Schulz's Adventures: Bookplates by Bruno Schulz]. Edited by Grzegorz Matusza and Roman Nowoszewski. Łódź: Łódzkie Towarzystwo Przyjaciół Książki, 2013.

Kuprel, Diana. "Errant Events on the Branch Tracks of Time: Bruno Schulz and Mythical Consciousness." *Slavic and East European Journal* 40, no. 1 (Spring 1996): 100–17.

Kuryluk, Ewa. "The Caterpillar Car, or Bruno Schulz's Drive into the Future of the Past." In *The Drawings of Bruno Schulz*, edited by Jerzy Ficowski. Northwestern University Press, 1990.

Landau, Felix. *Love Letters of a Nazi Murderer in Lemberg and Drohobycz*. Yad Vashem, 1987.

Latek, Stanisław, ed. *Bruno Schulz: New Readings, New Meanings*. Montreal: Polish Institute of Arts and Sciences in Canada / Kraków: Polish Academy of Arts and Sciences, 2009.

Lewi, Henri. *Bruno Schulz, ou, Les stratégies messianiques*. Paris: La Table Ronde, 1989.

Lipszyc, Adam. "Najoryginalniejsza książka o Schulzu, jaką do tej pory napisano." *Wielogłos* (Polyphony) 1, no. 15 (2013).

Lower, Wendy. *Hitler's Furies: German Women in the Nazi Killing Fields*. Houghton Mifflin Harcourt, 2013.

Lukashevich, Olga. "Bruno Schulz's *The Street of Crocodiles*: A Study in Creativity and Neurosis." *Polish Review* 13, no. 2 (1968): 63–80.

Malcolm, Janet. "Graven Images." *New Yorker*, June 8, 1987.

Mark, Sabrina Orah. "Cracked Fairy Tales and the Holocaust." *Paris Review* blog, Oct. 8, 2018.

Markowski, Michał Paweł. *Powszechna rozwiązłość': Schulz, egzystencja, literatura* [The promiscuity of all things: Schulz, existence, literature]. Kraków: Jagiellonian University Press, 2012.

Meyer-Fraatz, Andrea. "Söhne und Väter: Überlegungen zu einer thematischen Konstante bei Franz Kafka, Bruno Schulz und Danilo Kiš." In *Mundus narratus: Festschrift für Dagmar Burkhart zum 65. Geburtstag*, edited by Renate Hansen-Kokoruš and Angela Richter, 359–74. Frankfurt: Lang, 2004.

Michalska, Magdalena. "Ukradli Schulza!" *Gazeta Wyborcza*, May 26–27, 2001.

Miłosz, Czesław. "A Few Words on Bruno Schulz." *New Republic*, Jan. 2, 1989.

———. *The History of Polish Literature*. University of California Press, 1983.

Miron, Susan. "Bruno Schulz Redux." *Partisan Review* 59, no. 1 (1992): 161–66.

Misiak, Anna Maja. "Im Schatten von Bruno Schulz." *Neue Zürcher Zeitung*, August 8, 2008.

Mönch, Regina. "Die Märchen im Spielzimmer der SS Rekonstruiert in Berlin: Die Bilderkammer des jüdischen Malers Bruno Schulz." *Frankfurter Allgemeine Zeitung*, May 13, 2013.

Mortkowicz-Olczakowa, Hanna. "Bruno Schulz: Wspomnienie" [Bruno Schulz: A reminiscence]. *Przekrój* 67 (March 23, 1958).

Nadeau, Maurice. "Bruno Schulz." In *Présences polonaises: Witkiewicz, constructivisme, les contemporains*. Centre Georges Pompidou, 1983.

Neau, Jessy. "*La mannequination:* Un procédé moderne d'érotisme chez Bruno Schulz." *Slavica bruxellensia* 9 (2013).

Nelson, Victoria. "An Exile on Crocodile Street: Bruno Schulz in America." *Salmagundi* 101–02 (Winter–Spring 1994): 212–25.

————. "Leaving by the Closet Door." *Salmagundi* 150–51 (Spring–Summer 2006): 294–302.

Newton, Adam Zachary. "Bruno Schulz's Murals, Oyneg Shabes, and the Migration of Forms." In *Eastern Europe Unmapped: Beyond Borders and Peripheries*, edited by Irene Kacandes and Yuliya Komska. Berghahn Books, 2017.

Ó Ceallaigh, Philip. "Bruno Schulz: The Shadow of the Word." *Los Angeles Review of Books*, Nov. 19, 2018.

Ozick, Cynthia. *The Messiah of Stockholm*. Knopf, 1987.

————. "The Phantasmagoria of Bruno Schulz." *Art and Ardor: Essays*. Knopf, 1983.

Pacewicz, Piotr, and Uri Huppert. "Czyj jest Schulz? Polemika w sprawie Fresków z Drohobycza." *Gazeta Wyborcza*, June 4, 2001.

Paloff, Benjamin. "Who Owns Bruno Schulz?" *Boston Review*, Dec. 1, 2004.

Panas, Władysław. *Księga blasku: Traktat o kabale w prozie Brunona Schulza*. Lublin: Towarzystwo Naukowe Katolickiego Uniwersytetu Lubelskiego, 1997.

Panas-Goworska, Marta. "Szkolni koledzy z Drohobycza" [School colleagues from Drohobycz]. *Newsweek Historia* 2 (2022): 66–73.

Pemwieser, Karoline. *Von "gilgul," Golem und Wunderrabbis: Motive der chassidischen Volksliteratur in Bruno Schulz, "Cynamonowe sklepy."* GRIN Verlag, 2011.

Perez, Rolando. "Bruno Schulz: Literary Kabbalist of the Holocaust." *Occasional Papers in Jewish History and Thought* 20. Hunter College of the City University of New York, 2002.

————. *The Divine Duty of Servants: A Book of Worship Based on the Artwork of Bruno Schulz*. Cool Grove, 1999.

Peter, Stefanie. "Denkmalschwund: Bruno-Schulz-Fresken gestohlen." *Frankfurter Allgemeine Zeitung*, May 28, 2001.

Piętniewicz, Michał. *Między mitem a kiczem: O prozie Brunona Schulza* [Between myth and kitsch: On Bruno Schulz's prose]. Wydawnictwo Adam Marszałek, 2020. (Polish.)

Polonsky, Antony. *The Jews in Poland and Russia*. 3 vols. Oxford University Press, 2010–12.

————. "Polish-Jewish Relations and the Holocaust." *Polin* 4 (1989).

Powers, Denise V. "Fresco Fiasco: Narratives of National Identity and the Bruno Schulz Murals of Drogobych." *East European Politics and Societies* 17, no. 4 (Fall 2003): 622–53.

Pritchett, V. S. "Comic Genius." *New York Review of Books*, April 14, 1977.

Prochaśko, Jurko. "Der Streit um das jüdische Kulturerbe in Mitteleuropa. Der Fall Bruno Schulz." In *Antisemitismus und Erinnerungskulturen im postkommunistischen Europa*, edited by Bernd Kaufmann and Basil Kerski, Osnabrück, 2006, 157–68.

Prokopczyk, Czeslaw, ed. *Bruno Schulz: New Documents and Interpretations*. Peter Lang, 1999.

Radzilowski, John. "Thieves Stealing from Thieves, Victims from Victims: The Culture, Morality, and Politics of Stolen Art in Twentieth Century Poland." *Polish Review* 61, no. 4 (2016): 3–17.

Raphaeli, Zvi. *HaBayit Shebo Hitgorer Bruno Schulz* [The house where Bruno Schulz lived]. Renaissance, 1975.

Reich-Ranicki, Marcel. "Bruno Schulz: Die Zimtläden." *Neue Deutsche Hefte* 88 (July–Aug. 1962): 131–33.

Robertson, Theodosia S. "Bruno Schulz and Comedy." *Polish Review* 36, no. 2 (1991): 119–26.

————. "Time in Bruno Schulz." *Indiana Slavic Studies* 5 (1990): 181–92.

Rosdy, Paul, dir. *The Last Jew from Drohobycz (Der letzte Jude von Drohobytsch).* 2011. Film, 94 min.

Rosiek, Stanisław. *Odcięcie: Szkice wokół Schulza.* Gdańsk: Słowo / Obraz Terytoria, 2021.

Roth, Philip. "Conversation in New York with Isaac Bashevis Singer about Bruno Schulz." In *Shop Talk: A Writer and His Colleagues and Their Work.* Houghton Mifflin, 2001. Originally published as "Roth and Singer on Bruno Schulz." *New York Times,* February 13, 1977.

————. *The Prague Orgy.* Jonathan Cape, 1985. Also published as "Epilogue: The Prague Orgy," in *Zuckerman Bound.* Farrar Straus Giroux, 1985.

Rothenberg, Samuel. *Brief über die Vernichtung der Juden in Drohobycz* [A letter on the extermination of Jews in Drohobycz]. Translated by Naomi Silberner-Becker. München, 1992. Published in Polish as *List o zagładzie Żydów w Drohobyczu.* London: Poets and Painters Press, 1984. Republished in *Biuletyn SPZD* 21 (2017). (A copy of the Polish original is in Central Zionist Archives, Jerusalem, K14\298.)

Rothfeld, Becca. "Territory of Dreams: The World of Bruno Schulz." *Nation,* July 29, 2019.

Russell, James R. "Harvard Death Fugue: On the Exploitation of Bruno Schulz." *Zeek: A Jewish Journal of Thought and Culture,* Jan. 2004.

Sadova, Victoria. "Why Did Europe Talk About Bruno Schulz and Drohobycz?" *Progress* [Поступ], June 14, 2001.

Sagnol, Marc. "Enfance, kitsch et mannequins: L'expérience magique de Walter Benjamin et Bruno Schulz." *Les temps modernes* (2006–07): 132–48.

————. "Les lieux de Bruno Schulz: Drogobytch et Truskawiets." *Les temps modernes* 629 (2005): 151–78.

Sandauer, Artur. *On the Situation of the Polish Writer of Jewish Descent in the Twentieth Century.* Translated by Abe Shenitzer and Sarah Shenitzer. Magnes Press, 2005.

Sander, Martin. "Das Vorgefühl des Untergangs." *Neue Zürcher Zeitung,* March 20, 2013.

————. "Entführte Bilder, versperrtes Denkmal: Die Ukraine und das galizische Erbe von Bruno Schulz." In *Europas Mitte. Mitteleuropa. Europäische Identität? Geschichte, Literatur, Positionen,* edited by Barbara Breysach. Berlin: Logos Verlag, 2003.

————. "Wie gefunden, so verschwunden." *Neue Zürcher Zeitung,* June 13, 2001.

Sawicki, Nicholas. "A Painting, an Artist, and a Case for Restitution." *Ukrainian Weekly,* July 22, 2001.

Schönfelder, Andreas. "Die Kraft der aufreizenden Vergeblichkeit. Gedanken zu Bruno Schulz." *Silesia Nova,* 2012.

Schönle, Andreas. "*Cinnamon Shops* by Bruno Schulz: The Apology of Tandeta." *Polish Review* 36, no. 2 (1991): 127–44.

————. "Of Sublimity, Shrinkage, and Selfhood in the Works of Bruno Schulz." *Slavic and East European Journal* 42, no. 3 (Autumn 1998): 467–82.

Schulz, Bruno. *Chanuyot Kinamon, Be'siman Shaon Hachol.* Translated by Uri Orlev, Rachel Kleiman, and Yoram Bronowski. Schocken, 1979.

————. *Księga listów* [Book of letters]. Edited by Jerzy Ficowski. 3rd ed. Gdańsk: Słowo / Obraz Terytoria, 2008.

————. *Księga obrazów* [Book of Images]. Edited by Jerzy Ficowski. Gdańsk: Słowo / Obraz Terytoria, 2012.

————. *Listy, fragmenty, wspomnienia o pisarzu* [Letters, fragments, memories of the writer]. Edited by Jerzy Ficowski. Kraków: Wydawnictwo Literackie, 1984.

————. *Opowiadania: Wybór esejów i listów* [Stories: Selected Essays and Letters]. Edited by Jerzy Jarzębski. 2nd ed. Wrocław: Ossolineum, 1998.

————. *Szkice krytyczne* [Critical Sketches]. Edited by Małgorzata Kitowska-Łysiak. Lublin: UMCS, 2000.

Shallcross, Bożena. "Pencil, Pen and Ink: Bruno Schulz's Art of Interference." In *The Heart of Nation: Proceedings of PIASA International Congress*, edited by James Pula, 57–68. Polish Institute of Arts and Sciences of America (PIASA) / Columbia University Press, 1994.

Shendar, Yehudit, and Eliad Moreh-Rosenberg. "The Republic of Dreams—Bruno Schulz: Wall Painting Under Coercion." *Yad Vashem Newsletter*, Spring 2009.

Shore, Marci. *Caviar and Ashes: A Warsaw Generation's Life and Death in Marxism, 1918–1968*. Yale University Press, 2006.

Silberner, Regina. *Strzępy wspomnień: Przyczynek do biografii zewnętrznej Brunona Schulza*. London: Oficyna Poetów i Malarzy, 1984. Published in German as *Erinnerungsbruchstuecke: Ein kleiner Beitrag zur Biographie von Bruno Schulz*. London: Poets' and Painters' Press, 1984.

Singer, Isaac Bashevis. "Burlesquing Life with Father: Bruno Schulz, *The Street of Crocodiles*." *Washington Post*, Dec. 22, 1963.

————. "A Polish Franz Kafka: A Review of *Sanatorium Under the Sign of the Hourglass*," *New York Times Book Review*, July 9, 1978.

Singer, Isaac Bashevis (under the pen name Icchok Warszawski). "A buch fun a poilisher-yiddishn schrayber in English." Review of *The Street of Crocodiles*. *Forverts*, Dec. 1, 1963.

Skrzypczyk, Aleksandra. "Bruno Schulz i muzyka. Próba biografii akustycznej pisarza" [Bruno Schulz and Music: An Acoustic Biography]. *Teksty Drugie* (2022): 329–33.

Słucki, Arnold. "Bruno Schulz." *Eklogi i psalmodie*. Czytelnik (1966): 59–60.

Snyder, Timothy. "The Causes of Ukrainian-Polish Ethnic Cleansing 1943." *Past and Present* 179 (2003): 197–234.

Speina, Jerzy. *Bankructwo realności: Proza Brunona Schulza* [The bankruptcy of reality: Bruno Schulz's prose]. Towarzystwo Naukowe w Toruniu: Prace Wydziahi Filologicznego-Filozoficznego, 1974.

Stala, Krzysztof. *On the Margins of Reality: The Paradoxes of Representation in Bruno Schulz's Fiction*. Almgvist & Wiksell, 1993.

Sznaider, Natan. *Jewish Memory and the Cosmopolitan Order*. Polity, 2011.

Szyszka vel Syska, Monika. "Creator's Freedom: Schulz's Late Projects." *Acta Universitatis Lodziensis / Folia Litteraria Polonica* (2017): 83–112.

Taylor, Colleen. "Childhood Revisited: The Writings of Bruno Schulz." *Slavic and East European Journal* 13, no. 4 (1969): 455–72.

Terranova, Nadia. *Bruno: Il bambino che imparò a volare* [*Bruno: The child who learned to fly*]. Illustrated by Ofra Amit. Orecchio Acerbo, 2012.

Thorne, Leon. *Out of the Ashes: The Story of a Survivor*. Bloch, 1976. Republished as *It Will Yet Be Heard: A Polish Rabbi's Witness of the Shoah and Survival*. Rutgers University Press, 2018).

Traynor, Ian. "Murals Illuminate Holocaust Legacy Row." *Guardian*, July 2, 2001.

Underhill, Karen. "Bruno Schulz and Jewish Modernity." PhD diss., University of Chicago, June 2011.

———. "Bruno Schulz's Galician Diasporism: On the 1937 Essay 'E. M. Lilien' and Rokhl Korn's Review of *Cinnamon Shops*." *Jewish Social Studies* 24, no. 1 (Fall 2018): 1–33.

———. "Ecstasy and Heresy: Martin Buber, Bruno Schulz and Jewish Modernity." In *(Un)masking Bruno Schulz: New Combinations, Further Fragmentations, Ultimate Reintegrations*, edited by Dieter de Bruyn and Kris Van Heuckelom, 27–47. Rodopi, 2009.

———. "Modern Midrash: A Poetics of Exegesis, Empathy and Encounter (Bruno Schulz)." In *Being Poland: A New History of Polish Literature and Culture since 1918*, edited by Tamara Trojanowska, Joanna Niżyńska, and Przemysław Czapliński, 347–55. University of Toronto Press, 2018.

———. "Next Year in Drohobycz: On the Uses of Jewish Absence." *East European Politics and Societies* (Aug. 2011): 581–96.

———. "What Have You Done with the Book? The Exegetical 'Encounter' in Bruno Schulz's Graphic Works." *POLIN: Studies in Polish Jewry* 28 (2016): 323–49.

Updike, John. "Bruno Schulz, Hidden Genius." *New York Times Book Review*, Sept. 9, 1979. Also published as the introduction to Bruno Schulz, *Sanatorium Under the Sign of the Hourglass*. Penguin, 1979.

———. "The Visionary of Drohobych." *New York Times*, Oct. 30, 1988.

Warska, Katarzyna. *Schulz w kanonie: Recepcja szkolna w latach, 1945–2018* [Schulz in the canon: School reception, 1945–2018]. Słowo / Obraz Terytoria, 2021.

Watt, Daniel P., and D. T. Ghetu, eds. *This Hermetic Legislature: A Homage to Bruno Schulz*. Ex Occidente, 2012.

Witkiewicz, S. I. "An Interview with Bruno Schulz." Translated by Lou Weiss and Tom McDonald. *Pequod* (1984): 16–17, 144–48.

Wolfram, Gernot. *Der Fremdländer*. Munich: Deutsche Verlags-Anstalt, 2003.

Woźniak, Marcel. *Egzekutor*. Warsaw: Filia, 2022.

Wygodzkil, Stanislav. "Bruno Schulz." In *Encyclopaedia Judaica*, edited by Michael Berenbaum and Fred Skolnik. Vol. 18, 2007.

Zagajewski, Adam. Preface to *Letters and Drawings of Bruno Schulz with Selected Prose*, edited by Jerzy Ficowski, 13–19. Harper & Row, 1988.

Zemel, Carol. "Modern Artist, Modern Jew: Bruno Schulz's Diasporas." In *Looking Jewish: Visual Culture and Modern Diaspora*, 53–79. Indiana University Press, 2015.

Zimmerman, Joshua D. *Contested Memories: Poles and Jews During the Holocaust and Its Aftermath*. Rutgers University Press, 2003.

INDEX

ABOUT THE AUTHOR

Benjamin Balint is the author of *Kafka's Last Trial* (W. W. Norton), awarded the 2020 Sami Rohr Prize for Jewish Literature, and the coauthor, with Merav Mack, of *Jerusalem: City of the Book* (Yale University Press). He regularly writes on culture for *The Wall Street Journal* and the *Jewish Review of Books*, and his translations from the Hebrew have appeared in *The New Yorker* and *Poetry International*.